AMERICAN INDIAN CONSTITUTIONAL REFORM AND THE REBUILDING OF NATIVE NATIONS

American Indian Constitutional Reform and the Rebuilding of Native Nations

Edited by Eric D. Lemont

 UNIVERSITY OF TEXAS PRESS
Austin

Requests for permission to reproduce material from this
work should be sent to Permissions, University of Texas Press,
P.O. Box 7819, Austin, TX 78713-7819.
www.utexas.edu/utpress/about/bpermission.html

∞ The paper used in this book meets the minimum requirements
of ANSI/NISO Z39.48-1992 (R1997) (Permanence of Paper).

LIBRARY OF CONGRESS CATALOGING-IN-PUBLICATION DATA
American Indian constitutional reform and the rebuilding of Native
nations / edited by Eric D. Lemont.— 1st ed.
   p.   cm.
  Includes index.

   ISBN-13: 978-0-292-71317-8 (pbk. : alk. paper)

   1. Indians of North America—Legal status, laws, etc.—United
States. 2. Indians of North America—Politics and government.
I. Lemont, Eric D. (Eric David), 1969–
  KF8221.A44 2006
  342.7308'72—dc22
                                    2005032407

To my parents, Harvey and Betsy Lemont

CONTENTS

PREFACE

The movement of American Indian nations and Alaska Native villages to revise and replace their constitutions has been of keen interest to those of us at the Harvard Project on American Indian Economic Development.[1] Internationally, a large and growing body of academic research has demonstrated the crucial importance of governmental institutions for promoting economic growth and social well-being. The work of the Harvard Project shows that this finding also holds true for American Indian nations. Since the 1980s, the Project's research has shown that the nature and effectiveness of governing institutions is a crucial, although often neglected, component of successful long-term development. This research has found that the success of American Indian nations in realizing their economic and social goals rests largely on the exercise of their de facto sovereignty: when they—and not the U.S. government—control, manage, and determine their futures. A critical foundation underlying such effective assertions of self-governance is the creation of strong governing institutions that match traditional understandings of how political authority and decision-making should be organized.

Notably, academic findings concerning the importance of governmental institutions have occurred concurrently with a flurry of constitutional reform initiatives throughout Indian Country. The U.S. government's policy since 1975 of enhancing American Indian nations' opportunities for self-governance has led numerous Indian nations to amend their constitutions—many of which were drafted by the U.S. Government in the 1930s and 1940s. Like emerging democracies in Eastern Europe and Africa, American Indian nations are creating new constitutions to foster greater governmental stability and accountability, to increase citizen support of government, and to provide a firmer foundation for economic and political development. In short, constitutional reform initiatives have been one of the most important examples of the exercise of self-governance by American Indian nations.

Given the practical and academic value in learning more about specific areas of American Indian constitutional reform, the Harvard Project launched a one-year research project in 2000 investigating the constitutional and governmental reform experiences of the Cherokee Nation of Oklahoma, the Hualapai Nation, the Navajo Nation, and the Northern Cheyenne Tribe. The key component of this research consisted of in-depth interviews with leading constitutional reformers from each of the four nations. This research concluded with constitutional reformers from eighteen American Indian nations participating in an international symposium held in 2001 at Harvard University's Kennedy School of Government.

A consensus quickly formed among symposium participants to develop a forum where practitioners and researchers could continue this valuable process of information sharing. In 2001, the Harvard Project launched a unique working group comprised of constitutional reformers from twelve American Indian nations and several of Indian Country's leading academics in the areas of Indian law and tribal government. Over the next two years, these experienced and committed individuals shared their experiences and their ideas for strengthening American Indian constitutions and constitution-making processes. Many of the firsthand accounts in this book are drawn from their papers and presentations.

The rich and layered questions that American Indian reform leaders are wrestling with cannot be captured in a single paper, a single report, or even a conventional book. A comprehensive and accurate presentation of the insights that have been shared by tribal constitutional reformers over the past several years demanded that this book possess the following two characteristics.

First, it is interdisciplinary. While legal scholars are well represented, the book also includes the perspectives of two sociologists, two political scientists, and an economist. This diversity of viewpoints helps capture not only the legal aspects of tribal constitutional reform but also its historical, cultural, political, and economic facets.

Second, it relies extensively on tribal leaders' firsthand accounts. Those looking for a quantitative or "unified theory of constitution-making" will not find it within these pages. All too often in academia, related events are swept together and categorized under a single label. Such sterile generalizations cannot possibly do justice to the voices of those who have spent their lives in the trenches of reform. The firsthand accounts provide the most comprehensive and accurate picture to date of what is happening on the ground. I hope that the emotion, passion, and wisdom they contain will succeed in providing the inspiration necessary for true understanding and real change to occur.

NOTE

1. Several chapters in this book, including my own, refer to the 562 federally recognized Indian tribes and villages in the lower forty-eight states and Alaska collectively as *American Indian nations*. The reference to nations acknowledges the political sovereignty of American Indian tribes and Alaska Native villages and their performance of a broad range of governmental functions. Authors of other chapters prefer the use of *Indian tribe* or, in David Wilkins's instance, *First Nations*.

AMERICAN INDIAN CONSTITUTIONAL
REFORM AND THE REBUILDING
OF NATIVE NATIONS

INTRODUCTION

$\mathbf{H}$assen Ebrahim, the former Executive Director of South Africa's Constitutional Assembly, writes that a constitution "must be a reflection of a people's history, fears, concerns, aspirations, vision, and indeed, the soul of that nation."[1] In many ways, this book is about the soul of American Indian nations.

Tremendously important and exciting changes are taking place within the 562 federally recognized American Indian nations and Alaska Native villages in the United States. On the one hand, centuries of land seizures, physical relocations, chronic disease, and federal policies of assimilation (and even termination) have taken their toll. The 2.4 million American Indians and Alaska Natives have disproportionately high rates of poverty, unemployment, teenage suicide, alcoholism, and high school dropouts. On the other hand, the past several decades have brought nothing less than a historical revolution. Especially since the commencement of the U.S. government's policy of Indian self-determination in 1975, Indian nations have seized opportunities to exercise their powers of self-governance. For the first time, a large number of Indian nations—distinct political entities with inherent sovereignty recognized by the U.S. Constitution, Congress, and the courts—are determining their own economic, political, and cultural futures. Many American Indian nations have taken over responsibility for managing and delivering a wide range of government programs and services in areas as diverse as health, education, gaming, economic development, housing, and environmental management. The great increase in governmental responsibilities assumed by tribal governments over the past thirty years has produced larger government bureaucracies, workforces, and budgets. It has led as well to more frequent, sustained, and complex interactions with surrounding governments and private businesses. All of these developments demand stronger and more responsive government institutions.

The urgency of this demand is driving American Indian nations to reexamine the very foundations of their governments. For most, this involves the first step of taking a closer review of their written constitutions, many of which were introduced by the U.S. government as part of the Indian Reorganization Act of 1934 (IRA). Since its passage, more than a hundred Indian nations have adopted IRA constitutions. Countless others govern under constitutions modeled after IRA constitutions. While the IRA did not add to the sovereign powers of tribal governments, it did—for the first time—formally acknowledge those powers that the U.S. government would recognize. These include the power to form a government, define membership/citizenship, regulate the domestic relations of tribal members, prescribe rules of inheritance, levy dues, fees, and taxes upon tribal members and nonmembers doing business within the reservation (subject to conditions), remove or exclude nonmembers from the reservation, regulate the use and disposition of tribal property, and administer justice with respect to all disputes and offenses of or among tribal members (other than certain major offenses reserved to the federal courts). These powers continue to form the broad outlines of tribal government powers as recognized by the U.S. government.

IRA constitutions and those modeled after them by non-IRA Indian nations share certain structural weaknesses. Most centralize power in a small tribal council, lack provisions for separating power among branches of government, and do not provide for independent courts. In many cases, this centralization of political authority conflicts with tribal traditions of decentralized, consensus-oriented methods for allocating political responsibilities and engaging in collective decision-making. At the same time, the lack of effective and impartial courts has hampered American Indian nations' ability to fully realize the opportunities brought about by self-governance.

In addition to their structural weaknesses, IRA and IRA-style constitutions suffer from varying degrees of political illegitimacy within American Indian nations. Because large numbers of tribal members did not have the opportunity to read and understand these constitutions at the time of their adoption, the very basis of tribal government among many Indian nations has never enjoyed the broad-based support and legitimacy of the tribal citizenry.

The structural weaknesses and lack of legitimacy of IRA-style constitutions have contributed to well-publicized crises in tribal government. These crises have ranged from chronic government instability and allegations of corruption to full-blown constitutional deadlocks that bring daily government to a standstill. In response, a considerable number of the 562 federally recognized Indian nations in the United States are tackling a wide range of constitutional reforms, including revamping systems for electing tribal officials, restructuring tribal councils, developing and strengthening tribal courts, and rethinking mechanisms for separating power among branches of government. With dozens of American Indian nations having completed, currently undertaking, or planning major reexaminations of their constitutions, Indian Country is witness to a veritable wave of constitution-making and revision. Like other countries breaking free from the yoke of colonialism, Indian nations are increasingly charting their own course.

Importantly, the changes Indian nations are making to their constitutions are more than technical responses to mechanical insufficiencies. In many ways, they represent only the first attempt to resolve a more fundamental challenge, one that emerges again and again in tribal leaders' interviews, presentations, and conversations. It sometimes remains unspoken, hidden in the undercurrents running through a conversation. But just as often, it appears in the form of a question as pressing as it is difficult to answer: How can American Indians balance a largely spiritual, holistic, oral, family-based, consensus-oriented view of the world within a larger society that is secular, individualistic, written, and majoritarian? While federal policies of relocation and termination in the 1950s and 1960s threatened the very political survival of Indian nations, the current era of self-determination has confronted tribal leaders with this equally important, albeit more subtle, dilemma.

If any single solution emerges in the words of tribal leaders, it is the importance of retaining one's values, both individually and collectively. Tribal leaders' emphasis on values should not be surprising. A constitution must reflect a society's fundamental values if it is truly to serve as its highest law. In his landmark book, *The Origins of American Constitutionalism,* political scientist Donald Lutz reminds us that the genesis of a society's political values predates its written political documents. Indeed, a society's deepest values are born in its people's most ancient, primal, and unspoken worldview:

> Essentially a people share symbols and myths that provide
> meaning to their existence together and link them to some
> transcendent order. They can thus act together and answer
> the basic political questions: through what procedures do we
> reach collective decisions? By what standards do we judge
> our actions? What qualities or characteristics do we strive

> to maintain among ourselves? What kind of people do we
> wish to become? What qualities or characteristics do we seek
> or require in those who lead us? Far from being the reposi-
> tory of irrationality, these shared symbols and myths are the
> basis upon which collective, rational action is possible. Since
> these myths and symbols are frequently expressed in political
> documents, they tend to structure the form, determine the
> content, and define the meaning of the words in these docu-
> ments. . . . By studying the political documents of a people,
> we can watch the gradual unfolding, elaboration and altera-
> tion of the myths and symbols that define them.

Through detailed empirical research, Lutz traces the roots of the core American constitutional tradition back in time to earlier state constitutions, colonial charters, English church covenants, and, ultimately, the Old Testament. Viewed in this fashion, the U.S. Constitution is only the latest written expression of Western values that have been developed and modified over thousands of years.

In contrast, American Indian nations have been denied the luxury of seeing their own fundamental values organically incorporated into their political documents over the span of millennia. Native cosmologies, including oral origin stories and creation myths, that served as many Indian nations' original "constitutions" have been systematically attacked and weakened by federal policies of termination, relocation, and assimilation. Reform leaders therefore face a difficult dual challenge. They must first reaffirm (and in some cases rediscover) these core beliefs and then develop strategies for having them serve as the foundation of their governments. This difficult work of community and nation rebuilding is compounded by the entrenched presence of written constitutions developed by an outside nation—the U.S. government.

Moreover, the overwhelming legal, political, and cultural influence of the United States further compromises American Indian nations' ability to hold on to their identities and their values. The pressure to simply *move forward* and adapt is strong. Influential media newspapers and magazines question American Indian nations' sovereign status. Outside investors pressure them to develop courts and codes modeled after their state and federal counterparts. Finally, there are deep divisions within American Indian nations themselves over the extent to which traditional values and methods of political decision-making can and should be incorporated into new governing frameworks.

In the end, constitutional revision may prove sufficient for some American Indian nations to succeed in realigning tribal government with tribal values. For others, the process of reform may serve as an important tool for rediscovering these values. Most likely, the wave of constitution reform sweeping Indian Country will represent a critical starting point in American Indian nations' journey to retake ownership of their governments.

In Part I of this book, tribal leaders discuss the complexity of forces underlying their desire to reexamine their nations' governing frameworks. Although each firsthand account offers a unique perspective, the desire of American Indian nations to exercise sovereignty, promote economic development, and preserve their cultural identity is a recurring theme. Duane Champagne's chapter provides an in-depth discussion of these competing tensions and concludes that neither traditional forms of tribal government nor IRA constitutions nor the U.S. constitutional model can in and of themselves provide a solution. Instead, each Indian nation must skillfully synthesize elements from all three models to realize its own economic, political, and cultural goals.

In his chapter, David Wilkins cites the convergence of four trends prompting governmental reform in Indian Country: perceived inadequacies of the Western constitutional model of governance, a resurgence of traditionalism, internal crises and elite corruption, and broader state and societal developments over the past fifty years. At the same time, Wilkins notes three persistent quandaries that continue to constrain American Indian nations' ability to act decisively in the area of governmental reform: the ever-uncertain understanding of their legal rights vis-à-vis local municipalities and counties, state governments, and the U.S. government; the fundamentally conflicting tasks of providing much-needed social and educational services to their constituents while simultaneously developing and operating profitable businesses; and the fact that members of tribal communities are also state citizens and citizens of the United States.

In an important contribution to the scholarly literature concerning the origins of the IRA, the late Elmer Rusco provides additional insight into its legislative history and the first year of its implementation. Rusco also questions the conventional and often-repeated view, echoed by a number of contributors to this book, that the Bureau of Indian Affairs thrust a "model" IRA constitution upon unwilling tribes. Citing original archival material, Rusco argues that some of the best-known problems of IRA constitutions, including their failure to reflect the specific cultural values of individual tribes, were not the product of the Bureau's malicious intent to control tribes or saddle them with boilerplate constitutions. Rather, they resulted from more mundane and benign problems of implementation, both administrative and political.

Part II of this book discusses common areas of revision among American Indian nations undertaking constitutional reform. The first section of Part II discusses American Indian nations' struggles to resolve issues of tribal membership and citizenship though tribal constitutional reform. Jaime Barrientoz speaks powerfully of how the Grand Traverse Band of Ottawa and Chippewa Indians' decision to share its gaming revenue with its members has injected a divisive set of economic considerations into the Band's debates over membership criteria. Le Roy Shingoitewa stresses the cultural aspects of membership within the Hopi Tribe and the Tribe's determination to retain its cultural identity in future generations. Albert Hale, a former president of the Navajo Nation, connects the debate over membership and citizenship to the political sovereignty of American Indian nations. Hale argues that members of American Indian nations must define themselves as citizens of a nation rather than members of a tribe if they are fully to exercise their governing powers and ensure their continued existence.

To be sure, the topic of membership and enrollment is complex and suffused with often competing concerns over identity, distribution of economic resources, and jurisdictional authority. All too often, commentators and tribal leaders alike lock into one of these concerns to the exclusion of other, equally valid, aspects of the membership debate. Through detailed case studies and policy analysis, Carole Goldberg's chapter draws out the conflicting pressures American Indian nations face to alternatively expand and contract their criteria for enrollment. Goldberg's parsing of the complex and layered nature of this heated issue will be sure to help focus future discussions. Judge Joseph Flies-Away, a member of the Hualapai Nation, offers a compelling case study of his nation's experience with its constitutionally based blood quantum requirement.

The creation of more stable, effective, and culturally legitimate governmental institutions is the focus of the second section in Part II. Joseph Kalt's chapter focuses on the empirical connection between strong, stable, and culturally appropriate government institutions and enhanced economic and political development. Stressing the cultural fluidity of the rule of law, Kalt underscores the importance of Indian nations' aligning their constitutions with their own most deeply held beliefs and values.

This section on the reform of governmental institutions concludes with case studies of two Indian nations that have undertaken such large-scale constitutional engineering. Carroll Onsae discusses the Hopi Tribe's current initiative to realign its sixty-year-old IRA constitution with the political systems embedded in deeply held Hopi religious and traditional beliefs. Onsae reports that much of the reform process involves the redelegation of political authority to the Tribe's twelve local villages. Steven Chestnut, a longtime lawyer for the Northern Cheyenne Tribe, discusses why and how the Tribe substantially revamped its courts and its tribal council in a large-scale constitutional revision process in the mid-1990s.

Part III of this book discusses the process of tribal constitutional reform. Unfortunately, Indian nations' most important constitutional goals can be left unrealized because of the sheer difficulty of developing effective processes of reform. Some of the very characteristics of IRA-style constitutions that Indian nations most want to amend—centralized power in the hands of relatively small tribal councils, underdeveloped mechanisms for separation of powers among branches of government, and the absence of independent courts—often serve as institutionalized obstacles to the initiation and implementation of effective government reform. The general disengagement from politics and tribal government of many tribal members further hampers attempts for broad-based change. As a result, many Indian nations have seen the self-interest of incumbent officeholders combine with citizen apathy to prevent productive reform from taking place.

Two critical issues related to the development of effective processes of American Indian constitutional reform are citizen participation and the politics of reform. Citizen participation in constitutional reform processes is the topic of the first section of Part III. Reform leaders such as Sheri Yellowhawk of the Hualapai Nation, Lenny Dixon of the Lummi Nation, and Theresa Two Bulls of the Oglala Sioux Tribe argue that the success of a reform process—and ultimately the acceptance and legitimacy of a new or revised constitution—rests on providing citizens with both a grounded education in tribal government and the real opportunity to participate in the development of new and revised constitutions. Based in part on these firsthand accounts, my own chapter disentangles some of the reasons tribal members may choose not to participate in reform initiatives. My chapter concludes with suggestions for increasing citizen participation and understanding based on the experiences of different American Indian nations.

The second section of Part III discusses the universal difficulty of managing the politics of reform. Drawing from his own experiences and observations—as well as best practices from the fields of negotiation and community organizing—Steven Haberfeld's chapter discusses strategies for mediating conflict and generating ownership in new and revised constitutions. Martha Berry's firsthand account and my own chapter discuss the Cherokee Nation's success in developing and proposing a new constitution in the middle of a searing constitutional crisis. In 1999, the Nation formed an independent constitution commission and held a nine-day constitution convention. The inclusiveness and independence of these two institutions—combined with innovative strategies for achieving maximum citizen education and participation in the reform process—provide one model for other nations interested in pursuing constitutional reform. In addition, convention debates over the boundaries of citizenship, patterns of political representation, and methods for achieving separation of powers reflect the substantive challenges faced by Indian nations as they have diversified and assumed greater governmental responsibilities over the past several decades.

NOTE

1. Hassen Ebrahim, *Soul of a Nation: Constitution-Making in South Africa* (Capetown: Oxford University Press, 1998), Introduction.

PART I

Duane Champagne

One   REMAKING TRIBAL
CONSTITUTIONS
*Meeting the Challenges of Tradition,
Colonialism, and Globalization*

Native communities in the United States, like all contemporary governments, are confronted with globalized markets, politics, and culture. Globalization is multidimensional and is more than the expansion of global markets, but also includes intensified exchanges of culture, information, international law, and human rights.[1] If Native peoples are going to assert their nationalities and maintain their cultures they will need to have strong leadership and government organization capable of representing and defending their interests at local, state, and national government levels. Furthermore, Native peoples will need to develop a degree of economic development capable of supporting their assertions of sovereignty and self-government while loosening their dependence on federal funds and administration.

Confronted with these realities, many tribal communities want more sustainable economic development, stronger assertions of tribal sovereignty, stricter protection of tribal lands and rights, and greater efforts to ensure the sustainability of their communities and cultures. Many tribal communities have come to realize that none of these goals can be achieved under flawed and outdated constitutional governments. If tribal communities want to assert greater control over their economic, political, and cultural lives, they will need more effective forms of government. For many communities, there is a growing sense of crisis and a movement to remake tribal constitutions.

As tribal communities wish to take their affairs into their own hands, they will be confronted with the dilemmas of trying to make serviceable governments out of traditional and colonial models of political organization and constitutions. Most likely, neither a traditional nor a colonial nor even a U.S. form of government will be sufficient for most tribal communities to solve the crisis in tribal government organization. Many traditional Native forms of government and political process are not suitable to managing market, bureaucratic, and competitive relations with state and local governments.[2] At the same time, colonial forms of government, like the Indian Reorganization Act (IRA) constitutions, originated as appendages to federal Indian administration and are not designed to stand independently in protection of Native communities and their political, cultural, or economic interests. Even the U.S. constitutional model that is often offered to tribes has its drawbacks. Differing Native and Western worldviews as well as tribes' unique historical and contemporary situations preclude its easy or stable adoption by tribal governments.

For these reasons, the solution to new tribal governments and constitutions will draw on elements from all three forms of prior government experience, although some new synthesis of organization will be required. This situation is both exciting and threatening. There is no single template that will work for most tribal governments or communities, since most have unique cultural and institutional arrangements and histories. If there are hundreds of tribal governments in crisis and in need of change, then there are potentially hundreds of unique solutions. This presents many exciting possibilities for experimentation and innovation, but also suggests the potential for many failures.

Along with the lack of a clear blueprint for reform, Native communities will confront inevitable disagreement over the scope and pace of change and even whether new forms of tribal government and constitutions are a means to achieving community and cultural preservation. As important as the substantive constitutional alternatives available to tribal nations is the process that tribal nations adopt in their reform efforts.

Many Native communities are very small and a full-scale tribal government may not be reasonable. There are more than 560 federally recognized tribal communities in the United States, and about 330 of them are in Alaska and California, where most of the tribal communities are villages or small rancherias, often with fewer than three hundred members. While small communities open interesting possibilities for processes of direct political participation, often based on traditional forms of government, such small communities cannot look to the U.S. Constitution or other full-scale government as a model. In many other communities, colonial IRA constitutional governments or non-IRA constitutions have operated for more than sixty years and are often taken by many community members as the given government. This provides another source of resistance to change. While the globalization of markets, politics, and culture is real and affects all communities on the planet, many tribal communities may not believe they have the resources to meet the challenge of change.

For these and other reasons, the actions of many tribal communities do not suggest immediate change or response to an increasingly competitive world market, globalization of culture, and national and local competition. As strong as these external crises are, new constitutions, or revival of old forms of tribal government, may not be for every Native community at this time. They may be deferred to the future when a more local crisis develops that indicates an immediate need for change. If the general community is not well disposed for changing its constitution or creating a new one, then little can be done to create a stable new constitution or government. Enduring or institutionalized social change in Native communities must rest on the foundation of strong consensual support and community-wide participation.

This chapter gives an overview of the different constitutional models—traditional, U.S., and colonial—that tribal nations are wrestling with and discusses how each may or may not assist in tribal governments' efforts to confront twenty-first-century challenges. Equally important as these substantive constitutional alternatives is the process that individual tribal nations choose to implement their reforms. This topic will be addressed in depth at the end of the chapter.

I. A DIFFERENCE OF WORLDVIEWS: TRADITIONAL, U.S., AND COLONIAL CONSTITUTIONS

Traditional Worldviews, Traditional Tribal Governments

Native traditional forms of government are inextricably tied to Native worldviews. For many Native peoples, the universe is a sacred place and the powers and beings in the world are gifts from a powerful but unknowable Creator or primary force of the universe. The Creator is a benevolent gift giver who through intermediary powers and spirits provides culture and knowledge to the people and informs them of the sacred rules and direction of the universe. In Native worldviews, the world is a sacred gift and to disturb it through remaking the earth and reconstructing social and political relations is to disturb the divine order of the universe and incur this-worldly disaster. There is considerable autonomy of individual action in many Native communities but, in contrast to the Western view, Native individualism takes place within the cosmic order of purpose and balanced powers. Ideally, each individual is respected as an autonomous force and purpose in the universe and part of the unknowable divine plan of the Creator. Thus, each individual is seen as a sacred power with the right to speak in public and be heard by her community members.

Similarly, social and political groups also are respected as autonomous cultural and political units. The roles played by individuals, families, clans, bands, or nations are often spelled out in Creation teachings and are unique to each tribal community. Because Native social and political relations are part of the cosmic balance of the universe, the separation of religious views and political order is an alien concept.

Across many tribal communities, tribal worldviews traditionally led to loose and decentralized forms of government, with considerable autonomy reserved to local groups such as villages, lineages, clans, and bands. The relative political and economic autonomy of many of the bands, villages, clans, and regions gave each subgroup considerable independence. Local groups often made their own decisions and there was little requirement for agreeing to collective decisions. Because of the decentralized and egalitarian nature of Native communities, decision-making was dependent on a process of negotiation. If there was an overall agreement or consensus, then all went forward. But usually not all agreed, and those that did not consent to a decision did not have to comply with the will of the majority. They were free to make their own choices and follow them.[3]

Often, the decentralized and consensual political forms of many Native communities worked very well in the political environment before the coming of Europeans. But the new colonial governments were more centralized and commanded more resources than most tribal governments, which proved insufficiently powerful to manage political, and especially land, relations with colonial governments, and later the United States. Tribal governments and communities did not integrate well with markets, did not promote internal markets, and could not field warriors for extended times, as men had to return to their families and communities to hunt, fish, and help provide sustenance. While several large confederacies of Indians were formed under Iroquois, Miami, and Creek leadership, and by Tecumseh in 1805–1812, Native forces could not stem the economic and political expansion of the United States.[4] Their decentralized and often consensual form of organization and political relations could not resist U.S. state bureaucracies, market economy, and nation-state organization.

For many communities where traditional forms of political relations have been lost, forgotten, or supplanted by Western or U.S. forms of government, the wholesale return to traditional forms of political organization is not practical or desirable. While there are many spiritual, organizational, and consensual processes that many tribal governments still retain from traditional political forms, the wholesale retention of traditional political organization and leadership is much better suited for managing internal social and cultural relations than managing relations with the outside world. Most traditional political forms do not centralize authority nor manage internal or external markets. Consequently, they are not well suited to the contemporary challenges of competitive and globalized markets, bureaucracy, and political competition at the local, state, or national levels.

If going back to an entirely traditional society is not possible, many significant aspects of traditional society, culture, and government may nonetheless be preserved in new creative arrangements. The critical factor is ensuring that innovations not only meet the demands of markets and political competition but also are accepted as preserving and continuing a community's fundamental values and institutional arrangements. Pueblo communities like Cochiti and Acoma, discussed later in this chapter, provide some interesting examples.[5]

U.S. Worldviews and the U.S. Constitutional Model

Another model offered to tribes considering constitutional revision is that of the United States. The U.S. constitutional model is what American policy has offered Native communities. In general, and especially in recent years, Native communities have kept the U.S. model in mind, since it is the model most often taught and espoused in U.S. society.

It is important to note at the outset that the values underlying the U.S. Constitution often are at odds with the values and institutional relations of most Native traditions. The U.S. Constitution has a strong emphasis on individual goals and rights. The basic assumption about human nature is that people are self-interested and are willing to seek power and domination at any opportunity.[6] Any person or group that can gain power and suppress the values and rights of others will do so. Furthermore, the U.S. Constitution is designed to allocate power through many specialized departments and institutions. Power to make political decisions is delegated to elected officials. The community votes for officers, but the government officials, appointees, elected officials, and hired workers carry on the daily tasks of government. Markets, where most economic production and exchange occurs, are regulated, but not controlled, by government. Churches and religion are largely compartmentalized and separated from the business of conducting government. Religion, community, and economy enjoy a degree of separation and specialization. While regulated by the government in limited degrees, they have a certain level of autonomy.

There are a variety of cultural assumptions taken for granted in the making of the U.S. Constitution that are not applicable for most Native communities. One primary goal of the U.S. Constitution is to create a legal and protective framework for development of a national market and to encourage accumulation of property and wealth. Institutionally, the U.S. found that by the late 1780s the Articles of Confederation were not adequate to manage a variety of national tasks, such as creating a national market, managing international military, diplomatic, and economic relations, forming an active central authority, and providing stability and union among the various states.[7] Many of these weaknesses were responded to by specific constitutional provisions. The U.S. Constitution creates a centralized authority to manage national and international markets, military organization, Indian affairs, diplomacy, and international relations, while providing a framework for legal and economic unity among the states.

In some ways, Native communities today face similar challenges, including the need to develop internal and external market relations and the need to support and distribute wealth created through trade and industry. Furthermore, if political competition from federal, state, and local governments demands that tribal governments centralize authority to manage and respond vigorously to political and economic issues, then there must be a corresponding development of checks and balances to ensure that power is not abused or monopolized.

Nevertheless, there are many compelling reasons not to believe that the U.S. constitutional form can be adopted directly by most Native communities. There are many differences in the historical and contemporary situation of Native communities, indicating that while Native communities may borrow concepts from the American experience, it is unlikely that the American constitutional model will be easily or stably adopted by Native communities seeking stronger Native governments.

Historically, the early U.S. government had more freedom to choose its path of political development, since its origins were accompanied by the overthrow of British rule and the establishment of self-government. In contrast, Native communities reside within the cultural and political hegemony of United States laws and policies. Native communities are constrained by the history of external rule and by the constraints of U.S. law and culture on choices for social and political development. Native communities start constitutional reform after a history of cultural and institutional colonialism. Most Native communities are willing to build upon what has gone before, for better or worse. Nevertheless, the initial obstacles for most Native communities contemplating reform are in many ways more numerous than those found in the early U.S. republic.

Even more important, the conflict between Native and Western worldviews makes it difficult to envision the widespread adoption among tribal governments of the U.S. constitutional model. For many Native communities, humans are not seen as self-seeking economic and political actors, but often have religious, ceremonial, or community tasks set as their life missions. Individuals seeking knowledge about their future and purpose in life have vision quests, or participate in ceremonies according to the traditions of their community. Once a task is given, either socially or through ceremonial seeking, that person is often dedicated to his mission, usually serving a collective purpose that helps ensure the survival or well-being of the community or family. Native values do not emphasize individual accumulation of wealth and reinvestment for greater profit.[8] In most Native communities, accumulation of wealth on an individual basis is not a primary value; in fact, people who hoarded wealth were considered stingy and often ostracized.[9] Most tribal communities emphasize sharing, exchange, and giveaways, so that wealth is shared throughout most of the community. Although there were elaborate networks of exchange throughout North America well before the arrival of the Europeans, no Native community created and sustained capitalist markets.

The values and norms against individual accumulation and profit making often continue in many Native communities and have real consequences in the way tribal economies and governments interact. Many tribal communities and governments have chosen to foster capitalism primarily for its benefits to the entire community, not for the success of individual entrepreneurs.[10] This often takes the pattern of tribal government control over most reservation economic enterprises. In other instances, special commissions or tribal corporations are created to manage economic development in ways that avoid the direct interference of tribal government. Many of these arrangements are analogous to U.S. corporations. But the collective orientations and values embodied within them, as well as their goals, are derived from tribal values and institutional preferences, which in the end are decidedly non-Western. Economic development and entrepreneurship are seen as a collective enterprise, designed not to benefit individual capitalists, but to benefit the community as a whole. Profits, as in most federally regulated gaming enterprises, are distributed among the tribal members. While economic development is a primary goal for many tribal communities, individual capitalism is often a secondary goal to collective business investment and return.

Furthermore, as discussed earlier, the institutional arrangements of most Native communities emphasize the interrelatedness of religion, community, economy, family, and moral relations. The American separation of church and state and economy and government generally does not find a counterpart in Indian Country. While many of the colonial government structures imposed some separations similar to U.S. institutional arrangements, much of the instability found in Native tribal governments is related to some degree to the lack of tribal support for American-style compartmentalized institutional relations, culture, and values.

Without shared culture, values, and institutional relations, Native communities will be hard pressed to implement and sustain viable political governments and communities that are merely adaptations of U.S. institutional and cultural models. Because the U.S. constitutional model, taken wholesale, does not reflect the values, traditions, understandings, and institutional preferences of most Native communities, it cannot be taken wholesale as a solution to tribal constitution building.

Colonial Governments and IRA Constitutions

A third model—and the one currently in place in the largest number of Native communities—is colonial government organization and constitutions. Colonists and the American government have often tried to remake tribal governments in their own images.[11] Finding Native government too decentralized, with too many local authorities and leaders, and consensual decision-making processes too slow, deliberate, and cumbersome for their tastes and needs, early European and American agents worked to establish more centralized authorities and to discourage traditional government forms and political processes. Women, who often participated in Native councils, were increasingly excluded from political and economic issues in the European manner.[12]

During the 1880–1934 period of assimilation, the Bureau of Indian Affairs assumed and exercised considerable control over tribal governments and communities. The Bureau discouraged Native traditions, language, government, and religion while encouraging the adoption of American lifestyles. Native traditional governments based on band, family, lineage, clan, village, or regional organization often were pushed into the background. In their place, U.S. agents and missionaries held out the American democratic political model, establishing business councils in many tribes and often appointing the leadership. In other cases, tribes were encouraged to adopt constitutional governments, which often placed considerable oversight in the hands of the Indian administration of the U.S. government.

Many tribal constitutions were forerunners to the Indian Reorganization Act (IRA) constitutions initiated in the early 1930s. Although the IRA alleviated many of the culturally more oppressive aspects of the government administration of culture, ceremony, and religion, it continued the policy of transforming and Americanizing tribal governments. IRA constitutions, bylaws, and governments were largely imposed by government officials. Often, there were votes within tribes to approve IRA constitutions. But many elections were structured with heavy Indian service influence—and without widespread community consensus or participation.

While the original intention of the IRA may have been to provide tribal communities with modern governments that would allow them to participate more fully in democratic, American-style political processes, IRA constitutions and other similar constitutions generally have proven to be limited tools for the exercise of self-government. To a large extent, they were designed to allow the Indian administration to more effectively manage relations with Indian communities rather than to provide Native communities with governments capable of protecting their interests and culture through assertions of economic development and national sovereignty. The decades that followed the introduction and adoption of IRA constitutions did not witness an improvement in this situation. Budget cuts, World War II, and the emergence of termination policies during the 1940s and 1950s continued to limit the development of tribal governments and constitutions.

Admittedly, the IRA vested some decentralized tribes with a stronger infrastructure and greater government organization.[13] For the most part, however, even where IRA constitutions have become accepted, their failure to sufficiently encompass traditional tribal values and institutions, their incomplete design (especially in terms of lack of checks and balances), and their dependence on federal support and administration have failed to serve tribal needs.

First, IRA constitutions created a direct relation between the tribal citizen and the tribal government. This followed from the U.S. model, where the community is composed of individual voters who have access to the state through the federal government, and also through the mediation of local and state governments. Unfortunately, by viewing the community as a collection of individual voters, IRA constitutions ignored traditional political groupings and social-cultural relations within the community. This bypassing of traditional sources of authority and methods of political decision-making has contributed to political instability within many tribal governments to this day.

Second, IRA constitutions suffered from significant structural flaws, even by the standards of the U.S. government and mainstream Western political theory. Some of the main difficulties include the absence of checks and balances and the relative absence of separation of powers among executive, legislative, and judicial branches.[14] Many IRA governments did not develop courts, and those that did often subordinated them to the tribal council. Furthermore, the executive in most IRA constitutions was not allocated significant powers over legislation or administration. The executive, or tribal chair, often had no voting power in the tribal council, and did not have direct power over the administration of the tribal government. With a weak executive and weak court, the legislative branch, or tribal council, usually held plenary powers. The tribal councils were often small and unicameral, generally consisting of less than ten elected members. In such situations, six members, often called a "six pack," created a majority on the tribal council, and then managed administration, court, and executive decisions. Generally, no community initiative or action by the court or tribal chair could inhibit the actions of a majority of tribal councilors. Such monopolies of power often led to unchecked actions that were widely unsupported in the community, and often led to election of new councilors in the next election—a situation tilted toward unstable and ineffective tribal government. Since tribal councilors were elected directly by community members, tribal government actions became politicized and were often considered arbitrary by tribal members, further exacerbating tribal government instability and ineffectiveness. The continued exercise of control over tribal enterprises by some tribal governments has led as well to the politicization of tribal economic ventures, and to relatively unsatisfactory results in terms of profitable economic development.[15]

Since many Native communities continue to find themselves with Indian administration–inspired governments, many community members will find it hard to propose a clear break with the old constitution and government. As great as the need may be for making tribal governments more effective and culturally acceptable, proposing to implement such changes in practice may appear radical. The suggestion of drastic changes complicates discussions for creating acceptance or consensus. Change ultimately may depend upon the degree to which the broader community believes that change is the lesser of evils. In such cases, the current colonial constitutions will serve as the starting point for change. Building on the colonially imposed governments, making them more responsive, effective, and culturally acceptable, but not rejecting the colonial tradition entirely, may be a pragmatic path for most Native communities.

II. CRISIS, INNOVATION, AND TRADITION

The crises confronting contemporary Native communities are similar to those faced by the makers of the U.S. Constitution. Many Native communities do not believe their current governments are capable of managing the economic, political, and cultural issues that confront them in the twenty-first century. Many tribal governments lack checks and balances, cultural and institutional support from their communities, active executive powers and leadership, and general administrative capability. Tribal governments may need to centralize greater authority in the executive like the United States, but then work out a stronger set of checks and balances to avoid misuse or abuse of powers. Even those tribal governments that, in varying degrees, follow the model of separation of powers among legislative, executive, and judicial departments will need to more clearly define the relation of community to government and business to government.

Since traditional, colonial, and U.S. constitutional models do not work directly as models for Native constitutional revision, tribal communities likely will draw on all three government forms known to them. Solving Native constitutional crises will require the selective borrowing and creative synthesis of those institutions and concepts that are agreeable to each specific community. Approached in this fashion, constitutional reform can play a significant role in helping to create governments more effective in preserving nationality and identity. In this section, several possible patterns of institutional change and constitution reform are explored.

Centralizing and Balancing Authority

The U.S. Constitution confronted its economic and political challenges by creating a stronger central government, a stronger executive power, incorporation of states into the constitution, regulation of markets, and promotion of accumulation of wealth and protection of life and property. The U.S. Constitution created a stronger executive than the Articles of Confederation because the Founding Fathers did not believe the old government was capable of managing military, economic, and diplomatic issues. They saw a vigorous executive responsible for the everyday administration of government as a necessity for achieving appropriate action, which could not happen in the legislative branch. Such concentrations of power, however, need checks and balances, usually in the form of a clear separation of powers and duties with the other two branches of government. Otherwise, executive power can be abused and not used in the collective interest of the nation or community.

As the world has become more globalized and competitive politically, economically, and culturally, the need within tribal governments for enhanced executive capability similarly is seen as a means to enhance government performance and efficiency. Many tribal communities realize that their traditional, and often retained, means of reaching decisions are not effective in responding to bureaucratic and political issues that confront tribes on the local, state, and federal levels. This is one argument for concentrating greater power in the executive—as long as there are attendant checks and balances on the concentrations of power. However, Native communities traditionally did not concentrate power in the hands of a central leader. Likewise, IRA governments and constitutions often do not have strong executives. In many tribal governments it is the legislative branch, and not the executive branch, that handles daily administration. So the notion of concentrated administrative power in the hands of an executive may be alien to many communities.

If Native communities do decide to select this path for reform, they will need to look seriously into issues of checks and balances among governmental branches. Currently, most tribal governments do not have checks and balances among the tribal council, judiciary, and executive. In most cases, the tribal council has plenary power, while both the executive and the judicial branches are powerless or underdeveloped. Tribes will have to choose which centralizations and delegations of powers they feel comfortable with and create their system of checks and balances accordingly.

Recognizing Traditional Sources of Decision-making

DELEGATION OF POWERS TO LOCAL COMMUNITIES

In addition to checks and balances among branches of government, concentrations of authority to meet the challenges of globalization could be strengthened if paired with increased local authority. IRA governments and other tribal constitutions often ignore local community powers, thereby promoting conflict between the elected government and social and political forces that are not formally represented within the tribal government. Including local and traditional forms of organization in a constitutional framework may help ensure more accurate representation of community social power and add another layer of checks and balances within a constitutional plan.

The Navajo have recently begun a process of delegating power to local chapters in a way that generally reflects the power of traditional local bands composed of related families.[16] Dividing and redistributing the powers of government to local groups, such as families, bands, clans, villages, or regions, may go far toward dividing the plenary powers of central tribal governments and weaving more social and traditional powers into the fabric of tribal government. This kind of inclusion is analogous to dividing powers among the federal, state, and local levels, and is a means of distributing administrative powers and responsibilities. States were powerful forces in the formation of the U.S. Constitution, and tribal communities cannot ignore the powerful social and political bases within their own communities.

BICAMERALISM

Elected tribal councils likewise will need to share power and submit to checks. This can take the form of separation of powers as in the American government, or can be achieved through the creation of bicameral houses, with oversight by the general council. Two houses of a legislative body reduce the possibility of forming a majority in the council with de facto plenary political powers.

Just as important, two houses allow for the representation of different social groups. The IRA constitutions purposefully bypassed tribal villages, clans, bands, families, and regions in favor of direct voting and representation through individuals. This very much follows the American form of individual rights and democracy. At the same time, the exclusion from government organization and participation of major and still powerful social groups has often led to government instability. Communities where there are still active and strong traditional social groupings may want to consider a two-house structure. Just as the U.S. Constitution includes states as representative bodies within the legislature, and the two houses, the Senate and the House of Representatives, arose from a debate between large, powerful states and smaller states, the same method can be used by tribal communities to include their traditional and still active social and political power bases in the new government.

If a community finds it appropriate, it may want to create a lower house of the tribal council that is elected by the membership and, as a check, an upper house that represents the interests of significant traditional groups in the community such as women, elders, clans, families, villages, bands, or regional groupings. Depending on the historical and institutional organization of a tribal community, the legislature may be composed of more than two houses representing different social and political groupings.

The drawback of the multiple-house approach is that there are more steps and time expended to process and approve legislative acts. Legislation may not move quickly, if at all. Furthermore, more time and commitment is required from tribal members who serve in the legislature, although this may not be an issue if the members are representing and protecting strong and traditional interests within the community.

Where tribal communities have lost their original social and political organization, where members have adopted Christianity or other aspects and understandings of American life and culture, or where there has been a revival of non-operational traditional groupings, bicameralism may not be an effective means of developing a government. Other tribal governments have not adopted bicameral houses because IRA constitutions rarely included them and because they are considered complicated and unwieldy. Nevertheless, in certain circumstances a bicameral council can provide an effective check on the exercise of plenary powers by a tribal council.

SPECIAL CONCERNS OF SMALL TRIBAL COMMUNITIES

Just how much government apparatus a tribal community can bear may depend on it size. There are more than 560 federally recognized tribal communities in the United States, and about 330 of those communities are in Alaska and California, where most of the tribal communities are villages or small rancherias with fewer than 300 members. While small communities open interesting possibilities for processes of direct political participation, often based on traditional forms of government, such small communities cannot look to the U.S. Constitution or other full-scale government as a model.

Lacking the need to support an elaborate government like the U.S. Constitution, with several branches of power, many small tribes have opted for including all tribal members as the "general council" of the tribe. Often this method has been a tradition for the community, and provides a mode of direct participation for all adult members. The general council plan, consisting of all adult voting members, has the advantage of being congruent with tradition, and does not delegate powers to a small group. The community retains plenary powers, but must agree to checks and must be willing to delegate powers to a smaller committee (either a tribal council or executive committee) for effective administration and government action on behalf of the community.

The success of this method has depended very much on the organization of the executive and other branches of government, as well as the organization of relations between the government, community, and economy. The Pechanga of California has managed its gaming success through a harmonious relationship among the general council, the tribal council, and the Pechanga Development Corporation.[17] However, if the general council retains plenary powers to act in most or all situations, the general council method may lose stability and effectiveness. The Crow Nation struggled for many years with the opposite problem. Its general council often found itself subordinated to the powers of the executive branch, which administered the day-to-day operations of the Nation in between quarterly meetings of the general council.

With respect to the judiciary, small tribal communities without the resources to establish full civil and criminal courts may opt for peacemaker courts, or circuit courts with other tribes in a court consortium. Courts will also need powers of interpretation and relative autonomy to make decisions.

Incorporating Traditional Values

The opportunity to remake a constitution is a great chance to incorporate community traditions, organization, and values directly into the constitution. The degree to which a community can incorporate such concepts will depend on the degree to which such values and understandings are currently retained within the membership of the community.

RETHINKING RELATIONSHIP OF GOVERNMENT
TO ECONOMY

There is generally a close relation in Native communities between community, government, and economy. The values of Native communities do not support individual forms of capitalist accumulation, and so the American model of open markets and individual entrepreneurship may not work in many communities. Many Native communities have to make choices in order to survive in the global political and economic competition of the contemporary world. One possibility is to opt for accepting Western market values of individual accumulation and business orientations. While this is possible, and some communities may do so, most

Native communities likely will not make such a choice, since it runs counter to long-held values and institutional relations.

The difficulty of a close match among community, government, and economy is the interference of government and community relations in economic management, which may severely impede market competition and efficiency. Observers of Native economic development can relate stories of business failures owing to nepotism or tribal government management. Many tribal communities, and most gaming communities, however, have not opted for individual entrepreneurship, but rather for tribal control of large economic investments and enterprises within reservation communities. If a collective form of tribal capitalism is the preferred arrangement of many tribal communities, since it better reflects their values, motivations, and institutional relations, then tribal communities confront the dilemma of creating competitive market-oriented business enterprises. Tribes such as the Ho Chunk of Nebraska, the Mississippi Choctaw, and numerous gaming tribes have experimented with collective forms of tribal capitalism, and have enjoyed reasonable success.[18] For other tribes, where location and demographics do not allow strong gaming or other development, economic growth may continue to prove difficult. Nevertheless, if tribal communities are going to be successful, their government and economic organization must reflect their fundamental values and ways of organization, and this possibility tends to preclude direct adoption of Western institutional and constitutional forms. At the same time, it opens the way for many potentially creative solutions for managing globalized economic relations while still retaining cultural and political sovereignty and preserving tribal community identity and organization.

The pueblos of Cochiti and Acoma exemplify innovative approaches. Both Cochiti and Acoma run stable governments with profitable businesses, which raise considerable funds for their communities. Both pueblos maintain traditional forms of ceremonies, leadership patterns, and clan-religious organization. Acoma even manages a casino. They do this by separating capitalist enterprises from clan-religious community organization and delegating management to the appointed tribal leadership.

In both cases, the government is organized through traditional clans and religious societies. The government leaders are chosen for one-year terms as governor and lieutenant governor by religious leaders belonging to specific clans. Each clan has specific duties within the community, and different leaders are chosen each year. The Acoma are thinking about writing a constitution, but their view of writing a constitution is to record procedures for selecting pueblo leadership through clans and religious societies. They wish to write down their traditional method of community-clan organization and their processes of selecting leadership.

Business organization is separated from community clan-religious organization, so that good management techniques can be used to make profits. The capitalist enterprises work under the management of the annually appointed governors, and are seen as necessary for sustaining and maintaining the collective community. The simultaneous management of traditional clan-based and religious community is not seen to contradict management of capitalist enterprise, as predicted by Western modernization theory. Rather, capitalism is seen as organized for the collective well-being and preservation of the community, an unfortunate necessity in a globalized market system.

The two pueblo cases, both with stable and enduring traditional religious communities, exemplify creative solutions that tribes may develop in order to defy the need to change both economy and government. They demonstrate how institutional forms of government and community may well be preserved in a globalized market system. Success depends on a tribal nation's desire to preserve its values, religion, and institutional relations.

RETHINKING RELATIONSHIP OF GOVERNMENT TO COMMUNITY

Consideration should be given to the secular nature of American government when compared to the interrelatedness of religion, family, culture, economy, and community in Native nations. The secular form of government, while a product of Western Enlightenment philosophy and history, is not well understood in many Native communities. IRA constitutions created secular governments and ignored the holistic and interrelated organization of most Native communities. Separation of church and state as a principle does not make sense for most Native communities, where community and political issues historically were closely tied to ceremonial cycles and understandings of and relations with powerful spirit beings in the cosmic order. Humans and Native communities have a role to play in the plan of the cosmic moral order, and Native governments served the purpose given to them through creation stories and through the spirits and powers of the cosmic order, which represented the direction and path of the Great Spirit, in some Native traditions. Many Native governments have adopted secular forms, usually given by the Indian administration, and many Native peoples would prefer that government again represent the spiritual task set to them in their histories and creation stories. Thus government, for many Native communities, cannot take the secular form intended and advocated by the American government and policies.

In the process of remaking tribal constitutions, many, although not all, tribal communities may want to restore their tribal symbolism and purposes based on the place where they received their stories and instructions. Native communities are expressions of governments and cultures that precede the formation of the American governments, but they are also expressions of cultural and community values and identity that many communities will want expressed in their governmental institutions. How many communities will balance secular organization and concentrations of power with tribal values and culture will prove very interesting. While modernization theory suggests that government and religion should be separate, many communities, such as the Cochiti and Acoma pueblos, may find creative and enduring methods to retain community and religion and uphold efficient and effective governments.

COURTS

The organization of the judiciary and the laws of the government should reflect the values, institutions, and culture of the tribal community. Consequently, the constitution should reflect the methods of judicial procedure acceptable to the community. Peacemaking, elder and family concerns, conflict resolution, and community healing are often higher priorities than incarceration and adversarial assertions of legal rights.

Moreover, courts, when considered as part of a system of checks, will need to have built-in constitutional powers to ensure autonomy from executive and legislative powers. Courts need powers to interpret the constitution and to operate as referees between executive and legislative branches in regard to constitutional and legal issues. In most tribal governments, judiciary branches are often subordinated to tribal council powers. Tribal courts need greater financial and organizational support and assurances in their role as interpreters of the law and the constitution.

III. THE PROCESSES OF TRIBAL CONSTITUTION–MAKING

The current policy of self-determination gradually has opened many possibilities for greater tribal decision-making in government issues, economic development, and reclaiming and preserving tribal traditions and communities. How and to what extent a tribe turns to constitution-making as a tool to realize these possibilities depends largely on the specific interests and mobilization of its community.

The consent of the community to the new constitution is of vital and central importance, and the formation of such consent is a long tradition in most Native communities. If the community is not asked to form or re-affirm a constitutional plan, then there will be relatively little commitment and support for the constitutional arrangement. Indeed, one can argue that the absence of functionality and tribal community support of many IRA constitutions derives at least in some part from the absence of community consent at the time of their introduction in the 1930s.

There are numerous difficulties associated with achieving consensus formation and community consent. First, it takes considerable time to debate issues and develop a consensus, especially if there are many sub-groups. The process for forming a constitution, however, must ultimately reside in the community as a whole, and the constitution must be formed with a clear sense of the common understanding and values within the community.

A second obstacle to consensus is the entrenched nature of many tribal constitutions. Unlike the U.S. experience in the 1780s, Native communities are not working on a blank slate. The U.S. constitution reformers worked against the relatively weak Articles of Confederation, which was in a crisis of resources, leadership, and organization that threatened the continuity of the early American republic. Contemporary Native communities are not immediately threatened with dissolution and chaos, and tribal governments often have bureaucratic and financial support from the U.S. government. Many elders are not willing to change government organization, having worked for or having participated in the formation of the Indian service governments.

Moreover, in many IRA governments there are weak executive and judiciary branches that leave plenary power in the hands of a majority coalition of tribal councilors. Such majorities may see constitutional change as threatening, especially the creation of stronger judiciary and executive branches, as well as checks and balances on the use of authority and power. Such situations may generate considerable debate and controversy over the methods, possibilities, and substance of constitutional reform. Existing tribal leaders and tribal governments will have a strong interest in the processes of constitutional change, and therefore they must be included in the processes of negotiation and proposed change. Reform efforts that cannot secure tribal government support and participation may well fail or encounter considerable opposition. This may mean that constitutional reform movements must gain tribal government approval and allow the tribal government to play a role in the negotiations for reform.

Third, there may be fundamental uneasiness among segments of tribal populations about having constitutional governments at all, in any form. Much of this decentralized and consensual way of decision-making and social action is still apparent today. The imposition of majority rule and delegated powers is often opposed by groups that continue to adhere to cultural worldviews and maintain their own sense of independence and autonomy from a constitutional government, especially in many communities where Indian administration constitutions were adopted with majority rule or other methods that did not incorporate Native processes of consensus formation.[19]

Finally, tribal communities are now multicultural and express a variety of values and orientations, such as Christian, Native American Church, traditional, and Western educational and scientific knowledge. The cultural complexity of contemporary tribal communities significantly increases the difficulties of negotiating sustainable constitutional reform. Again, the present-day multicultural character of tribal communities differs greatly from the U.S. constitution's assumption, at the very beginning, that everyone shares the same cultural background—British, in the U.S. case in the 1780s.[20] Multicultural Native communities have a greater likelihood of disagreeing over fundamental issues of social and political organization. When formulating a constitutional government, such disagreements at the level of cultural worldview or cultural epistemology can greatly inhibit or possibly prevent the formulation of a generally agreeable constitutional document. Contemporary Native identities, loyalties, and epistemologies are multidimensional. Consequently, finding common ground can be complicated and very difficult in some communities. Furthermore, even traditional communities do not generally have strong collective or national commitments and loyalties, but rather traditional identities and loyalties that are usually local and specific to clan, family, band, or locality.

In response to these obstacles, some tribes have begun processes of constitutional revision through constitutional conventions, referenda, and reform committees aimed at obtaining community acceptance and commitment. Most IRA constitutions and bylaws require revisions or amendments through the rules spelled out in the existing organic documents. If tribal communities want to remain engaged with their present constitutions or bylaws, then they will need to work through those rules. In many cases, there are existing rules for change, although the need for a major revision of constitutional concepts and organization is rarely foreseen, and may make working through the existing arrangements cumbersome. Other tribal constitutions may allow considerable leeway in making major revisions, largely by not specifying the rules for a major constitutional revision, and in those cases tribal communities and governments may wish to develop ad hoc methods of reform, such as constitutional conventions, or representative constitutional committees to propose changes. Small communities, with tribal members readily available and willing to participate, have the possibility of convening a general council of the entire voting membership to decide on possible constitutional revision. Where such matters traditionally are decided by a meeting or negotiation involving the general community or major subgroups, such methods may help ensure support for constitutional revision, and future participation and commitment.

Constitutional reform can be a slow and deliberate process, which lends itself to Native methods of consensus formation. Developing strong support for proposed constitutional changes through traditional methods of community consensus building may well help ensure strong and enduring support for a new or revised constitution. Waiting for the processes of consensus building to take shape may be wiser than hurrying to create constitutional change in a crisis atmosphere. While crisis situations confront Native governments and peoples, most communities must reach a general agreement that the current government organization is not sufficient to meet present and future challenges before there will be strong support or motivation for change.

Native peoples generally prefer consensual decision-making with respect to developing a governing document. The time and processes needed to create consensus and agreement may be well suited both for community expectations and long-term support for constitutional reform. In the end, the Native traditions of patience, process, respect, and consensual negotiation may well be the surest path to developing the community support and participation necessary to uphold reformed tribal governments and constitutions that will protect Native cultures, communities, and interests in future centuries.

NOTES

1. David Held, *Global Covenant: The Social Democratic Alternative to the Washington Consensus* (Malden, MA: Polity Press, 2004), x–xi.

2. See, for instance, Tom Holm, "The Crisis in Tribal Government," *American Indian Policy in the Twentieth Century,* ed. Vine Deloria, Jr. (Norman: University of

Oklahoma Press, 1985), 142, 186; Robert Porter, "Crisis Pending: Governance in Tribal America," *Native American Law Digest* (August 1999): 5–7; Ian Wilson Record, "Broken Government: Constitutional Inadequacy Spawns Conflict on San Carlos," *Native Americas* (Spring 1999): 10–16; Gerald Monette and Robert Lyttle, "The Crisis Is Constitutional," *Native Americas* (Spring 1999): 64.

3. Champagne, *Social Order,* 28–34; John Reid, *A Law of Blood: The Primitive Law of the Cherokee Nation* (New York: New York University Press, 1970), 29; George Snyderman, "Behind the Tree of Peace: A Sociological Analysis of Iroquois Warfare," *Pennsylvania Archeologist* 18 (1948): 23–29; John Noon, *Law and Government of the Grand River Iroquois* (New York: Viking, 1949), 28.

4. R. D. Edmonds, *The Shawnee Prophet* (Lincoln, NE: University of Nebraska Press, 1983), 92–93, 189; Frank Speck, *The Iroquois: A Study in Cultural Evolution. Bulletin No. 23* (Bloomfield Hills, MI: Cranbrook Institute of Science, 1945), 31; Henry Schoolcraft, *Indian Tribes of the United States,* vol. 6 (Philadelphia, PA: J. B. Lippincott, 1857), 310; Barbara Graymont, *The Iroquois in the American Revolution* (Syracuse, NY: Syracuse University Press, 1972), 47; Arthur Parker, "The Code of Handsome Lake," in *Parker on the Iroquois* (Syracuse, NY: Syracuse University Press, 1968), 45; Duane Champagne, *Social Order and Political Change: Constitutional Governments among the Cherokee, the Choctaw, the Chickasaw and the Creek* (Stanford, CA: Stanford University Press, 1992), 164–171; Duane Champagne, *American Indian Societies: Strategies and Conditions of Political and Cultural Survival* (Cambridge, MA: Cultural Survival, Inc., 1989), 124–127.

5. Joseph Kalt, "Presentation," *Tribes Moving Forward: Engaging in the Process of Constitutional and Governmental Reform* (Cambridge, MA: JKF School of Government, April 2, 2001), 40–44; Joseph P. Kalt, "Sovereignty and Economic Development on American Indian Reservations: Lessons from the United States," in Royal Commission On Aboriginal Peoples, *Sharing the Harvest: The Road to Self-Reliance—Report of the National Round Table on Aboriginal Economic Development and Resources* (Ottawa: Minister of Supply and Services and Canada Communication Group Publishing, 1993), 44; Personal Communication, Acoma Pueblo Presentation (Acoma Pueblo, NM: Acoma Pueblo, 1998).

6. Alexander Hamilton, James Madison, and John Jay, *The Federalist: The Famous Papers on the Principles of American Government,* ed. Benjamin F. Wright (New York: Barnes and Noble Books, 1996), 355–359, 378–379.

7. Ibid., 98, 106, 110, 113, 124, 128–131, 138–141, 156, 159, 162–164, 186, 199; David R. Palmer, *1794: America, Its Army, and the Birth of the Nation* (Novato, CA: Presidio Press, 1994), 30–84.

8. See note 4.

9. Max Weber, *The Protestant Ethic and the Spirit of Capitalism* (New York: Charles Scribner's Sons, 1958), 59–60; Dean Howard Smith, *Modern Tribal Development: Paths to Self-sufficiency and Cultural Integrity in Indian Country* (Walnut Creek, CA: AltaMira Press, 2000), 80–82; E. E. Rich, "Trade Habits and Economic Motivation among the Indians of North America," *Canadian Journal of*

Economics and Political Science 26 (1960): 53; Arthur Ray, *Indians and the Fur Trade* (Toronto: University of Toronto Press, 1974), 68; Adair, *Adair's History*, 394–396, 444; Thomas Norton, *The Fur Trade in Colonial New York, 1686–1776* (Madison, WI: University of Wisconsin Press, 1974), 70; Roul Narrall, "The Causes of the Fourth Iroquois War," *Ethnohistory* 16 (1969): 58–59; Paul Phillips, *The Fur Trade,* vol. 2 (Norman: University of Oklahoma Press, 1961), 524; Sherman Uhler, *Pennsylvania Indian Relations to 1754* (Allentown, PA: Donecker Printing Co., 1951), 61.

10. Smith, *Tribal Development,* 71–90; Joseph S. Anderson and Dean Howard Smith, "Managing Tribal Assets: Developing Long-Term Strategic Plans," *American Indian Culture and Research Journal* 22 (Summer 1998): 139–149; Stephen Cornell and Joseph P. Kalt, "Sovereignty and Nation Building: The Development Challenge in Indian Country Today," *American Indian Culture and Research Journal* 22 (Summer 1998): 187–214; Peter Ferrera, *The Choctaw Revolution: Lessons for Federal Indian Policy* (Washington, DC: Americans for Tax Reform Foundation, 1998).

11. Champagne, *Social Order,* 56–67; C. A. Weslager, *The Delaware Indians* (New Brunswick, NJ: Rutgers University Press, 1972), 419; R. J. Ferguson, *The White River Delaware.* Ph.D. diss., Ball State University, 1972, 166.

12. Mary Jane Jim, "Racism and the Alternation of the Role of Indigenous Women in Decision-making," *Indigenous Peoples, Racism and the United Nations,* ed. Martin Nagata (Sydney, Australia: Common Ground Press, 2001), 123–130; Raymond Fogelson, "Cherokee Notions of Power," in *The Anthropology of Power: Ethnographic Studies from Asia, Oceania, and the New World,* ed. Raymond Fogelson and Richard Adams (New York: Academic Press, 1977), 191–193; James Adair, *James Adair's History of the American Indians,* ed. Samuel Williams (Johnson City, TN: Watauga Press, 1930), 153.

13. Special Edition on IRA Governments, *American Indian Culture and Research Journal.*

14. Kenneth R. Philp, ed., *Indian Self-Rule: First-Hand Accounts of Indian-White Relations from Roosevelt to Reagan* (Salt Lake City, UT: Howe Brothers, 1986), 28, 47, 76, 84–85, 94, 100, 104–107; Clyde Kluckhohn and Robert Hackenberg, "Social Science Principles and the Indian Reorganization Act," in *Indian Affairs and the Indian Reorganization Act: The Twenty Year Record,* ed. William Kelly (Tucson, AZ: University of Arizona Press, 1954), 32.

15. Duane Champagne, "American Bureaucratization and Tribal Governments: Problems of Institutionalization at the Community Level," *Occasional Papers in Curriculum Series* (Chicago, IL: Newberry Library, 1987), 174–222.

16. Office of Navajo Government Development, "Navajo Nation Government Book" (Window Rock, AZ: Navajo Nation, 1998), 33–40; David Wilkins, *The Navajo Political Experience* (Tsaile, AZ: Dine College Press, 1999), 101–169.

17. Duane Champagne, "Socio-Cultural Responses to Coal Development: A Comparison of the Crow and Northern Cheyenne," *Research in Capital and*

nent: Native American Economic Development, Vol. 10, ed. Carol Ward and v Snipp (Greenwich, CT: JAI Press, 1996), 131–146; Fieldwork, May :changa Band of Mission Indians; see also the history of the Pechanga ment Corporation at *www.pechanga.com/development.*

:cutive director of Ho Chunk Inc., "Ho Chunk Report at Honoring Na- iference," February 2002, Santa Fe, New Mexico; Ferrera, *The Choctaw* '.

V. Young, *A Political History of the Navajo Tribe* (Tsaile, AZ: Navajo Com- ollege Press, 1978), 59, 108, 114–118; A. Williams, "Navajo Political *Smithsonian Contributions to Anthropology,* Vol. 9 (Washington, D.C.: in Institution Press, 1970), 60–62; Edward H. Spicer, *Cycles of Conquest* .Z: University of Arizona Press, 1962), 228.

lton, *Federalist,* 89–97; Palmer, *1794,* 87–93.

David Wilkins

Two   SEASONS OF CHANGE
Of Reforms, Melees, and Revolutions in Indian Country

Indigenous nations, like all human collectivities, are fluid and dynamic polities in a perpetual, if futile, quest for long-term stability and security. Human nature—rational or irrational, noble or ignoble, innately conservative or essentially progressive—limited and finite natural resources, and changing demographics are three of the major factors that historically have served as effective deterrents of long-term stasis and continuity in the community life of Homo sapiens. There are simply too many unknown dimensions and unknowable factors that mitigate against indigenous or nonindigenous communities' locating that perfect place of balance and harmony in their ever-changing interpersonal, interracial, and interspecies relations.

Thus, for aboriginal peoples, no Shangri-la existed before European invasion and settlement. And certainly none has existed since the invasion of North America and its subsequent developments—depopulation from diseases, internecine wars, genocidal and ethnocidal policies aimed at the extinction of indigenous life and culture, and the ongoing problems of tribal economic dependency and federal political dominance. Together, these developments have shattered the possibility of tribal peoples' comfortably evolving on their own imperfect terms.

That said, First Nations have proven remarkably adept at adjusting to their changed conditions. By retaining essential elements of traditional institutions, modifying existing institutions and attitudes, and even generating new institutions, they are strengthening their own governments while sustaining and even enhancing the relative sovereignty of their nations in their political affairs with the intruding polities that have settled in their midst.

THE CONTEXT OF AMERICAN INDIAN
CONSTITUTION-MAKING AND REVISION

Although indigenous nations are sovereign polities, their peoples, lands, resources, and rights have been and still are directly affected by the political, economic, and cultural decisions and activities of the federal and state governments and the American public. Specifically, indigenous nations face at least three persistent quandaries that dramatically affect both their ability to respond to the expanding and diverse needs of their constituencies and the external exercise of their governing powers. Just as important, these quandaries significantly affect their decisions about whether or not to change their organic documents or otherwise engage in minor, moderate, or, in some cases, profound institutional changes.

First, indigenous governments confront uncertainty over the boundaries of their political sovereignty. On the one hand, they inhabit autonomous territorial units—reservations, rancherias, pueblos, or so-called "dependent" Indian communities—in which the federal and state constitutions are largely inapplicable. This is due to the reality that all tribal nations have a preexisting sovereignty, and most have a treaty relationship with the federal government and predecessor European states affirming their independent political status.[1]

On the other hand, the U.S. government retains a significant direct and indirect presence in the internal affairs of Indian nations through the exercise of its trust responsibility. While indigenous nations have a genuine desire to exercise self-determination, the federal government still sometimes defines its trust responsibility paternalistically, denying tribal governments the right to make their own political and economic decisions. The Bureau of Indian Affairs' response to the current trust fund scandal[2] exemplifies its desire to retain economic dominance over funds that should be handled by individual Indians, or tribal governments in the case of collectively held indigenous funds. With respect to constitution-making and revision, the Bureau has similarly come under attack for interfering in tribal nations' internal decisions. Tribal nations' ambiguous relationship with the federal government is exacerbated by the inconsistent manner in which the federal government has dealt with tribal governments—sometimes enhancing tribal sovereignty, sometimes acting to diminish tribes' governing powers.

Second, if government-to-government relations between tribal nations and the U.S. government are constantly changing, issues of citizenship are equally complex. American Indians and Alaskan Natives are citizens of their own indigenous communities, which are recognized as extra-constitutional governments. But by the middle of the twentieth century, through various treaties and congressional acts, individual Natives also acquired the status of being U.S. citizens and citizens of the state that came to encompass their aboriginal homelands. Individual Natives thus have a treble citizenship status that theoretically entitles them to the benefits of each and holds them responsible to each of the three governments. I say theoretically, however, because the Supreme Court has held on a number of occasions[3] that while Indians are indeed U.S. citizens, it is an attenuated or partial citizenship because the federal government can wield virtually unfettered authority over tribal citizens and their aboriginally held property and their religious sites and traditional ceremonial practices. Moreover, the Fifth and Fourteenth Amendments' due process and equal protection clauses are not extended to tribal members who reside within Indian Country.[4]

Finally, and most pertinent to this discussion, tribes as governments face the fundamentally conflicting tasks of providing much-needed social and educational services for their constituents at the same time as they are involved with attempting to develop and operate profitable and competitive businesses. In their efforts to balance these two different roles, tribal political leaders encounter complications from within their own membership and outside their territorial boundaries that do not similarly confront states and the federal government. The difficulties that have arisen for successful gaming tribes, for example, encompass intratribal, intertribal, intergovernmental, and tribal-corporate conflicts that exemplify what can occur when a government is also a community's principal employer, which is the case with a majority of First Nations.[5]

With this backdrop we turn now to examine those factors that are compelling a number of tribal nations to engage in either minimal, moderate, or in some cases profound governmental or constitutional alterations. Importantly, despite all the uncertainty, instability, and ambiguity discussed above, not every indigenous nation is actively engaged in governmental reform. So the question of why some First Nations are not actively engaged in constitutional reform is an equally valid research question that this essay does not address. This is a crucial empirical question, however, that does eventually need to be systematically studied.

To touch upon it if only briefly, we could begin by hypothesizing about the factors that have led to the relative governmental stability in some indigenous communities:

- Small populations conducive to political stability;
- Strong kinship systems and strong cultural identity;

- Ample natural resource endowments;
- Strong financial health due largely to gaming or other economic development;
- A well-educated citizenry with clearly outlined and enforced civil liberties and property rights;
- Tribal elites committed to respecting the sovereignty of their people;
- A relatively uncontentious relationship with local, state, and federal governments;[6] and
- Separation of powers and effective checks and balances (as opposed to unitary systems lacking such features).

What we do know by observing the indigenous landscape is that some tribal nations have maintained fairly stable governments for long periods of time. Some have endured for decades, from the Indian Reorganization Act forward. Others, including the Iroquois Confederacy and the Pueblo traditional governments, have prospered for centuries, dating back to pre–contact era tribal political systems.

A majority of indigenous governments, of necessity, evolved from their precontact types of government to transitional forms of rule in the wake of pressures brought on by colonial and neo-colonial forces, to contemporary types of governments that may or may not exhibit state-like features such as written constitutions. On the other hand, an un-specified[7] number of indigenous governments still exhibit original or traditional structures and views of governance that directly link to ancient times, although certain adaptations have been made in the course of history. One report, in fact, concluded that "each tribe has retained, in varying degrees, traditional, cultural, and religious societal practices which influence the manner and form in which the tribal government is operated."[8]

Of course, in some tribal communities where there is little or no move-ment for political and constitutional reform, this may have less to do with the tribes' relative democratic stability and comfort with the reigning sys-tem than with the fact that a deep apathy or malaise is present, mitigating against any action to change or modify the existing political institutions or organic documents. Such indigenous inertia or passivity means that despite the protests of a few there is simply not enough desire to change the governing status quo.

THE BEGINNINGS OF CHANGE

As noted earlier, aboriginal peoples have always exhibited the willingness and the required skills necessary to modify their political and social institutions when conditions warranted such changes. And while precipitating events varied widely and across time from nation to nation, certain developments—such as reservation confinement, forced allotment of lands, and the constraints as well as opportunities unleashed by John Collier's Indian Reorganization Act—typically led to important if variable changes in the structures and functions of indigenous governments.

Since the late 1950s, many First Nations have been rocked by a profound if sporadic set of events, personalities, and state and societal factors that have left them in an almost constant state of flux, including termination and relocation policies, the War on Poverty and the Civil Rights movement, indigenous social and political/legal activism, federal self-determination policies for tribal peoples, Reagan-era policies, and the Indian gaming phenomenon. Each of these factors has played a dramatic role affecting a number of tribal nations and their governing systems. Tribal leaders, segments of committed or disaffected tribal communities, and individual tribal policy entrepreneurs have voluntarily and involuntarily responded to this maelstrom of laws, events, human personalities, and attitudes by engaging in a wide array of discussions and developments that have led to or are leading to important governmental changes for many tribal communities.

I move now to discuss four of the major sets of factors prompting the variable changes that are occurring in tribal governance: (1) structural and philosophical inadequacies (for many tribes) of the Western-style constitutional systems established in the 1930s and beyond; (2) state and societal developments in the last four decades that have spurred tribal governmental changes; (3) a resurgence of traditionalism among some tribes; and (4) internal political, economic, and moral crises that compel governmental change.

Before discussing these four factors, it is important to note a final factor, actually a set of innovative and deeply committed individuals, persons John Kingdon called *policy entrepreneurs.*[9] In Kingdon's model of how particular policies get placed on the congressional agenda, policy entrepreneurs are individuals who advocate for particular proposals. They may be found at various levels of the policy community. Their defining characteristic, according to Kingdon, "is their willingness to invest their resources—time, energy, reputation, and sometimes money—in the hope of a future return. That return might come to them in the form of policies of which they approve, satisfaction from participation, or even personal aggrandizement in the form of job security or career promotion." [10]

Evidence in Indian Country indicates that in a number of cases there are indigenous constitutional or political reform entrepreneurs who often initiate the discussion and lead the developments that culminate in governmental change in tribal communities. These individuals may be tribal chairmen or chairwomen, council delegates, traditional clan leaders, church leaders, businessmen or -women, tribal educators, young, typically college-bound or college-educated youth who are interested in moving the tribe in a different political direction; or they may be individuals who belong to interest groups or organizations with a desire to influence a tribal government's organic document for a variety of reasons.

Inadequacies of the Western Constitutional Model of Governance

When commentators address the issue of what is prompting tribal government reform in Indian Country, the most common response typically involves a discussion about John Collier's personal and professional background, his vision of a "Red Atlantis" for Indians, and a policy description and analysis of the relative philosophical and institutional strengths and weaknesses of the Indian Reorganization Act (IRA) of 1934. This line of analysis usually includes a discussion of how and why the original bill was introduced, the tortured process the bill went through in the congressional committees, the Indian Congresses Collier organized throughout Indian Country as he sought to convince tribes why they should approve the bill, the electoral and constitutional aftermath as tribes voted to approve/disapprove the act, and finally how tribes who approved the act went about adopting constitutions, charters, and by-laws. [11]

We learn from a majority [12] of these studies that there were a number of deeply problematic aspects of the voting and constitutional processes as they were carried out on many reservations, and later in Alaska and Oklahoma. First, the Secretary of the Interior retained and actually gained additional discretionary powers over tribal governments. Second, traditional tribal leaders and vestiges of organic tribal governance were, some have argued, effectively supplanted by the newly constituted tribal governments, following the reputed "model" constitution developed by the Bureau of Indian Affairs. Third, Collier created a voting scenario for the membership of Indian reservations which counted nonvoting Indians during the election process as approving the ratification of the IRA rather than as not approving it. Finally, "for the many American Indian nations with histories and cultures of decentralized, consensus-oriented, and deliberative methods of decision-making, IRA constitutions' centralization of power in small tribal councils acting by divisive majority rules with few checks and balances has been a difficult transition."[13]

Since the IRA (or the IRA-like statutes passed in 1936 specifically applying a version of the IRA to Oklahoma and Alaskan Natives) is such an important federal policy in the pantheon of laws and policies enacted by Congress, many people assume that it had a direct bearing on all aboriginal peoples. The act, however, applied only to those tribes that voted to accept its provisions, and not every tribe that adopted the IRA also opted to develop a written constitution.

In fact, Elmer Rusco recently pointed out that "down to 1999 a substantial number—approximately half—of all Native American societies in the United States are ruled by governments not based on written constitutions."[14] Thus, only about 45 percent of First Nations currently operate under the auspices of the IRA or the Alaska or Oklahoma versions of the IRA. But for those tribes with IRA or IRA-type constitutional governments, one or a combination of these factors appears to be the motivating force producing some degree of constitutional reform.

Of course, a number of tribes were organized under written constitutions long before the IRA—most notably the Five Civilized Tribes of present-day Oklahoma.[15] And some indigenous communities adopted constitutional governments post-IRA that are not based explicitly on that act. These communities have encountered a fair share of structural and philosophical problems as well, although the issues and, in some cases, crises fomenting the change vary widely from nation to nation. The Cherokee Nation of Oklahoma, for example, has been at the forefront of constitutional reform in recent years, though for different reasons that will be addressed momentarily.[16]

State and Societal Developments

Indigenous nations throughout their evolution, but particularly in the last half-century (1953–2003), have been confronted by, and have unleashed from within their own communities, forces that have propelled economic, cultural, political, and governmental changes that are constantly reshaping Native communities. Contradictory federal policies, such as termination in the 1950s, the Indian Civil Rights Act of 1968, the 1975 Indian Self-Determination and Education Assistance Act, the Indian Self-Governance policy of the late 1980s and early 1990s, and the Indian Gaming Regulatory Act of 1988, have served alternately as opportunities and constraints for indigenous nations. The significant apprehension in tribes created by the federal termination policy in the 1950s, for instance, deterred any widespread attempt to strengthen tribal constitutions. In contrast, the confidence and economic opportunities brought about by self-determination contracts, self-governance compacts, and gaming over the past three decades have served as catalysts for changes in tribal governance. Tribes have made necessary changes in their governing institutions both to validate their relative political independence and to make improvements in the effectiveness of their political and economic systems. Constitutional revisions are making tribal leaders more accountable to their constituencies and federal patrons by returning to separated political powers, by creating tribal judiciaries or giving tribal judges greater independence, and by improving venues for freedom of information and speech.

Besides these national policies, a more favorable social and political climate, influenced by liberal and progressive social attitudes, and sparked by the black civil rights activism of the 1950s and 1960s and the environmental movement of the 1960s and 1970s, also helped to create an atmosphere that led to governmental reform opportunities for some tribes. Simultaneously, college, postsecondary, and professional training, funded in part by the War on Poverty and Great Society programs and state-sponsored programs, generated an important if statistically small surge in the number of Indians receiving law and business degrees and doctorates in various fields who assumed political, economic, and cultural leadership roles in many tribes. An outgrowth of these developments was the creation of a number of Indian interest group organizations and associations, including the Native American Rights Fund and the Council of Energy Resource Tribes, among others. These diverse groups helped to exert pressure on tribal governments to improve their stability, accountability, and representation.

The militancy of Red Power Indian activists and an invigorated Indian youth movement also played an important role. Individuals like Vine Deloria, Jr., Clyde Warrior, Dennis Banks, Russell Means, and Gerald Wilkinson, and organizations like the American Indian Movement and the National Indian Youth Council, compelled some tribal governments to respond and to institute some measure of governmental change.[17]

Resurgence of Traditionalism

In some indigenous communities in recent decades, segments of tribal communities, representing different economic classes, cultural clans, and other interests, have became more committed to retaining or in some cases resurrecting so-called *traditional* forms of governance resting upon distinctive cultural values. These groups, or, in some cases, handfuls of dedicated individuals, typically disavow any interest in having their governing systems modeled after Western-style or majoritarian democracies, which emphasize opposition rather than consensus and exclusion rather than inclusion. Instead of being satisfied with a bare majority, they seek to maximize the size of a governing majority.

By *traditional* I mean institutions or values that are rooted in, based on, or styled after precontact indigenous thoughts, actions, and structures. Traditional institutions and values build upon (1) the idea of tribes as kinship groups bound together in a complex interweaving of social relationships based on language, clans, and ceremonial practices, (2) the idea that personal autonomy is essential to societal stability and must be protected and respected, (3) the idea of the nation's spiritual, physical, and emotional connection to one's homeland, (4) the idea that the political and economic world of the community cannot and must not be separated or distinguished from the spiritual world, (5) the idea that sovereignty must be vested in the community—the people—and not in individual leaders or specific institutions, and finally, (6) the idea that the primary thrust of traditional governance is more judicial than legislative in nature and more adjudicatory than prosecutorial in purpose.

Of course, the notion of what constitutes "traditionalism" varies widely from tribal nation to tribal nation. The term depends, at a minimum, on the interaction and exhibition of several factors—the particular nation and its population size; the kinship system in place; the community's natural and artificial resource endowments; the types of external governing institutions, and the timing and extent of the tribes' political, economic, social, and cultural relations with European and Euro-American colonizing powers and their affairs with the states that have encompassed indigenous boundaries and peoples.

In the last several decades a number of aboriginal communities, or segments thereof, have implemented or are seeking to implement governmental reform as a direct result of this surge of "traditionalism." First, several tribal nations are seeking to revive traditional values through their court systems. Segments of the member nations of the Iroquois Confederacy have established a Peacemaker Court and have sought to reinvigorate other traditional governing forms and values. The Navajo Nation has also established Peacemaker Courts, which are actually dispute resolution centers based on traditional mediation techniques practiced by Naataanii (traditional leaders). The Office of the Commission on Navajo Government Development also has worked to construct a set of ideas and institutions that would explicitly fold Dine (Navajo) culture and tradition into the Navajo Nation's current three-branch system of government, possibly through the creation of a fourth branch.[18]

Third, several tribal nations are seeking to tie their traditional values directly to their written constitutions. Members of the Grand Traverse Band of Ottawa and Chippewa Indians who are working to revise and modernize their constitution intend to have tribal elders write their constitution's preamble in the Ottawa language. As tribal member Jaime Barrientoz put it: "We're doing it in the Ottawa language and, by doing that, we're also preserving and locking into the future some of our language. We will always have that in our Constitution . . . and feel that is very important because that's who we are and that's the identity of who we are" (presentation at October 12, 2002, Executive Session on American Indian Constitutional Reform, John F. Kennedy School of Government, Harvard University).

Internal Crises and Elite Corruption

Within the last thirty years a burgeoning number of intra-tribal conflicts and a deepening level of corruption by tribal elites has evidenced itself in different parts of Indian Country. Examples abound. First, Wounded Knee II in 1973, which focused, in part, on the conflict between the tribal chairman, Dick Wilson, and his supporters in and around the town of Pine Ridge, South Dakota, and a large segment of more traditional, treaty-oriented Lakota who lived away from Pine Ridge, supported by many young Oglalas and the American Indian Movement.

Second, developments in Navajo country, which pitted former chairman Peter MacDonald and his allies against a majority of the tribal council and a number of Dine citizens who had become frustrated with the MacDonald regime (two Navajos were killed in a riot-type situation in 1989). Third, at Akwesasne, Mohawk Nation, in New York State, and at Kahnawake Mohawk Territory south of Montreal, Canada, an internal conflict focusing in part on the ideological, spiritual, and economic differences among several Mohawk groups led to violent conflict that culminated in the deaths of several Mohawk members.[19]

Fourth, a virulent segmentation fractured the Lumbee Nation in North Carolina into multiple and deeply competitive groups that ultimately led to the formation of several new groups, including the Hatteras Tuscarora and the Cherokee of Robeson & Adjoining Counties. The core Lumbee group then experienced an even more debilitating bifurcation when the Lumbee Regional Development Association split with the Lumbee Tribe of Cheraw, with both groups vying for political, economic, and cultural power over the tribe's constitutional process, the membership roll, and federal funds earmarked for the nation.[20]

Fifth, the Cherokee Nation of Oklahoma experienced a devastating constitutional crisis, precipitated by the actions of the principal chief, Joe Byrd, in the late 1990s, that for an extended period of time had the Cherokee Nation's government in a state of anarchy.[21]

Whether this seemingly chronic tribal divisiveness and elite corruption is an outcome of the inexorable tide of modernization, a direct or indirect result of colonial and assimilative federal policies aimed at indigenous absorption, a byproduct of contemporary phenomena like gaming and the tensions that capitalism can invoke, a consequence of the internal social and cultural dynamics inherent in various tribal cultures, or some unpredictable combination of several or more of the above factors, is difficult to say and is beyond the scope of this essay.[22]

In some cases, the tribal membership was moved to push for governmental changes because of an alleged or real concentration and abuse of political and economic power in the hands of certain tribal policymakers. In other cases, the reform process was already slated to occur and the elite corruption happened to coincide with a previously called-for convention. In the case of the Cherokee Nation, a preexisting constitutional provision, Article XV, section 9 of the 1975 constitution, mandated that a constitutional convention be submitted to the Cherokee Nation's citizenry every twenty years. In still other cases, like the Lumbee Tribe's situation, the pursuit of external validation in the form of federal recognition and an internal desire for exclusive political and economic power led first to the construction of a constitutional form of government and then to intense and dizzying conflicts over who was actually going to be in control of the newly formed government.

CONCLUSION

Constitutional change in Indian Country ranges from slight tweaks of existing frameworks to additions of new structures and constitutional principles to radical creations or transformations of governments. There are nearly as many reasons motivating indigenous communities to pursue (or not pursue) governmental changes as there are tribal nations. In this essay, I identified and discussed four of the major sets of change agents. Of course, with more than 560 federally recognized tribes, some 50 or more state-recognized tribes, and more than 100 groups petitioning for federal recognition, this effort certainly overlooks other equally important reasons that have inspired or compelled Native peoples to seek to change, scrap, or develop anew their organic forms of governance. This is not unexpected, given the heterogeneity of indigenous America.

The question of *why* Native communities pursue governmental change is but the first of three phases of the important process leading to a deeper understanding of constitutional change. In succeeding sections the book next addresses *what* are the most significant areas of reform and *how* are American Indian nations navigating the process of political reform.

Tribal communities and their political leaders, whether creating or contending with overt and destabilizing political, cultural, legal, or economic forces that threaten their governing capacity or political and moral accountability, or simply as a result of the ceaseless and spontaneous evolution and development that inheres in all human collectivities, have shown themselves willing and prepared to make strategic and timely decisions regarding their basic governing systems. As Frantz Fanon optimistically noted in discussing the state of African nations in their early decolonizing years, the people "are equal to the problems which confront them."[23]

The situation of indigenous nations is, of course, more complicated than that of African nations because we have yet to experience, and most likely never will experience, complete decolonization. The distinctive and still oppressive and paternalistic system of internal colonialism that indigenous nations experience continues to be a plague on their self-governing aspirations. That reality, however, will never completely stifle the creative or dynamic powers of indigenous self-governance that tribes still struggle to wield. It is this understanding of inherent, if constrained, sovereignty that keeps tribes moving forward but ever mindful of the past and present.

NOTES

1. See, e.g., *Talton v. Mayes,* 163 U.S. 376 (1896).
2. See *http://narf.org/IIM.html* for an overview and description of the trust fund controversy from the perspective of the Native American Rights Fund, the Indian

interest organization that is spearheading the class-action litigation on behalf of many of the Indian claimants.

3. See, e.g., *U.S. v. Nice,* 241 U.S. 591, 598 (1916), which held that an enfranchised Indian allottee was still subject to vast congressional power since "citizenship is not incompatible with tribal existence or continued guardianship, and so may be conferred without completely emancipating the Indians or placing them beyond the reach of congressional regulations adopted for their protection."

4. Vine Deloria, Jr., and David E. Wilkins, *Tribes, Treaties, and Constitutional Tribulations* (Austin: University of Texas Press, 1999), chapters 6 and 7.

5. David E. Wilkins, *American Indian Politics and the American Political System* (Lanham, MD: Rowman and Littlefield, 2002), 57.

6. This factor produces a tribal leadership and Native citizenry that are confident of their political, legal, economic, and cultural status and thus less likely to be defensive.

7. I say "unspecified" because, to date, there has been no comprehensive study of all indigenous governments to determine what their actual systems were like, how they changed over time, and what their present forms and functions are.

8. U.S. Congress, *American Indian Policy Review Commission: Report on Tribal Government* (Washington, D.C.: U.S. Government Printing Office, 1976), 28.

9. John Kingdon, *Agendas, Alternatives, and Public Policies* (Boston: Little, Brown, 1984), 129.

10. Ibid.

11. See, e.g., Vine Deloria and Clifford M. Lytle, *The Nations Within: The Past and Future of American Indian Sovereignty* (New York: Pantheon Books, 1984); Theodore H. Haas, *Ten Years of Tribal Government under the Indian Reorganization Act* (Chicago, IL: Haskell Institute Printing Service, 1947); Graham D. Taylor, *The New Deal and American Indian Tribalism: The Administration of the Indian Reorganization Act, 1934–1945* (Lincoln, NE: University of Nebraska Press, 1980); Curtis Berkey, "John Collier and the I.R.A.," *American Indian Journal* 2, no. 7 (July 1976): 2–7; and Elmer R. Rusco, *A Fateful Time: The Background and Legislative History of the Indian Reorganization Act* (Reno, NV: University of Nevada Press, 2000), for a sample of the various viewpoints that have been expressed on the IRA.

12. Elmer R. Rusco adopts a very different posture than most IRA chroniclers. In contrast to what many writers have asserted about the federal government's "imposition" of the constitutional framework on tribal nations, Rusco posits with considerable support in his recent study that there was no "model" or "boilerplate" tribal constitution developed by the Bureau of Indian Affairs that was then imposed on tribal peoples.

13. Eric Lemont, "Developing Effective Processes of American Indian Constitutional and Governmental Reform: Lessons from the Cherokee Nation of Oklahoma, Hualapai Nation, Navajo Nation and Northern Cheyenne Tribe," 26 *American Indian Law Review* (2001–2002): 147.

14. Rusco, *A Fateful Time,* 301.

15. But see also the Seneca Constitution of 1842, the Osage Constitution of 1881, and the Red Lake Band of Chippewa Constitution of 1918.

16. See Jay Hannah, "The 1999 Constitution Convention of the Cherokee Nation," 35 *Arizona State Law Journal* (2003): 1.

17. See, e.g., Vine Deloria, Jr., *Custer Died for Your Sins: An Indian Manifesto* (Norman, OK: University of Oklahoma Press, 1969, 1988); Emma R. Gross, *Contemporary Federal Policy toward American Indians* (New York: Greenwood Press, 1989); Joane Nagel, *American Indian Ethnic Renewal: Red Power and the Resurgence of Identity and Culture* (New York: Oxford University Press, 1996); and Troy Johnson, Joane Nagel, and Duane Champagne, eds., *American Indian Activism: Alcatraz to the Longest Walk* (Urbana, IL: University of Illinois Press), 1997.

18. Office of the Commission on Navajo Government Development, "Engaging the People of the Navajo Nation in the Process of Nation Building" (July 26, 2001, unpublished).

19. Gerald A. Alfred, "From Bad to Worse: Internal Politics in the 1990 Crisis at Kahnawake," *Northeast Indian Quarterly* 8, no. 1 (Spring 1991): 23–31.

20. See *Lumbee Tribe of Cheraw Indians, et al. v. Lumbee Regional Development Association,* 95 CVS 02047 (General Court of Justice, Superior Court Division, January 11, 1999).

21. See Eric Lemont, "Overcoming the Politics of Reform: The Story of the 1999 Cherokee Nation of Oklahoma Constitution Convention," 28 *American Indian Law Review* (2003): 1; Jay Hannah, "The 1999 Constitution Convention of the Cherokee Nation," 35 *Arizona State Law Journal* (2003): 1.

22. But see Robert B. Porter, "Strengthening Tribal Sovereignty through Peacemaking: How the Anglo-American Legal Tradition Destroys Indigenous Societies," 28 *Columbia Human Rights Law Review* (Winter 1997): 235. Porter argues that the process of Western colonialism of Native peoples is the most significant culprit causing tribal fragmentation.

23. Frantz Fanon, *The Wretched of the Earth* (New York: Grove/Weidenfeld, 1991), 193.

Elmer Rusco

Three THE INDIAN REORGANIZA-
TION ACT AND INDIAN
SELF-GOVERNMENT

There is a widespread view in Indian Country that the
Indian Reorganization Act of 1934 set back self-government for Native
people in the United States. According to one aspect of this conception,
the IRA, seen in overall terms, was another national statute pushing in the
direction of forced assimilation. In other words, its intent was to require
Native Americans to abandon their own governing institutions and cultural distinctiveness and "assimilate" to the general culture of the United
States.[1]

A particular aspect of this negative view of the IRA deals with its impact on the right of Native Americans to govern themselves. Graham D.
Taylor and several other scholars have argued that this statute forced cookie-
cutter non-Native governments on most tribes or nations. Specifically,
it is asserted that a "model constitution" was presented to Native societies
around the country, which most of them accepted. Supposedly this document reflected non-Indian values and conceptions of governance, with the
result that "IRA governments" were alien intrusions on traditional patterns of governance. For example, it is charged that Native American governments before the IRA were traditional ones relying on consensus, but
that EuroAmerican-oriented written constitutions were based on majoritarian premises.[2]

In my view, this conception of the impact of the IRA on Indian self-
governance is seriously flawed, although no thorough and comprehensive
study of how this important statute affected Indian self-government is yet
available. The wider conception that this act was intended to promote assimilation rather than preservation of Native American cultural integrity
is even more flawed. Most of the differing opinions on these questions
arise from the fact that the IRA, although simple in most of its specific
sections, dealt with a wide range of matters affecting Native Americans.
Much of this confusion has also, in the past, resulted in part from the lack

of a thorough and detailed knowledge of the events during the drafting, consideration, and passage of this complex statute.

This chapter will discuss several aspects of the evidence about the views discussed above. My book about the Indian Reorganization Act up to the time of its passage in 1934—*A Fateful Time: The Background and Legislative History of the Indian Reorganization Act*—provides the most thorough account of the IRA until just before its implementation began. The first part of this chapter briefly summarizes the major findings of this work, based on twenty years of research, largely in National Archives records.[3] The second part provides new evidence, based on records in the papers of Felix Cohen, on the first year of efforts to implement the governance provisions of the IRA. Finally, some material is provided (intertwined with information about the first year) about the general outlines of the organizational effort subsequent to the formal establishment of the Organizational Division within the Bureau of Indian Affairs in the spring of 1935. This is an area of inquiry about which relatively little serious research has been carried out.

BUREAU ATTITUDES TOWARD NATIVE SELF-GOVERNMENT BEFORE THE IRA

There is no doubt that, for several decades before John Collier became Commissioner of Indian Affairs in 1933, the leadership of the Bureau of Indian Affairs (BIA) was strongly committed to the ultimate goal of assimilation for all Indians. Part of the worldview of the top layers of the BIA during this long period was that the federal government should no longer recognize and deal with Indian governments. Instead, the objective of Bureau leaders, particularly after passage of the General Allotment Act of 1887, was to "break up the tribal mass," in a famous phrase by President Theodore Roosevelt. Under this policy of assimilation, the Bureau placed priority on interacting primarily with individual Indians, not tribal governments.

The goal of assimilation also stemmed in part from Bureau leaders' assumptions about the status of tribal governments in the early decades of the twentieth century. There was widespread acceptance in Washington of the "vacuum" theory—the notion that a substantial proportion of several hundred Native American societies no longer possessed governing structures at all. Even John Collier, who knew a great deal about Indians and strongly valued their ability to govern themselves, several times opined that varying but significant proportions of Native societies no longer had effective governing systems.

Notwithstanding this formal policy, available evidence reveals that from 1920 to 1933, Bureau leaders often dealt with what they considered to be legitimate tribal governments, despite their ideological commitment to dealing only with individual Indians. Three reasons explain this surprising result. First, despite all the assaults on Native self-government over many decades, a great many governments which were essentially traditional in their structure were still present and functioning during the 1920s and early 1930s.[4] Given this fact, it would have been impossible for the Bureau to have avoided completely dealing with these governments.

Another reason for Bureau de facto dealings with existing Native American governments in the dozen years before the IRA was that judges and attorneys still adhered to traditional conceptions of the nature of Indian self-governance. The core of this legal tradition, developed in the first third of the nineteenth century, was that Native American societies were recognized as self-governing; Indian governments were the contemporary forms of the governments of once wholly sovereign societies. The sovereignty-based legal tradition influenced substantially how U.S. courts interpreted assimilation-oriented legislation. For example, the General Allotment Act contained provisions stating that Indians who became private owners of former reservation lands as a result of allotment were to become U.S. and state citizens. But the U.S. Supreme Court ruled that such persons did not automatically become citizens of the United States when they obtained fee title to these lands. The court ruled that the standing interpretation of Indian law was so strong that it could only be overturned by a specific action of Congress.

Finally, Bureau leaders dealt with Native governments, and even organized new ones, when they believed such actions would further Bureau goals. Informal, case-by-case dealings between the Bureau and Native governments left much discretion in the hands of Bureau employees. Because there were no statutory restraints on this policy, the Bureau could, and did, in several instances ignore existing legitimate Native governments in favor of new governments organized on its initiative, because the latter were more amenable to Bureau desires. For example, the BIA created the present Navajo Tribal Council during the 1920s to consent to lease Navajo lands for oil exploration and development. This government survived and has evolved into the present government of the Navajo Nation. In the 1920s the Bureau tried, unsuccessfully, to organize a U.S. Pueblo Council to replace the All-Pueblo Council, which had been organized by leaders of the Pueblos. In yet another instance, the Bureau superintendent of the Flathead Reservation reported incorrectly that a tribal council organized years earlier on this reservation no longer existed; he then attempted to organize a new government. The reason for his actions clearly was that the legitimate reservation government opposed Bureau plans to build a dam for power generation on the Flathead Reservation.

LEGISLATIVE HISTORY OF THE IRA

The events which led to passage of the IRA had several aspects. However, there is no doubt that John Collier played a central role in the late 1920s and early 1930s in the preparatory work which led to this statute. Moreover, after Collier became Indian commissioner in 1933 he led the drive that led to IRA passage. An examination of his life, career, and writings leaves no doubt that Collier was passionately committed to reversing the previously dominant assimilation policy, because he thought not only that Native Americans had a right to preserve their cultures but that their civilizations could help the wider culture to survive. This involved acknowledging, strengthening, and even in some cases encouraging the formation of such Indian governments in cases where tribal government had ceased to function. It also led him to condemn Bureau "absolutism" over Indians and to seek ways to curb the power of the Bureau over Indian lives.

Self-government cannot be divorced from other aspects of Indian life and policy, however. Beginning with publication of the Merriam Report in the late 1920s, a consensus developed among persons knowledgeable about national Indian policy that the allotment policy had had a powerful effect in reducing the Indian land base. Therefore, some kind of reform of this policy was necessary to preserve the Indian-owned land necessary to survival of Native self-government. But allotment also had the effect of generating divisions within Native societies. Some Indian ranchers or farmers were successful on the portions of tribal land which had become their property, with important but unanticipated effects that appeared later.

John Collier, his reform organization, and a small number of Native American societies that worked with him offered various reform proposals in the few years before 1933. Always these proposals included reform or abolition of the allotment policy—the cornerstone of national policy toward Indians since 1887—and supporting Native American self-governance in some fashion. Collier tried to influence the Rhoads-Scattergood administration, between 1929 and 1933, to move in these directions, without success. After becoming commissioner, Collier thought he should take advantage of the unusual opportunity at the beginning of the New Deal to break congressional logjams by getting Congress to adopt a thorough and systematic reform of statutory law, starting with abolition of the allotment policy. This delayed introduction of a reform bill until early 1934 and introduced into the planning process attorneys, chief of whom was Felix S. Cohen, previously not acquainted with Indian policy. Cohen became the principal intellectual leader of this reform effort, within the general structure of Collier's views. Cohen also quickly became a strong advocate of the right of Indians to govern themselves.

However, the attempt to enact the omnibus reform bill, largely drafted by Cohen, turned out very differently than Collier and the Bureau leadership group he had chosen anticipated. For one thing, the bill ran into strong initial opposition from the Senate Indian Affairs Committee, led by Montana Senator Burton K. Wheeler. The Senate committee refused to allow Collier to make his case before it or otherwise consider the bill for two months, and ultimately forced Collier to abandon the original bill in favor of a streamlined version worked out in large part between the Bureau and Senator Wheeler.

Another extremely important reason for the early stalemate of the reform bill was the initial failure of the Collier administration to consult with Indians on the content of the bill, and the resulting negative response when this was done. The commissioner probably relied on his own pro-Indian views—aimed at reversing the assimilationist-oriented policies of several decades—as well as the knowledge that passage of a reform bill was highly likely in the unusual political climate of the early New Deal. In this climate, Collier knew that if President Franklin D. Roosevelt endorsed it the bill could become law with little regard to other factors. He did not realize that the contents of such a bill had to be worked out in Congress.

Just before introduction of the bill, Felix Cohen became aware of the danger of failing to obtain Indian involvement and secured Collier's approval to send out a long description of the goals of the administration's proposal to superintendents and Indians, including Native governments. The January 30, 1934, "Self Government" circular solicited Indian opinions about the Bureau's ideas. No doubt Collier was surprised to find that this first contact with Indians over the contents of a reform bill did not produce a wave of support for the measure. Instead, there was much opposition to it and much more suspension of judgment, until Indians could understand what the long and complex bill dealing with many areas of policy actually meant. The evidence for this response comes from a special Wheeler-Howard file in the National Archives, but it is apparent that Indians were communicating the same responses to senators and representatives.

One response by the Bureau was to hold an unprecedented series of Indian congresses in every part of Indian Country, to answer questions and build support for the bill, but also to solicit Indian ideas about the content of the bill. The ten congresses did result in many suggestions; ultimately the Bureau suggested thirty amendments to its bill, a number of which became part of the final act. The Congresses also generated majority support in Indian Country for the general ideas behind the bill. Tabulations of the degree of this support—usually based on statements by Indian governments—demonstrated such a change in the views in Indian Country toward Collier's reform efforts. The content of the bill was determined by melding Collier's views, those derived from Indians, and those of Senator Wheeler after Collier had stated his willingness to abandon the original draft bill.

Another very important result of the belated consultation with Indians was the inclusion in the final act of the one provision which came clearly from members of the House Committee on Indian Affairs. The original draft bill stated that it would not apply to the New York Indians, who clearly desired such an exemption. However, the House committee extended the possibility of such an exemption to every Native American society. Moreover, the provision selected to reach this result, Section 18 of the act, required an election on every reservation or in every tribe, allowing individual Indians to vote for or against application of the act to their societies. The major impact of this provision on the implementation of the self-government provisions of the IRA is discussed below.

Senate opposition and early lack of Indian support clearly at one point threatened the possibility that any bill reforming Indian policy could be passed in 1934, and we have direct evidence that this was so from the chief drafter of the initial bill. In a letter written August 1, 1934, to a Bureau official in Denver, Cohen excused his inaction on work he had promised earlier by noting his "expectation that the Wheeler-Howard bill would not be passed at the last session or, if passed, would not include a provision for tribal incorporation."[5]

It is highly important, however, that several goals of the original draft bill were not significantly contested during the progress of the bill through Congress. Two of the most important were the end of the allotment process, already suspended by Secretary of the Interior Harold Ickes, and the statements of the goals of the self-government provisions of the bill.[6]

The abolition—not just reform—of allotment was accepted without recorded protest from the beginning of the legislative process. It is also clear throughout the period when the IRA bill was before Congress that the legislators accepted the explicit recognition in the bill that the existing body of judge-made law concerning Indians was the principal source of the power of Native governments.[7] Senator Wheeler, during committee hearings, opined that Native societies no longer possessed real governments, but there is no evidence that any other member of the Senate or House agreed with this view.

The explanation of the draft bill that became the IRA elaborated the draft bill's conception of inherent tribal authority. The draft stated that constitutions created under authority of the proposed act would exercise almost entirely authority that the legal tradition of tribal sovereignty had recognized as belonging to Native governments since important decisions of the U.S. Supreme Court in the early nineteenth century. Nothing in the record of hearings before the Indian Affairs Committees or in the debates on the floor of both houses of Congress indicates that this provision was challenged. That legislators understood this fact and did not quarrel with it is strongly indicated by the fact that the IRA explicitly granted only a small number of new powers to Indian governments, only one of which was significant. Moreover, most statements by senators or representatives as the bill moved through Congress featured repeated statements that the bill was not intended to "impose" any form of government on any Native American society or to require any society to adopt a written constitution.[8]

Completing this picture is the fact that passage of the IRA was followed quickly by an opinion by the Solicitor of the Interior Department chiefly written by Felix Cohen.[9] The "Powers of Indian Tribes" opinion boldly stated the legal theory that the provision of the IRA referring to the authority of tribal councils "does not refer merely to those powers which have been specifically granted by the express language of treaties or statutes, but refers rather to the whole body of tribal powers which courts and Congress alike have recognized as properly wielded by Indian tribes, whether by virtue of specific statutory grants of power, or by virtue of the original sovereignty of the tribe in so far as such sovereignty has not been curtailed by restrictive legislation or surrendered by treaties." The opinion pointed out that some of these powers rested on custom rather than formal statutes but that this was also true of the authority of governments of many nation-states. It listed nine major areas in which tribes had such authority, including the right to determine their own form of government.[10]

In summary, the IRA clearly did not create but rather acknowledged the authority of existing Indian governments. The view that governments created under authority of the IRA owed their powers to the act is untenable. The detailed history of how the values and ideas of John Collier ultimately resulted in the IRA establishes beyond doubt that the self-government provisions of the IRA not only recognized and endorsed the existing pattern of judge-made Indian law but also were intended to enlarge, not restrict, Native rights to govern themselves. Also, there is strong evidence that neither the Bureau officials who had drafted the initial bill and largely worked out the details of the final bill nor the Congress intended any campaign to require all Native American societies to adopt written constitutions or change or abolish their existing governments.

Although Senator Wheeler and some others in Congress continued to promote assimilation as an ultimate goal, nothing in the act or its history as it became law supports the notion that its overall purpose was congruent with the assimilation-based legislation of the previous several decades. In fact, the act taken as a whole obviously aimed at reversing the disintegrative effects of the previous allotment policy and enlarging the possibility that Native American societies could retain their cultural distinctiveness and self-governing capacities.

EARLY IMPLEMENTATION OF THE SELF-GOVERNING PORTIONS OF THE IRA

It is now possible to add to this summary of the meaning of the IRA for self-government at the time of its passage significant material on how the Bureau of Indian Affairs attempted to implement the self-government provisions of the IRA during the first year after its passage. This evidence comes from the Felix S. Cohen Papers, which were not available to researchers before 1989. Part of this large collection—105 boxes—is organized as Series I. This series consists of documents Cohen worked with or produced as an assistant solicitor of the Interior Department, during which time he served as a key figure in the drafting and early implementation of the IRA.[11]

Importantly, Cohen did not enjoy significant financial or human resources to implement the IRA. Although the act included a section authorizing an appropriation to fund efforts to implement its organizational provisions, including the drafting of tribal constitutions, Congress did not in 1934 actually approve any such appropriation. This meant that the Bureau had to find ways to start such work without additional personnel.[12] In any case, at some point after or possibly before June 18, 1934—the date when the IRA became law—an organization committee, with Felix Cohen as chair, was put in charge of the effort.[13] None of the committee members had his or her normal duties completely suspended, although, in a handwritten draft memorandum to Collier—discussed below—Cohen stated that he had spent about five-sixths of his time on this assignment. Only one and one-half staff positions were assigned to the committee.[14]

The Referendum Campaign and Its Impact

One of the first duties of the BIA after passage of the IRA was to conduct a referendum on every reservation within a year after passage of the act. Section 18 of the IRA stated that the statute would not apply "to any reservation wherein a majority of the adult Indians, voting at a special secret-ballot election duly called [within one year after passage of the act] by the Secretary of the Interior, shall vote against its application."[15] Although the legislative history of the IRA makes clear that the BIA never intended to carry out an organizational effort that would press uniform proposals of any kind on all reservations and tribes—and nothing in the act required that it do so—the referendum requirement did necessitate organizing an election everywhere. Initially, these elections were to be completed within a year of the act's passage, but in 1935 a statute amending the IRA extended the period for completion of the process to June 18, 1936. Because it had no field staff, the committee headed by Cohen was not in charge of organizing and conducting these elections. Instead, some superintendents were designated area leaders to do this work. In practice, essentially all superintendents must have been involved in the effort.

Section 18's requirement of tribal elections to adopt the IRA was the product of substantial Indian input, as noted above. Ironically, its actual effects were to confuse implementation of the self-government provisions of the act, to exert pressure on tribes to accept the IRA and adopt written constitutions, and to increase federal involvement in tribal governance to some extent. These results—some intended and some not—occurred for several reasons.

First, a process potentially resulting in the adoption of a constitution obviously could not begin until the group in question had had a chance to approve or reject the IRA. Since the period of referendum elections lasted longer than a year, many tribes or reservations could not begin work on this aspect of the new law for a substantial period. As late as March 6, 1935, Collier sent out a five-page letter to Indians and field personnel which stated that, because no funds had been appropriated for organizational purposes, the "Indian Office is . . . unable at the present time to send advisers to each tribe to assist in the task of drawing up constitutions, by-laws and charters. It will be several months before all the tribes that desire help in this way will receive it."[16] Furthermore, if a reservation or tribe rejected the IRA, initially the programs authorized by the BIA could not be implemented within this society.

Second, Section 18 provided no possibility of a second vote if a society that had rejected the IRA decided later to reverse its decision. This meant that the Bureau was under pressure to provide adequate information everywhere in Indian Country about the IRA and the programs it wished to carry out under it, lest Indians vote for exclusion before they had sufficient understanding of the new Act.[17] Almost necessarily, the referendum process pushed Bureau officials away from neutrality during the election process and toward "selling" the IRA.

The Bureau does not seem to have antagonized many Indians by excessively advocating rather than simply educating. However, undoubtedly there was substantial variation in the way that the vote was carried out among hundreds of societies, and some Indians must have resented pressure not to reject it. More significant was the probable effect of attitudes of the Bureau's field force regarding tribal organization. Between the lines of instructions from Washington to field personnel was the message that they should work hard to avoid rejection of the IRA. For example, an October 20, 1934, letter from Collier "To Superintendents and Area Leaders" was clear on this issue. It stated, "It is quite evident from the questions, letters and telegrams being received by the Office from Service officials, that the material sent out, *including the act itself,* has not been sufficiently considered, read and studied by them. Unless this is done and done earnestly, we certainly cannot hope for success." While stating that the memo was not meant to be "critical" and that the Office realized "that the field is carrying a heavy load," it ended with this statement: "May we have your cooperation and assurance that you are giving the act and the explanatory material the consideration and attention they must have?"[18] It is a reasonable hypothesis that experience with having to promote acceptance of the IRA in many cases led superintendents and other Bureau personnel to feel that similar advocacy of tribal constitution-making was expected of them. Graham Taylor noted that "the notion of reinstituting tribal organizations along traditional lines and providing for their gradual assumption of greater responsibilities was distorted by the requirement of immediate referenda among the Indians for inclusion in the program" and that this requirement "served to force the pace of tribal organization."[19]

Third, the difficulty created by the danger that significant numbers of Indians might irrevocably reject the IRA and then later decide to accept it ultimately resulted in a policy position that aroused controversy. On the advice of Interior Solicitor Margold, the Bureau adopted a dubious interpretation of what would constitute rejection. On October 15, 1934, the solicitor was asked by Assistant Commissioner Zimmerman to answer twelve questions about the meaning of the IRA. On October 20, he replied to the first five questions, which had dealt with Section 18. His major conclusion was that rejection of the IRA could occur only if "a majority of all *eligible* Indians on that reservation cast their ballots against the application of the act." An obvious alternative interpretation was that the decision to reject the IRA could be taken by a majority of those *actually* voting on the proposition. The practical effect of this ruling was that on some reservations it was held that the IRA had not been rejected, even though more ballots were actually cast against rather than for the IRA.[20]

Although Solicitor Margold reaffirmed his finding of the previous October on February 5, 1935, Secretary of the Interior Harold Ickes requested a ruling on the legality of Margold's position two days later from Attorney General Homer Cummings.[21] In a February 13, 1935, letter to Ickes, Cummings indicated his dissatisfaction with Margold's ruling.[22] Suggesting that a final settlement on this issue by the courts might take years, the Attorney General proposed "the enactment of a clarifying statute or resolution," and offered to help with such action.[23]

The Bureau did seek a legislative clarification, and this produced a change from Margold's original interpretation of this issue. When the statute extending the time to conduct referendum elections was enacted in 1935, it included a provision changing the rule so that "a majority of those actually voting shall be necessary and sufficient to effectuate . . . exclusion, adoption, or ratification" of the IRA, but only if not less than 30 percent of "those entitled to vote" had actually cast ballots. However, this solution still left open the possibility that in some circumstances the act would not be rejected even when a majority of voters favored such action—if less than 30 percent of eligible voters participated in the referendum, a negative vote would not be considered to be a rejection.[24] There can be little doubt that in at least a few cases Indians were offended by being told that the IRA had been accepted by their tribe or reservation in spite of the fact that more votes were cast for rejection than for acceptance.[25]

Fourth, the referendum process forced early decision-making about questions of importance to constitution-making. As will be noted below, Cohen and the organizing committee encountered many questions about the meaning of the act and about its relation with existing federal law. Such questions inevitably arose, and inevitably were seen as of central importance by attorneys. For example, the "Rules and Regulations Governing Elections under the Reorganization Act," first issued August 20, 1935, dealt extensively with questions such as the "eligibility of voters," including the question of minimum age for voting, what residence meant in a tribal context, and how tribal membership was to be determined. Several of these questions were obviously central to self-government, and raised many questions about the extent to which nationwide rules or local, culturally sensitive rules should be followed. A reasonable hypothesis is that the referendum process necessarily short-circuited proper attention to resolution of issues of this kind, given the time constraints in conducting the elections. This probably affected the nature of ultimate Bureau choices on matters affecting tribal organization.

Governing Powers of Tribes under IRA Constitutions

One of the most important documents produced during the first few months after passage of the IRA was the "Powers of Indian Tribes," an opinion written by Cohen and approved in October 1934.[26] The "Powers" opinion reports Cohen's well-documented conclusion that existing law—mostly judge-made law accepting and interpreting traditional laws of many Native American societies—acknowledged sweeping, inherent powers which a tribal constitution might assign to the governing body of the group. In short, the opinion expressed the clear view that Native American societies possessed many powers besides those few specifically granted by the IRA. The treatment of tribal authority to govern Native American societies in this opinion presents a theory of the relevance of the IRA to tribal sovereignty. Pointing out that "it is a fact that State governments and administrative officials have frequently trespassed upon the realm of tribal autonomy," it stated that "these trespasses have not impaired the vested legal powers of local self-government which have been recognized again and again when these trespasses have been challenged by an Indian tribe." It went on to say that "the Wheeler-Howard Act, by affording statutory recognition of these powers of local self-government and administrative assistance in developing adequate mechanisms for such government, may reasonably be expected to end the conditions that have in the past led the Interior Department and various State agencies to deal with matters that are properly within the legal competence of the Indian tribes themselves."[27] One of the important unanswered questions is the extent to which Indians were aware of this document during the 1930s. Cohen's report, noted below, that there was at least one dramatic incident demonstrating that Indians were sometimes deliberately kept from reading it raises a question about wider knowledge of the "Powers" opinion on the part of those most directly affected by it.

Another issue concerned the powers of tribal governments to assume government functions previously handled by the Bureau. The draft bill in early 1934 had stated its goal of permitting tribal governments to take over Bureau functions, with federal funding. Although this proposal was dropped in the watered-down bill that finally passed Congress, Cohen continued to assume that devolution was one of the goals of Indian organization. Cohen stated this goal at various times while he headed the Organization Committee. For example, the undated "Organization Program," which stated deadlines for each needed task, referred to the "long range program for gradual assumption of agency duties" by tribal governments. The cover letter for the draft of the "Basic Memorandum" sent to Commissioner Collier on November 19, 1934, spoke of "the extremely complex and difficult problem of erecting workable systems of local government fit to take over many of the responsibilities now borne by the Indian Office."

Cohen's reason for assuming there was a legal basis for this expansion of tribal control over Bureau functions even though the IRA did not embrace this goal was stated clearly in the "Powers" opinion. In that document, in a section headed "The Power of an Indian Tribe to Supervise Government Employees," he called attention to the existence of a statute giving the Secretary of the Interior authority to move in this direction. This law stated that when the Secretary thought "any of the tribes" were "competent to direct the employment of their blacksmiths, mechanics, teachers, farmers, or other persons engaged for them, the direction of such persons may be given to the proper authority of the tribe." The opinion pointed out that a "previous administration" had asked for the repeal of this statute, but that Congress had not acted on this request. It asserted that a number of court decisions had held that "an Indian tribe may impose upon such employees the duty of enforcing the laws and ordinances of the tribe."[28]

While it would be surprising if John Collier did not think this a worthy goal, he did not openly adopt it as administration policy. He had approved this approach in the draft bill, and it was highly consistent with his overall approach to preserving tribal self-government. It is highly likely that one reason for not doing so was concern about congressional response to such action. He certainly knew that a comprehensive provision for devolving Bureau functions to tribal governments was deleted from the draft bill. He also knew that the powerful Senator Wheeler was opposed to efforts along these lines. Not until the passage of the Indian Self Determination and Education Assistance Act in 1975 did Congress finally pass a law allowing some devolution of Bureau functions to tribal governments.

A Movement away from "Model" Constitutions

Although a full account of how the Organization Division approached the writing of constitutions and charters cannot be dealt with here, some aspects of this question are relevant to the views noted in the beginning of this chapter.[29] Graham D. Taylor, in his 1980 book on the impact of the IRA, made assertions about the process followed by the BIA in implementing the organizational provisions of the act. Taylor wrote that "a model constitution was prepared [in Washington] and teams of lawyers were sent around the reservations . . . to tailor the constitutions to the particular tribal situations they encountered."[30] The notion of a model constitution has been very influential with scholars; a number of writers on Native American policy have accepted this conclusion, usually citing Taylor's book.

I believe that these views are fundamentally inaccurate. Taylor provides no notes stating where a copy of the model constitution can be found, and there is no evidence that there was such a document. I have never seen one, nor have I found clear references to such a document. Instead, as will be demonstrated below, there is evidence that, during and after the initial stages described above, the decision was made not to produce a model constitution.

The Cohen Papers provide data for following the process by which the Bureau decided how to implement Sections 16 and 17 of the IRA during most of the first year after passage. Admittedly, the Bureau toyed initially with the idea of a model constitution. An undated Bureau document headed "Action necessary to implement the Wheeler-Howard Act" assumes the desirability of "model" constitutions and charters.[31] Another undated "Organization Program" document also seems to be moving in the direction of model documents. Setting a series of deadlines beginning July 2, it mandated that by September 1, the "preparation of model constitutions, by-laws and charters" was to take place. Importantly, the document notes that several "models" were to be sent out to "interested tribes with guides for study and discussion" because a number of factors, including anthropological data, legal questions, the abilities and dispositions of Bureau field personnel, and "Indian statements on desires for specific powers," would all require flexibility in constitutions.[32]

However, the first clear-cut product of the Organization Committee, the "Immediate Program for Organization of Indian Tribes" dated July 31, 1934, signals an unmistakable shift away from the utilization of model constitutions. It states clearly the intent of the committee to work only with tribes or reservations most interested in organization or reorganization and most likely to be able to benefit from organizational activity. The goal of the committee was to work with "about 30 tribes" initially, with the hope that as many as twelve constitutions, by-laws, and charters could be adopted by January 1, 1935.[33] The bases for selection of these thirty cases were stated to be "the wishes of the Indians and their intelligent understanding of the problems of self-government, as expressed by their action on the Wheeler-Howard Act, their responses to the Circular of January 20, and other office correspondence," as well as the "sympathy and ability" of superintendents, the "economic conditions permitting a community organization independent of land purchase," and "the comparative simplicity of the task of organization (as where present constitutions are functioning in a satisfactory manner)."

This document reveals that the committee was no longer thinking in terms of a single "model" constitution.[34] Two specific strategies for moving to the committee's goal were outlined. First, it proposed to study the "actual operation" of existing tribal constitutions. It cited about forty such tribal constitutions that had been "approved or [were] awaiting approval by the Indian Office." Second, once these existing tribal constitutions were studied from several aspects, "a general comprehensive memorandum" was to be drafted. The memorandum would

> contain an outline of the various topics to be dealt with in a constitution and, under each heading, any extant constitutional provisions which may serve as a model, any extant constitutional provisions which may serve as horrible examples, and reference to any data showing actual experience with and criticism of relevant constitutional provisions. Where no existing constitutional provision is entirely adequate, a model provision or series of provisions for different circumstances should be drafted.

Eventually such an outline—minus inclusion of possible constitutional provisions—was produced by the Bureau and used for years in helping tribes develop constitutions.[35] The difference between this outline and a model constitution is that the outline merely suggests topics that might be considered, but does not require or, in most cases, advocate particular constitutional structures or provisions. For example, the outline notes that each tribe or reservation should determine in a constitution the rules for deciding who will be a member of the society, but offers no sample provision on this question, and the section on bills of rights describes what such a provision could do without indicating that all constitutions must have one, let alone suggesting the content of such a part of the constitution. Indeed, a study of all tribal constitutions in the "Lower 48" as of the end of 1981 showed great variety in the treatment of civil liberties in these documents.[36]

These facts notwithstanding, Taylor's description of the Bureau's organizational effort not only refers to a model constitution which seems not to exist, it also contains inaccuracies in its description of the Bureau's interactions with tribes regarding constitutional development.

Regarding the reference to a model constitution, it is true that in 1935, and after creation of the Organization Division, Cohen sent to Organization Division head Joe Jennings an eight-page model constitution "based upon the draft which you turned over to me" with corrections. But, Cohen stated, "Personally I feel that it would be a mistake to furnish this outline to any Indian tribes, who would naturally be tempted to regard it as compulsive rather than suggestive." He did suggest it might be turned over to Bureau employees working with several tribes meeting a number of criteria he suggested, the most important of which was that "there is no functioning social control within the tribe."[37] As noted above, however, there is no evidence known to me that such a model constitution was ever sent to either field personnel or Indians working on constitution-making.

In addition, Taylor's assertion that "teams of lawyers" descended on Indian reservations is erroneous. Organization Division field agents who were not attorneys—a number of whom were Indians—were sent into the field after the division became organized to meet with Indians to find out whether they wanted written constitutions and, if they did, what such documents should contain. Then draft constitutions were sent to Washington to be checked by a small group of attorneys, who were to be sure the documents were legally correct. After the lawyers had made suggestions, the Indians who had drafted the constitutions were advised to make changes. Sometimes they accepted the proposed changes. In other instances they resisted doing so and prevailed, sometimes with the assistance of superintendents. Finally, the Indians involved had to approve the constitution in an election before it went into effect, although the approval of the Secretary of the Interior was also required.

These steps in the process, as well as information on how to adopt charters, were outlined to "Superintendents, Tribal Councils, and Individual Indians" in a document dated March 6, 1935. My experience with tracking constitution-making in the Organization Division files convinces me that these procedures were actually followed.[38] My impression is that the review by attorneys did have a substantial impact on the content of IRA constitutions, but the actual process was a long way from adapting a model to local conditions.[39]

My assertions above about how constitutions were written are based on study of a significant number of the documents in the Organization Division's files in the National Archives Building, but there are still many more files unexamined. As with so many other important matters, what is needed is more research. Graham Taylor's book does not report in-depth case studies of constitution-making on any reservation or tribe. His longest chapter describes a number of divisions within Native American societies, existing at the time of passage of the IRA, which made agreement on constitutional matters difficult. His account identifies a number of situations in which reservations were jointly occupied by two or more tribes, creating cultural and linguistic divides. Taylor also notes divisions between full-bloods and mixed-bloods on at least some reservations plus several other sources of division, including those between Indians who owned allotted lands and others who did not, and those between formally educated and traditionally educated Indians.[40]

His treatment of these divisions is sound, and it would be difficult to disagree that these divisions sometimes hampered organizational activities going on in the 1930s or produced flawed results in some instances in which written constitutions were adopted in spite of the divisions. For example, Taylor discusses at several places conflicts between Navajos and the office, which account in part for the fact that this large and important tribe—now officially the Navajo Nation—has not to this date adopted a written constitution. However, his attempt to find quantitative evidence of the impact of two of these divisions produced unsatisfactory results, probably because of the paucity of adequate comparative data.[41]

However, Taylor does not discuss the actual writing of constitutions in detail anywhere, nor does he give a thorough account of the actual content of written tribal constitutions adopted during this time or at other times. He makes a point of asserting that the IRA constitutions were essentially the same in the granting of powers to tribal governing structures, but his data on this do not support such an assertion. For example, he does not report any tribal constitution listing all of the powers enumerated in Cohen's "Powers" opinion, nor does he report unanimous inclusion of any of these. I suspect that he mistook the identical wording of statements about specific powers incorporated into many IRA constitutions for unanimity on content. The legalistic language was a product of review by the legal team in Washington, but Taylor presented no proof that the constitutions were carbon copies of a model constitution. In a footnote, he reports that his conclusions about the content of constitutions come from a sample of twenty-two constitutions evaluated in a master's thesis (which I admit I have not yet read) and twenty others selected by himself, presumably without overlap.[42] But he presents neither information about how these samples were chosen nor any quantitative study of the features of these constitutions.[43]

Few in-depth studies of the actual impact of the IRA on Native governance have appeared since Taylor's pioneering effort, although it is possible that there are studies of this sort unknown to me. Loretta Fowler's excellent study of governance among Northern Arapahoes at Wind River deals with a Native American tribe which has to the present rejected written constitutions, and it puts the situation after 1934 in the context of a long history of governing practices in that society. When we have a significant number of such studies, firmer conclusions can be drawn about the questions discussed in this chapter. Also, we need more studies of how Bureau leadership approached the many aspects of Indian governance during the Indian New Deal. Both more comparative studies of the actual content of tribal constitutions and more detailed studies of how IRA constitutions came to be are necessary before definitive conclusions can be drawn.

Problems of Implementation in the Field

The Organization Committee from the middle of summer 1934 to spring 1935 worked hard to resolve various legal and related questions and also collaborated with various Indian tribes interested in adopting constitutions, insofar as such cooperation could be carried out from Washington.[44] Here it is important to note that Cohen felt the Organization Committee never received adequate cooperation from other officials of the Bureau in its attempt to collect information in aid of the organization effort. Cohen complained specifically of the Bureau's hesitancy to clarify its policies regarding Native self-government as well as its lack of assistance in procuring much-needed statistical information from tribes.[45]

At the end of November 1934, frustrated by the difficulty in acquiring both statistical information and a definitive interpretation of the IRA, Cohen resorted to writing the "Basic Memorandum on Drafting of Tribal Constitutions." This was initially a ninety-seven-page document "to outline legal possibilities in the drafting of constitutions under the Wheeler-Howard Act," as the cover memorandum to Collier referred to it. Cohen stated his desire that approval of this document would enable constitution-writing to advance more rapidly. He wrote Collier: "I feel that when we have reached a tentative agreement on the general questions of policy taken up in this memorandum, we shall be able to proceed in rapid fashion to deal with particular constitutions which have been submitted to us from many sources."[46] Cohen continued to add to it, and eventually it grew to 222 pages.[47] Ultimately, neither Commissioner Collier nor Secretary Ickes ever formally approved the "Basic Memorandum." However, this does not necessarily mean they opposed it. Cohen obviously was an able and hard-working person who showed no signs of being aware that not everyone could match his output.

Nevertheless, the document outlines clearly the attitude toward tribal organization under the IRA of Cohen and the Organization Committee. It begins by stating that it "is made to offer useful suggestions" to Indians and "members of the Indian Service" who may be "engaged in drawing up constitutions." After stating that it will provide information on "various constitutional provisions that Indians themselves have prepared," the "Basic Memorandum" in its long form rejects the idea of a model constitution: "For the present, the Indian Office will not furnish Indian tribes with 'model constitutions.'" Two fundamental reasons are given for this approach. First, "the situation of the various Indian tribes . . . is so variable that no single constitution prepared by the Indian Office could possibly fit the varied needs of the different Indian tribes."[48]

Second, such a model constitution, even if it were accepted, "would be only an adopted child and not the natural offspring of Indian hearts and minds." Cohen stated that "what the Indians themselves create they will understand," but there could be no assurance that they would accept "a form of government manufactured in Washington." Asserting that past tribal constitutions have "frequently" been "prepared by" the Office, he wrote that these "have been merely scraps of paper. This has not been the case where the Indians themselves have determined the forms of their own self-government." Even offering suggestions in these matters is justified only on the ground that because in the past "most of the Indian tribes" have been denied both "the right to manage their own affairs" and even "a *voice* in these affairs," many tribal members "do not have very much practical knowledge or experience of the tasks of government."

The discussion of specific topics in the "Basic Memorandum" follows the same strongly pro–self-government orientation. For example, it notes that "each tribe must consider for itself how far it wishes to preserve its own ancient traditions of self-government." Cohen pointed out that "before the coming of the white man" each tribe not only had its own officers but also determined its own laws and dealt with "relations with other tribes, the problem of making a living, [and] the problem of guiding and controlling the use of property so as to eliminate want within the tribe." The Basic Memorandum noted three possible "levels of self-government." These levels ranged from requiring all decisions of an Indian governing body to be approved by the Secretary of the Interior through requiring such approval for only some exercises of tribal power to "the greatest degree of self-government that could be attained under existing law [which] would give the tribal government complete independence of the Interior Department." While it notes that even in the last case Congress could "nullify any tribal ordinances or resolutions," the Basic Memorandum concluded that "which of these levels of self-government a tribe will achieve through its constitution must depend upon the desires, capacities and experience of the Indians themselves." [49]

On March 5, 1935, Felix Cohen wrote Collier the important four-page memorandum referring to "unfinished business" in the work of the Organization Committee that has been noted above. He began by complaining that information the committee needed in its work—statistical data from another division of the BIA and answers to three memos concerning policy questions written in November 1934—had not been provided. He also complained that the Basic Memorandum had not been approved, which left the committee unable to be sure what administration policy was on key questions. [50] Moreover, the "Powers" opinion, which had been approved in October, had not been properly distributed. He wrote that he had "been informed" that "division heads have not seen" it, and implied that the opinion had also not reached Indian eyes. Stating that "while I realized that this opinion would not be suitable for general distribution to Indians, I expected that it would be furnished to the heads of divisions, who alone can plan the manner of transferring powers back to the Indian community, and that some abstract at least would be furnished to those Indians who were anxious to know what the provisions of the revised Wheeler-Howard Act meant."

The handwritten draft of this memorandum to Collier states: "I am told by the present Chairman of the Navajo Council that a copy of this memorandum which he began to read in the anteroom of your office was taken from his hands."[51] The memo actually sent to Collier stated that "the matter was brought to my attention in a rather shocking way when an extremely intelligent and discreet Indian who had been authorized to work on the drafting of a tribal constitution complained to me that he had not been permitted to read a copy of this memorandum in your office although it is a public document available to anybody on request."

In a third reference to this incident, published in 1949, Cohen wrote that after approval and issuance of the "Powers" opinion,

> I learned to my dismay that all copies of the opinion in the Indian Office had been carefully hidden away in a cabinet and that when an Indian was found reading this opinion, the copy was forthwith taken from his hands and placed under lock and key. Incidentally, the Indian whose reading was thus interrupted had spent more years in school and college than the men who controlled the lock and key. The Indian Office was sure that the opinion, if released to the public, would be most disturbing. I suppose they were right. . . . Its suppression was equally disturbing to me.[52]

The importance of this dramatic incident is greater than it seems on its surface. The central leadership of the Collier BIA was well aware while struggling with implementation of the IRA that many of its employees were either ignorant of the ideas behind the IRA or disagreed with them. Two memoranda from top leaders in October 1934 demonstrate their acute awareness of this problem. Walter V. Woehlke wrote on October 13 that

> in the Field we have some ninety odd superintendents, very few of whom even know that the policy has changed or what the new policy is. I doubt whether more than half a dozen are fully familiar with the details of the reconstruction plan as laid down in the Indian Reorganization Act. Many of them are not in sympathy with what they consider the objectives of the Bill to be. Others are antagonistic toward the plan and new policy. Along side of them we have thousands of field employees in practically the same mental condition.

He went on to wonder how the new and ambitious policy could be implemented, given these circumstances, writing that "this is a great emergency in the Indian Service," but also suggested that it was "the greatest opportunity ever offered the Service."[53]

Ward Shepard, who had played an important role in shaping the draft bill sent to Congress, wrote on the same day:

> as [Assistant Commissioner] Zimmerman has truly said, there is probably not one single superintendent who thoroughly comprehends the Wheeler-Howard Act and the policies back of it. . . . Moreover, as Armstrong said in open meeting yesterday, none of the Division Chiefs in Washington fully understand either the Act or the policies back of it.

Few other documents indicate that this question was given formal attention by top Bureau policy-makers, but they clearly were aware of the problem raised in these statements.

In any big bureaucracy, large-scale turnover in personnel during a short period is rare, and clearly this did not happen in the BIA when Collier came into office. In the first few months after he took office, only five of the top twenty-two general positions in the Bureau were new, and only 16 out of 106 superintendents were newcomers.[54] Because few non-Indians knew much about Native American life while few Indians were considered qualified for administrative positions, most of the important Bureau leaders were holdovers from the previous Bureau. The Cohen incident shows that at times even important decisions not in tune with the views of the Bureau's leadership could take place. Combined with the fact that the required referendum process pushed the field force into action with little time to educate the key officials and/or win them over, the necessity to reverse policy and make big changes quickly through a bureaucratic structure not wholly in agreement with ultimate objectives must have been seriously handicapping to Collier and his top leadership. A more measured program which began with those Native American societies already knowledgeable about the program and sympathetic with it would probably have led to greater success at accomplishing changes in line with the principles of the IRA. Some of the urgency would have remained without the referendum process. As Taylor has noted, hostility in Congress toward the new policy also increased pressures for rapid progress, lest a new majority in Congress or a change in the White House lead to abandonment of the entire effort.[55]

Cohen's March 5 memorandum went on to point out that, nine months after passage of the act, "no tribe has yet been organized and no general policy has been enunciated looking toward the performance of our legislative promises."[56] He stated his own belief that "tribal organization . . . is the only thing of permanent value that the Government can give to the Indians. Everything else is benevolent despotism; everything else that is given another administration can take away." Cohen then wrote that it "is quite possible that the fault [for the slow pace of organization] is my own," and stated that he had suggested when asked to head the Organization Committee that "it would be better to have a regular member of your staff in charge of this work. However, I shall be glad to continue work either as Chairman of this Committee or in any other capacity, if you think that this work is important and can suggest any way of making it effective."[57]

It is not known what else may have been going on to lead to this extraordinary memorandum, which must have been read by Collier as a resignation, even though the final form was not explicit on this point.[58] On April 10, Cohen sent Collier a formal memorandum in which he offered "my resignation as chairman of the Tribal Organization Committee," since Cohen's successor, Joe Jennings, was "now able to take up definite administrative responsibility in the matter of tribal organization."[59] Jennings headed a new organization division within the Bureau for the next few years.[60]

It is certainly possible that this change in leadership was in part due to a lack of administrative skills on Cohen's part. Cohen's brilliance led him to profound and important written reports, but it is difficult to see how many of his studies—such as the "Basic Memorandum"—could have been used in the field, with either Indians or administrators. However, two other conclusions about this change are apparent.

First, in 1935, at about the time of Cohen's resignation, the Bureau secured the first congressional appropriation[61] specifically earmarked for organizational work. A "Memorandum for the Secretary" from Solicitor Margold reported the appropriation and recommended using part of it to hire at least two attorneys in the solicitor's office to work on tribal organization. The memo went on to indicate that the plan was still to work with a minority of Native societies; it stated that the goal was to "incorporate as many as 100 different Indian tribes without making 'legal mistakes.'"[62] With funds for organizational work provided, the hiring of field personnel for such work became possible for the first time. Perhaps this would have meant replacement of Felix Cohen as the central person in this effort (without Cohen's resignation) by a person with administrative experience.

Whether the transition from a committee headed by him to a division also meant a change in approach toward the organizational questions discussed above is not yet clear. While discovering what was going on in terms of basic policy is not easy because of the way Bureau records were kept in this period, no doubt more research on this problem would tell us more than we know now about this important question.

Second, even without knowing the contemporary attitudes of Commissioner Collier and his group of top aides on these questions, it seems highly likely that Felix Cohen's approach to Indian organization was not fully embraced by them at this time. For example, there was the question of the goal of devolving Bureau functions to Indian governments and the unapproved Basic Memorandum.

Finally, it is clear that Cohen's retirement from leadership of the organizational effort did not lead to his departure from the solicitor's office or the field of Indian policy. Not only did he continue to give legal advice on specific constitutional proposals from tribes, but before his retirement from the solicitor's office in 1948 he wrote the brilliant and very important *Handbook of Federal Indian Law* and continued to be an advocate for Indian rights. In other words, his resignation from this important role was not due to idiosyncratic personal goals, nor did it result from personal animosities. The extent to which his departure from leadership of the organizational effort resulted from policy changes departing from his fundamental ideas remains to be investigated.

CONCLUSIONS

A brief statement of the evidence presented above supports the following conclusions. First, John Collier and his administration sought comprehensive reform of Indian law through passage of an omnibus statute in 1934. Principal goals of this law were to strengthen tribal self-governance and reduce Bureau control over Indians, not weaken self-government or impose EuroAmerican political ideas or concepts on all or even most Native societies. Another important goal was to encourage Indian societies to improve their economic status within reservations protected from dissolution by abolition of the allotment policy.

Second, both the draft bill—later changed in major ways—sent to Congress in early 1934 and the Indian Reorganization Act signed into law in June were clearly based on the stated premise that Native American governments retained substantial numbers of governing powers inherited from their pre-EuroAmerican sovereign status. The IRA cannot be construed to be the source of authority for any Native nation, nor is there any evidence that the Bureau intended to get reservations or tribes to assert such powers according to any preconceived pattern.

Third, the initial organizational strategy of the Bureau—during almost a year after passage of the IRA—was to offer assistance to a few reservations or tribes wishing to adopt constitutions and charters; initial plans were to assist thirty societies in these efforts in the first wave, with the expectation that perhaps only twelve would actually make changes. In other words, there was no plan to impose any kind of organizational structure across Indian Country.

Fourth, the inclusion of Section 18 in the IRA, requiring that an election be held within every Native American society to give Indians an opportunity to reject the act, demonstrated that Indians were important in the legislative process leading to the act. However, ironically, Section 18 may have led a number of Bureau superintendents to conclude that their job was to push constitutions, charters, and an economic program on all or most such societies.

Fifth, Felix Cohen, the leader of the Bureau's organizational effort during the first ten months after passage of the IRA, wanted to implement the act in such a way as to achieve devolution of Bureau functions to tribal governments. However, the IRA did not include proposed provisions to accomplish such an objective. There is good reason to believe that Commissioner Collier never agreed with Felix Cohen that this should be a stated goal of the Indian New Deal, although it is also not likely that he rejected this idea as a long-range goal. Not until the 1970s did Congress adopt this goal in major legislation.

Sixth, in the spring of 1935, after appropriations for this work were finally approved, an Organization Division headed by Joe Jennings was established, to replace the initial effort, which had been controlled by a committee chaired by Felix Cohen. Almost all constitutions adopted by Native American societies during the 1930s were written after creation of the Organization Division.

Seventh, we do not know very much about the process of constitution-making after the initial period, which ended with Cohen's resignation as chair and the appropriation of funds to create a new unit to carry out the work. But we do know that Graham Taylor's overall description of the process of constitution-making is incomplete and in some respects inaccurate. There is no hard evidence that the organizational effort beginning with the appointment of Joe Jennings included the preparation and use of a "model constitution." In the field—on reservations—it was led chiefly by nonlawyer employees of the Organization Division, who were supposed to discover what tribes or reservations wanted in terms of governance (if they wanted a constitution at all). They were then to produce, in cooperation with Native leaders, a rough draft embodying these ideas. Attorneys in Washington played a role only after draft constitutions were written. The draft constitutions had to be approved by a vote of the members of a reservation or a tribe, and also by the Secretary of the Interior.

In short, although decades have passed since passage of the IRA, it is still premature to draw definitive conclusions about the direct impact of this statute on Indian governance in the hundreds of Native American societies. Certainly it is not the case that almost all Native American societies have written constitutions which are essentially the same. Overall data on the patterns of Native governance in recent times are scarce, but the most complete report I have found, compiled in 1981, reports that only 45 percent of Native American societies in the United States had written constitutions drawn up under authority of the IRA or the 1935 Oklahoma act.[63] There are still a large number of Indians governed by unwritten constitutions, although we know even less about these structures than we do about written constitutions.

I will end this already-too-long chapter with two simple pieces of advice to Native Americans interested in enhancing self-governance today. First, whatever was done during the 1930s is not as important as what Native Americans want and need today. Whether Indians want to retain traditional structures, modify them, retain constitutions adopted during the 1930s, or adopt new constitutions, their best judgment about what to do should not be significantly controlled by decisions made two-thirds of a century ago.

Second, the one aspect of the Indian Reorganization Act that does limit Native American constitution-making is the provision that tribal constitutions and amendments to them must be approved by the Secretary of the Interior. Whether this provision can be repealed has not been determined, but doing so would, as Felix Cohen realized, go a long way toward reducing the role of the federal government in the governing of Native American societies.

NOTES

1. This statute is often called the Wheeler-Howard Act, after its formal sponsors in both houses of Congress. "IRA" is used as the title here because assigning major

responsibility to Senator Wheeler and Representative Howard does not reflect the realities of the legislative history of the law.

2. Graham D. Taylor, et al., *The New Deal and American Indian Tribalism: The Administration of the Indian Reorganization Act, 1934–1945* (Lincoln: University of Nebraska Press, 1980).

3. Elmer Rusco, *A Fateful Time: The Background and Legislative History of the Indian Reorganization Act* (Reno: University of Nevada Press, 2000).

4. No overall survey of the nature of Native American self-governance during this period was found, in part because most of the records of the Bureau on these matters are contained in files organized on a tribal basis. I was surprised to find almost no central, overall decision-making records in the National Archives. But a Bureau survey of tribal business councils in the late 1920s disclosed that the most common form of government reported by superintendents at this time was some form of traditional government, even though they had not been asked to report governments of this type.

5. Felix S. Cohen Papers at Yale University, Series I (hereafter Cohen Papers), Box 7, Folder 98, Cohen to Louis C. Mueller, August 1, 1934.

6. Other features of the initial bill—notably a title calling for the creation of a new system of federal Indian courts, provisions designed to devolve Bureau functions to Indian governments, and several provisions providing for involuntary return of allotted lands to tribal ownership—were opposed and dropped.

7. Collier's first specific proposal on Indian self-government had been a 1932 bill to authorize the organization of tribal councils, which explicitly stated that tribal councils which might be organized under the bill would possess the "authority vested in Indian tribes or tribal councils by existing law." In other words, the authority of Native governments would not be created by the bill or by administrative action. The proposal sent to Congress by the Collier administration in early 1934 called for the issuance of charters by the Secretary of the Interior to Native American societies requesting them. These charters—a new idea not accepted in the final act—could have provided for constitutions creating governments or corporations dealing with economic matters. The constitutions created by such charters were to be the inheritors of the authority provided for by "existing law." The explanatory material accompanying the original draft made clear that the already existing powers of Indian tribes would be the basis for the authority of Indian governments. The cumbersome, new, and confusing notion of charters was dropped after introduction—fortunately, since no one could be sure what charters would mean in practice.

Ultimately, the IRA in two sections authorized tribes to draw up and approve both constitutions establishing new governmental structures and charters—given a new meaning—extending the economic powers of corporations to tribal governments. Section 16, referring to constitutions, stated that these had to be approved by the Secretary of the Interior and amended through the same process, but clearly Collier hoped that the governments created by these constitutions could subsequently not be abolished, even by Congress. He was mistaken on the latter point, but his view demonstrates how strongly he wanted to protect Native American governments.

8. This aspect of the measure was most prominent in floor discussions in both the Senate and the House. Members were made aware that the original draft bill had been essentially dropped in favor of a shorter version, and member after member used this fact to assert that the chief meaning of this drastic change had been to make the bill voluntary rather than compulsory.

9. In a memorandum to Commissioner Collier dated March 5, 1935, Cohen wrote that he had devoted most of his time during July and August to researching this question and producing a draft, which was "carefully examined and critically revised first by Mr. Flanery, then by Mr. Wiener and finally by Mr. Margold." Cohen Papers, Box 49, Folder 741.

10. "Powers of Indian Tribes," *Opinions of the Solicitor of the Interior Department,* 55 I.D. 14 (October 25, 1934): 445–477.

11. It would seem that these records should have been turned over to the National Archives and Records Service many years earlier, but obviously Cohen kept these materials when he left the BIA in 1948. Only many years later did his widow, Lucy Kramer Cohen, turn them over to the Beinecke Rare Book and Manuscript Library at Yale University, along with other material documenting Cohen's life and career. Much, though not all, of this part of the Cohen Papers was examined by the author on December 7–10, 1993.

There is no question that the Cohen Papers are a rich source for many topics related to Native American law and policy. Jill E. Martin has written an excellent account of Cohen's role in producing the *Handbook of Federal Indian Law,* largely based on them. "'A Year and a Spring of My Existence': Felix S. Cohen and the *Handbook of Federal Indian Law,*" 8 *Western Legal History* 1 (Winter/Spring 1995): 35–60.

12. We do not know when the strategy for meeting this problem was devised; probably Bureau officials knew for some time that the revised bill would be passed, but it is not known when it learned that there would be no funds to implement it.

13. The committee's other members were Fred H. Daiker, a long-time top Bureau official who in 1933 was Junior Assistant to the commissioner; John R. T. Reeves, Chief Counsel to the Bureau in the previous and Collier administrations; Walter V. Woehlke, a new appointee who was one of Collier's top aides; and a Mrs. E. Smith, about whom I know nothing. Anthropologist Dr. Duncan Strong was named adviser to the committee, reflecting Collier's desire to involve scholars from this discipline in Indian policy-making. "Immediate Program for Organization of Indian Tribes," July 31, 1934, Cohen Papers, Box 8, Folder 117, *Official Register of the United States, 1933* (Washington: Government Printing Office, 1933), 57. Presumably all except Cohen, who continued to be an assistant solicitor for the Interior Department, were Bureau employees. The Cohen Papers, so far as I can determine, do not include any notes of meetings of the committee.

14. A Mrs. Welpley filled the full-time position, assisted initially in the half-time position by a Mr. Drift and then by Paul W. Gordon. Unsigned and undated memorandum in Cohen Papers, Box 49, Folder 741. This memo differs from the one actually sent in several respects; see below. Mrs. Welpley apparently was hired by the Bureau about the beginning of August 1934. Gordon had been director of education for Alaska in the previous administration. *Official Register of the United States, 1932* (Washington: Government Printing Office, 1932), 60. A memorandum by Mrs. Welpley dated October 4, 1934, says that she had been a Bureau employee for about two months by that time. Cohen Papers, Box 8, Folder 117.

15. While not opposing a provision allowing tribes and reservations to initiate a process which would allow rejection of the IRA, the BIA opposed having a universal vote on this issue, but lost in Congress.

16. Felix Cohen, "To Superintendents, Tribal Councils, and Individual Indians," Cohen Papers, Box 8, Folder 118.

17. Abandoning a strategy of piecemeal, gradual implementation of the act required expenditure of a great deal of time, energy, and money by the BIA, all of which were in short supply and could have been devoted to other efforts. The referendum campaign took place when the Bureau was simultaneously expanding its activities and losing employees. Appropriated funds for the Bureau had decreased from a high of over $27 million in fiscal year 1929 to a little over $16 million in fiscal year 1932. Since Collier's administration also spent less tribal funds than the previous one, the result was necessarily a significant drop in Bureau personnel, from a high of 6,638 regular employees on July 1, 1931, to 5,565 by July 1, 1934—a decline of over 16 percent.

18. National Archives Building, Record Group 75, Records of the Bureau of Indian Affairs (hereafter NAB, RG 75), Central Classified Files, 1907–1936, File 17722-1935-066.

19. Taylor, *The New Deal and American Indian Tribalism*, 31, 144.

20. Felix Cohen, Cohen Papers, Box 6, Folder 78. The solicitor's opinion, implicitly recognizing the difficulties this result might cause, went on to state that if the Secretary of the Interior "should find that the number of ballots cast at such an election was too small to represent fairly the views of those entitled to vote," he was authorized to call for a second election, to give the Indians "a second opportunity to exclude themselves." However, the results of the second election were to be interpreted following the same rules as those applying in the first election.

21. National Archives Building, Record Group 48, Records of the Department of the Interior, Central Classified File, 1907–1936, 5–11, Administrative, General, 1929–1936, Part 10.

22. He suggested that Margold had been correct about "the punctuation of the sentence" but then went on to say that "punctuation alone is not an infallible guide in statutory construction." He pointed out also that there was some reason, based on congressional testimony, to believe that "the statute was not intended to be applied to any Indian reservation until approved by a majority of the Indians

concerned." He suggested that "if the Act applies until rejected, there may be a question whether the prior legislation which it supersedes, if effective, will be in force after rejection of the Act."

23. NAB, RG 75, unnamed file in the Wheeler-Howard File.

24. Public Law 147, 74th Congress, approved June 15, 1935.

25. An alternative Bureau strategy to deal with the possibility that the IRA would not apply to significant numbers of Indians was to find exemptions from this exclusion for parts of the act, and ultimately for the entire act. The most important step in this direction was an opinion from the solicitor that the very important section of the IRA ending the allotment policy applied to all parts of Indian Country, whether or not a tribe had rejected the IRA. Senator Wheeler had during Senate consideration of the bill agreed with Collier that educational benefits provided by the act should be extended to individuals even if their tribe had rejected the IRA, and this policy was followed at an early date. Loretta Fowler, in her study of governance among the Northern Arapahoe on the Wind River Reservation, stated that "by the end of 1936 . . . the new legislation and the resultant BIA policies and programs had begun to affect all tribes, whether they accepted the act or not," but I have been unable to find any precise point at which rejection of the IRA became in effect a nullity. However, it is clear that this eventually happened. Fowler, *Arapahoe Politics, 1851–1978* (Lincoln: University of Nebraska Press, 1982), 172.

26. This represented the first step toward the eventual writing by Cohen of the first *Handbook of Federal Indian Law*.

27. "Powers of Indian Tribes," 454.

28. Ibid., 476.

29. While I ended *A Fateful Time* with passage of the IRA, I had originally intended to describe its early implementation, especially with respect to tribal governance. Moreover, I had intended to write a book on implementation of the act in the Great Basin. For these reasons, I collected much material from the National Archives on this topic, and will briefly report much of what was learned from this research. I have also written a number of articles on the formation and approval of constitutions in Nevada, most of which have been published. Most of this research involved careful study of documents in the Organization Division File. I have notes from and copies of materials from the National Archives on constitution-making for a number of Great Basin tribes plus several special cases, including the Santa Clara Pueblo and the Hopi Reservation.

30. Taylor, *The New Deal and American Indian Tribalism,* 37. He also asserted that "during the early stages of tribal organization, the Interior Department's legal division prepared a model constitution that was supposed to form the basis for discussion between Indian delegates and bureau advisers in preparing specific tribal constitutions" (p. 96) and referred to a model constitution at other places.

31. This document seems to have predated the organization committee. It assigns various duties to specified individuals, not all of whom were later committee members; Cohen Papers, Box 3, Folder 34. Regarding constitutions, the memo

states that Daiker, Cohen, and Paul L. Fickinger, the Bureau's assistant director of education, were to "prepare a skeleton or model constitution and set of by-laws to fit an Indian tribe of intermediate size, say about 2000 members." This model constitution was to be written so that it could be adapted to smaller and larger tribes and "to the needs of both primitive and advanced tribes."

The memo also states that Cohen, Reeves, and Fickinger were to "produce a model charter which may be applicable for the incorporation of a majority of the tribes, keeping in mind the need of simplicity." It notes that "special charters" for such tribes as the Red Lake Chippewas, the Menominees, the Klamaths, and the Pueblos might be necessary. In fact, Cohen drafted a model charter during the next few months, which clearly served essentially as "boilerplate," undoubtedly because the purpose was to endow tribal governments with many of the powers of non-Indian corporations; neither the simplicity desired early on nor much variety could in fact be maintained in these documents. Cohen, in his annual report of his activities dated July 29, 1935, states that during the year he had prepared "a model charter for general use in the incorporation of Indian tribes." Cohen Papers, Box 49, Folder 741.

32. Cohen Papers, Box 9, Folder 120.

33. Cohen Papers, Box 8, Folder 117.

34. By the middle of 1935, there were several statements from Bureau leaders reporting explicitly that there was no such document. For example, a letter from Assistant Commissioner William Zimmerman to a Pima Indian written May 6, 1935, contains this statement: "You say that you have never received a copy of the administration's proposed constitution. The Office is not issuing any form of constitution for the adoption of the Indians. It is our idea that the Indians at the proper time and in conjunction with representatives of the Washington Office should work together and prepare the type of constitution and by-laws which the Indians want and which will be consistent with the provisions of the act and the opinion of the Solicitor." Noting that part of this process had already taken place with the Pima Indians and that a draft constitution had been developed, Zimmerman wrote, "it does not follow that you must adopt the Pima constitution or any other." NAB, RG 75, Central Classified Files, 1907–1936, File 17722-1935-066.

35. This seven-page document has been encountered in many places. See Cohen Papers, Box 8, Folder 106.

36. Elmer R. Rusco, "Civil Liberties Guarantees under Tribal Law: A Survey of Civil Rights Provisions in Tribal Constitutions," *American Indian Law Review* 14 (1989): 269–299.

37. Cohen Papers, Box 8, Folder 106.

38. Cohen Papers, Box 8, Folder 118.

39. A model charter was developed and used in the manner suggested by Taylor, as noted above, and it appears that some constitutions approved earlier were used by some field agents at times as a starting point for discussions.

40. Taylor, *The New Deal and American Indian Tribalism*, 82–85, 39–62.

41. Ibid., 41–44, 151–158.

42. Ibid., 177.

43. Graham Taylor is a historian. There may be disciplinary reasons why he paid little attention to the mechanics of constitutions and governments. A political scientist such as myself automatically begins by considering constitutions and their contents important when dealing with serious questions of the nature of governance in various societies.

One reason for Taylor's approach was that he properly linked the organizational information with information about Indian New Deal efforts to improve Indian life economically. While he admits that in some cases the latter programs meshed with invigorated tribal governments to produce substantial positive effects, in many cases the results were meager or ineffective. While the inability to make massive improvements in the reduction of Indian poverty may well be related to difficulties in the Indian New Deal effort to increase self-governance, it is certain that much of the difficulty in these matters resulted from limited congressional support in the form of appropriations and from a considerable amount of hostility from key quarters in Congress. Taylor reports that Collier's departure from the commissionership in 1945 was forced by budgetary threats; ibid., 142.

44. The latter activity is only partly documented in the Cohen Papers, probably because the small Washington staff could not work with very many tribes, but also because many materials dealing with this area of interest are contained in individual agency files of the separate Organization Division File in the National Archives Building.

45. Series I of the Cohen Papers documents the effort to acquire more information to aid the organizational effort. One example of this search for information is the October memo (noted above) asking twelve questions about the meaning of the IRA; this was initially only partially answered by the solicitor, although the other questions were answered in December. On July 17, Cohen sent to Commissioner Collier a draft of a form—developed by the organization committee—for collecting statistical information from tribes "to be used in the work leading up to the granting of constitutions and charters." Cohen stated that the data collected in this fashion would be placed in a "general organization file for each tribe" and summarized in a "statistical abstract." Assistant solicitor to Collier, Cohen Papers, Box 6, Folder 75. In his memorandum to Collier of March 5, 1935, Cohen reported that this statistical information had not been gathered by that time. Referring to the July 17 memo, he wrote that the data were available in the statistics division and that the committee had requested much of the data from this division. However, he had been informed by the head of this division that producing this information would take one employee a week and that she "could not spare anyone for this purpose, at least for a long time to come." Cohen remarked that the director had "apparently never been informed of the responsibilities" of the committee and "therefore probably considered me an officious intermeddler." Cohen Papers, Box 49, Folder 741. This memo also referred to memoranda of November

19, 22, and 27 asking for policy decisions relating to the work of the committee, and asserted that replies had never been received. He stated that while members of the committee had "ventured to answer certain questions raised by the constitutional conventions at Yuma, Gila River, and San Carlos, last December, . . . as yet the Indians concerned do not know whether these opinions were correct statements of departmental policy." On July 12, a questionnaire was sent out to superintendents seeking information about the governing experience and present structures of tribes or reservations. A substantial number of replies were received; they can be found in individual files in the records of the Organization Division. A copy of the cover letter for this questionnaire can be found in Box 9, Folder 122, "Indian organization/Indian organization-Anthropological Data/1933−34." These files also contain replies from anthropologists about governance in many tribes; these were acquired during the drafting process.

46. Cohen Papers, Box 7, Folder 100.

47. Box 7, Folder "Indian-Org/Basic Memorandum on Indian org."

48. Cohen Papers, Box 7, Folder 101: 1−2.

49. "Basic Memorandum," 38.

50. Cohen Papers, Box 49, Folder 741.

51. The combination of identifying the Indian involved as the chairman of the Navajo Tribe with the statement that he was well educated establishes that the individual must have been Thomas Dodge. He was the well-educated son of Henry Chee Dodge, chairman of the tribal council for much of the 1920s. Thomas Dodge was elected to this position in 1934 and served until 1936. Donald C. Parman, *The Navajos and the New Deal* (New Haven: Yale University Press, 1976), 39, 160; Cohen Papers, Box 49, Folder 741.

52. Cohen wrote that, after realizing that Chief Justice John Marshall, Pope Paul III, and Bartholomé de las Casas "had all received the same treatment. . . . I was relieved to find myself in such good company, and so, instead of resigning, I distributed copies of the opinion where I thought they would do the most good." Lucy Kramer Cohen, ed., *The Legal Conscience: Selected Papers of Felix S. Cohen* (New Haven: Yale University Press, 1960), 307.

53. NAB, RG 75, Office Files of John Collier, file "Regional Organization." See also Taylor, *The New Deal and American Indian Tribalism*, 112−113.

54. Rusco, *A Fateful Time*, 180.

55. Taylor, *The New Deal and American Indian Tribalism*, 141.

56. The first constitution to be approved was that of the Flathead reservation of Montana, which reached this stage on October 26, 1935. Only eight more tribal constitutions were approved during the remainder of 1935.

57. In the unsigned handwritten memo quoted above, Cohen had stated clearly, on the first page, that he was resigning. He wrote: "Regretfully I have come to the conclusion . . . that this work has been futile, and that it is therefore incumbent upon me to offer you my resignation as Chairman of the Tribal Organization Committee."

58. Nine days after the March 5 memorandum, Cohen sent a memorandum to Solicitor Margold in which he mentions having had discussions over lunch with Commissioner Collier. Cohen then wrote: "I feel very strongly" that a Mr. Joe Jennings should be appointed to "a regular administrative post charged with the single task of carrying through the tribal organization program." He also wrote that he would be happy to be relieved of his administrative duties, although he would like to "continue work on the legal phases of the organization program." Cohen Papers, Box 49, Folder "Personnel Files/Official Status."

59. Cohen Papers, Box 49, Folder 741.

60. Graham Taylor states, incorrectly, that the Organization Division was established in 1936 and that at its founding it was headed by Fred Daiker; *The New Deal and American Indian Tribalism,* 37. Obviously Taylor did not know of this early stage in the organization effort. Daiker was listed in the federal government's *Official Register* for 1935 and 1936 as an Employment Supervisor, while neither Jennings nor any head of the Organization Division was listed for these years. I believe that Jennings continued to head the division for several years.

61. This first congressional appropriation was for $150,000, although the authorized appropriation was $250,000.

62. June 6, 1935. Cohen Papers, Box 49, Folder 741.

63. Rusco, *A Fateful Time,* 301.

Firsthand Accounts

WHY ENGAGE IN CONSTITUTIONAL REFORM?

Albert Hale, Former President, Navajo Nation
Sheri YellowHawk, Council Member, Hualapai Nation
Steve Brady, Sr., Former Member, Northern Cheyenne
  Tribe Constitutional Reform Committee, and Instruc-
  tor, Northern Cheyenne Government and History
Larry Foster, Former Chair, Navajo Nation Commission
  on Government Development
Michelle Dotson, Executive Director, Office of Navajo
  Government Development
Le Roy Shingoitewa, Chair, Hopi Tribe Constitutional
  Reform Committee
John Peters, Jr., Executive Director, Commonwealth of
  Massachusetts Commission on Indian Affairs, Member
  of Mashpee Wampanoag
Ross Swimmer, Former Principal Chief, Cherokee Nation
  of Oklahoma, and Former Assistant Secretary, Indian
  Affairs, U.S. Department of the Interior
Leonard D. Dixon, Former Outreach Coordinator,
  Lummi Nation Constitutional Reform Committee

ALBERT HALE, FORMER PRESIDENT, NAVAJO NATION

[Navajo introduction] I'm a member of the Salt Clan.
For those of you who love to eat with salt, I'm your man. I'm also born
for Bitter Water. My fathers are of the Bitter Water Clan. My paternal
grandparents are of the Tall House people, and my maternal grandparents
are of the Walkabout Clan. So that's who I am.

I'm reminded of a story, and I've told this story before because it really points out to me the problem that we have in terms of looking at the same thing and having different interpretations. We think we're talking about the same thing, we think we understand each other, but we really don't. And constitutions are just another one of these issues. If I delivered this presentation in Navajo those of you who don't speak Navajo would not even know what I was talking about. And the same with Navajos who live in the Navajo Nation, or Cherokee who are traditional, or the Hualapai who are traditional and have no English education. If I did this presentation in English they wouldn't have a clue of what I was talking about, all the different concepts.

There was a dispute, or a discussion, over who was the smarter of the two races, Indian people or white people. The white person said, "We're smarter because look at all the things we did. We came across the big waters, explored and conquered many, many worlds. What have you done, Indian?" Couldn't say a word. Didn't know what they've done that could outdo that. Finally the white guy said, "Look at all those tall buildings; we're smarter because we made those. We thought about them, we constructed them. Now look at the computers, we built those. You know what, we're even smarter because we sent a man to the moon. What have you done, Indian?" The Indian just stands there, looks at his feet, wiggles around a bit not knowing what to say. Finally he said, "We're smarter, because, let me tell you what, we're going to send a man to the sun." And the white guy said, "That's impossible, that guy's going to burn up before he gets there." And the Indian guy, sort of baffled, stands there for a while and finally said, "We're going to send him at night." [Laughter]

You know, this is two different ways of looking at the same thing and coming up with different perceptions about it, different interpretations, different worldviews. In the context of what we're talking about, constitutional reform, we all have to understand that it is, bottom line, an exercise of sovereignty. That's the bottom line. With constitutional reform we're talking about Indian nations doing what they have to do, or can do, in forming a structure that will bring them together, and to address common problems through a mechanism. That's what we're talking about. But even when we talk about that sovereignty, we have different interpretations, we have different perceptions about it. We're not on common ground when we talk about sovereignty, and then the step beyond that, exercising sovereignty. We're all on different levels of interpretation.

When we talk about constitutional reform and forming a government we're talking about an exercise of sovereignty. In that process, one of the things we should always keep in mind as members of Indian nations, as developing Indian nations, is that we all have a role in that development. We all have an input. We all have something to contribute. But in my experience, especially when I was president of the Navajo Nation, one of the things that I found out was even those of us who are members of Indian nations, or leaders of Indian nations, don't understand what sovereignty is, we don't know what it means. So we run to Congress, and we say to Congress, "You owe me this because I'm a sovereign entity. You have to deal with me because I'm a sovereign nation. You have to deal with me in a certain way because I'm a sovereign nation." But when it really comes down to getting questioned about that we can't really respond because we have become comfortable and, above all, we have accepted other peoples' definition of our sovereignty. By that I mean court decisions—the federal government defining for us what our sovereignty is. But that's not sovereignty. When we go to somebody else and we say, "Can you tell me, as a sovereign entity, what I can do?" That's not sovereignty. Sovereignty is having the ability to go to that person and say to that person, "I can do this because I'm sovereign. I don't need you to approve my constitutional charter." The question shouldn't be is that document, the constitution that you have produced, acceptable to the federal government? What will the Secretary of the Interior say? Will the Secretary of the Interior approve this document? That shouldn't be the question.

The question should be, as a sovereign entity, as a truly sovereign nation, is this constitution, this form of government, acceptable to us? To our people? That should be the question. And that should be the only question. And if it is acceptable to our people, to your people, then it is and that's the way it should be. That is sovereignty. That is the exercise of sovereignty. We have to have the courage to exercise that sovereignty. But we don't now as Indian people, as Indian leaders. And you know why? In my mind because we have been so long under a colonial power that our minds have been colonialized. To truly take that step we need to take that initial step of decolonizing our minds, of getting away from saying, "Is this acceptable to the federal government?" We have to get away from that. Only then can we adopt governments, or forms of governments, or constitutions that truly reflect our culture, that can be truly culturally based and supported, and can stand the test of time. Otherwise they'll fall down. Otherwise they'll fall down.

You look at the IRA tribes. They adopted the form of constitution that's spelled out in the IRA Act, the Indian Reorganization Act. So, if you look throughout Indian Country at those tribes that have adopted those IRA forms of government and constitutions, what do you see?

Dual developments of government—one that's recognized through the IRA, and one that's recognized by tradition. And at some point it conflicts, it comes to a head. The conflict at Navajo. The conflict at Cherokee. The conflicts in the Pueblos, where there are dual systems of government that have developed as a result of that. The only way I see that we can make this accommodation, or this consistency between our culture and a traditional form of government on the one hand and a constitutional or a modern day form of government to meet modern day needs on the other hand, is to bring these two together so that the culture, the tradition, the values that are uniquely Navajo, or Cherokee, or Pueblo, can support that government, that form of government. Otherwise you can't support that government.

If you look across the country, look at the governments that were supported by the United States. What happened? They ultimately fell because the people didn't support them. They're gone now. So we need to decolonize our minds. Well, what does that mean? To me it means we have to recognize what we say, the words that we use. In Navajo the teaching is to be careful with your words because words are sacred, words are powerful. The words that we talk, the language that we talk in Navajo is given to us by the Holy People, so you need to be careful with those words. So we try to be. The words that we use reduce our sovereignty. On the one hand we refer to ourselves as tribes. Take a look at what that means. On the other hand we refer to ourselves as nations. If we continue to refer to ourselves as tribes, you know what we do? We limit our sovereignty, because when we talk about tribes we're only talking about our members. We're only talking about a group of people that has tradition, values, and language in common. That's inconsistent with sovereignty because, as I understand sovereignty, as I understand nation, the word *nation* supports the notion of sovereignty. Because if you're a nation you have the ability within your lands, within your boundary, to adopt laws that will govern everybody in that jurisdiction, not only your members. But if you consistently refer to yourselves as a tribe, people from the outside will consistently treat you as a tribe and limit your sovereignty. That's why it's important that we start the process of referring to ourselves as nations, because when we start referring to ourselves as nations, we expand our sovereignty. We can exercise jurisdiction over everyone who comes within our land, regardless of his or her racial background. We need to start doing that. I think that is the reason why the federal government continued to refer to us as the Navajo tribe before we made the change to referring to ourselves as the Navajo Nation.

So we have to move in that direction, decolonizing our minds, getting out of that. Remember, when you're writing a constitution you're exercising your sovereignty. And when you write those words, expand your sovereignty. Protect it. That's what the federal government does. That's what the state government does, because they're always fighting Indian nations when we assert our sovereign rights. They want to limit our rights as sovereign entities because they want to expand theirs. We shouldn't just sit back and let that happen. We should fight back. When we form our own government, we should exercise that sovereignty, and expand it, and act as true sovereign entities. Don't just talk the talk, walk the walk. Don't just say you're sovereign and be afraid to be sovereign. Be sovereign, act sovereign; only that way will people treat you as sovereign. Only that way.

And let me tell you some of the other things that have to happen in the context of decolonizing our minds. If you look at the history of Indian people, one thing we have in common is the atrocities we had to suffer at the hands of the Europeans. Again, this goes back to the use of words and description. Why do you think they called us savages? Why do you think they called us heathens? Why do you think that they've labeled us and the oral histories of our creations as stories and not as history? The reason why is they wanted to minimize us, to make us subhuman. It's easier to steal from savages because they don't know what the heck they're doing. It's easier to kill a savage than a human. It's easier to justify that. That's what I mean when I say look at those words. Look at the words that the federal government uses, that the dominant society uses to describe you. They call you the Hualapai tribe because that's the way they want you to be. They don't want you to exercise your sovereignty. And when they continue to treat you as a tribe, and describe you as a tribe for years, you'll end up in cases like *Oliphant* where the Supreme Court said tribal courts do not have criminal jurisdiction over non-Indians. Why? Because we've always dealt with them that way. Because the BIA and the government has always treated Indian tribes as not having jurisdiction over non-Indians. That was the reason for that decision.

So all I'm telling you is that you have to walk the walk. In this process of reform, do that, and you will enhance and advance your sovereignty, instead of just talking about it. Do that and you'll begin to take that step towards truly being sovereign, and towards that achieving of a mechanism that can really reflect your values, your culture, your tradition.

One thing that we were trying to do in the 1989 amendments to Title 2 of the Navajo Nation Code is exactly that. We recognized that we needed to expand our sovereignty through these documents, through these amendments, and that's what we tried to do. The other thing that we tried to do in the Title 2 amendments was to create a process of continuing to reform the Navajo Nation government. One real important thing that we recognized, which is the basis of constitutional government as I understand it, is that the government exists because it's consented to by the people who are governed. But you know what? For Indian people, we have never consented for the federal government to govern us. We never have. So what does that mean with regard to Indian people? We have adopted forms of government that were put out there for us by the federal government. And in taking that form of government, and adopting it, internalizing it, and using it to govern our people, we never gave our people the opportunity to consent to be governed by that form of government. So we have never given that basis, or that opportunity to our people to consent to a particular form of government. We continue to do that to this day. I support the revision of constitutions, I support the constitutional and governmental reform that's going on in Indian Country, but it has to come from that basis. It has to come from the people in order for that government to survive. The Navajo Nation government was a government that was taken from the federal government, adopted as the Navajo Nation government, and then added on to. We need to address that too.

So, I'm talking to you at two levels. One is the exercise of sovereignty with regard to your relationship with the federal government, our relationship with the federal government, and the second is our exercise of our sovereignty in our relationship with our own citizens.

And again, back to using words. When we talk about sovereignty and tribal sovereignty—and I don't want to be critical of any of the people who are writing academic articles—but as I was flipping through the documents here I saw tribal sovereignty side by side. To me they're inconsistent. Why are you using them together? You're perpetuating that thing that I just talked about. They shouldn't be used together. It should be Indian nation sovereignty instead of tribal sovereignty. When you say "tribal sovereignty," immediately what comes to my mind is that this is just for tribal members, it's not for those people who are found within the territorial jurisdiction of Indian nations. It's inconsistent with concepts of nationhood and nation building. So I beg you, those of you who are in academia, when you are writing papers, watch out for these things. Don't refer to us as tribes when you're trying to build our nationhood, or advance our sovereignty. Refer to us as nations. If you refer to us as nations then we won't be talking about enrollments. And we won't be having conflicts and discussions about he's only a quarter Navajo, and therefore he's not eligible for enrollment. We won't be talking about that. If we're dealing with ourselves as nations, what will we be talking about? Citizenship. Citizens of Navajo Nation, not enrolled members in Navajo Nation. Expanding that sovereignty and building that sovereignty is necessary to becoming a true nation so that you can then, you can look at these problems. Look at the problems of economic development and the internal obstacles stemming from our government structures and the obstacles brought about by the federal government as your problems. You can start dealing with those obstacles and removing them because they're inconsistent with nation building. They're inconsistent with sovereign status.

If you work from that basis, then you can truly become sovereign.

SHERI YELLOWHAWK, COUNCIL MEMBER,
HUALAPAI NATION

They [elders] keep talking about it [bringing back tradition] and I feel bad about it when I respond to it because I say, "How are you going to do that when we are so far gone? We don't live in wickiups anymore. We don't ride horses or walk around anymore. We don't have any medicine people anymore. And even the tribes that do, they all charge. We shop in the grocery store. We go to the clinic for our medicine. And we're third or fourth generation physically, emotionally, sexually abused. How are you going to deal with all that and then want to go back to these traditional ways?" They're going to have find a way, instead of just saying we're going to go back—because that's what they always talk about, "You have to go back." You're not going back anywhere. That's gone. You're going to have to find a way to bring some of that forward. And incorporate it into the lives now. They need to get away from "we're going to go back to this." Because there's nothing to go back to. That's all gone. . . . The state of the community and the way that we've been brought up has not been traditional and how are you all of a sudden going back to that? And I think it's going to take the young people

*to find out what it was and bring it forward and incorporate it
into our lives now.*
YOUNG TRIBAL COUNCIL MEMBER

*Sometimes they forget they are Indian. They want so much
to be in the mainstream. Tradition doesn't carry too much
weight.*
ELDER AT SAME TRIBE

I'm the young tribal council member in the above passage. I believe
there's five aspects of culture: government or leadership, education, family, religion, and economy. Tribes have been fighting the assimilation that
the BIA has facilitated and modeled with respect to the first two aspects,
government/leadership and education, and many of our councils right
now currently resemble these models. Our education system consists of
public or BIA schools, and they're teaching our children all the realms of
Western civilization. We might have a little bit of a language program,
might have a little bit of a basket-making program, but there are no real
teachings in the school of our culture or language. So our children are
no longer taught their role in the tribe. A long time ago we were raised
to have a role, we had a purpose, and now we don't really have a sense of
purpose inside our tribe. So our new constitution would need to address
that. What are the people's purpose[s] inside the tribe?

Our family systems have even been separated into individual family
units. We didn't live like that before. We were one big family, and now
we're these little bitty, separate family units of all kinds of varying sorts. I
mean, you might have one parent, two parents, four parents, no parents,
grandparent, and a whole array of kids related by all different ways, and
when you try to talk to somebody else's kid you end up getting in trouble. It used to not be like that. I used to get yelled at down the road by
somebody else's mom and dad and I listened to them. Nowadays, when I
try to do that I get cussed out, so things have really changed.

Our religion has been replaced by churches and visiting missionaries.
Our economy is no longer based on survival. Our economy used to just
be we're going to eat, and we're going to be healthy, and we're going to
survive. And now it's business. It has been transformed into the capital-
istic model of the United States, which is kind of strange for us because
I think Indians were generally socialists. They always focused on how to
meet everybody's needs. It conflicts with us when we're trying to go into
business, when we're trying to get money to sustain ourselves. It's a

different concept because it used to be we were trying to get food to sustain ourselves. It conflicts with the way that we think currently. We need to take that into consideration.

Some of us are standing around and talking about the tribes, and talking about white people this, and white people that. I can't stand that. It just makes me crazy, because it confuses me when somebody is saying that but yet they have a cell phone in their pocket, and then they're going outside and they're driving away in a car, and you're thinking, "But who gave you that, or how did you get that?" You bought, with money, the same system that these white people are using. So, I think we also need to address our hypocrisy and our own racism because Indian people are incredibly racist, and they don't even realize it. We need to start addressing that because it gets in the way of our progress and whatever is left of our culture, because it exists in varying degrees within each tribe. Some tribes are still rich in their culture and their language, and some tribes are not, and they have little bits and pieces that they're trying to hang onto.

But what we need to do is whatever you have left of your culture, whatever you have left of your language, needs to be incorporated into these constitutions, and into our future activities for our children instead of standing around and talking about it because that's what happens in our council meetings. Somebody talks about being full-blooded Hualapai, and I look at him and think, "But you have facial hair, you cannot be full-blooded Hualapai." These things go through my mind. And how do you know for the last ten thousand years you came straight down from one person, one lineage? These things go through my head and we need to stop blaming each other and yelling at each other about these things and start preserving our culture, our language, and our constitution, so that it will continue.

I went to a meeting and we were talking about team building. One tribal member stood up and said, "Well, that's a white way of teaching." I thought about that after that meeting, and I thought how is it that you come together, everybody has a purpose, everybody has a task and a role, and they all have a common purpose. How is that white? Isn't that what we used to do to survive a long time ago? It's probably my fault because I should have said it a different way and then it would have made a connection in somebody else's mind.

I think that our constitutions should require that our elected leaders learn the language because we need to preserve it. I've been trying very hard to learn the language, and it's hard because I don't have anybody in my family that speaks it fluently. I have to pick it up here and there. But I think we need a harsher requirement because otherwise we're going to lose our language. I don't think that we should go so far as to where we're going to exclude some of our people from office because they haven't had the opportunity to learn or be exposed to the language. I think that it should be included somewhere in the constitution that it's required of elected officials to learn the language and to be exposed to it. I don't know how. You know every time I say something in Hualapai they laugh, and then they say, "Say it again, say it again," and they want to tease me about it and that kind of makes me not want to say things. But then that's kind of our Hualapai way—we like to tease, and we like to laugh. So I try to just get over it and keep going on with it.

STEVE BRADY, SR., FORMER MEMBER, NORTHERN CHEYENNE CONSTITUTIONAL REFORM COMMITTEE

My name is Steve Brady. My Cheyenne name is Night Wolf. I'm a headsman of the Crazy Dog Society, first of all. I belong to the traditional system, the traditional Council of Chiefs, and the traditional military societies. This system has been in existence for centuries upon centuries, perhaps thousands of years. It goes to the very core of our existence in terms of identity, in terms of culture, in terms of language. I was involved in the constitutional reform process for the Northern Cheyenne tribe from about 1990 until about 1996. I sat on a committee. I also chaired the committee, and then the tribal council later appointed me as a coordinator to coordinate the daily affairs of the constitutional amendment process.

This thought, or this notion of including traditional systems into contemporary written systems is very difficult thing. It's heavy duty. It's not light. It's not to be taken lightly at all. It's far reaching, profound in many ways. While I have been involved in the amendment of this Indian Reorganization Act system, this written system, I've also been involved extensively in the rebuilding of our traditional systems, and that's been probably almost thirty years of my life. It's been a long time. A couple of generations. My predecessors that I worked with also wanted to see the rebuilding, the regeneration of our traditional system. It's been a long time coming and we still have a long way to go.

Whether or not it will ever be written down, codified, I don't know. I don't know that we have enough paper to actually do that. It's a vast, extensive system. It covers much spirituality, traditional laws, laws that have existed since time immemorial, or beyond memory. The prophets who brought us the traditional systems from our sacred sites and our holy covenants that we still have, sacred arrows, the sacred hat. I've been a covenant keeper before and I know the sacredness of these responsibilities for our people, and it's a very, very difficult responsibility. You carry all of the people with you and I would say it's different than being an elected official, far different.

Our traditions are still very, very meaningful. Very meaningful. You can't put into words the spiritual meaning of these responsibilities. And while the written constitution guides us, and certainly in some ways protects us, and maybe in some cases is a hindrance in our existence, in much the same way the traditional covenants guide us and protect us. And if you don't understand them, they appear to be regressive, but they're not. They're the very, very fundamental definition of who we are, and what we're all about, and where we come from.

Centuries before the coming of [the] white man, we knew that he was coming. We knew that there was going to be the coming of the horse and to welcome them. And we were also told that the white man was going to take everything that we had. Sadly so, it has come to reality in many, many ways. Millions upon millions of buffalo have ceased to exist from the northern reaches of Canada where we used to go, down into Texas. We can no longer do that. The boundaries, all of the rivers have Cheyenne names from the Missouri River down to Palo Duro Canyon in Texas. Our people are scattered all over. We have battle sites that have very, very historical contexts. The locations of where we used to go, our territory.

When the Sand Creek Massacre occurred on November 29, 1864, we came to a stark realization that the white man was here. He completely wiped out our traditional system, our traditional band systems. Twice I've testified before the United States Senate on the Sand Creek Massacre, and we finally got it set aside as a National Historic Site. This only happened in November 2000 after two letters came forth from cavalry officers that were written about a week and a half after Sand Creek and that described in very graphic detail what occurred to the Cheyenne women at Sand Creek. The dismembering of people, children, things like that.

All of this occurred during Abraham Lincoln's administration and since then our traditional system has been severely weakened because our band system was pretty much wiped out, and with it our method for selecting our traditional council of chiefs. It's been a very, very difficult process since then, and it's within memory of my family. My family was there. But nonetheless, we continue to carry on. We still have our sacred covenants with us.

In 1879, our reservation was established by executive order. It was expanded in 1884 and, subsequently, in 1900. Then in 1926 Congress passed a law called the Northern Cheyenne Allotment Act, and by the time they got done allotting land on the Northern Cheyenne Reservation, it was about 1932–1933. Incidentally, our tribal members, for some reason or another, petitioned for allotment to the U.S. Congress. Shortly thereafter the Indian Reorganization Act was passed in 1934. And for some reason or another our people decided to vote for an IRA-type constitution which repealed the allotment system. So, within a very short time, our people petitioned Congress for allotment and, all within the same breath, also voted for an IRA constitution. So, I am not certain that all the messages were carried across to where our people understood them. I do believe that the Indian Reorganization Act system is a system that quite often conflicts with traditional systems and was intended to do away with them. Whether or not the people really knew what they were voting on when they voted for an IRA constitution in 1935 remains in question.

The only thing that alludes to our culture in our IRA government is that the tribal council supports our culture, and that's about the extent of it under the enumerated powers of the tribal council. Will we be able to blend the traditional system and the contemporary written system together? I don't know. I don't think that it's doable at this point, and I don't think that we're able to put it down in writing because of the profound significance, the far-reaching implications of doing so. In addition, we would also need to have extensive authorization by the covenant keepers, the council of chiefs, and the military societies. If it's going to be put into written format, it's going to require some very, very lengthy, detailed discussion. There's very specific, traditional, legal protocol that has to be adhered to. We haven't decided to put that into written, legal format. It exists. It exists. Many, many people, anthropologists, lawyers, archeologists, historians have written about our traditional system. It is very well documented in terms of historical context, but in terms of formal, written, constitutional format, it hasn't been done. There has to be a tremendous amount of protocol, lengthy protocol, and to the extent of even breaking traditional law.[1]

The other thing that is going to be difficult is having jurisdiction over major crimes. It's going to be difficult. It was taken away from us through the Major Crimes Act, among others. So there's a lot of legal implications. The idea of living on a reservation in a fixed location is another. We used to be a nomadic people.

And so there is so much, so much. I've been working in both areas for a long time and I can see the conflict, and I can see the two systems complementing each other from time to time. So, we've got a long ways to go. The United States isn't ready to let us go yet either. Our traditional system is based upon two covenants and if the United States wants to truly recognize our traditional system then it has to surrender much of the occupied territory that it has because it pertains to our sacred sites in the Rocky Mountains, and over in the Black Hills and into the Great Lakes region. Nor are we ready to absolve the United States of its fiduciary obligations. It's a difficult task. It's good to hear that other tribes are wrestling with these issues, that we're not alone. Colonialism has had devastating consequences, terribly devastating. My generation is probably the last generation of fluent speakers for our language and we're trying to regain control of that. So much has to be done in a very short time and you don't want to hurry the process because you're afraid of making mistakes. But I think that we're going to probably make some mistakes along the way and I hope that we can learn from them.

LARRY FOSTER, FORMER CHAIR, NAVAJO NATION COMMISSION ON GOVERNMENT DEVELOPMENT

[Navajo introduction] My name is Larry Foster. I'm with the Navajo Nation. My clan is Red Running into the Water; that's my mother's clan. My father's clan is One Who Walks Around clan. I've been with the Navajo government for a long time. Coming back from the private sector, I was enticed to move back home from the West Coast. I planned to go home for five years and then go back to the West Coast. Well, I'm still there.

I served as an advisor to tribal councils, to tribal chairmen and tribal presidents. I chaired the Navajo Commission on Government Development for about ten years and worked with a lot of our tribal programs. I've left the tribe now. I do international work, a lot of work with the United Nations. I do work in Russia with three Native tribes, down in South Africa with the Zulus, all over, helping people build indigenous governments.

In the past, pre-treaty, we didn't have enrollment problems. It wasn't until the U.S. government came in and started issuing us census numbers. That's when we started having enrollment problems. Pre-treaty, when a non-Navajo married a Navajo they became a part of our people, they had property rights, and it stayed within the clans. So basically, a lot of this is that we forget who we are. We try to act so much like the white man. We want to copy him so much that we're over here spinning our wheels.

I'll tell you a story. One time I was way up in the mountains with the medicine men. All the medicine men and the medicine ladies came together and they went to a mountain called Chuska Mountain. They asked me to come up there. At the time I was still on the Navajo Nation Commission on Government Development and they wanted to hear from us what we were doing. "Which direction are you leading us?" they asked. I explained to them what we were doing. I told them that we started a really aggressive program of educating ourselves, and that some of the younger generation were saying, "The white man is so far ahead, so sophisticated, has the technology in place, and we're so far behind."

I sat in the hogan with the elders and they thought about it. In the end, you know what they told me? They said, "What the young people are saying might be true. But we think we are in the right place. It's just that the white man has moved so far ahead that he's going off the cliff. Eventually he's going to kill himself. You look at the air, the pollution, the water. Everything is polluted. We need to be patient. So long as we have our nation, so long as we have four sacred mountains for ourselves, we'll be OK. Let the rest of the world go off the cliff."

So they're saying go back to who you really are. As I said earlier, what has been pushed on us with enrollment is an issue now, but if we go back to our traditional concepts we won't have enrollment problems. If my daughter marries a Sioux, her decision will be, does she go to South Dakota or is he going to come to Navajo? If he comes to Navajo, traditionally he'll become a part of our nation. And traditionally I would think that the Sioux would also reciprocate if my daughter went up north. So that's how we dealt with it in the past.

We started dealing with governmental reform to prevent a political crisis. We knew that we were going down that road where sooner or later we were going to hit that crisis. Like I said, I started looking at government reform in 1976 and it took about 13 years to hit that crisis. But in our traditional way, we have our songs, we have our chants, the blessing ways. We call it *hozho*—that means everything evolves around life, the natural laws. There are songs in place. They're not written down but are in our memory. It's in songs. That's our natural laws. The medicine man that sits on our government reform commission tells us it's just like we have sacred medicine bundles. I wear my hair tied up because it's part of our medicine bundles back home, and these are medicine bundles brought from the sacred mountains. Everything in life—water, air—everything in life that evolves around us comes through the bundles. And they tell us in our tradition that every four years we have to open these medicine bundles up and put light back into them, put life back into them. We look at it and say what else needs to be done. That's done by clan, by families. My family does that. Every four years we have a ceremony. We bring in all our relatives. We do a ceremony. We open the bundles. We have prayers. Basically, it's like a self-inventory. Are we OK? What do we need to do to get back? If we're not OK, what do we need to do to get back in harmony? The medicine man that sits on our commission tells us that we have to use that concept because we're never going to be perfect. Everything is changing.

But we have the basic laws in place and use the principle that you're always going to have to do an inventory periodically. So that's why I was interested in what the Cherokees are doing because they do a periodic inventory of reviewing their constitution every twenty years. To me, that would be a periodic inventory, reviewing where you are as changes take place and time goes by. That's kind of how the governmental reform commission works. They may not move as fast as people want it to go. They may decide, "Hey, let the rest of the world fall off the cliff. We'll be OK so long as we're in the sacred mountains."

The other thing too is that in looking at this self-inventory, one of the things we said when I chaired the commission was that all we're trying to do is structure. We're not trying to change the government from the top down, and force things on people. My thought, based on my teachings, was that we needed to go to the local people, do it from the grassroots level up. Build it from the ground up. It's like building a home. You have to first lay the foundations. To us our chapters of local government were our foundations, so we started from the ground up and that's where the 1998 Local Governance Act came in, giving more power back to our local communities.

So I think we're taking one step at a time and moving along so that we know where we're going. Basically we're moving ahead but we don't know how fast we'll go because of 300,000 Navajos, we have three main factions. We have the Christians, one-third, we have about 100,000 traditional Navajos that just believe in the Navajo way, and we have approximately 100,000 Navajo that believe in the Native American Church. So we have three factions to deal with. Then, in the next two years, we're probably going to see half of our Navajo population living off reservation. So we're going to have to balance that. It's going to take time.

MICHELLE DOTSON, EXECUTIVE DIRECTOR,
OFFICE OF NAVAJO GOVERNMENT DEVELOPMENT

I just wanted to mention that the Navajo Nation does have a very good court system in place. The law of preference is customary law, whereby, if there is a conflict that needs to be resolved, the courts will look to how customarily they dealt with those issues. Until recently there seemed to be that balance, we were able to deal with those issues through the court system and judge-made law if need be. But in the recent year or so the current leadership within the Navajo Nation council has decided, been concerned—and the intent is good—that our children are growing up and we're not teaching them our value systems. There's a movement to think about putting it in the books to maintain it. But there's a big argument on the other side that if we do that we're going to lose something, because once you put it into writing it'll change the nature of your customary law. And something about Navajo is that we have such a wide area that some traditions vary from one area to another, and to codify and put something in writing would create tremendous conflict. So my commission is trying to balance that. How do we recognize the need to ensure customary law? How do we make sure we recognize this for future generations, but by the same token, not mess it up by putting it in writing? So, you're right, there is a tension and the commission is right in the middle of it.

LE ROY SHINGOITEWA, CHAIR, HOPI TRIBE
CONSTITUTIONAL REFORM COMMITTEE

Well, in dealing with tradition and culture, among my people, we are dealing with twelve separate villages within our group. We have some villages, approximately three, who still recognize in our language what we call *kikmongwi*. The English word is the chief. And the leaders of the other nine villages are recognized either as governors or a board of directors.

So, based on that, our job is now to try to provide that common traditional rule among all the villagers as to how they would choose their leadership. I'll give you an example. Based on our constitution right now, there's a section that says *kikmongwi* will certify. Well, for those villages that don't have a *kikmongwi,* that doesn't hold any meaning anymore. So now we're having to change that language, and yet still retain the authority of the *kikmongwi* in other villages. There's going to be language that says if a village chooses to still govern by the traditional form of government, they may so choose. But there's got to be language so that that authority and respect is still there for the traditional form. So, as we work on Hopi with the constitution, it's not simply the English language that we're putting into this. We're having to try to interpret some of the things that we un-derstand in the Hopi way, so that the language we put in there still keeps the traditional role of village leaders and the Hopi Tribal Council.

I think one of the things somebody said was that we're just trying to find a way of running a better organization at the tribal council level. Each village will still have the autonomy to run their village the way they so choose. To me, as time changes, it becomes a real critical factor that the respect for each of those villages has to remain, and the people have to understand that the constitutional language has to be broad enough that it's going to cover those areas of concern.

One of the things about constitutions is that you can't make them so specific that you leave everybody out. In some ways I do understand what President Hale was talking about earlier about nations. I guess being a Hopi, I don't see any difference between being a Hopi Tribe or Hopi Nation because to me I'm a Hopi. I'm a Hopi. There's not a tribe to me, or there's not a band to me. Culturally, I'm a Hopi, and so anybody that's within our boundaries who are associated through Hopi, becomes a Hopi.

Our other concern is being able to have jurisdiction over others who are on the reservation. They should answer to our rules, just like every-body else. Tradition rules and the legal language has to be set up so that they cover everybody on the reservation. Because I would expect, and our constitutional reform committee expects, that everyone who lives on the Hopi reservation needs to respect and abide by the Hopi law. But the Hopi has also always had rules that we live by. There's religious rule and there's traditional rule. What we have come to find out is that for all of us who have grown up being Hopi, and have listened to the ways of the Hopi, it's simple to internally understand these rules. It's what we've always lived by. But to convey that to someone who is not of our tribe, or who is not of our Indian way of thinking, in the outside world things must be placed on paper. And once it's put on a document, when you visibly give it to the government, or to any outside entity, they know these are the rules by which we live. Sometimes this is contrary to our Indian way because everything is oral. A lot of rules are oral and that's what has been ingrained. So I guess my point is that when the topic of traditional culture comes up you have to try to find a peaceful middle ground where those that consider themselves really traditional and those that are progressive will still meld.

I'm an educated fool, OK? I put it that way because I went to a lot of schools. But on the other side I'm traditional because I still take part in the ceremonies that I have at home. So it makes me no different from others. I have a role that I must play. I have a clanship. I have that responsibility. And being of that clanship I know that one of my responsibilities is working with the constitution because I think that's why I was trained to do that. But on the other side I also respect those of my elders who still really try to practice the way that they were taught. Because sometimes as we get educated that education takes the forefront. We forget there's still the other part of us that we need to remember. That's why when I heard the prayer the other day I think all tribes who are in the traditional way, we don't singularly look out just for ourselves or for our people. We look out for everybody in the world. Everything that's alive. That's for everybody. And so our constitution has to be for everybody. They may come visit us someday. As long as they know we have something that we live by then I would respect them if I go to their part of the country, go to the Cherokees, go up to Cheyenne. I would respect and have to live by their rules. That, to me, is what the constitution would embody culturally and traditionally.

JOHN PETERS, JR., EXECUTIVE DIRECTOR, COMMONWEALTH OF MASSACHUSETTS COMMISSION ON INDIAN AFFAIRS, MEMBER OF MASHPEE WAMPANOAG

We've been running our government for quite some time and have been doing it in a different way that is consistent with the U.S. system. But I think of the years, of the excuses they used why they wouldn't invest into Native communities, and it was basically because Indian nations didn't have a system in place where companies could feel confident about investing without the fear of losing their investment. They were unable to collateralize.

I look at constitutional development as a process we're going through in order to set up a government so that these investors will feel comfortable about investing in us, and have some assurance that they would get their money back out of it. So the constitution really isn't about us, it's really about them, and about them having confidence and investing in us. So, as far as trying to incorporate traditions into this form of government, I see it as sort of a conflict. I think the conflict that the United States has found with respect to a separation of church and state is something that I think we're going to have as well.

Things that happen in our community are going to continue to happen in our community. The peer pressure and the influences that we have among each other will continue. I know in my own community we have to step up the pace a little bit in order to have influence on our youth and try to get them to go in a stronger, more traditional direction, and to stop doing some of the things that outside influences have on them. But I don't think it's particularly necessary to put this in the constitution. I think some of the principles that we feel are important to guide our kids, and our adults and so forth need to be put in place, but it doesn't necessarily have to be written down.

ROSS SWIMMER, FORMER PRINCIPAL CHIEF,
CHEROKEE NATION OF OKLAHOMA, AND FORMER
ASSISTANT SECRETARY, INDIAN AFFAIRS,
U.S. DEPARTMENT OF THE INTERIOR

It seems to me that there a couple of things here that are in play, but the most important theme that runs through this whole constitutional development is called economy. The Hopi were the only ones that brought up the issue of ethnicity, and there have been discussions of nationhood. But that's quite different from ethnicity. Anyone who goes on the Hopi reservation should become a Hopi under the tribe's nationhood, but that doesn't necessarily mean they are ethnically Hopi. But as we talked about Navajo, if you go on the Navajo reservation and you recognize a person as a citizen of that nation, then they are. If you go to Mexico, you become a Mexican citizen, you can do that.

But the economy, I think, is what drives constitutions and our case in point is very interesting. From 1906 until 1975, the Cherokee Nation

did not have a constitution. Why? Nothing changed. No law changed.
Nothing said, why don't you all write a constitution? Why don't you
write one in 1940? Why don't you write one in 1920? Why didn't you
write one in 1970? It wasn't an issue. Why? There was no economy.
Why would you need a constitution? Everybody is essentially assimilated,
so they're all enjoying the economy of the greater state of Oklahoma,
and their county, and their city. So there really wasn't a need for a
constitution.

Well, what brought that need about? In 1970 the Great Society was
born and suddenly millions and millions of dollars started funneling out
to Indian Country. Indian people became eligible for that money. Well,
how were they going to get it? They were only going to get it if there
were some kind of organization there that could distribute it, so we
needed a constitution. We had to figure out who was going to run that
organization. How it was going to be organized. Jaime Barrientoz [Vice
Chair of the Grand Traverse Band of Ottawa and Chippewa Indians] has
got the same problem. The Grand Traverse Band may not, in the past,
have had a great need for a constitution, but all of a sudden they're into
all this gaming money, so they've got to have a way of determining who's
eligible for it. What greater reason to become a member of a tribe than
to get a per capita distribution?

I just recognized a tribe last year through Congress. It's interesting because guess what the first issue [was] that came up with this newly recognized, brand-new tribe? Are we going to allow dual membership in our
tribe or are we going to exclude it? I asked the question, why do you
care? It's economic. What happens if we get into gaming? If we can keep
all of these people that are members of other tribes out of our tribe, and
only have our tribe enrolled, they have to give up a lot but we'll keep
our numbers down. If we keep our numbers down, and we get into
gaming, we'll have fewer people to distribute the funds among.

So I think that we have to be realistic whether it's Africa and dia-
monds, or whether it's Indian tribes and gaming. The real driving
force here is economy. It could be land-based economy, it could be
preserving territory, but the purpose for tribal constitutions, perhaps,
needs to be put in a different context and thought of in a different
context than a governance context.

States developed constitutions. Once a state is created you need a
governance framework. In law the simplest constitution was a handshake,
and then we went to a written partnership, and then we went to corporations. But you have to have a way of dealing with the outside world.

The problem I have with unwritten constitutions, or the handshake, you might say, between two business deals, is that tribes have to present themselves in some kind of format that the rest of society and the world can understand. You have to have some kind of written document, assuming you have an economy for which you need a written document. If you're too poor, or if, as at one point in our history, land is communally owned and nobody has title, there isn't as much to disagree about. But we have to recognize that the economies are driving a lot of what we do today. We can talk about a lot of high-sounding ideals, and keeping our tribes together, but it's money, and power to a certain degree. But if there's no money there's no power.

LEONARD D. DIXON, FORMER OUTREACH
COORDINATOR, LUMMI NATION CONSTITUTIONAL
REFORM COMMITTEE

There are a few words that I could leave with you on the subject of whether or not culture is a barrier to tribal government or not. We are a society that was rooted in subsistence, and because of that subsistence we're not disassociated from the environment in which we live. We're still very much connected in that, and we still practice that, and then we go to the council meetings and sit around the tables and discuss how we're going to relate to the outside governments. That's why we structure ourselves so that they recognize who we are, and give our own selves that merit. That's the whole reason why we have a tribal government. It isn't to govern ourselves. It's so we can communicate with the other governments—that they recognize who we are in our sovereignty.

We still participate in our ceremonies. We still have our canoes. I pull a war canoe for the Lummi Nation. We compete against the Canadian Indian nations all the time in the Pacific Northwest. There are a lot of teachings that go with that canoe pulling. It's not just a sport. It never was a sport. There are a lot of things you can only learn if you're involved in that cultural activity. There are things that we really involve our younger generations [in] that come up through the years with that.

I was speaking some of the language that I'm learning as a young person. I'm thirty-one years old. I didn't try to learn the Lummi language until I was about twenty-four. It became really important because it gave me that sense of connectivity to be able to speak the same words that were spoken in our area for thousands and thousands of years. It does something to an individual. It wakes you up. I heard it discussed earlier about the connection with the animals and the plants, that they won't recognize you, they won't know you unless you can call them by their names in your own language. How does that all tie in with tribal government? Is there a separation between church and state? That's the conundrum of walking in two worlds. How do we adapt from subsistence social structures to one of consumerism and capitalism, and then try to be successful in both worlds? It's a difficult task. As a young person I'm seeking answers, and I don't think there is an easy answer. But I think talking with each other like this is a very good start in that process. [Indian spoken]

NOTE

1. Norma Gourneau, former vice chair of Northern Cheyenne Tribe and member of constitutional reform committee: "Let me give you an example of that. Under traditional law there are certain roles for men, and there are certain roles for women, and we grow up knowing what those roles are. In the constitution, the written constitution, there's a role in there for women and I'm able to participate in that. So if you try to bring the two together I think there will probably be a lot of conflict, more conflict. I understand my role as a woman in the traditional sense, and that's just how it is, you know. I wouldn't want to change it. I abide by it. But I have a different role when it comes to the constitutional process, and what he's talking about is there's a lot more issues involved in that than just the one with the roles."

Mr. Brady: "It's kind of like, almost like oil and water."

PART II

Carole Goldberg

Four   MEMBERS ONLY

Designing Citizenship Requirements
for Indian Nations

Indian nations' constitutional reform efforts encounter
some of their most paralyzing conflicts over criteria for membership.[1]
Three years ago, I initiated the Tribal Legal Development Clinic at UCLA,
whose purpose has been to assist Indian nations in building their legal in-
frastructures. This Clinic has provided free consulting and drafting services
to Indian nations seeking to establish or modify tribal constitutions, codes,
or justice systems.[2] As the Clinic embarked on several constitution drafting and revision projects, controversies over membership—or citizenship,
as we preferred to call it—readily and regularly escalated from negotiable
differences among tribal participants to heated stalemates or irresolvable
conundrums.[3] In some instances, to the dismay of tribal folks, students, and
faculty alike, these difficulties doomed the entire enterprise.

As the work of the Clinic has proceeded, law review articles have been
attacking ancestry-based tribal membership requirements and advocating
substitution of "nonracial" criteria such as cultural affiliation or residence.[4]
These articles seem to draw force from an ideology that requires assaults
upon all legal provisions that can possibly be characterized as racial in
nature.[5] To support their positions, these authors assert, sometimes erro-
neously, that existing blood quantum requirements are federally imposed
rather than "traditionally" tribal,[6] implying that tribal law can be authentic
and entitled to respect only so long as it adheres to practices that predate
European contact. This critique of tribal citizenship provisions necessitates
a searching examination of the historical and contemporary choices that
Indian nations have available and are making regarding citizenship. Insofar as these choices reflect contemporary concerns of tribal communities,
there is no reason to deny their legitimacy merely because they depart
from "traditional" measures.

My aim in this chapter is thus twofold: (1) to spur a discussion
among tribal law scholars and practitioners about the legal, economic, and

cultural factors associated with drafting tribal citizenship provisions; and (2) to equip Indian nations with knowledge of the law, both tribal and federal, that may enable them to more effectively design tribal citizenship provisions. As demonstrated below,[7] after years of meddling with tribal constitutions, federal law and bureaucrats increasingly defer to Indian nations in establishing such provisions. However, this key component of self-determination may be unavailing to Indian nations if they cannot deploy it effectively to achieve community values and objectives. Rather than offering a particular prescription for such provisions, this chapter draws out implications and consequences of various alternative formulations, hoping to facilitate the decisions of Indian nations.

This chapter begins in Part I with three illustrative case studies of Indian nations struggling to develop citizenship requirements, drawn from the experience of the Clinic and other sources.[8] In Part II, it considers the features of federal law that have contributed to tribal difficulties in designing citizenship provisions and that continue to affect tribal citizenship choices. Part III addresses practical dilemmas, values, and objectives that Indian nations may want to reflect upon in developing their citizenship requirements. And in Part IV, the chapter offers some drafting options that may help Indian nations navigate their way out of treacherous struggles over citizenship. Obviously, different Indian nations will think about citizenship differently. Citizenship is intimately entangled with fundamental cultural, social, economic, and political dimensions of tribal life, which vary from tribe to tribe. However, it is possible and productive to pose the following general and instrumental question: if Indian nations want citizenship requirements to serve a particular set of values and purposes within their community, what kinds of citizenship provisions will most effectively achieve those ends?

I. CASE STUDIES OF TRIBAL CITIZENSHIP STRUGGLES

A. Tribe A

Indian nation A is a small California tribe, one of more than thirty-five that experienced termination in the 1950s.[9] As a result of tribal success in litigation,[10] the government-to-government relationship between Tribe A (as well as many other terminated tribes) and the United

States was restored. To regularize its tribal government, this Indian nation sought to promulgate a constitution.

The threshold question confronting any such endeavor is who may participate in designing the new government. Given the wrongful intervention of the United States in terminating the tribe, one natural assumption would be that anyone who qualified for tribal citizenship according to the criteria that existed before termination would be eligible to participate, at least so long as that individual was not claiming citizenship in a different tribe or was willing to switch citizenship upon completion of the new constitution. In fact, for purposes of governmental organization, the Bureau of Indian Affairs was willing to recognize individuals who satisfied membership criteria under any rancheria's pre-termination governing documents.[11] In the absence of such documents, it might be expected that the new constitution could be established by individuals reliably identified with the tribe. Indeed, because of census lists prepared in connection with earlier litigation to settle land claims by California Indians, a number of rolls or lists exist from the early decades of the twentieth century up to the 1970s that identify California Indians by tribal affiliation.[12] Consultation with tribal elders would be another way to establish a reliable set of tribal members for purposes of government formation.

Instead, the United States took the position that it would deal only with a government constituted by the distributees of land at the time of termination and their direct or lineal descendants, the group acknowledged in the "untermination" litigation.[13] Tribe A had not had a governing document prior to termination. So when the individuals who fit this description from Tribe A came together to agree upon the terms of their constitution, the citizenship provision they first proposed mirrored the Bureau's criteria for constitution formation. Any number of individuals listed on various census rolls as members of Tribe A, including a full sibling of one of the distributees, were excluded from citizenship under this proposed term. These individuals and their ancestors often had good reasons for not living on the reservation or rancheria at the time of termination. The very improvements needed on these parcels and promised by the United States at the time of the Rancheria Act made life there extremely hard. Jobs were scarce, poverty was grinding, and many residents consequently left the government-surplus handouts and ramshackle housing on the rancheria to eke out a living as farmworkers or in factories.[14] But many of the distributees who could participate in the constitutional drafting process felt these individuals should not have left the community for better opportunities and that they were returning to glean benefits of tribal membership that they had too readily abandoned.

There was probably no legal obstacle to Tribe A's using the termination-inspired criteria as its citizenship requirements.[15] Certainly the use of such criteria would fulfill the aspiration of the framers of this constitution to maximize tribal and federal benefits for their own family members. However, the Clinic also undertook to explain to these organizers some of the implications of instituting such a provision, including the likely political reverberations and weakened legitimacy as excluded members (especially the sibling) sought sympathy from the non-Indian public through the press;[16] the symbolic assault on tribal sovereignty if the language of termination were folded into a tribal document; the loss to tribal social solidarity from excluding close family members; and the inflexibility that would result from freezing citizenship criteria into constitutional language at this early stage in the tribe's reconstitution. Eventually those sitting at the table spoke favorably of provisions that directly included the sibling,[17] that identified the distributees and their descendants without using the termination-era vocabulary, and that allowed for passage of future tribal statutory citizenship provisions that could supplement those articulated in the constitution itself.[18]

B. Tribe B

Tribe B is a small to medium-sized Indian nation that established a constitution in 1936 under the Indian Reorganization Act.[19] Its membership provision, which has not been changed since that time, offers citizenship to anyone whose name appears on a census roll of the reservation dating back to the early decades of the twentieth century; any children born to a tribal member who resides on the reservation at the time such children are born;[20] and anyone made eligible for membership (including by adoption) pursuant to a future ordinance enacted by the tribe and approved by the Secretary of the Interior. No such ordinances have been enacted. Thus, the citizenship requirements of Tribe B are based on lineal descent from individuals on a fixed list, subject to the further requirement of parental residence on the reservation at the time of the birth of the children.

Tribe B wanted to update its constitution, to eliminate unnecessary roles for the Secretary of the Interior, and to reflect changes in the community and its social, political, and economic requirements. When it came time to discuss the membership or citizenship provision, elected and appointed tribal leaders broached concerns about both broadening and narrowing the requirements. The residence requirement was criticized because of the inadequate size of the tribal land base, which forced many to live off-reservation in a nearby town. Furthermore, the search for education and training had led some tribal members to leave the reservation during their childbearing years, causing them to forfeit tribal membership for their children. Some tribal leaders confronted the specter of their own grandchildren becoming disqualified for citizenship because the parents of their grandchildren (i.e., their own children) resided off-reservation. Because Tribe B had substantial (though not lavish) gaming revenues, one might expect tribal leadership to be very cautious about expanding citizenship.[21] However, because they could not predict in advance whether their own grandchildren would qualify under the existing criteria, some were inclined toward greater inclusiveness.[22]

Others raised concerns about eliminating the residence requirement and leaving only lineal descent as the criterion for citizenship, on the grounds that individuals with little connection to the tribe would potentially dominate its voting and office-holding. With the allocation of gaming revenues at stake, they worried that individuals living off-reservation would opt for per capita distributions rather than investment in reservation infrastructure such as schools, public safety, and housing.[23]

While it was easy for the participants to agree on removing the requirement for the Secretary to approve tribal membership ordinances, the consensus halted there. The Clinic viewed its job as pointing out the likely origins of the parental residence requirement in Department of the Interior directives,[24] advising the tribe about the possibility of establishing a residence requirement for voting and office-holding rather than citizenship, and suggesting other ways the tribe might sustain cultural coherence while maintaining more inclusive citizenship provisions.

C. Tribe C

Tribe C has a large population but a small land base. Its current constitution, which was *not* promulgated under the Indian Reorganization Act, allows membership to anyone listed on a roll prepared in the twentieth century for a land claims judgment distribution, as well as all descendants of those individuals, provided that they possess one-fourth or more Indian blood. Notably, the one-fourth Indian ancestry need not be from Tribe C, but presumably could be from any tribe. Such ancestry provisions can be found in a number of tribal constitutions, sometimes attached to additional requirements of some lesser percentage of ancestry from the tribe in question.[25]

Tribe C is reexamining and revising its constitution, having elected representatives to a constitutional convention charged with a broad mandate. One concern that has been brought before the convention is the problem of providing adequate educational, health, and other services to the growing numbers of children who fail to satisfy tribal citizenship criteria. Although the convention has not yet finished its work, it considered an innovative solution to this dilemma that simultaneously tightens and relaxes the blood quantum or ancestry requirement: voting membership and entitlement to distribution of tribal funds or property would be limited to descendants from the designated roll who have one-fourth or more ancestry from the tribe itself (not just *any* Indian ancestry); but medical and educational benefits would be available to nonmembers who are lineally descended from individuals on an assortment of tribal rolls, several predating the list.[26] Whether the BIA would be willing to treat such individuals as tribal citizens for purposes of receiving federal benefits restricted to tribal members[27] is uncertain. The contemplated provision distinguishes between those members who satisfy the blood quantum requirement ("full members") and those who are only lineal descendants. Those in the latter group are not labeled "partial" members, but that seems to be what they are. Certainly the draft describes this group in the constitution's section on "Membership." But it does not follow that the individuals in this group will qualify for membership-based federal services.

Tribes A, B, and C are all struggling to accommodate the often competing internal demands of cultural cohesiveness, communal well-being, and intergenerational inclusiveness. Yet these conflicts also arise within a context of legal structures and commands fashioned by an external force: federal law and policy. Often this law creates incentives or disincentives toward inclusiveness. Hence Part II of this chapter is devoted to examining the federal framework for adoption and revision of tribal citizenship provisions.

II. FEDERAL LAW AND POLICY AFFECTING TRIBAL CITIZENSHIP PROVISIONS

A. Forms of Direct Federal Control

Contemporary federal judicial and administrative decisions regularly note that tribal citizenship is a matter for tribal governments to determine.[28] The United States Supreme Court made this point emphatically in its 1978 decision in *Santa Clara Pueblo v. Martinez*,[29] when it rejected a claim under the Indian Civil Rights Act of 1968[30] that challenged a tribal citizenship provision.[31] More recently, in *Rice v. Cayetano*,[32] the Court indicated that tribal voting eligibility provisions (closely related to citizenship) would receive more relaxed constitutional scrutiny than those propounded by states or the federal government.[33] The Bureau of Indian Affairs affirms that "an Indian tribe has the right to determine its own membership for tribal matters."[34]

Historically, federal law and policy took a more active role in directing Indian nations' citizenship requirements. The Indian Reorganization Act of 1934 specified that the Secretary of the Interior must approve all constitutions of tribes organized under its terms.[35] Although the act did not dictate the specific provisions for inclusion in tribal constitutions, the Bureau of Indian Affairs quickly developed models that it pressed upon the more than 150 tribes that "chose" organization under the act by not mustering more than half the eligible voters to reject its terms.[36] The Bureau's policy on citizenship (which it labeled "membership") provisions quickly emerged in a circular distributed by the Secretary of the Interior and signed by the Commissioner of Indian Affairs.[37] While recognizing that the Indian Reorganization Act itself did not dictate who could qualify for tribal membership under a tribal constitution, the Secretary noted that the act provided a definition of "Indian" for purposes of determining who could take advantage of the authority to establish a constitutional government in the first place.[38] This definition referred to all persons of Indian descent who are members of federally recognized tribes, all descendants of such members residing on any reservation as of June 1, 1934, and any other person "of one-half or more Indian blood."[39] According to the Secretary, this definition expressed a "definite" congressional policy "to limit the application of Indian benefits [under the act] to those who are Indians by virtue of actual tribal affiliation or by virtue of possessing one-half degree or more of Indian blood."[40] From there, the Secretary leaped to the conclusion that the Department's policy should be "to urge and insist that any constitutional provision conferring automatic tribal membership upon children hereafter born, should limit such membership to persons who reasonably can be expected to participate in tribal relations and affairs."[41] To clarify this policy, the Secretary offered several illustrations of appropriate membership limitations, including requirements that both parents be tribal members, that the parents reside within the reservation, or that the children have a minimum blood quantum.[42] Even more specifically, the Secretary directed that where only one parent is a member and the parents live off the reservation, the minimum blood quantum requirement for children's membership should be "one-half degree Indian blood."[43] The circular authorized provisions for the adoption of nonmembers only upon secretarial approval for each applicant, unless the person was of Indian descent and related by marriage or descent to a tribal member. To conclude, the Secretary declared that not only departmental agents, but also the Indians themselves, must understand the importance of these limitations for "their own welfare, through preventing the admission to tribal membership of a large number of applicants of small degree of Indian blood."[44]

This policy found its way into tribal constitutions that required approval under the Indian Reorganization Act, such as the constitution of Tribe B.[45] But even as to tribal constitutions promulgated outside the terms of the Indian Reorganization Act, and even for Indian nations that have chosen not to promulgate constitutions at all, this set of requirements could be introduced by the Bureau of Indian Affairs through the wide-ranging influence of that agency over tribal budgets and essential services.

Beginning in the late 1960s, federal policy formally aligned itself with ideals of tribal self-determination. Federally imposed membership or citizenship provisions cannot be reconciled with such a policy. By the 1980s, Indian nations were beginning to seek greater control over their own governing documents, and challenged the Bureau's refusal to approve amendments that departed from policies such as those articulated in Circular 3123.[46] In 1988, Congress amended the Indian Reorganization Act to require secretarial approval of all tribal constitutional amendments unless they conflicted with federal law.[47] However, this shift did not have the effect of eliminating Bureau preferences for tribal membership provisions or eliminating opportunities for the Bureau to introduce its preferences into tribal constitution-making. Despite the pronouncements of the Supreme Court in *Santa Clara Pueblo v. Martinez*[48] and of Congress in the 1988 amendments to the Indian Reorganization Act, federal involvement in tribal decision-making about citizenship is alive and well.

This involvement manifests itself most vividly when federal decision-making intersects with definitions of tribal citizenship. As the chief of the Bureau's Division of Tribal Government Services wrote in 1998,

> The Bureau of Indian Affairs exercises its authority to
> intervene in enrollment matters when the tribe is prepar-
> ing a membership roll for distribution of tribal assets held in

> trust [by the federal government], when Federal interests are
> involved, such as challenges to a Secretarial election, or when
> the governing document authorizes the Secretary of the In-
> terior's involvement, such as an appeal from an adverse tribal
> decision. Even then, however, our decision would be based
> on the tribal constitution or other organic documents such as
> constitutions and bylaws, articles of association, ordinances,
> and resolutions.[49]

Thus, for example, when the Secretary of the Interior was required
to sponsor an election for amendment to the Indian Reorganization Act
constitution of the Lac Courte Oreilles Band of Lake Superior Chippewa
Indians, the Bureau of Indian Affairs refused to approve changes to the
Tribe's membership provisions that substituted lineal descent for a blood
quantum requirement.[50] According to the Bureau, the wrong class of voters had been allowed to vote on approval of the amendments.[51] Underlying the Bureau's resistance to the change, however, was antipathy to the
idea of reducing or eliminating minimum blood quantum requirements.[52]
In a letter to the tribal governing board chair, the deputy commissioner
expressed "concern about eliminating the blood quantum in favor of mere
descendancy."[53] According to the deputy commissioner, tribes are understandably tempted to increase their numbers because federal benefits are
directly tied to the population of tribal members.[54] But to do so by lowering blood quantum "without regard to the extent to which the persons
have actually maintained meaningful, bilateral relations with the tribe"
is to risk weakening "the very logic and foundation of tribal jurisdiction
and sovereignty."[55] The letter ended by offering thinly veiled threats of
termination if Congress or the courts conclude "that a tribe has so diluted
the relationship between [its] government and its members that it has 'self-
determined' its sovereignty away."[56] Evidently the Bureau took its normally
interventionist approach too far in this case. In overturning the Bureau's
disapproval of the amendments, a federal court ruled that "[t]he bureau
cannot be guided by the results it favors in its relationship with Indian
tribes, especially when its role is as carefully proscribed as it is in Secretarial
elections."[57] Clearly, however, the Bureau is inclined to do so whenever a
federal role can be found or stretched into existence.

Other illustrations of room for federal involvement in tribal membership decisions can be found in the Bureau's need to determine whether a
tribal government is a proper partner in the government-to-government
relationship that exists between Indian nations and the United States.

A case in point is the controversy between several Oklahoma tribes and the United States over the legitimacy of membership and voting rights for descendants of freedmen—freed black slaves who lived with the tribe. The position of the United States is that federal law, namely post–Civil War treaties made with these tribes, affords the freedmen and their descendants rights that the tribes may not deny. For example, because the Oklahoma Seminole adopted a referendum limiting the full membership rights of freedmen, including the vote, the Bureau has been unwilling to recognize the leaders chosen through a tribal election and has been administering federal programs directly rather than through the tribe.[58]

Not only may federal treaty interpretations prompt the Bureau to insert itself into tribal citizenship decisions, but so may Bureau interpretation of the dictates of the Indian Civil Rights Act of 1968.[59] For example, if an Indian nation were to adopt or amend its Indian Reorganization Act constitution to include a citizenship provision denying citizenship to individuals whose parents are not married, the Bureau could decide not to approve the amendment based on concern that such discrimination against illegitimates would violate the equal protection provision of the Indian Civil Rights Act.[60]

Thus federal law and policy continue to exert an effect on tribal citizenship requirements directly through the actions of the Bureau in administering federal programs and executing directives built into tribal constitutions themselves, such as review of enrollment disputes or approval of constitutional amendments. Federal bureaucrats' preferences, including their hostility toward lineal descent provisions for citizenship and antagonism to naturalization of non-Indians,[61] can be introduced through such means.

B. The Context of Federal Incentives and Indirect Control

Apart from its direct intervention to prescribe or limit tribal citizenship determinations, the federal government has established legal rules that create incentives for Indian nations to fashion their citizenship provisions in particular ways. The system of federal incentives does not always point consistently in the same way. Often different federal measures create incentives leading down divergent paths. Sometimes a single statute may introduce two contrary incentives, depending on the particular Indian nation's values or objectives. While some commentators claim that federal law, especially the Indian Gaming Regulatory Act,[62] is pressing Indian nations toward more exclusive, racially based citizenship criteria,[63] their analysis is unidimensional and too simplistic. By focusing on a single federal statutory scheme, they ignore competing pressures from other federal provisions, discussed below. The implications they draw from the Gaming Act also represent only a subset of possible consequences. Thus, it is important to identify the various federal laws potentially impinging on tribal citizenship choices and the types of magnetic forces they exert on the design of tribal citizenship criteria.

I. FEDERAL STATUTES TYING BENEFITS TO MEMBERSHIP

Beginning with the Non-Intercourse Acts of the late 1700s and through enactment of the 1934 Indian Reorganization Act, federal law has treated "Indians" as a class without regard to proof of tribal enrollment.[64] Blood quantum[65] or recognition by a tribal community as an Indian typically sufficed to open the door for such benefits as Indian preference in BIA employment,[66] college scholarships,[67] and exemption from state criminal or taxing jurisdiction.[68] Over the past three decades, Supreme Court decisions and federal statutes have increasingly tied benefits to more formal tribal membership or eligibility for such membership. Whether these enactments push tribes in the direction of tightening or loosening tribal citizenship requirements varies, however, depending on the type of benefit at stake under the federal law.

A case in point is the Indian Child Welfare Act of 1978.[69] For its special rules regarding exclusive tribal court jurisdiction, transfer of cases from state to tribal court, and Indian preference in adoptions to apply, the child must be a member or eligible for membership.[70] Although federal regulations provide that membership is not synonymous with enrollment,[71] federal and state courts deciding Indian Child Welfare Act cases have checked to see whether a purported "Indian child" satisfies formal tribal criteria for enrollment.[72] Thus an Indian nation interested in securing its future generations may seek to expand eligibility for membership in order to encompass a broader class of children.

Another case in point is the Bald and Golden Eagle Protection Act,[73] which allows the Secretary of the Interior to issue permits for tribal members to possess eagles or eagle parts, thereby exempting them from federal laws that outlaw transport or possession of such items.[74] Federal regulations restrict access to these parts to enrolled members, thereby excluding some individuals who have close connections to the tribe through birth or adoption.[75] If this exclusion produces impediments to the operation of tribal ceremonies, because some of the most important ceremonial leaders are not enrolled members, it may press the tribe toward more inclusive citizenship provisions. Since the supply of eagles and feathers will probably not diminish for existing enrolled members as a consequence of such expansion, the Indian nation may be receptive to broader citizenship through adoption or some other means for ceremonial users.

Where monetary benefits from federal assistance programs are at stake, the resulting incentive for Indian nations may depend on federal funding levels. If funding is ample, expanding to accommodate all eligible individuals, then the incentive may be to expand citizenship. If appropriations tend to be static or declining, then an Indian nation may be tempted to contract citizenship in order to protect benefit levels for existing members.

The advent of tribally sponsored gaming on reservations has created another set of federally structured benefits that turn on tribal enrollment. The Indian Gaming Regulatory Act of 1988[76] (IGRA) enables Indian nations to take advantage of their inherent powers to generate revenue from gaming enterprises. Indian nations that possess the advantage of location have been able to reap large revenues.[77] Under IGRA, tribal gaming may only be carried out by tribally controlled entities, and the revenues may be used only for tribal governmental purposes or for distribution to tribal members.[78] Tribes seeking to make per capita distributions must do so pursuant to a plan approved by the Secretary of the Interior.[79]

Rand and Light argue that "IGRA's gaming revenue provisions . . . create a real incentive for tribes to limit their members. . . . Obviously, the fewer members, the bigger the pot."[80] Attempting to document their point with a few case studies drawn from news reports and court cases, they conclude that "the incentives created by Congress may well become the overriding factor in the membership determinations of gaming tribes."[81] In fact, they point to only one tribe, the Eastern Band of Cherokee, who have increased their blood quantum requirement since the advent of tribal gaming.[82] Some others have been welcoming the newly interested members attracted by the prospect of per capita payments.[83] Neath goes further, claiming that IGRA has inspired a wholesale racialization of tribal membership criteria, as tribes use minimum blood quantum requirements to limit the number of recipients of per capita distributions.[84]

Such observations do not capture the full range of tribal considerations with respect to citizenship, and do not even reflect the complex incentive structure presented by IGRA. As with other federal benefits that turn on tribal membership, this one pushes in two separate directions. The desire to enjoy a larger portion of a fixed asset pool may prompt more restrictive citizenship requirements, including those based on blood quantum; but the desire to pass on these benefits to one's descendants, including those born of intermarriage with non-Indians, may militate in favor of relaxed blood quantum and other requirements.

2. COURT DECISIONS TYING JURISDICTIONAL RULES TO TRIBAL MEMBERSHIP

Court decisions have also tied the application of rules concerning tribal and state jurisdiction to tribal membership, creating an incentive for tribes to enlarge their criteria. Until the Supreme Court's 1980 decision in *Washington v. Confederated Tribes of the Colville Reservation*[85] and its 1990 decision in *Duro v. Reina,*[86] most courts and commentators assumed that the jurisdictional doctrines of federal Indian law distinguished Indians from non-Indians, not members from nonmembers.[87] This lack of distinction drew inspiration from the federal Indian Country criminal statutes dating back to the eighteenth century, whose application never rested on formal tribal enrollment.[88] Indian ancestry and acceptance by any tribal community would suffice.[89] Without repudiating these interpretations of the federal Indian Country criminal statutes, the Rehnquist Court has shifted course for purposes of state and tribal jurisdiction. In *Colville,* the Court upheld a state sales tax on cigarette purchases by nonmembers, defined as anyone not enrolled in the tribe.[90] And in *Duro,* the Court rejected tribal criminal jurisdiction over nonmember Indians.[91] Although Congress has effectively overturned *Duro,*[92] the Court continues to render decisions allocating state and tribal civil jurisdiction based on the member/nonmember distinction.[93]

For Indian nations seeking to maximize their control over reservation territory and to exclude competing state claims, it may be valuable to broaden citizenship criteria. Otherwise, state rather than tribal law will hold sway over a broader class of individuals with respect to taxation, zoning of fee land within reservations,[94] judicial jurisdiction over reservation-based claims,[95] and a host of civil regulatory practices. For example, broader membership criteria may enable the Indian nation to apply its law and exclude application of state law to the growing number of children of intermarried members, some of whom may be ineligible for citizenship under existing constitutional provisions.[96] Finally, broadening citizenship may enable Indian nations to exercise effective authority over non-Indians who commit violent acts against tribal citizens with whom they share family or intimate relations. If tribal criminal jurisdiction is valid in the eyes of the Supreme Court only over tribal members, then Indian nations should be able to gain such jurisdiction in intimate violence cases by expanding tribal citizenship to include spouses and intimate partners.[97]

3. RECOGNITION AND TERMINATION LAWS

Some federal laws seem to demand active involvement by tribal members in the tribe's communal life in order for benefits to be dispensed to those members. Laws of this type may prompt tribes to require communal or cultural involvement as a condition of citizenship or even continued citizenship, either in addition to or in lieu of criteria based upon descent. For example, federal administrative[98] and judicial[99] criteria for federal acknowledgment and recognition heavily emphasize members' participation in tribal cultural and political activities. Under the Department of the Interior's "mandatory criteria" for federal recognition, one requirement is that "[a] predominant portion of the petitioning group comprises a distinct community and has existed as a community from historical times until the present."[100] To satisfy this criterion, tribes may present evidence of regular social interaction and intermarriage within the group as well as "[s]hared sacred or secular ritual activity encompassing most of the group" and "[c]ultural patterns shared among a significant portion of the group that are different from those of the non-Indian populations with whom it interacts, . . . [including] language, kinship organization, or religious beliefs and practices."[101] Another mandatory criterion is that the group "has maintained political influence or authority over its members."[102] A tribe can fulfill this criterion by demonstrating that "[t]here is widespread knowledge, communication and involvement in political processes by most of the group's members."[103]

The upshot of all these prerequisites for federal recognition is that if a tribe seeking that status defines itself too broadly based on descent and kinship alone, the chances increase that recognition will be denied. It may be more difficult, for example, to demonstrate "political influence or authority" over a larger descent-defined group. Such participation is far more likely to survive decades of federal denial and neglect if the group is defined according to close family ties and actual involvement in ceremonies, political meetings, and social gatherings. Thus, for example, the Gabrieleno/Tongva Nation of the Los Angeles basin, who have initiated the federal recognition process administratively and are the subject of proposed federal recognition legislation,[104] have excluded from their organizing group some individuals who consider themselves Tongva by descent. Not surprisingly, these excluded individuals are displeased with their treatment.[105] But the Tongva seeking recognition will be able to make their case more effectively under prevailing federal criteria if they confine the petitioning group to those who are more closely related and actively involved in communal activities. They would presumably be free to broaden membership criteria following recognition,[106] but the impulse to limit benefits to their own descendants may inhibit any later expansion of citizenship.

The impact of federal termination laws on tribal citizenship criteria has already been presented through the experience of Tribe A.[107] Termination often triggered a sell-off of tribal assets to a fortuitously defined set or "roll" of tribal members. Where restoration of such tribes has been ordered or voluntarily established through federal legislation, the group empowered to reinstitute tribal government has often followed federal dictates derived from the termination process rather than more inclusive tribal conceptions of belonging. Consequently, a truncated group is sometimes positioned to reaffirm its sole entitlement to tribal political rights and the federal benefits attending them.

4. FEDERALLY CREATED TRIBAL ROLLS

The phenomenon of federally devised lists or "rolls" of citizens is not confined to the termination/restoration process. Beginning in the late nineteenth century, various federal laws compelled the Department of the Interior to compile such lists for purposes of distributing Indian allotments and land claims judgments.[108] In other words, these lists attended the dismantling of tribal land bases. Professor John Lavelle has powerfully pierced the misconception that these laws imposed blood quantum requirements.[109] Nevertheless, these laws did exert a force on tribal governing documents, offering a convenient starting point for citizenship criteria that turn on lineal descent.[110] Unfortunately, these federally mandated lists are sometimes inadequate and incomplete, excluding some people with deep and continuous tribal connections, whose ancestors failed to show up for the sign-ups because their traditional beliefs counseled nonparticipation or for other culturally based reasons. Dean Rennard Strickland relates the poignant story of a Seminole woman who could not qualify for an Indian scholarship program because she could not document her Indian ancestry based on federally compiled rolls.[111] Her Seminole grandmother, who barely spoke English, had resisted enrollment and hidden from the enrollment parties because she did not believe that the tribal land base should be broken up.[112] As Strickland points out, "[h]er granddaughter could not qualify to enroll in law school under the Native American Scholarship program because the tribal rolls were closed to her despite her historic Indian-ness." [113] The impact of such omissions becomes magnified with each generation. Once a roll is established as the basis for citizenship, it becomes politically difficult to expand citizenship beyond its confines.

Federal law thus creates a constraining and rewarding framework within which Indian nations must produce the citizenship requirements. Some of the constraints are architectural in nature, such as the federal rolls created for purposes of allotment and land claims settlements. Some federal statutes and judicial decisions require Indian nations to weigh material and other consequences of expanding or contracting citizenship rules, both for current members and future generations. Although Indian nations clearly face federal incentives and pressures, the forces affecting these nations do not press them toward a single set of citizenship requirements. The direct and indirect influence of federal law on tribal citizenship requirements is rarely conclusive and often points in multiple directions. How Indian nations filter and translate these pressures and forces of indirect control will depend on internal tribal considerations.

III. TRIBAL CONSIDERATIONS IN DESIGNING CITIZENSHIP PROVISIONS

Despite federal efforts to shape tribal citizenship, Indian nations have considerable freedom of action in articulating citizenship criteria. What are some of the most important considerations that these nations have taken and should take into account in choosing among alternative formulations?

A. *"Traditional" Conceptions of Belonging*

Recent commentators have chided contemporary tribal governments for holding to minimum descent or "blood quantum" requirements for citizenship, observing that such provisions depart from traditional (read precontact or early postcontact) North American tribal practices.[114] These authors point out that tribal membership traditionally depended more on social incorporation into clan or kinship group than on ancestry, and that inclusion of members of outside groups was common.[115]

These criticisms imply that Indian nations' membership practices were static during the precontact period, and that tribes err when they depart from such precontact practice. Even assuming that membership criteria remained constant before contact, a questionable assumption, it does not follow that Indian nations today should continue to adhere to those criteria. Supposing that earlier practices are the only ones that can be justified today is another way of promoting what some have called the "menagerie theory of Indian law that treats Indian reservations as historic human zoos."[116] It denies that traditions are vital and dynamic in response to changing conditions.

Consider the reasons why Indian nations today might prefer some type of blood quantum or minimum percentage of ancestry requirement, even though absolute criteria of that type were not part of historical practice. First, Indian nations today may anticipate that outsiders are more culturally different from insiders than in precontact North America. In that earlier time, warring tribes or trading partners may have shared more in terms of technology, values, and social understandings than Indians and non-Indians share today. The fact that some Indian nations today reduce their minimum blood quantum requirements for individuals belonging to other tribes may reflect such an analysis.[117] Second, tribes may have been more willing to adopt outsiders at a time when they were less likely to feel threatened that the adoptees' worldview and culture would overwhelm their own by virtue of material power and sheer numbers.[118] Third, earlier practices of adoption and incorporation may also have been shaped by concerns for population loss due to warfare and disease[119] that do not preoccupy some tribes today.

There may be good reasons to question minimum blood quantum requirements, but departure from tradition probably isn't one of them. In fact, biological relationship has always formed some part, often a significant part, of tribal belonging. Extended kinship groups or clans formed the basic units of nearly all tribal societies. Indeed, for anthropologists, a social structure based on kinship is the defining characteristic of a tribe, as opposed to some other form of political organization, such as a state.[120] For outsiders to be incorporated into a tribal system, they must be assimilated to some family-like role and/or find their place in a prevailing clan system.[121] Conversely, biological descendants can be disqualified from membership if they lack requirements for clan belonging.[122] And biological outsiders can qualify for membership under some circumstances if a family or clan had an established ceremony or other means by which kinship or clan roles could be assumed.[123] But these exceptions do not destroy the dominant rule that proper descent is the key to tribal belonging, and a person possessing such descent could far more readily establish membership than someone who did not.[124] Thus, for example, Gould's and Neath's ideas of entirely substituting some cultural affiliation requirement for descent[125] is no less a departure from tribal "tradition" than exclusive reliance on biology or blood quantum to define tribal citizenship.

B. Maintaining Numbers and Maximizing Political Impact

For some Indian nations, high blood quantum requirements coupled with rising Indian intermarriage rates portend a sharp diminution in tribal numbers, if not outright tribal extinguishments.[126] For tribes seeking political influence within federal and state governments—perhaps to increase their land base by having the United States take their fee land into trust, to establish funding programs benefiting their members, or to ensure protection of their sovereignty—size matters.[127] Larger numbers of citizens help the tribe by buttressing the non-Indian public's perception of Indian nations as governments rather than small clubs. A government with only a few dozen or even a few hundred citizens is anomalous in today's world. Furthermore, larger numbers can boost the leverage effect of tribal organization. Lower transaction costs mean that a tribe of five hundred can speak with more political effectiveness than five hundred otherwise identical individuals. If speaking for a thousand is not much more costly to achieve than speaking for five hundred, then potential political influence can easily be doubled. One of the largest Indian nations, the Cherokee, has worked to expand its numbers in order to enhance its national and state-level influence.[128]

C. Maintaining Cultural Cohesion

An influential work by legal scholar Rebecca Tsosie and former Comanche Tribal Chair Wallace Coffey urges Indian nations to rank what they call "cultural sovereignty" as their highest priority.[129] This term refers to "the effort of Indian nations and Indian people to exercise their own norms and values in structuring their collective futures," and "the battle to protect and defend tribal cultures from the multitude of forces that threaten the cultural survival of Indian nations."[130] Central to the achievement of cultural sovereignty is a tribal citizenry committed to engagement with a living tradition. Language revitalization, aesthetic immersion, storytelling, reliance on elders' knowledge, and repatriation all contribute to cultural sovereignty. A precondition for all these activities, however, is a knowledgeable or at least positively disposed tribal electorate, whether it is geographically based or knitted together by other means.[131] Tribal citizenship requirements that advert to such knowledge and cultural engagement, or generally reliable surrogates for those characteristics, might facilitate the process of achieving cultural sovereignty. Conversely, more inclusive citizenship requirements may draw in members with less vigorous cultural ties, reducing the likelihood that cultural sovereignty, as opposed to material or political advancement, becomes the highest communal priority. Thus, except where family ties and the gravitational force of culture are extremely strong, lineal descent requirements could afford controlling influence to individuals with no cultural connection at all.

Some Indian nations' constitutions already allow for incorporating those with close but nonbiological ties to the communities, mainly through adoption.[132] But it may be clumsy business for tribes to attempt to achieve cultural sovereignty through exclusive reliance on cultural ties as the basis for citizenship. Residence, language fluency, community service,[133] elders' certification, and ceremonial participation are all possible bases for establishing a more culturally assertive citizenry. These kinds of criteria, however, come unnervingly close to replicating the criteria set forth in state courts' "existing Indian family" standard for application of the Indian Child Welfare Act.[134] In California, the courts have gone further, deeming the act unconstitutional as applied to Indian children whose parents do not "maintain a significant social, cultural or political relationship with their tribe."[135] These state courts have taken it upon themselves to determine individuals' relationships with their tribes by examining such contacts as subscription to a tribal newsletter. What seems presumptuous when undertaken by state courts may be less troubling when the deciding authority is a tribal enrollment board. However, even then, serious problems remain.

First, who would be afforded the opportunity to demonstrate adequate cultural ties? Would an Indian nation be obliged to give a hearing to anyone who learned the language and rituals? If so, tribes might be overwhelmed with applications for citizenship, especially well-off gaming tribes. Would a different standard be applied to close relations of tribal members in order to expedite administration and to recognize the significance of family ties? If so, the use of a cultural fluency or cultural ties criterion would not escape the wrath of those who oppose all "race-based" classifications.[136]

Second, how, and at what intervals, would prospective tribal members have to demonstrate their cultural ties in order to prove their right to citizenship? Would children be given an opportunity to draw closer to their culture than their less interested parents? What would be the status of these children until such time as they were prepared to stand for review of their cultural ties? What about individuals who go through a youthful period of rejecting their culture, but then decide to return? Would they be able to reapply? There is great potential for community divisiveness if the extent of one's cultural fluency is transformed into grounds for disenrollment or exclusion from citizenship.

One way to respond to some of these concerns is to designate a particular surrogate for cultural ties, such as reservation residence, and let that stand for the more complex determination. The problem with this response is that it is likely to miss many culturally connected individuals who need to live away from the reservation for one reason or another, such as the tribal member who is teaching the tribal language in an American Indian Studies program at a university in her state. Reservation residence in particular is a problematic criterion, because the Indian nation, in its capacity as landowner, can decide to restrict who can reside within the tribal territory.

Third, the whole idea that individuals can "prove" their tribal membership through demonstrations of cultural fluency or "lose" it by forgetting the culture is anathema to many tribal worldviews. According to these worldviews, belonging to a "people" is not an affirmative choice of the individual, but rather a condition of one's birth. Thus, for example, the Tlingit of Sitka believe that adoption in the sense of termination of parental rights and establishment of new such rights is impossible. Once one is born into a clan, it is impossible to separate from it, even in death.[137]

Those who argue for cultural affiliation as the sole criterion for tribal citizenship do not fully appreciate the nature of such societies and the difficulties attached to culturally based citizenship criteria. As a means for excluding people with clan and kinship ties by birth, such criteria actually abrade culture. As a wholesale means for including people who lack clan and kinship ties, culturally based criteria could overwhelm Indian nations with wannabes. While culturally based criteria might be sound bases for overcoming residence requirements of otherwise eligible tribal citizens, or for overcoming arbitrary consequences of other citizenship provisions, Indian nations might want to look to vehicles other than citizenship to advance cultural sovereignty.

D. Maximizing Benefits for Those Who Have
Sustained Affiliation

Some, perhaps many, tribal citizenship disputes reduce to conflicts pitting those who have remained actively involved with the tribal community during difficult times against those who moved away, often because of those very hardships. Gaming success magnifies such potential conflicts, because it presents Indian nations with the choice between per capita distribution of revenues[138] and investment in tribal infrastructure and services, primarily benefiting those living on or near the reservation. Thus, those currently enrolled may have an incentive to exclude potential citizens who are unlikely to live and participate within the reservation community. Furthermore, longtime contributors to reservation life may view more recent applicants for citizenship as securing windfalls, regardless of whether these applicants demonstrate willingness to return to the reservation. In the view of existing citizens, the proper solution may seem to be closing the rolls.

Gaming is not the only wellspring of conflict among established reservation citizens and new applicants. Other limited resources prompt the same difficulties. For example, if an Indian nation with a small land base considers expanding citizenship to encompass all lineal descendants, it must confront tough decisions about how to allocate land assignments for reservation homesites. Tribal health and education benefits are likewise limited, posing the same trade-offs. A broader citizenry may mean a broader group empowered to make these allocation decisions, thereby threatening the position of established citizens.[139]

Not surprisingly, those who have remained active in tribal communities are often loathe to diminish their own power base and share resources. They also have some legitimate claims that they deserve some recompense for sacrificing personal interests in the name of tribal survival. But as the example of Tribe A demonstrates, contrary interests also emerge, resisting inertial forces favoring existing members.[140] For example, those who left can solicit sympathy from the non-Indian media, generating political pressures contrary to tribal interests, including gaming interests. And citizenship criteria that are too restrictive based on blood quantum or residence can squeeze out the children or grandchildren of those who never left, or exclude those who may leave for legitimate tribal purposes, such as to get an education or build up political capital. So Indian nations should carefully weigh the justifications for exclusivity based on characteristics of existing citizens. As this chapter suggests below, legal requirements affecting voting, entitlement to benefits, or officeholding may be more appropriate ways to ensure support for tribal infrastructure development or to reward those most instrumental in sustaining tribal communities.

E. Securing Future Generations

A tenet of most tribal cultures is the collective obligation to render today's decisions on behalf of future as well as present generations.[141] This dictate is often expressed as a requirement to assess consequences of current choices for the "seventh generation." These choices could include decisions about who belongs to the tribal community, and therefore who can benefit from it both spiritually and materially. Contemplating current rates of intermarriage,[142] some citizens of Indian nations may worry that their high minimum blood quantum requirements will strip their descendants of identity, of access to tribal culture and resources, and of rights within federal Indian programs. As indicated above, for these tribal citizens, relaxing blood quantum requirements, at least for their own descendants, can make sense.

IV. DESIGN OPTIONS FOR TRIBAL CITIZENSHIP

A comparative study of Indian nations' constitutional citizenship provisions yields several standard types: (1) place of birth (or parents' domicile at time of birth); (2) lineal descent from a tribal member listed on a base roll (may be matrilineal, patrilineal, or bilateral); (3) minimum percentage tribal descent (expressed as blood quantum, often referring to percentage of descent from a person who was living in North America before European contact, but sometimes expressed as minimum percentage of descent from a person listed on a base roll); (4) minimum percentage of Indian descent (expressed as blood quantum, and usually a means of reducing the requirement for minimum percentage of tribal descent); (5) adoption or naturalization (sometimes limited to tribal descendants, Indians, or relatives of existing members); (6) no dual citizenship; (7) future citizenship criteria by tribal statute or ordinance.

Some of these provisions are obviously inconsistent with one another (e.g., lineal descent and minimum percentage tribal descent), and not every Indian nation makes use of each one. But these are the most common features of Indian nations' citizenship requirements.

It would be a mistake, however, for Indian nations to view this existing array as the exclusive set of tools for addressing the kinds of considerations explored in Part III of this chapter. Different kinds of citizenship provisions may prove useful, as may constitutional measures addressing related matters, such as voting rights, officeholding rights, allocation of representation, the right of return, and rights to tribal benefits such as land assignments or tribal healthcare. These provisions may function to differentiate rights of groups of citizens or create multiple categories of citizenship.[143] The following suggestions are offered with deference to and respect for individual Indian nations' norms and values, which are the only true guide for legitimate governance. In the past, these nations have struggled to sustain their own visions of community in the face of federal controls and pressures described in Part II of this chapter. The discussion below offers ideas drawn from specific tribal experiences and international practice that may provide further raw material for Indian nations to employ in this transformative process.

A. Addressing Potential On-Reservation, Off-Reservation Conflicts

If an Indian nation is troubled by the prospect that broadened citizenship criteria will empower nonresident tribal members at the expense of reservation-based investment in education, physical infrastructure, and law enforcement, making citizenship turn on residence (or durational residence) is not the only option. Other alternatives include limiting voting and/or officeholding to those domiciled on or near the reservation, prohibiting absentee voting, and structuring representation so that off-reservation citizens have a smaller voice than their numbers would otherwise allow. Each of these alternatives augments the political influence of reservation residents. But the latter option is particularly appealing for Indian nations that do not want to send a message of exclusion to individuals who are maintaining tribal ties at a distance. Consider the example of the Cherokee Nation, which recently undertook a massive constitution revision process.[144] The Cherokee have a large population base living outside their historic reservation. Of approximately 220,000 enrolled Cherokees, nearly 40 percent live outside Oklahoma, mostly in California, Texas, Kansas, Arkansas, and Missouri.[145] To address this situation, the current draft constitution establishes fifteen geographically based districts for representation on the legislative governing body, and allocates two districts to off-reservation citizens who vote for these seats on an at-large basis. All citizens may vote for the executive branch officers.

Another way to signal inclusion of those who live off-reservation is to provide potential members with what is known as a "right of return."[146] Such a right would enable anyone who satisfies broad criteria (for example, lineal descent) to take an active measure to affirm citizenship, if not by establishing permanent domicile within the tribal territory, then by assuming some obligations of citizenship, such as taxation or community service. Such a provision would maintain ties and identity for individuals who are not in close geographic proximity to the tribal community, while reserving rights of citizenship for those who make a more substantial commitment.

B. Benefits-Related Provisions

Indian nations often have two competing concerns about the distribution of tribal benefits. If citizenship is defined too broadly, there may not be enough to go around. If it is defined too narrowly, their own descendants may be the ones excluded if present rates of intermarriage persist. But using citizenship criteria as the vehicle for addressing these concerns may be too crude a method.

For example, if allocation of land assignments and other tribal benefits is a concern, then it may be possible to build allocation criteria for these benefits into the constitution at the time of adopting broader citizenship criteria. In that way, the allocation criteria are protected against easy amendment or repeal by the newly enlarged citizenry. If the Department of the Interior has review power over a tribal constitution based on the Indian Reorganization Act or some other federal law, the tribe may need to attend to possible violations of the Indian Civil Rights Act.[147] Thus, for example, allocation criteria based on gender would be denied approval. However, creation of priorities based on such considerations as duration of reservation residence or availability of other land assignments within the same family would doubtless pass muster while addressing allocational concerns.

For Indian nations concerned with excluding their future generations from tribal benefits, one possible solution is the one under consideration within Tribe C—to separate eligibility for benefits from citizenship. Under a provision of this type, lineal descendants lacking sufficient blood quantum to qualify for citizenship would nonetheless be entitled to specified benefits, such as scholarships or land. In effect, such a provision commits the group of voting citizens to allocate benefits beyond their limited group. At the same time, it maintains decision-making power within the established group, which possesses a greater degree of tribal ancestry. Viewing such ancestry as an appropriate surrogate for tribal cultural identification and practice, this approach has the advantage of maintaining cultural cohesion while providing for future generations. An important caveat, however, is that this solution is likely to function more effectively for tribal than for federal benefits. To the extent that federal law ties federal benefits and special jurisdictional rules to tribal membership, then these beneficiary recipients will not qualify. However, if the tribal constitution establishes multiple "classes" of members—some entitled to full citizenship including voting, others entitled only to benefits—rather than prescribing a group of noncitizen beneficiaries, the problem of qualifying under federal law may diminish.

C. Expanded Adoption Provisions

Relatively expansive adoption provisions for lineal descendants or those with socially appropriate relationships to tribal citizens may be an appropriate way for Indian nations to accommodate all of the concerns expressed above, but on a case-by-case rather than a categorical basis. Such provisions have a long history in Indian communities, and the United States has sometimes been willing to treat adoptees as tribal citizens for purposes of federal law, even without regard to lineal descent.[148] More expansive provisions could be written to allow for demonstrations of adequate commitment to tribal culture and community, by a variety of means.[149]

Such individualized determinations do, however, place a heavy burden on tribal communities, which are rarely in a position to compensate individuals who must hear these applications initially or as a reviewing authority. Furthermore, if past experience is any guide, these determinations can become divisive and heavily politicized. Thus, it may be helpful for an Indian nation wishing to adopt this course to establish criteria amenable to relatively clear-cut demonstration.

V. CONCLUSION

Since the 1988 amendments to the Indian Reorganization Act, Indian nations have had far greater freedom to reexamine their constitutions in order to bring them into closer alignment with community needs and values. Experts in economic development have demonstrated that this kind of alignment is key to producing more legitimate and stable tribal governments, capable of charting the proper course between material and cultural goals.[150] Yet constitutional reform often flounders over fundamental issues such as the definition of citizenship. This chapter offers Indian nations some case studies and analyses that may prove helpful in reaching agreement on citizenship measures. It also offers a perspective on prevailing academic and tribal controversies over blood quantum provisions in Indian nations' constitutions, suggesting that they may sometimes have a legitimate place in tribal governing documents. As citizenship is a key constituent of individual identity and tribal cultures, the only appropriate decision-maker is each tribal community.

NOTES

Carole Goldberg is Professor of Law and Director of the Joint Degree Program in Law and American Indian Studies at UCLA. Support for writing this article came from the Dean's Fund of the UCLA School of Law. This article first appeared in the April 2002 edition of the *Kansas Law Review*.

1. Eric Lemont, "Developing Effective Processes of Constitutional and Governmental Reform: Lessons from the Cherokee Nation, Hualapai Nation, Navajo Nation, and Northern Cheyenne Tribe," *American Indian Law Review* 26 (2001–2002): 147; see also Rob Carson, "Membership in Indian Tribes Becoming Increasingly Important Divisive Issue," *Tacoma News Tribune,* February 17, 2002, A1 (reporting some controversies over membership criteria).

2. In the course of extending these services, the students (teams of law students and M.A. students in American Indian Studies) develop skills in cross-cultural legal representation and legal drafting.

3. I came to believe that the term *membership* is used in tribal constitutions rather than *citizenship* because the Bureau of Indian Affairs did not treat these constitutions as charters for governments. Rather, it viewed them as some variation on private associations or student councils, designed to instruct Indian people in self-government rather than to facilitate genuine self-determination. For example, the constitutions promoted by the Bureau typically have "by-laws" attached to them, something one finds in nonprofit or business associations, not governments. For an illustration of BIA resistance to constitutional reform substituting the term *citizen* for *member,* see Cherokee Nation Constitutional Progress Report, available at *www.cherokee.org* (February 2000). The Bureau has objected that such a shift would produce "confusion."

4. See, e.g., L. Scott Gould, "Mixing Bodies and Beliefs: The Predicament of Tribes," *Columbia Law Review* 101 (2001): 702 (concluding that the continued existence of most tribes may depend on eliminating race as an essential membership criterion); Mark Neath, "American Indian Gaming Enterprises and Tribal Membership: Race, Exclusivity, and a Perilous Future," *University of Chicago Law School Roundtable* 2 (1995): 689 (stating that if tribes continue abiding by racial membership requirements, they face shrinking population and stricter federal court scrutiny of tribal laws).

5. Carole Goldberg, "American Indians and Preferential Treatment," *UCLA Law Review* 49 (2002): 943.

6. See generally John P. LaVelle, "The General Allotment Act 'Eligibility' Hoax: Distortions of Law, Policy, and History in Derogation of Indian Tribes," *Wicazo Sa Review* 14 (1999): 251, 260–262 (analyzing the work of Marianette Jaimes-Guerro and Ward Churchill).

7. See Part II of this chapter.

8. Case studies drawn from the clinic or other nonpublic sources do not identify the Indian nation involved.

9. Termination occurred pursuant to the Rancheria Act, Pub. L. No. 85-671, 72 Stat. 619 (1958) amended by Pub. L. No. 88-419, 78 Stat. 390 (1964), codified at 25 U.S.C. § 465 (2000). Originally enacted in 1958 and amended in 1964, the Rancheria Act authorized the Secretary of the Interior to divide and distribute the assets of certain California Indian rancherias and reservations after the vote of a majority of the members of each reservation. Id. The purpose of this act was not to define Indians by tribal affiliation in a way that would strengthen tribal sovereignty, government, or self-determination. Rather, it was designed to identify generally California Indians who were users of land held in trust for them by the United States government. *Kelly v. United States Dep't of Interior,* 339 F. Supp. 1095, 1098–1099, n.8 (E.D. Cal. 1972). Once such Indians were identified, they received a distribution of the land and their special status as Indians, and the government-to-government relationship between their tribe and the United States could be terminated, thus allowing the United States to abandon its trust responsibility. An obvious objection to the Rancheria Act is that it ignored the interests of tribal members living off or near the reservation, even though the federal government owed a trust responsibility to all tribal members.

10. Several such lawsuits succeeded in producing "untermination" of tribes, including *Hardwick v. United States,* No. C-79-1710 SW (N.D. Cal. December 22, 1983) ("*Tillie Hardwick*"), available at http://sorrel.Humboldt.edi/asp/hardwick.html; *Table Bluff Band v. Watt,* 532 F. Supp. 56 (N.D. Cal. 1978); and *Duncan v. Andrus,* 517 F. Supp. 1 (N.D. Cal. 1977). These lawsuits resulted in adjudication or settlement of claims that the United States had failed to implement promises to improve the land of the terminated tribes. Among other things, these orders directed the United States to reestablish a government-to-government relationship with the seventeen tribes represented in the litigation. Additional background is available in *Hardwick v. United States,* Civ. No. 79-1710 SW, 1994 WL 721578, at *1 (N.D. Cal. Dec. 22, 1994).

11. *Alan-Wilson v. Acting Sacramento Area Dir., Bureau of Indian Affairs,* 33 I.B.I.A. 55, 1998 I.D. LEXIS 85 at *4 (1998) (ordering "untermination" of a tribe).

12. See, e.g., 25 U.S.C. § 657 (2000) (authorizing revision of the California Indian rolls). For example, a 1928 census list, available on microfiche, was intended to document California Indians with families alive when treaties were signed in 1851 and 1852. It lists more than twenty thousand California Indians, each assigned

a number by the Bureau that corresponds to the census interview form for that person. Another list, created in the late 1950s, exists in book form at the National Archives in San Bruno, California. In the 1970s the Bureau made another census, probably more extensive than the others, which is not easily accessible or organized into list form because it consists of a series of individual files located at the Bureau's Washington headquarters. Interview with Heather Singleton, Researcher, UCLA American Indian Studies Center (January 24, 2002). Ms. Singleton has been conducting research under a grant from the Administration for Native Americans on behalf of the federal recognition claims of the Gabrieleno/ Tongva Nation, the indigenous people of the Los Angeles basin. The history of California Indian land claims litigation is set forth comprehensively in Bruce S. Flushman and Joe Barbieri, "Aboriginal Title: The Special Case of California," *Pacific Law Journal* 17 (1986): 391.

13. Goldberg, "American Indians and Preferential Treatment." For an illustration of this problem involving a different tribe, see *Alan-Wilson v. Sacramento Area Director,* 30 I.B.I.A. 241, 1997 I.D. LEXIS 85, *recons. den.,* 31 I.B.I.A. 4, 1995 I.D. LEXIS 41 (1997). The settlement order in the largest untermination lawsuit, the *Tillie Hardwick* case, did not directly address the question of who would be entitled to participate in the formation of subsequent governing documents for the affected tribes. 30 I.B.I.A. 241, 1997 I.D. LEXIS 85, at *18–19. The Department of the Interior has taken the position that the BIA may take a more active role when a tribe is organizing its initial government than when an existing tribal government is shaping its citizenship provisions. *Burris v. Sacramento Area Director,* 33 I.B.I.A. 66 (1998), *Indian Law Report* 26 (1998): 7061, 7063.

14. For a similar story, see Kevin Fagan, "Outcasts of the Reservations," *San Francisco Chronicle,* April 10, 2000, A1 (discussing the plight of Indians who are not considered rightful heirs to their tribal legacies and therefore are not entitled to casino profits).

15. See discussion in notes 11–12 and accompanying text herein.

16. For illustrations of such press attacks, see Peter Hecht, "Amador Tribal Dispute Heats Up," *Sacramento Bee,* December 16, 2001, B1, and Fagan, "Outcasts of the Reservations." See also George Hostetter, "Indians Sign Petition in Tribal War," *Fresno Bee,* June 4, 2000, A1; George Hostetter, "Indians Bet on Public Support in Tribal Dispute," *Fresno Bee,* April 17, 2000, A1.

17. Citizenship was defined to include anyone who was a lineal descendant of a lineal ancestor of a distributee.

18. For unrelated reasons, the constitution was never promulgated by the tribe.

19. 25 U.S.C. §§ 461–479 (2000).

20. The requirement of parental residence likely traces to a Department of the Interior Circular, dated November 18, 1935, which specified such a requirement as highly desirable for tribal constitutions established under the Indian Reorganization Act in order to ensure that membership is limited to persons "who reasonably can be expected to participate in tribal relations and affairs." *U.S. Department*

of the Interior, Circular No. 3123, November 18, 1935 (copy on file with the author).

21. For such a view, expressed without systematic empirical support, see Kathryn R. L. Rand and Steven A. Light, "Virtue or Vice? How IGRA Shapes the Politics of Native American Gaming, Sovereignty, and Identity," *Virginia Journal of Social Policy and Law* 4 (1997): 381 (discussing the Indian Gaming Regulatory Act's effect on Native American tribes); see also Neath, "American Indian Gaming Enterprises and Tribal Membership," 694–702 (offering anecdotes about membership requirements in connection with gaming success).

22. This same situation prevails with respect to so-called "blood quantum" requirements, which can be found in many tribal constitutions. See Russell Thornton, "Tribal Membership Requirements and the Demography of 'Old' and 'New' Native Americans," in *Changing Numbers, Changing Needs: American Indian Demography and Public Health,* ed. Gary Sandefur et al. (1996), 103, 107 (offering a partial survey of tribal membership requirements which showed that two-thirds had some form of blood quantum requirement). Most often the requirement was one-quarter descent or less. Tribal members voting on whether to include such requirements must take account of possible disqualification of their future generations, based on intermarriage patterns that they cannot predict.

23. Under the Indian Gaming Regulatory Act of 1988, tribal citizens have a choice between per capita distributions of gaming revenues and use of the revenues for tribal governmental purposes. 25 U.S.C. § 2710(b)(2), (d)(1)(A)(ii) (2000).

24. See notes 11–12 and accompanying text herein.

25. Felix S. Cohen, *Handbook of Federal Indian Law,* ed. Rennard Strickland et al. (Charlottesville, VA: Michie Bobbs-Merrill, 1982), 23 n. 27.

26. Subsequent drafts of the constitution have dropped this provision.

27. Many federal regulations allow tribal membership to establish eligibility for services. See, e.g., Employment Assistance for Adult Indians, 25 C.F.R. § 26.1(g) (2001) (defining "Indian" for purposes of the regulation); Vocational Training for Adult Indians, 25 C.F.R. § 27.1(i) (2001) (same); Financial Assistance and Social Services Program, 25 C.F.R. § 20.1(n) (2001) (same).

28. See, e.g., *Apodaca v. Silvas,* 19 F.3d 1015, 1016 (5th Cir. 1994) (noting that federal government has left control of membership rosters to tribes themselves); *Smith v. Babbitt,* 875 F.Supp. 1353, 1360 (D. Minn. 1995) (providing that "[t]he great weight of authority holds that tribes have exclusive authority to determine membership issues"); *Torres v. Muskogee Area Dir.,* 34 I.B.I.A. 173, 1999 I.D. LEXIS 102 at *+ 8–9 (1999) (detailing the process by which tribes regulate their membership).

29. 436 U.S. 49 (1978).

30. 25 U.S.C. §§ 1301–1303 (2000).

31. 436 U.S. at 71.

32. 528 U.S. 495 (2000).

33. Id. at 518–523.

34. Letter from Chief, Division of Tribal Government Services, Bureau of Indian Affairs, to Leroy Salgado (September 24, 1998) (on file with author) (hereinafter "Salgado Letter").

35. 25 U.S.C. § 476.

36. See Russel Lawrence Barsh, "Another Look at Reorganization: When Will Tribes Have a Choice," *Indian Truth* 247 (October 1982): 10–12 (detailing the process and implications of passage of the act by voting tribes).

37. *Circular No. 3123,* U.S. Department of the Interior (November 18, 1935) (on file with the author) (interpreting section 19 of the Indian Reorganization Act, 25 U.S.C. § 479 [2000], and describing the term *Indian;* authorizes the Office of Indian Affairs to limit membership benefits for Indians based on tribal affiliation or degree of consanguinity).

38. Id.

39. 25 U.S.C. § 479.

40. *Circular No. 3123,* note 37 herein.

41. Id.

42. Id.

43. Id.

44. Id.

45. See notes 19–24 and accompanying text.

46. See, e.g., *Coyote Valley Band of Pomo Indians v. United States,* 639 F. Supp. 165 (E.D. Cal. 1986) (challenging the federal government's practice of withholding authorization of special elections until after the completion of a lengthy process for the review and modification of proposed tribal constitutions by the BIA).

47. Pub. L. No. 100-581, §§ 101, 102 Stat. 2938 (1988) codified at 25 U.S.C. § 476(c)(2) (2000).

48. 436 U.S. 49 (1978).

49. Salgado Letter, note 34 (brackets in original).

50. *Thomas v. United States,* 141 F. Supp. 2d 1185, 1192 (W.D. Wis. 2001).

51. Id. Specifically, absentee ballots had been permitted for the constitution amendment vote, but had not been allowed for the adoption of the original constitution. The Bureau's position was that the exact same class of voters had to vote on the proposed amendment as had voted on the original governing document.

52. *Thomas,* 141 F. Supp. 2d at 1200.

53. Id. at 1192.

54. Id.

55. Id.

56. Id. at 1192–1193.

57. Id. at 1203.

58. See John Rockwell Snowden et al., "American Indian Sovereignty and Naturalization: It's a Race-Thing," *Nebraska Law Review* 80 (2001): 171, 236; Wilhelm Murg, "BIA Announces Position on Seminole Dispute," *Native American Times,* January 1, 2002, 1.

59. 25 U.S.C. § 1302 (2000).

60. Id. § 1302(8).

61. See Snowden et al., "American Indian Sovereignty and Naturalization," 200–220.

62. 25 U.S.C. §§ 2701–2721.

63. Rand and Light, "Virtue or Vice."

64. Robert N. Clinton et al., *American Indian Law: Cases and Materials,* 3d ed. (Charlottesville, VA: Michie, 1991), 84.

65. Blood quantum has generally been interpreted to mean percentage of ancestry from a person who lived in North America before the sixteenth century.

66. 25 U.S.C. § 472; 25 C.F.R. § 5.1 (2001).

67. See *Zarr v. Barlow,* 800 F.2d 1484, 1491 (9th Cir. 1986) (holding that the BIA could not continue to apply the one-quarter-degree Indian blood test to determine eligibility for Indian higher education grants).

68. See, e.g., *United States v. A.W.L.,* 117 F.3d 1423, 1997 WL 397168 (8th Cir. July 7, 1997) (unpublished table decision) (concluding that defendant who had 15/32 Indian blood and was accepted by tribal community was an Indian under 28 U.S.C. § 1153).

69. 25 U.S.C. §§ 1901–1963.

70. Id. § 1903(3)–(4).

71. See 44 Fed. Reg. 67584, 67586 (November 26, 1979) (stating that enrollment is commonly used as evidence of membership in an Indian tribe, but it is neither necessary nor always determinative).

72. See, e.g., *Indian Tribe v. Doe,* 849 P.2d 925, 928 (Idaho 1993) (applying tribe's enrollment criteria to establish that the child was an Indian child for purposes of the Indian Child Welfare Act); *John v. Baker,* 30 P.3d 68, 73 (Alaska 2001) (concluding that, according to tribal law, the children were eligible for membership).

73. 16 U.S.C. § 668 (2000).

74. See *United States v. Dion,* 476 U.S. 734, 740 (1986) (summarizing the provisions of the act); 50 C.F.R. § 22.22 (2000) (stating requirements to qualify for a religious exemption).

75. See Brett Anderson, "Recognizing Substance: Adoptees and Affiliates of Native American Tribes Claiming Free Exercise Rights," *Washington & Lee Race and Ethnic Ancestry Law Journal* 7 (2001): 61, 62.

76. 25 U.S.C. §§ 2701–2721 (2000).

77. Rand and Light, "Virtue or Vice," 402–404; Mike Geniella, "Slots Pay Off Big for Indian Casinos," *Press Democrat* (Santa Rosa, Calif.), January 2, 2002; Dennis McAuliffe, Jr., "Casinos Deal Indians a Winning Hand," *Washington Post,* March 5, 1996, A1.

78. 25 U.S.C. §§ 2710(b)(2), (d)(1)(A)(ii).

79. Id. § 2710(b)(3).

80. Rand and Light, "Virtue or Vice," 421.

81. Ibid., 424.

82. Ibid., 423. Another example is the Fort McDowell Apache, who amended their constitution in 1999 to require one-quarter Fort McDowell Yavapai ancestry rather than the prior requirement of one-quarter Indian ancestry. Fort McDowell Yavapai Nation Constitution, art. III, § 2 (1999), available at *www.narf.org*.

83. Rand and Light note the example of the Mashantucket Pequots. Rand and Light, "Virtue or Vice," 422–423.

84. Neath, "American Indian Gaming Enterprises and Tribal Membership," 694–697. Skibine describes a similar effort to limit tribal membership by blood quantum when oil was discovered on the Osage reservation in the early twentieth century. Alex Tallchief Skibine, "The Cautionary Tale of the Osage Indian Nation Attempt to Survive Its Wealth," *Kansas Journal of Law and Public Policy* 9 (2000): 815, 818–819.

85. 447 U.S. 134, 160–161 (1980) (holding that the state may impose cigarette taxes on nonmembers as "nonmembers are not constituents of the governing Tribe").

86. 495 U.S. 676, 694–698 (1990) (holding that an Indian tribe does not have criminal jurisdiction over a nonmember). Congress acknowledged tribal criminal jurisdiction over nonmember Indians, effectively overturning *Duro,* in its 1990 amendment to the Indian Civil Rights Act. Pub. L. No. 101-511, 104, Stat. 189 (1990), codified as amended by Pub. L. No. 102-124, 105 Stat. 616 (1991) at 25 U.S.C. § 1301(2) (2000).

87. See, e.g., *Duro v. Reina,* 495 U.S. 676, 700 (1990) (Brennan, J., dissenting) ("[I]t does not follow that because tribes lost their power to exercise criminal jurisdiction over non-Indians, they also lost their power to enforce criminal laws against Indians who are not members of their tribe"); *Confederated Tribes of the Colville Indian Reservation v. Washington,* 446 F. Supp. 1339, 1371–1372 (E.D. Wash. 1978) (rejecting the member/nonmember distinction by stating "all Indians residing on a reservation are equally free from the state's excise taxation regardless of whether they are members of the tribe"), *rev'd,* 447 U.S. 134, 160 (1980) (adopting the member/nonmember distinction).

88. See, e.g., 18 U.S.C. § 1152 (2000) (addressing the laws governing criminal punishment of offenses committed in Indian Country).

89. See *United States v. A.W.L.,* 1997 WL 397168, at *1 (8th Cir. Jul. 7 1997) (citing the appellant's Indian ancestry and tribal acceptance of appellant as sufficient to establish jurisdiction over appellant).

90. 447 U.S. at 160.

91. 495 U.S. at 677, 688.

92. 25 U.S.C. § 1301(2) (2000); see *United States v. Enas,* 255 F.3d 662, 670–671 (9th Cir. 2001) (en banc) (holding that "*Duro* squarely conflicts with the 1990 amendments to the ICRA"), *cert. denied,* 122 S.Ct. 925 (2002).

93. See, e.g., *Strate v. A-1 Contractors,* 520 U.S. 438, 439 (1997) (holding that tribal court does not have jurisdiction over nonmember pertaining to an accident

that occurred on a state-maintained highway on a federally granted right-of-way over tribal land).

94. See *Brendale v. Confederated Tribes & Bands of Yakima Indian Nation,* 493 U.S. 887, 887 (1989) (mem.) (retaxing costs assessed for preparing joint appendix for earlier decision).

95. *Strate,* 520 U.S. at 439.

96. The high rate of Indians' intermarriage with non-Indians is discussed in Thornton, "Tribal Membership Requirements," 109–111.

97. See *Means v. Dist. Ct.,* 26 Indian L. Rpt. 6083 (Navaho, May 11, 1999) (considering jurisdiction in an intimate violence case); Snowden et al., "American Indian Sovereignty and Naturalization," 233–236.

98. See generally 25 C.F.R. § 83.7 (2001) (defining the mandatory federal criteria for being recognized as a member of an Indian tribe).

99. E.g., *Mashpee Tribe v. New Seabury Corp.,* 592 F.2d 575, 581–584 (1st Cir. 1979).

100. 25 C.F.R. § 83.7(b) (2001) (alteration in original).

101. Id. § 83.7(b)(1) (vi, vii) (alterations in original) (citations omitted).

102. Id. § 83.7(c).

103. Id. § 83.7(c)(1)(iii).

104. Gabrieleno/Tongva Nation Act, H.R. 2619, 107th Cong. (2001).

105. See Bill Hillburg, "Tribe Seeks Recognition from U.S.," *Daily News of Los Angeles,* December 23, 2001 (discussing a rival tribal council).

106. See notes 9–15, 28–61, and accompanying text.

107. See text accompanying notes 9–18.

108. See Clinton et al., *American Indian Law,* 84–85 (discussing allotment rolls); Bruce S. Flushman and Joe Barbieri, "Aboriginal Title: The Special Case of California," *Pacific Law Journal* 17 (1986): 391, 428–439 (discussing California judgment rolls).

109. See generally LaVelle, "The General Allotment Act 'Eligibility' Hoax."

110. For examples of tribal constitutions deploying such rolls in their citizenship definitions, see Cherokee Nation Constitution, art. III, § 1, available at http://www.yvwiiusdinvnohii.net/Cherokee/Constitution.htm, and Turtle Mountain Band of Chippewa Indians Constitution, art. III, § 1, available at http://www.narf.org/nill/Constitutions.

111. Rennard Strickland, "Things Not Spoken: The Burial of Native American History, Law and Culture," *St. Thomas Law Review* 13 (2000): 11, 15.

112. Ibid.

113. Ibid.

114. See, e.g., Russel Lawrence Barsh, "The Challenge of Indigenous Self-Determination," *University of Michigan Journal of Law Reform* 26 (1993): 277, 301–302 (advocating that Indians should identify themselves as a race rather than a culture); Gould, "Mixing Bodies and Beliefs," 718–719 (contrasting tribal blood

quantum requirements with traditional practices); Snowden et al., "American Indian Sovereignty and Naturalization," 199–200, 237–238.

115. See Gould, "Mixing Bodies and Beliefs," 719–720 (discussing how tribes consisted of members and nonmembers such as children of slaves who were received as tribal members); see also Snowden et al., "American Indian Sovereignty and Naturalization," 197–200. Carole Goldberg-Ambrose, "Of Native Americans and Tribal Members: The Impact of Law on Indian Group Life," *Law and Society Review* 28 (1994): 1123, 1129–1131 (discussing the varying degrees to which individuals and kinship groups recognized their participation in larger tribal tradition).

116. Clinton et al., *American Indian Law,* 561.

117. For a discussion of such provisions see Goldberg-Ambrose, "Of Native Americans and Tribal Members," 1139–1145. Provisions of this type often reflect the fact that the United States government arbitrarily divided individuals from closely related cultural groups into distinct political entities.

118. For discussions of the conflict between tribal and non-Indian worldviews in the context of dispute resolution and political organization, see Russel Lawrence Barsh, "The Nature and Spirit of North American Political Systems," *American Indian Quarterly* 10 (1986): 181; Robert B. Porter, "Strengthening Tribal Sovereignty through Peacemaking: How the Anglo-American Legal Tradition Destroys Indigenous Societies," *Columbia Human Rights Law Review* 28 (1997): 235.

119. See Goldberg-Ambrose, "Of Native Americans and Tribal Members," 1139–1145 (discussing the postcontact changes in Indian group life); Snowden et al., "American Indian Sovereignty and Naturalization," 197–199 (describing how Winnebago clans incorporated adoptees).

120. See generally Morton H. Fried, *The Notion of Tribe* (Menlo Park, CA: Cummings, 1975) (attacking the traditionally held conceptions of tribes); Barsh, "Another Look at Reorganization," 4 (stating that extenuated kinship played a role in maintaining the cohesiveness of Indian society).

121. See Wallace Coffey and Rebecca Tsosie, "Rethinking the Tribal Sovereignty Doctrine: Cultural Sovereignty and the Collective Future of Indian Nations," *Stanford Law and Policy Review* 12 (2001): 191, 198 (discussing how relationships connect Indians to other communities). Use of the term *adoption* rather than *naturalization* to describe this incorporation is thus no coincidence.

122. For example, in a society made up of matrilineal clans, the child of a tribal father and an outsider mother has no place in the clan structure and is ineligible for membership.

123. For a discussion of tribal adoption practices, see note 131 and accompanying text.

124. Of course, one might argue that in precontact tribal societies, cultural learning attended biological descent in a way that it need not today, given geographic dispersion, intermarriage, and assimilationist forces that affect tribal members.

125. See Gould, "Mixing Bodies and Beliefs," 769–770 (suggesting "tribes adopt at least some members because of cultural affinity"); Neath, "American Indian

Gaming Enterprises and Tribal Membership," 706–707 (same). Neath also suggests a community service component as a requirement for tribal citizenship. Ibid. To the extent that Gould and Neath are concerned that blood quantum requirements represent unconstitutional racial discrimination, adding a few tribal citizens based on adoption or naturalization cannot solve the problem. In several gender discrimination cases involving eligibility for government benefits, the Supreme Court has held that if women receive benefits based solely on their gender and men must prove entitlement, the statute violates equal protection. The fact that some men may qualify does not save the law from successful challenge. *Califano v. Goldfarb,* 430 U.S. 199, 207–208 (1977); *Frontiero v. Richardson,* 411 U.S. 677, 690–691 (1973).

126. Thornton, "Tribal Membership Requirements," 108–111.

127. For a vigorous debate about the desirability of Indian participation in federal and state politics, see generally John P. LaVelle, "Strengthening Tribal Sovereignty through Indian Participation in American Politics: A Reply to Professor Porter," *Kansas Journal of Law and Public Policy* 10 (2001): 533, and Robert B. Porter, "The Demise of the Ongwehoweh and the Rise of the Native Americans: Redressing the Genocidal Act of Forcing American Citizenship upon Indigenous Peoples," *Harvard BlackLetter Law Journal* 15 (1999): 107.

128. For a discussion of how the Cherokee have used their inclusive citizenship criteria to expand their numbers and increase political influence, see "Cherokee Losing Chief Who Revitalized Tribe," *New York Times,* April 6, 1994, A16. As former principal chief Wilma Mankiller points out, the Cherokee were divided about pursuing such a strategy: "The constitution [of 1976] which was supposed to unify the Cherokees did not do so. Regarding tribal membership, many people thought a requirement of one-quarter blood quantum should have been instituted. Others thought the Cherokees who lived outside the Cherokee Nation should not be allowed to vote in tribal elections. Some people objected to the inclusion of the Delawares and Shawnees. . . . Others objected to the exclusion of the Cherokee freedmen and intermarried whites." Wilma Mankiller, *Mankiller: A Chief and Her People* (New York: St. Martin's Press, 1993), 218. Neath mistakenly interprets the Cherokee Constitution as allowing for enrollment of individuals who cannot prove Cherokee descent. Neath, "American Indian Gaming Enterprises and Tribal Membership," 705–706. While he correctly points out that the Constitution provides for a registration committee to consider applications for enrollment, he inaccurately claims that this committee serves individuals with Cherokee cultural ties who are "unable to trace ancestry." In fact, the Cherokee Nation requires that all applications presented to the registration committee be accompanied by a Certificate of Degree of Indian Blood (CDIB) issued by the Bureau of Indian Affairs. See Cherokee Nation, *Tribal Registration,* at http://www.cherokee.org/Services.

129. Wallace Coffey and Rebecca Tsosie, "Rethinking the Tribal Sovereignty Doctrine: Cultural Sovereignty and the Collective Future of Indian Nations," *Stanford Law and Policy Review* 12 (2001): 191.

130. Ibid., 196.

131. As Coffey and Tsosie point out, some disenfranchised urban Indian groups, such as the Navajos in Phoenix, have sought recognition by their tribes, suggesting a request for a culturally based model of sovereignty. The authors are careful to note, however, that "it is up to each Nation to decide whether recognition of communities outside the reservation is consistent with its own norms and values of governance." Ibid., 199.

132. Tribal constitutional provisions governing adoptions vary greatly. The Nez Perce Constitution, for example, permits membership adoption, without specifying any limitations on who is eligible for adoption. Nez Perce Tribe Constitution, art. IV, § 2, available at http://thorpe.ou.edu. Rather, criteria for membership by adoption are to be specified by tribal ordinance. A similar provision appears in the Constitution of the Lower Brule Sioux Tribe, although adoptees must reside on the reservation. Lower Brule Sioux Tribe Constitution, art. II, § 2, available at *http://thorpe.ou.edu.* In contrast, some tribal constitutions provide that only Indians are eligible for adoption. See, e.g., Yavapai-Apache Nation Constitution, art. II, § 2(a)(2), available at *http://thorpe.ou.edu.* Some Indian nations allow adoptions only for spouses of members. See, e.g., Fort McDermitt Paiute and Shoshone Tribe Constitution, art. II, § 2(b), available at http://thorpe.ou.edu (requiring one-half blood degree from any tribe).

133. See Neath, "American Indian Gaming Enterprises and Tribal Membership," 704.

134. See, e.g., *In re Santos Y,* 110 Cal. Rptr. 2d 1, 26–27 n.15 (Cal. Ct. App. 2001) (listing cases accepting and opposing the doctrine), *vacated by* 112 Cal. Rptr. 2d 692 (Cal. Ct. App. 2001).

135. *In re Bridget R.,* 49 Cal. Rptr. 2d 507, 516 (Cal. Ct. App. 1996).

136. See generally Gould, "Mixing Bodies and Beliefs" (urging American Indian tribes to redefine the membership criteria from rule-based classification to preserve tribal cultures); Neath, "American Indian Gaming Enterprises and Tribal Membership" (opposing race-based classifications for tribal membership). This point is also discussed above in note 124.

137. *Hepler v. Perkins,* 13 Ind. L. Rptr. 6011, 6016 (Sitka Comty. Assoc. Tr. Ct. 1989).

138. Per capita distributions of gaming revenues must be made pursuant to a plan approved by the Secretary of the Interior. 25 U.S.C. § 2710(b)(3)(B) (2000); 25 C.F.R. § 290.10 (2001). The plan need not include all tribal members. But if the plan excludes some categories of members, the Indian nation must justify the exclusion, demonstrating that the plan does not arbitrarily discriminate or otherwise violate the Indian Civil Rights Act or other applicable law. 25 C.F.R. § 290.14(b) (2001).

139. For a discussion of the possibility of separating voting from citizenship, see notes 142–145 and accompanying text.

140. See notes 14 and 16 and accompanying text.

141. See, e.g., Oren Lyons, "An Iroquois Perspective," in *Native American History*, ed. Christopher Vecsey and Robert W. Venables (1980), 171–174 (discussing the mandate to "make [every decision] . . . relate to the welfare and well-being of the seventh generation to come"). This point is addressed in Ronald L. Trosper, "Traditional American Indian Economic Policy," *American Indian Culture and Resource Journal* 19 (1995): 65.

142. See Gould, "Mixing Bodies and Beliefs," 757–764 (addressing the threat that racial criteria pose to the continued existence of most tribes); Thornton, "Tribal Membership Requirements" (addressing the problems created for tribes under blood quantum requirements).

143. For a proposal to create multiple classes of citizens, see Snowden et al., "American Indian Sovereignty and Naturalization," 235.

144. See D. Jay Hannah, "1999 Constitution Convention of the Cherokee Nation: Process of a Sovereign People," www.ksg.harvard.edu/hpaied/pubs. Archives of the constitution convention are available at http://www.cherokee.org. Nonresident Cherokees participated fully in the constitution revision process and possessed preexisting citizenship rights, which may explain the attention to their concerns.

145. Pamela Brogan, "Cherokees Open Office for Access in Capital," *Tulsa World,* April 8, 2001.

146. In the State of Israel, for example, anyone who is a Jew by birth or conversion, or a specified degree of relationship to a Jew, is eligible to become a citizen by indicating an intent to settle in the state. Law of Return, 5710-1950, 4 L.S.I. 114 (1950), available in translation with amendments at www.mfa.gov.il/mfa/go.asp.

147. The Cherokee Nation, for example, has been denied federal approval of its new Constitution because of concern that its citizenship provision violates the Indian Civil Rights Act. Cherokee Nation Status Report 2001, at http://www.cherokee.org.

148. See Anderson, "Recognizing Substance," 76–77 ("[A] member of a non–Native American ethnotype may be deemed a legal Indian, even though ethnologically that person is clearly not Native American.") But see Snowden et al., "American Indian Sovereignty and Naturalization," 200–220 (describing the U.S. courts' preoccupation with blood quantum as "vampire law").

149. See text accompanying notes 27–30.

150. See, e.g., Stephen Cornell and Joseph P. Kalt, "Reloading the Dice: Improving the Chances for Economic Development on American Indian Reservations," in *What Can Tribes Do? Strategies and Institutions in American Indian Economic Development,* ed. Stephen Cornell and Joseph P. Kalt (Los Angeles: UCLA American Indian Studies Center, 1992). ("Each present instance of substantial and sustained economic development in Indian Country is accompanied by a transfer of primary decision-making control to tribal hands and away from federal and state authorities.")

Joseph Thomas Flies-Away

Five   # MY GRANDMA, HER PEOPLE, OUR CONSTITUTION

I see a lot of creative people on the reservation. They're caught in a paradoxical situation. They adhere to the values of what the grandmothers and grandfathers talked about, to be in tune with themselves, to be in tune with their environment . . .

This value system that I'm telling you about goes this way, and the other value system comes back the opposite way. I'm telling young Indian people that there is a place there, right down the middle. Not too far to this side, not too far to that side but down the middle between pairs of opposites."
APACHE MAN, *OUR VOICES, OUR LAND*

"Midt Midt Miya:m." ("Go straight, right down the middle.")
HUALAPAI ELDERS AND GRANDMAS ELNORA MAPATIS, LOIS IRWIN, AND ANNABELLE JONES

INTRODUCTION

My grandma, Lois Marie *Wildavs*[1] Irwin,[2] was a "full-blooded" Hualapai.[3] She was an enrolled member[4] of the Hualapai Tribe, although—other than attending the Valentine Indian School—she never resided on what is now the Hualapai Indian Reservation.[5] Her people, her father's and mother's relatives, lived near what is now the Town of Kingman and the Walapai Mountain area of Arizona. Her people, the Hualapai, descend from the thirteen Pai Bands who once occupied what is now northwest Arizona, the ancestral homeland of the Hualapai. Today, almost everyone of Hualapai blood is "related" somehow, and every tribal member can link himself with at least one of the band affiliations and families. The constitution of the Hualapai Indian Tribe—the *writing*—was born in 1934. It was revised first in 1955 and most recently in 1991. The *writing* attempts to define who we are as Hualapai and to describe our methods of governance, leadership, and organization. Our constitution—the content and character of our people—our culture(s), customs, and common practices, are what make the *writing* stay alive and be.

My grandma, her people, and our constitution share a personal commonality. They are related to each other in that they contribute to and affect my identity, who I am, where I belong, even who I am born for. Or, in the plural, who are we? Why are we here? Where do we come from? Where are we going? This identity curiosity becomes even more engaging when thought about in terms of tribal membership and tribal citizenship. But, before discussing issues of membership, citizenship, and tribal constitutions, we should ask, are these concepts even connected to an indigenous worldview or capable of expression in the Hualapai language? How can, or does, a *writing* allow tribes to more clearly define who they are? How can these *writings*—these constitutions—artfully demonstrate tribally specific expressions of public power, personal representation, and political will? And what development strategies or approaches are available to tribes as they, or we, build and rebuild government?

Similar reformative thought and thinking is occurring in places throughout the world. In some countries colonial governments are attempting to find contemporary ways to address indigenous issues constitutionally, or through legislation. In other places, such as the United States, indigenous people are empowered to create and construct their own constitutions and currently are engaged in complex processes of constitutional and governmental reform. Sometimes reform is subtle and occurs with little notice, methodical and dispassionate. Other times reform simmers and heats, until it explodes into a full-blown controversy or crisis.

In 1991, members of the Hualapai Tribe voted to revise our constitution for a second time. This new governing document afforded institutional change to the Hualapai government. The new constitution is periodically tested and challenged in various ways,[6] though the process is quite restrained. Tribal members often do not know when the constitution is being tested until it reaches a level of conflict that calls for the intervention of the Tribe's judicial branch. Even then it can be uneventful or uninteresting to all but a handful of tribal members. Tests of the Tribe's governmental and corporate sovereign immunity, election challenges, and leasing questions in regard to economic development have also been brought before the Huala-pai Judicial Branch in recent years, and more are expected as the Tribe con-tinues to develop its government and economy. As more and more mem-bers and nonmembers become familiar with the Hualapai Constitution, criticism and challenges are expected. Some have commented that cer-tain provisions in our constitution are inconsistent with Hualapai culture. Others point to sections that may hinder economic development.

But underlying all of these disputes is a deep-seated ambiguity over the boundaries of tribal membership. Who is Hualapai? Who has the right to participate in Hualapai political life? And who has the right to make politi-cal decisions on behalf of the Tribe?

As the Hualapai people and other indigenous nations venture forward in their community and nation-building journeys, tribal leaders and mem-bers must address these bigger and deeper issues regarding the political status of their nation, their government, and the essence and context of tribal membership. They need to ask whether membership is synonymous with citizenship as defined under democratic terms, and what can be done to better articulate their relationship or delineate their differences. Tribal leaders and their constituents must begin critically thinking about these difficult and controversial questions, which include the status of a tribe's democracy, especially as it relates to nonmembers. This chapter, this book, is written as a challenge, or motivation, to tribal leaders—and constitu-ents—to begin formulating their own ideas and policy on the issues raised here from a thoughtful and prepared position, rather than an undiscerning and defensive one.

In this chapter, I propose tactics to help strategically approach constitu-tional and governmental reform in the area of tribal membership. Though I suggest these strategies specifically to the Hualapai Tribe, I invite their application to other indigenous polities (nations) that are endeavoring to reform their governments via their constitutions. Procedurally, each tribal government must critically assess its understanding of what it means to be a tribe and what it means to be a nation. This assessment must be per-formed with well-reasoned consideration given to the relationships and ties between tribal member, community resident, and citizen. In order to gather data and information regarding current thinking about these terms, tribes must create methods to institutionalize data collection. These meth-ods should assess tribal and community members' perceptions about tribal politics, political processes, and their institutions. This information can help tribal leaders and members make more informed and enlightened decisions about government and the future of their nations and communities.

A substantive strategic step is to remove blood quantum requirements for membership from tribal constitutions and instead articulate them in tribal ordinances. Moreover, throughout the development of a membership ordinance, tribal framers must give great consideration to the rights and responsibilities of non-indigenous residents and the notion of *tribal citizenship*. Framers must begin fashioning policies on how nonmember participation in government can be or is provided for in the constitution, and within what parameters.

MY GRANDMA

My *goda*[7] would not have minded living in Peach Springs, the capital of the Hualapai Nation. But circumstances kept her in the state of California, two hundred miles west of Hualapai territory. There she raised twelve children and helped with some grandchildren. My *goda* did not impress upon her kids patriotic notions of citizenship of the United States, California, or any of the indigenous peoples from whom she and her kids descended. She voted rarely, if ever, in state or tribal elections and never explained to me the importance of voting or participating in government. Her daily efforts centered on clothing, feeding, and disciplining her children, and her husband. "Just don't get in trouble and have the police chasing you" is what I hear my grandma saying every once in a while. And though my grandma never mentioned the Hualapai Constitution or read it to me, or even talked about tribal or other government—other than the time Nixon resigned and she called us inside the house to watch his resignation—she told me stories, some sad ones, about her relatives and about going to a federal government–run school in Valentine, Arizona.

While I was growing up I always had this sense that we were different from other people, that I was different from the other kids. I was an *Indian*[8] kid, which was readily pointed out to me on some occasions. It was hard to explain to others how I am a Hualapai and a mixture of four other indigenous tribes and peoples. Early on I gained this realization that people are not the same, that there are many differences between groups and tribes of people. Unfortunately, some of us are made to feel the difference more than others. While we are already feeling distant and distinct this gap is widened by prejudice and ignorance of many people and leaders in the dominant white world and in indigenous America.

Some believe that Natives choose to separate themselves from mainstream America. This may be true to some extent. But it's not that

Natives ran away—not altogether. It was because they were pushed and kept away, kept at a distance. Most Anglo-Americans do not understand this. Maybe because "white people" many times made my *goda* feel excluded and different she stayed away from them, and would consequently say to me, "Don't trust white people." I was very impressionable when she first gave me this instruction, and for many years I was ambivalent about those she said we could not trust. Undoubtedly my grandma's experiences and upbringing tarnished her view of "*haygus,*"[9] and my own, for a while. But as I experience more of the world I am no longer immediately distrusting of someone just because of their race, or color, though this takes practice and patience.

Like many indigenous folks, I have a strong tie with my grandma. She was my power, my protector. I would cry loud and long every time I was forced to leave her side, sometimes being pulled away as I clutched her legs, yelling, "I don't want to go, I don't want to go." I would cry for about three hours after being torn from her side to the further threat of "I'll give you something to cry about" that my stepfather would yell in my ear. I cried long and loud at my grandma's wake and funeral, which took place only a couple of months before I graduated from college. My grandma did not call me much while I was in school. She rarely called in part because she did not have a phone until about the time I left for school. I got all my power and strength from her big bear hug that she would give me every time I saw her. What is clear and certain is that because of my closeness, my bond, and my devotion to my grandma I grew up believing I should do all I can for her people.

HER PEOPLE, OUR CONSTITUTION

The Hualapai Tribe is one of the more than 560 American indigenous nations the United States government recognizes as "distinct political communities." The Hualapai Tribe recognizes more than 2,800 members and controls nearly a million acres of land in the plateaus and canyons of northwest Arizona. The Tribe also owns state fee land adjacent to the reservation in Arizona and in Truckee, California. Of the 2,800 members, many of whom can trace their lineage to a chief or head man of a Pai Band, about 70 percent live on the reservation, where the total resident population is approximately 2,500. Of these 2,500 residents, approximately 1,800 are tribal members. The remaining residents are other indigenous Natives or non-Natives. It is interesting to note that at

Hualapai and in many other indigenous nations, the majority of the tribal membership and resident community is under twenty-five years old.

In the Hualapai language, "Hwal'bay" was the name used to identify the People of the Tall Pines—the Band. Initially there were thirteen bands of Pai (people), with Hwal'bay being one of these bands. Other bands had names such as the Red Cliff People, the Juniper Pine People, and the Mahone Mountain People. The U.S. government inadvertently named the whole Pai people Hualapai because the band chief that the United States identified as the main leader was the chief of the Hualapai Band (my great-great-grandfather). The name stuck and all members were to be known as Hualapai. Though most Hualapais know about this misnaming, they nevertheless have fully adopted the name *Hualapai* as their own.

In the past, the United States demanded that the Hualapai adopt the "white man's ways" in social affairs and governance. Though U.S. leadership enacted policies meant to assimilate and "civilize" the Hualapai and other indigenous peoples, history shows that these policies did not work, even after imprisoning the Hualapais for a few years. From first contact, the U.S. government has vacillated from a policy of assimilation to one of self-determination, back to termination, then back to self-governance. Though the Hualapai Tribe currently faces a federal policy that continues to promote tribal self-government and autonomy, especially in domestic and internal affairs, the U.S. Supreme Court has not been as supportive of indigenous sovereignty in recent court controversies.

In 1934, Hualapai tribal leaders chose to adopt an Indian Reorganization Act (IRA) tribal constitution. Though the IRA's concept of self-determination was appropriate and necessary, the government structure prescribed for the Tribe was not. The IRA constitution provided for a centralized style of government headed by a tribal council, which replaced our band and extended family system. Although Indian agents believed these reforms to be civilized and democratic, the imposed government design was not accordant to Hualapai culture and took the Hualapai away from its customary and traditional means of governance. Under the IRA model the Tribe began to hold elections and grant membership to tribal applicants in accordance with federal guidelines and the blood quantum requirement.

While the name "Hualapai Tribe" is still in our constitution, the name "Hualapai Nation" has been used in the past several decades to promote pride in the government by highlighting the fact that the Hualapai Tribe is at the minimum a "dependent domestic nation"[10]—i.e., a government with significant responsibilities, obligations, and duties. Today, departments and offices of the Hualapai Tribal Administration print the name "Hualapai

Nation" on their ink stamps, envelopes, and letterhead and communicate the term *nation* to many people from outside the reservation. In casual conversation members and nonmembers say "Nation" when referring to Hualapai, the government, and the reservation. Unfortunately, while it has become commonplace to type and employ the term *Nation,* Hualapais have yet to clearly define and articulate what the word *Nation* means in the present context, or what it should mean in the Tribe's future.

CONSTITUTIONAL BLOOD QUANTUM REQUIREMENT FOR TRIBAL MEMBERSHIP

Around the world countries and nations have developed criteria for citizenship. Some countries outline specific requirements for citizenship in their constitutions; others outline these requirements in statutes. Most countries condition the granting of citizenship on the satisfaction of certain requirements such as length of residency, language proficiency, and general government knowledge.[11] Most American indigenous tribal constitutions do not utilize the term *citizen,* instead requiring a degree of tribal blood in order to be enrolled as a tribal *member.* Other tribal constitutions allow documentation of lineage as a basis for membership. A handful of tribes allow for adoption of nonmembers into the tribe where the adoptee enjoys the rights and privileges of a member. Some tribes confer honorary membership to nonmembers without any associated rights or privileges.

The constitution of the Hualapai Tribe determines membership as a function of blood quantum. Article II, Section 1(b), of the Hualapai Constitution grants membership to "all persons of one-fourth (1/4) degree or more Hualapai Indian blood." Membership in the Hualapai Tribe is similar to citizenship in the United States or other countries—but it is definitely not the same. A member has the right to vote upon reaching the age of eighteen and is eligible to run for tribal council positions at the age of twenty-five. A member can vote merely if she shows up to an election (residency is not a requirement), while a candidate for council must prove residency for at least one year prior to the election. In contrast, nonmember residents of the reservation are limited in their participation in tribal government. Pursuant to the constitution, they do not have the right to vote and they cannot hold elected office. In addition, nonmember residents are subject to deportation or exclusion and are ineligible for tribal government programs.

The blood quantum standard was not created by the Hualapai people. The U.S. government established it to systematically track indigenous people in the United States and provide a basis on which to allocate land, rations, and other resources.[12] Perhaps counting "Indians" was necessary to keep track of the enemy; after all, the Bureau of Indian Affairs was first organized under the U.S. Department of War. This blood quantum requirement nevertheless has managed to survive into the era of self-determination, and into the Hualapai governmental framework through the constitution.

Today, many Hualapais desire to retain the blood quantum requirement in the constitution, although for different reasons than those of the "Indian Agents" who conceived of it more than a hundred years ago. Broadly speaking, Hualapais believe that by requiring a degree of blood for membership they can ensure that their culture will endure. After many years of oppression and forced change, the Hualapai people's concern for the loss of their culture is extreme. At one time in Hualapai history, children were forced to go to schools run by the U.S. government. The main purpose of these schools was not to educate but to assimilate and "civilize" them. At these schools Hualapai children, my grandma included, were punished for speaking their language and were told they could no longer practice their traditions and customs. The children were even told that these practices were backward and wrong. Not only were many aspects of the Hualapai culture lost during this period, so were many children![13]

Relatedly, the mandate of a blood quantum requirement stems from the need for the Hualapai to be in control of their destiny. The Hualapai come from a very strong and powerful people who managed their own affairs long before there was a United States of America and state of Arizona. After the Hualapais became tired of fighting with the U.S. Cavalry, they accepted new ways of life, including new ways to govern. In 1883, President Chester A. Arthur, through Executive Order, created the Hualapai Indian Reservation. Under strict and sometimes unsophisticated supervision by the Bureau of Indian Affairs, the Tribe has slowly learned to progress under the government model the United States government provided. These years of federal oversight and intrusion have nurtured a fear of losing control to outside entities and to outsiders. Mandating a 1/4 degree blood quantum requirement, tribal leaders and members believe, will protect the Tribe from these outsiders.

The fear of outsiders even extends to other Hualapais who have lived outside of the reservation in cities all their lives and have recently moved to the reservation. Every so often, tribal members will make statements at council meetings and elsewhere regarding their "full-bloodedness" and suggest that those Hualapais who have recently come to the reservation are not *real* Hualapais. Fortunately for the Hualapai government, these kinds of prejudice and petty politics are not prominent. If they were, tribal leadership and the people—through legislation or referendum—could have made further, even more prejudicial laws in this regard.

Many indigenous nations deal with this issue of identity under the ruse of blood quantum or culture. A few tribes have made stricter blood quantum rules in order for their members to run for council seats. A federal court has upheld a tribe's rule that candidates for tribal council must have a higher degree of tribal blood than other members.[14] The court found that the tribe had a cultural interest in making such a rule. Other tribal governments have endured extreme internal conflict and infighting over these issues. To date, Hualapai discourse and debate have been civil.

What is odd about this notion of degree of blood regulation at Hualapai and other indigenous nations is that it is not a traditional point of view. Hualapai people traditionally "adopted" non-Hualapai children from the outside and raised them as their own. Even children of enemy neighbors such as the Yavapai were adopted and raised as Hualapai. Of course, I cannot describe exactly or officially what Hualapais used to do long ago. I can only describe what I have learned over time, from personal knowledge, research, and subsequent speculation. I have heard and read about other tribes that allowed the adoption of others into their people who would then be considered a part of the tribe. The Navajo, for example, explain that most of their more than three hundred clans came from absorbing other peoples into their polity. I would argue that the Hualapais did the same, that they were accepting of others under certain conditions and there was no counting of blood quantum. Degree-of-blood membership, therefore, is not culturally accordant with the Hualapai people.

COMPLICATIONS ASSOCIATED WITH
RETAINING BLOOD QUANTUM

Today, the retention of Hualapai's constitutional blood quantum requirement is complicated by a number of broader trends. Intermarriage and mobility have resulted in fewer Hualapais living on the reservation who can satisfy the 1/4 Hualapai blood quantum requirement. At the same time, as the Hualapai Tribe works to expand its governmental authority over all residents—to tax, to zone, and to exercise civil jurisdiction—the limited constitutional rights of nonmember residents are brought into sharper focus. Indeed, the fact that nonmember residents are subject to Hualapai jurisdiction but do not have the right to vote or run for office raises questions about the democratic nature of Hualapai governance.

This situation is much more "discriminatory" than the circumstances resulting from differing state citizenship. A person from Arizona when traveling to another state for business or pleasure is subject to the jurisdiction of that state. An indigenous person who travels from her own tribal lands to another tribe's lands is also subject to that jurisdiction. However, the difference between state and tribal citizenship is that a person who moves from state to state can become a citizen of the new state. After a period of time he can then vote, run for office, and participate fully in the state and local government. If a tribal member moves from one "reservation" to another, becoming a nonmember resident of his new home, he is not eligible to vote or run for office, even after a long period of residency. The same holds true for a non-Native person. On a practical level, tribal constitutional limitation of nonmember participation in tribal government provides anti-Indian interests with arguments for further circumscribing the scope of the sovereignty exercised by tribes.

The remainder of this section further explores the complications associated with the Hualapai Tribe's retention of its constitutional blood quantum requirement.

Democracy and the Problem of Nonresidents

Does the Hualapai Tribe even profess to be a democracy? Do tribal leaders and members have a clear understanding of what democracy means other than the general notions commonly held and taught in school? To begin this inquiry it is important to have a definition or description of what democracy is, or should be. A literal translation for *democracy* is "people rule."[15] Democratic governments provide open elections in which opposition forces have a chance to obtain leadership power for a specific period of time. Democracies also afford their citizens various freedoms, privileges, and rights, as well as place a responsibility and duty on their citizens to obey the laws and uphold the constitution. Generally, if a nation shows evidence of competition, participation, and political liberties, it can be considered a democracy.

Are these criteria evident at Hualapai Nation? Let's begin with the last factor. Political scientist Georg Sorensen gives these as examples of political liberties: "freedom of expression, freedom of the press, and freedom to form and join organizations." [16] Article IX, Bill of Rights of the Hualapai Constitution, guarantees these and other liberties for all people and persons within the Hualapai boundaries. Moreover, Hualapai culture traditionally allowed for free expression by all members of the Tribe and was practiced prior to the colonization by the Europeans. Individual liberties then are provided for and guaranteed to all by the Hualapai Tribe. Sorensen's third suggested component is satisfied.

However, political participation and competition are more problematic. Philippe C. Schmitter has described citizenship as "democracy's most distinctive property." [17] The dictionary definition of a citizen is "a person owing loyalty to and entitled by birth or naturalization to the protection of a state or nation" or "a resident of a city or town, especially one entitled to vote and enjoy other privileges there." [18]

There are very few countries that have not defined citizenship either through their constitution or through their laws. Countries that have recently gained their political independence, such as Malta, have rather complex constitutional provisions for citizenship. Others, such as Kazakhstan and Slovenia, simply state in their constitutions, "citizenship of the Republic of Kazakhstan shall be acquired and terminated by law" and "citizenship of Slovenia shall be regulated by statute." [19] These and other nations from around the world have thought through the nature of citizenship and how it is to be granted.

The Hualapai Constitution states, "The membership of the Hualapai Tribe shall consist of (b) all persons one-fourth (1/4) degree or more Hualapai Indian blood." There is no mention of the terms *citizen* or *citizenship* in the tribal constitution. The Hualapai Constitution speaks only in terms of members and membership. For example, the constitution's *Preamble* states in part,

> We, the members of the Hualapai Indian Tribe of the Hualapai Indian Reservation, a federally recognized sovereign Indian Tribe, do hereby adopt this constitution in order to: govern ourselves under our own laws and customs for the common good and well-being of the Tribe *and its members, and to protect the individual rights of our members.* (Emphasis added.)

There is no reference made regarding residents as nonmember citizens. Only in the bill of rights does the constitution make reference to "people and persons" other than members.

There are many residents of the Hualapai Reservation who are not members of the Hualapai Tribe. These residents do not have the power to vote or seek office, and they are ineligible for various privileges such as land assignments and educational scholarships. What is the political status of a nonmember resident? What are the political rights of this group of people on the Hualapai Reservation? Are they citizens? New York University law professor Christopher Eisgruber asserts that "a resident of a polity is a citizen if and only if the resident is not subject to deportation and is entitled to vote after reaching adulthood."[20] At Hualapai, nonmembers can be removed—deported—from the reservation after a hearing.[21] By this definition, nonmember residents at Hualapai are not citizens.

Nor is there a naturalization mechanism or process to allow nonmembers to gain the right to participate fully in tribal government. Noted political scientist Samuel Huntington writes, "To the extent . . . that a political system denies voting participation to part of its society. . . it is undemocratic."[22] As examples, Huntington cites blacks in South Africa, women in Switzerland, and African Americans in the U.S. South as classes of people who were routinely denied voting privileges and political access. These countries, however, have revised their policies and procedures for voting in order to consolidate further their democratic governments. Hualapai has not yet begun to consider how to promote nonmember participation in the political process. The thinking is very raw and controversial. Even now, members who consider themselves full-blooded Hualapai complain that non-Hualapais are benefiting to their detriment. Once the issue of voting or holding public office is brought to the council for consideration, these tribal members will no doubt find fault with the proposition and may come to the table unable to discuss the issue reasonably.

Moreover, Schmitter states, "Citizenship . . . is not confined to voting periodically in elections. It also can be exercised by influencing the selection of candidates, joining associations or movements, petitioning authorities, engaging in unconventional protests, and so forth."[23] At Hualapai, though "meaningful and extensive competition among individuals and organized groups for all effective positions of government power" and "political participation in the selection of leaders and policies"[24] exist, political competition and participation exist primarily for members of the Tribe. Members of the Hualapai Tribe can vote and run for one of nine tribal council positions.[25] Nonmembers are unable to vote and compete for a council position.

Nonmembers certainly have the ability to influence politics at Hualapai by their support of political candidates and issues. Nonmembers can lobby council members on issues important to them and their families. Nonmembers can also be appointed to tribal boards and committees and consequently become very powerful and influential people. Nonmembers are not prohibited from campaigning for a candidate or speaking at tribal council meetings in support of a cause or in opposition to tribal government. Moreover, the Tribe hires many nonmembers even though the Tribe utilizes "Hualapai or Indian Preference" in its hiring decisions. Still, because they cannot vote and serve as council members, nonmember residents are not "citizens." How does this difference between the rights and privileges of tribal members and nonmembers affect the nature of democracy in Hualapai government? Does this nonmember-noncitizen dilemma disqualify Hualapai from being referred to as a true democracy?

Applying the criteria for democracy suggested above by Sorensen: If the Hualapai Tribe excludes nonmembers from voting and competing for council positions, how democratic is Hualapai government? Where does the Tribe fit on a democratic scale from 1 to 10? a 5? an 8? Does this exclusion of nonmembers prevent a score of 10? Would the score drop more given that this exclusion is explicitly expressed in the tribal constitution? What is a 10?[26] Political theorists' description of a 10 might be when a "democracy becomes routinized and deeply internalized in social, institutional, and even psychological life, as well as in political calculations for achieving success."[27] At this time there are no data and information to determine whether democracy is routinized and internalized at Hualapai. The author's assumption is that it is. "But for" the exclusion of nonmembers in the primary political processes (particularly voting and competing for office), the description fits. Hualapai is a democracy; however, it is a *degree-of-blood* democracy—not fully consolidated—and therefore not a 10.

Jurisdiction, Tribal Sovereignty, and the Problem of Nonresidents

The question of how democratic Hualapai's political system is is not an academic one. This issue brings to the forefront questions about the Tribe's ability to exercise its authority over nonmember residents despite their disenfranchised status.[28] Jurisdiction over all individuals who enter the Hualapai reservation and territory has always been of great concern to Hualapai tribal leaders.[29] Unfortunately, over the last century the U.S. government has carved away bits and pieces of tribal jurisdiction. Indigenous tribes already have lost criminal jurisdiction over non-Indians living on the reservation and maintain only civil jurisdiction, though that is under threat as well. A well-known indigenous law scholar and jurist, Frank Pommersheim, fears that nonresidents' limited participation in tribal government might offer an argument for further limiting the scope of tribal jurisdiction:

> I would not be totally surprised if, at some point, the (Supreme) Court just said tribes do not have any authority over non-Indian residents on the reservation. Non-Indians do not participate in the political life of the tribe, it is unfair to allow tribes to have authority over those individuals.[30]

The question of the extent of jurisdiction of tribal government over nonmember residents is now reaching key decision makers in tribal governments, the U.S. government, and the courts. It is forcing tribal leaders to begin questioning their very frames and forms of government as well as pressuring them to be creative and compromising in their nation-building process and journey. It is in the Hualapai Tribe's best interest to answer these questions and provide guidance and direction before the federal leadership and courts do.

Diminishing Degree of Blood

It is inevitable that if tribal members continue the current pattern of marriage to non-Hualapais, in time "Hualapai" children will not have a quarter Hualapai blood. Under these circumstances, a few hundred years from now blood quantum will have diminished and few individuals will be eligible to enroll under the current constitutional mandate. Over many more years the Hualapai Tribe will cease to exist because no one will be eligible for enrollment. The constitutional clause requiring 1/4 degree Hualapai blood will ultimately defeat the Hualapai Tribe. Due to the diminishing degree of Hualapai blood over a very long period of time, under the current constitution, the Hualapai Tribe is destined to disintegrate. Many of the indigenous nations that require 1/4 degree blood or more for membership have a population greater than that of the Hualapai Nation, such as Hopi (10,000), White Mountain Apache (8,000), and of course Navajo Nation (250,000). The life spans of these tribes may run considerably longer than Hualapai's under the blood quantum requirement. Still, over a longer period of time, these Indian nations may face a similar end.

Other American indigenous nation constitutions, such as those of the Wampanoag Tribe of Gay Head and the Choctaw Nation of Oklahoma, do not specify a degree of blood requirement for membership. An applicant for membership in these nations must prove lineage to a list of "full bloods" developed earlier in their history. In these two cases all descendants can be members. This practice ensures that their nations will continue growing because there is a source of members who share in the same past and culture.

MOVING FORWARD

Just as citizenship is a cornerstone of democratic government, culture is the centerpiece of Hualapai civilization and identity. As the Hualapai Tribe continues to develop into the Hualapai Nation, these notions of citizenship and culture collide and are separated by a degree of blood. To what extent does this cleavage prevent the building of a "consolidated" democracy at Hualapai? Or, do the Hualapai people desire to be fully democratic? These are delicate and controversial questions. Nevertheless, the community and nation-building process and journey require their provocation, no matter how hard or difficult it is to all the builders and travelers on their way.

The following strategies are suggested to ease the bumpiness of this part of the road and journey. They are presented to promote a deeper understanding of concepts such as membership, citizenship, and democracy as defined by the Hualapai people through their constitution. No predetermined destination or pre-designed map is available, however. Where the Hualapais—and other indigenous people—find themselves in the twenty-first century is fully dependent on their own decisions and wholly determined by their own destinies.

Discuss and Define the Difference between Tribe and Nation

Tribal leaders and tribal members must begin a conversation about the terms *tribe* and *nation* and produce a statement that clearly defines them: in the past, present, and future. They must ask themselves, "What is the vision for the Hualapai nation—for hwal'bay ba:j?" Because culturally the Hualapai people were grouped in bands throughout northwestern Arizona, a nation concept may or may not be applicable. How do the Hualapai language and culture describe nation and tribe and how do they distinguish between the two? Is a nation simply a large group of people and a tribe or a band a smaller group? Or is there a deeper difference? How does the current structure of the Hualapai government change or contribute to the evolution of these words and concepts? The Hualapai people must investigate these words and their meanings and develop and define them under current contexts and circumstances.[31]

Discuss and Define the Difference between "Tribal Member," "Nonmember Resident," and "Citizen"

Leaders and members must begin a conversation about the meanings of and differences between *tribal member, nonmember resident,* and *citizen,* and produce a policy statement for each term. Having a clear understanding of the differences between tribal member and nonmember is critical to the future of Hualapai's developing democracy. The Tribe must articulate to its members and the outside world why nonmembers are not allowed to vote or to hold office. Not doing so allows others to easily criticize the Hualapai government as discriminatory and undemocratic. It also is fuel for the fire for those bent on extinguishing tribal sovereignty. Over time, as the Tribe continues to develop its own democratic system, members may want to begin allowing nonmembers more participation in government under their own creative terms and constructs. But this cannot occur unless tribal leaders and members have a clear understanding of the differences between Hualapais and non-Hualapais. It cannot occur unless tribal leaders understand what it means to be a Hualapai citizen.

It will be useful to this conversation for tribal leaders and members to review other tribes' membership criteria and other countries' citizenship criteria. By reviewing tribal and international constitutions and legislation, leaders and members will recognize the volume and depth of the consideration given to these concepts. This analysis, together with a general reading about the elements of democratic citizenship, will provide a good basis on which leaders and members can begin forming their own perception of how the term *Hualapai citizen* might be defined.

Institutionalize Data Collection

The Tribe must create a means to institutionalize data collection methods that not only record census-like demographic information but also public opinion information assessing member and nonmember residents' perceptions of political processes and institutions at

Hualapai. Tribal leaders can use this information to make more informed and enlightened decisions about Hualapai government and the future of the Hualapai Tribe. This data collection must become institutionalized in order for the Hualapai government to better plan for the future.

A tribal committee can determine the specific type of data needed and the procedure by which it should be compiled. After tribal leadership approval, the Tribe's enrollment office, in conjunction with the Election Board, should be directed to be its caretakers. Because the enrollment office is already responsible for keeping track of enrollment data, this task can be easily assumed and managed. The office should make, at a minimum, yearly presentations in person or by document to the tribal council and people.

Codify Membership Requirements in an Ordinance— Not the Constitution

Article II of the Hualapai Constitution—Membership— should be amended by deleting the specific requirement for 1/4 blood quantum and replacing it with the statement, "Membership shall be determined by law." A revised Hualapai constitution was adopted by the Hualapai voters in 1991. The vote was 141 for and 33 against. Only 174 tribal members voted in this election. Many Hualapai members were unaware of the passage of the new constitution. Some question its validity due to the small number of members who voted to approve it. Yet others complain that the constitution is not culturally accordant. The most pressing concern is that the document does not seem to be owned by the people. The constitution seems to be a mere piece of paper. The tribe's constitution should be much more than that, even if many are not comfortable with various clauses. The constitution should create a foundation on which the nation can continue to grow and develop. Given the questionable legitimacy of the constitution, it appears inadvisable to place the controversial topic of membership within its confines. For this reason alone, the requirements for membership should be outlined in a law rather than the constitution.

There is also a practical reason for moving membership requirements from the constitution to an ordinance. A constitution is a document used to describe and outline the general frame and form of a nation's government.[32] It articulates a nation's fundamental principles and convictions.[33] The relatively fixed nature of a constitution can promote permanency, stability, and consistency. Philosophically, changes to constitutions should not be ad hoc and routine.

Practically, the universal difficulty of passing constitutional amendments makes it problematic to include constitutional clauses that are likely to be revisited, such as a blood quantum requirement. Article XV of the Hualapai Constitution directs that 30 percent of the eligible voters must vote to approve a constitutional amendment. To date, the Tribe has held only a few elections where 30 percent of the voters have participated. Even if this hurdle were to be cleared, Article XV further requires that the U.S. government, through the Secretary of the Interior, approve the proposed amendment as well.[34] Because it is likely that members will want to amend the Tribe's membership requirements over time—probably by lowering the degree of blood requirement—it is best to delineate the requirements for membership in legislation. A membership ordinance simply is easier to amend than is a constitution.

Debate the Scope of Nonmember Resident Participation in Tribal Government

How can participation of nonmember residents in tribal government be provided for, and under what special contexts and circumstances? Are such residents eligible to vote? Can they hold elected office? Giving clear consideration to the concept of nationhood, tribal leaders and members must consider the status of nonmembers, many of whom are related to members and are long-term residents. The Tribe can be creative in developing ways to involve all residents in government without giving up its culture or giving up control to outsiders. In time these residents may even demand more privileges and rights, though there exists no current pressure from any source thus far.

The Hualapai must begin discussing this question in order to be ready to make clear and thoughtful decisions later, when this issue will arise or even explode. From this discussion, the Tribe can begin formulating a basis on which a citizenship ordinance can be developed with consideration to nonmember resident participation in government. For instance, perhaps nonmember residents may be granted the opportunity to vote after residing on the reservation for at least ten years. Perhaps one of the nine seats on the tribal council could be open to a nonmember resident candidate who must still run against other members for the one seat. In these ways the Tribe could extend the opportunity for real political participation. There are many other possible scenarios, many years away from now. The idea here is to push the thinking and debate to generate the best possible ideas for possible implementation at some later date—if the Tribe decides to do so.

CONCLUSION

My grandma may not have concerned herself with all this detail as she had so much to do just to feed her children and encourage sobriety for her husband, my grandpa. She would, however, appreciate the fact that these details could help her people, her relatives, to survive further as a people and a nation. She had so many sad memories through her own experiences and those shared with her by her elders. But she savored stories of survival and endurance despite the efforts of the United States government to do them in. I believe she would be proud that I am helping to strengthen and prepare Hualapai for an even more powerful future just by asking a few questions.

These questions include: what will the nature of Hualapai Nation's sovereignty be in the twenty-first century? Will the Tribe's sovereignty continue to be unclear and uncertain? Or will it eventually be clarified? And to what end? Is it possible that the Hualapai Tribe, over a long period of growth and development, will gain further independence and control? Can the Tribe ever generate the resources needed to be fully self-reliant, self-determined, and independent? This discussion may be more meaningful after years of economic development, once the Hualapai Nation accumulates greater wealth through strategic resource management.

Once the economy at Hualapai is strong and allows for a greater ability to provide a stable and prosperous government, how will the political treatment of nonmembers affect the potential for the United States to look favorably on further Hualapai independence and autonomy? What does the tribal leadership need to begin thinking about in order to address these bigger-picture questions? What kinds of education and studies must be initiated for tribal members in order for them to think fully and deeply about the nature of our *less than 10,* or unconsolidated, democratic system and government?

These questions together suggest that it is prudent for Hualapai leadership, and indeed the Hualapai People, to begin thinking critically about the future and to start searching for some answers. By engaging in a focused study of what it means to be a nation and a citizen of a nation, and whether the constitutional blood quantum mandate is a contribution to good government or a roadblock to its success, we may find some answers. Blood should not make the difference. Belief in one's people should.

NOTES

1. Or Willetts. My great-grandfather's name was changed from Wildavs to Willetts in boarding school.

2. Married name (a whole other story there).

3. Or Hwal'bay: People of the Tall Pines.

4. Term used to officially identify an individual as a member of a particular tribe.

5. Created by Executive Order in 1883.

6. *Vaughn v. Hualapai Tribe; Bravo v. Hualapai Tribe.*

7. Hualapai word for mother's mother, or grandma.

8. I no longer use the term *Indian* to describe my background unless it is necessary.

9. Hualapai word for Anglo-American.

10. See *Worcester v. Georgia,* 31 U.S. 515 (1832).

11. Debra R. Shpigler, J. D., *How to Become a U.S. Citizen* (Peterson's, 2002).

12. See *United States ex rel. West v. Hitchcock,* 205 U.S. 80 (1907) (determining membership in order to allot land), and *Stephens v. Cherokee Nation,* 174 U.S. 445 (1889) (determining membership in order to allocate funds).

13. The Hualapai Tribe is luckier than other tribes, however. Other indigenous peoples have lost, or are losing, their language and culture, which is now merely recorded in books. In the 1970s, innovative and insightful tribal members developed a model bilingual education program in the local school that combined tradition and technology. Later the Tribe would develop and administer a cultural resources office and program. The Hualapai language is taught to children in the local school and to adults through the local community college. Fortunately, the Tribe's elders speak Hualapai fluently, though they cannot read or write in Hualapai. The younger children are learning how to do so. It is no longer likely that the Hualapai language and culture will completely die away.

14. See *Daly v. United States,* 483 F.2d 700 (8th Cir. 1973).

15. Georg Sorensen, *Democracy and Democratization: Processes and Prospects in a Changing World* (Westview Press, 1993), 3.

16. Ibid.

17. Philippe C. Schmitter, "Civil Society East and West," in *Consolidating the Third Wave Democracies: Themes and Perspectives,* ed. Larry Diamond, Marc F. Plattner, Yun-han Chu, and Hung-mao Tien (Baltimore, MD: Johns Hopkins University Press, 1997), 243.

18. *American Heritage College Dictionary,* 3rd edition: Countries around the world provide for citizenship in their constitution or by law after the applicant resides in the country for a period of years; for instance, five years in India, ten in Japan and Zambia, and fifteen in the Kingdom of Nepal.

19. Slovenia, moreover, provides for "special rights" for foreigners, and voting rights are determined by statute.

20. Christopher L. Eisgruber, "Birthright Citizenship and the Constitution," *New York University Law Review* (1997): 58.

21. See Article V (u), *The Powers of the Tribal Council:* "to enact ordinances providing for the removal or exclusion of any nonmember of the Tribe whose presence may be injurious to the members of the Tribe, and to prescribe conditions upon which nonmembers may remain within the territory of the Tribe, Provided, That all actions of exclusion or removal shall be done by court proceeding."

22. Samuel Huntington, *The Third Wave: Democratization in the Late Twentieth Century* (Norman, OK: University of Oklahoma Press, 1991), 7.

23. Schmitter, "Civil Society East and West," 243.

24. Sorensen, *Democracy and Democratization,* 13.

25. Hualapai Constitution, Article VIII—*Elections*—Section 5, *Qualifications for Office.*

26. An instrument such as the Freedom House Survey or Beetham's Democratic Audit could be used to make this calculation.

27. Larry Diamond, quoting Linz and Stepan in the Introduction to *Consolidating the Third Wave Democracies: Themes and Perspectives,* ed. Larry Diamond, Marc F. Plattner, Yun-han Chu, and Hung-mao Tien (Baltimore, MD: Johns Hopkins University Press, 1997), xvii.

28. Tribal courts have also heard arguments in this area. For example, in 1999 a case was argued before the Navajo Nation Supreme Court challenging the Navajo Nation's jurisdiction over a nonmember Indian (an Oglala Sioux). The Petitioner, Russell Means, argued that the Navajo Nation did not have jurisdiction over him partly because he was not allowed to participate in government by voting and holding elected office though he resided within the Navajo Nation for approximately ten years. The Navajo Nation Supreme Court ultimately held that the Navajo Nation did have jurisdiction over Means on the basis of a treaty with the United States and because Means had assumed tribal relations with the tribe by becoming an "in-law."

29. See Article I of Hualapai Constitution—*Jurisdiction of the Hualapai Constitution.*

30. Frank Pommersheim, "Democracy, Citizenship, and Indian Law Literacy," *Thomas M. Cooley Law Review* (April 1997): 466.

31. An example of a Strategic Workplan is available from the author.

32. Joseph Flies-Away, unpublished manuscript, "Constitutional Development and Reform among American Indigenous Nations: Why Creative and Culturally Accordant Constitutions Contribute to Functional Frames and Forms of Government"; see Daniel Webster and Donald Bell, "First Principles for Constitution Revision," *Nova Law Review* (Fall 1997).

33. "A constitution may properly be regarded as a document in which the people set forth the structure of the government, including any powers they wish

to convey to the government from themselves, and including any instructions they wish to include about how those powers are to be distributed, retained, altered, or removed." Webster and Bell, "First Principles for Constitution Revision," 409.

34. Article XV states that "no amendment shall become effective until approved by the Secretary of the Interior or until deemed approved by the Secretary by operation of law."

Firsthand Accounts

Jaime Barrientoz, Chair, Grand Traverse Band
    Constitutional Reform Committee
Le Roy Shingoitewa, Chair, Hopi Tribe Constitutional
    Reform Committee
Albert Hale, Former President, Navajo Nation
Larry Foster, Former Chair, Navajo Nation Commission
    on Government Development
Ross Swimmer, Former Principal Chief, Cherokee Nation
    of Oklahoma
John Peters, Jr., Executive Director, Massachusetts
    Commission on Indian Affairs
Carrie Imus, Vice Chair, Hualapai Nation
Linda Havatone, Former Council Member, Hualapai
    Nation
Martha Berry, Delegate, 1999 Cherokee Nation of
    Oklahoma Constitutional Convention

JAIME BARRIENTOZ, CHAIR, GRAND TRAVERSE
BAND OF OTTAWA AND CHIPPEWA INDIANS'
CONSTITUTIONAL REFORM COMMITTEE

My name is Jaime Barrientoz. I'm the vice chairman for
the Grand Traverse Band. I've been involved with constitutional reform
since I came into the tribe as a council member in 1997. I've been working through this process ever since then as the chairman of the Constitutional Reform Committee. It seems like a long time, but yet it's gone
by fast. We've made some great improvements to some of the things that
we've wanted to see in the constitution that reflects the people's wishes
and the people's will.

I came into office in 1997 and prior to that time there had been talk about changes that needed to be made in the government—changes with the separation of powers, changes with the jurisdiction, changes with membership. Where does a person begin? You have these ideas and you have these goals in mind. You have these hopes and dreams that things can change for the future of the tribe, but where do you begin?

Who are the Grand Traverse Band people? We're a band of Ottawa and Chippewa Indians. Chippewa translates Ojibwe so we're the Ottawa and Ojibwe people of the Grand Traverse Band. We're from northern lower Michigan in a very beautiful place called the Grand Traverse region. We're people of the woodlands, of the water. We're fishermen. We got our name because of the Grand Traverse Bay.

People often ask me, "Are you Ottawa and Chippewa? Are you half and half? How did you come up with Ottawa and Chippewa?" Well, the story that was told to me is that a long, long time ago an Ottawa warrior had a relationship with a Chippewa woman who was married to a tribal Chippewa member. And the Ottawa warrior and the Chippewa man confronted each other and had a fight. The Ottawa brother killed the Chippewa male in this scuffle and this was going to create a war between the Chippewa and the Ottawa tribe. The leaders had to come together and try to resolve that because the people and the families were fighting. Our Ottawa leader and the Chippewa leader decided at that time, hundreds of years ago—because we were sorry as a nation that this happened—that we would forever call ourselves the Ottawa and Chippewa people. So that's how we got the name of the Grand Traverse Band of Ottawa and Ojibwe Indians. And ever since then, more Chippewas and more Ottawas got together and we eventually merged our tribes together. That's the story that was told to me and it's the story that I tell everybody. There are other Chippewa tribes and other Ottawa tribes, but that's how the Grand Traverse Band history came about.

We adopted an IRA constitution. We're an IRA tribe. Like many tribes, we have one of those template-type constitutions. Back in the 1970s and 1980s we had to adopt this because we had to move forward. There were a lot of people living without power, without water, in shacks, without employment. To get federally recognized and to get funding for our community, we had to adopt something and that's what we did to get started. It was more forced on us, I guess.

We've been successful with the IRA constitution since 1980 and it has helped us get to where we are today. Our tribe has been able to do fairly well in separating the three government institutions within the tribe.

We have a fully functioning tribal court. We have an appellate court that enforces the laws of the tribe. We have a law enforcement department that's more than adequate. But in order to move forward, we felt that we needed to change the constitution because it really didn't have the values or the wishes of the people in there. We got federally recognized in 1980. In 1983 we got gaming, and ever since 1983 until today we've been a thriving community and we've outgrown this constitution. And we need to move forward.

The previous chairman, George Bennett, had the idea, had the vision to change the constitution. He came to me and he knew that I was young and willing and determined to get that done as well. He asked me if I would chair the committee and move this along, and I said yes. And not having anything really to do with government, more with the gaming side of issues, I thrust myself into it and just started reading the materials, listening to people, and having a series of meetings with people and brainstorming to gather other ideas and input from people. I went to the council and asked to have this Constitution Reform Committee formed, and I told them why. I had the constitution with me and pointed directly to many things in our constitution that no longer apply to us, that are contradictory to one another, that are very vague in some areas.

I think somebody said, "Let's do this reform in a year or so." That was four years ago. I didn't realize when I first got involved exactly how important this was. I just figured, "Oh, it's just words in a book and I need to change those and make them look better and strengthen them up." But I really didn't know, I really didn't grasp that we're in the middle of changing the foundation of the government of the nation of our tribe. And realizing that I'm a lay person. I'm an electrician by trade and I went to school to be an electrician, got out of school and became a politician. How that happened I don't know, but either way it was a shocker. I approach my task with dignity and pride of the Grand Traverse Band people, who we are, where we come from, and how we've grown, and I listen to the people.

We hear a lot of talk about corruption in government but, at the Grand Traverse Band, we feel that we are living up to the constitution and even trying to exceed it in some areas by being open and being honest and talking with the people, because we reach out to them. Our tribal council initiated the constitutional reform effort. It wasn't initiated by community members. We are very committed to what we're doing. We've totally bought into this. This is something we know we need to do for the future and we're working on that today. The tribal council is behind it and the members that we've elected to sit on this committee are all behind it, and that's so important. I'll tell you the truth, not all the members on the committee trust me, not all the committee members trust Sam McClellan [another committee leader], and they don't trust us together either. But they have faith that by working together and putting our minds together, that we can come out with something that reflects what the Grand Traverse Band is and who we are.

Many of my critics and my political opponents say, "This is taking too long. Jaime is not capable of doing it." But it is my belief that with a document as important as the tribal constitution, our living, breathing document, that sometimes the shortest way home is the longest way there. So therefore I want to make sure that what we're doing is appropriate and right for the future. I don't want to have a six-month time frame to amend the constitution because six months, in my mind, is enough time to get a valid survey going. We've done surveys. We've done good surveys, but we still have a lot more educating to do with the membership. So we're having a series of public hearings. We're going to go out there and meet the people. We're not going to have a meeting in one central location that's a hundred miles or seventy-five miles from a person's residence. We're going to go within five miles of their residence and have a meeting and reach out to them. That's how we move forward.

SOVEREIGNTY AND IDENTITY

When we first started this process in 1997 we had the idea of making wholesale changes to the constitution and throwing it in the lap of the members and saying, "Vote yes or no on it." As we got more experience and grew through the process, we soon discovered that we needed to take it step by step and take it section by section and move forward through a systematic process.

We said, "What is the most controversial issue? What is the issue that we need to take care of today, right now, in order to move forward?" We decided that it was the membership issue and our ability to act as a sovereign nation. We felt the first thing we needed to do is define the identity of our people, who our people are. Our people have been shipped off to boarding schools and it's been beaten out of them and it's been taken away from them and we need to bring that back for our people and for our ancestors, for the ones that have passed on. They're shining on us and they're helping to drive us forward in that direction.

Sovereignty to us means being able to control your own destiny, having an identity and being who you are. And that comes with your language and your culture and your traditions. To me, what sovereignty is is who are you? We're the Ottawa and Chippewa people, the Ottawa and the Ojibwe people, and we speak that language, and that's who we are. The most valuable treasure that we have is our language. We respect our elders that have been able to hang onto that and carry that on for us because it's so important. And I encourage other tribes to look at that because it's something that will be lost if we don't do something about it.

Like I was saying earlier, our constitution is a template constitution. It has a preamble that's very basic and like most IRA constitutions or those modeled after them, it starts out by saying:

> We, the members of the Grand Traverse Band of Ottawa and Chippewa Indians, in order to organize for our common good and govern ourselves under our own laws and maintain and foster our tribal culture, to protect our homeland, to conserve and develop our natural resources and to insure our rights guaranteed by treaty with the federal government, do establish and adopt, as an incident of our sovereign powers, this constitution for the government, protection and common welfare of the Grand Traverse Band under the authority of the Indian Reorganization Act of June 18th, 1934, as amended.

That's our preamble. But essentially, those are white man words. And we're having a problem where we're losing our language, the Ottawa language. So we're working with our elders to translate our preamble into the Ottawa language. It's going to be written in the Ottawa Indian language as we see it. That's one of the major unique changes that we're making to the constitution. We're doing it in the Ottawa language and, by doing so, we're also preserving and locking into the future some of our language. We will always have that in our constitution, in the Ottawa language, and feel that is very important because that's who we are and that's the identity of who we are.

This idea didn't come from me. It came from the people, the local people that live within the Grand Traverse Band service area, the members of the tribe. They said, "We need to do something to preserve our language. How can we do this?" We thought about putting the whole constitution in the Ottawa language. But not everybody would be able to understand it so we have to use the white man's language to be able to communicate to everybody. Having said that, we're still going to put our preamble in the Ottawa language and focus on that education because it's so important.

We're also going to take out Article 18 requiring the Secretary of the Interior to approve our constitution. The first thing that we're going to do is ask the Secretary of the Interior to take himself out of our process. It just hinders our ability to act as a nation. Because we looked at the constitution and we said, "We're a sovereign nation, we're a government, we're a country here within a country. Yet we have to send our constitution, after our citizens have voted on it already, to an agency, an administration within the federal government, to have it approved?" When our people talk, that should be the final say. When our people say this is what we want, we shouldn't have to go to some administrator in Washington and say, Can we do this? When our people talk, we should just do that, because they elected us to do that and that's what we're going to do.

I heard somebody say, "Where do we want to go in a hundred years? Where we want to go is where we were a hundred years ago." That's so true. Albert Hale, the Navajo leader from Arizona, spoke about decolonizing our minds and getting back to our traditional ways and exercising our sovereignty, asserting our sovereignty, rather than always going to the government and asking them for their permission to do something. The Grand Traverse Band is a nation. Each tribe is its own separate nation and we just need to assert ourselves and be that, be a nation, and respect other tribes and nations just as we used to. Moving forward like this is how we are going to exercise sovereignty for Indian people in this country. I totally believe that.

MEMBERSHIP AND ENROLLMENT

We have an adoption provision in our constitution where we can adopt an individual into the tribe as long as they have 1/8 Grand Traverse historic blood and a total of 1/4 Indian blood. When we established our per capita law distributing our gaming revenue to members of the tribe we had many Indian people wanting to get adopted into our tribe to receive our benefits. They were not even Grand Traverse Band members. They were Indians from other tribes that had 1/8 Grand Traverse blood and the other 7/8 from other tribes. They were full blood Indians with 1/8 GTB rolling into our tribe to receive the gaming benefits because in our tribe we distribute per capita checks. And they were being adopted into the tribe because they were friends of council members, friends of the chairmen or whatever. Even though they're not historically Grand Traverse Band members they're receiving benefits as though they are Grand Traverse Band members. It's an equal distribution. Fifty percent of the net revenues are distributed equally to the 3,500 members and that's a lot of money.

So people were enrolling into our tribe just for that reason and we had to address it. Our membership was on the rise and it created a lot of disruption in the community. Because a lot of the people who never wanted to associate with the Grand Traverse Band, or even say that they were Indian before throughout their adult life, all of a sudden came home and said, "Yeah, I'm your brother or sister Indian and I want to be enrolled." Really it was just for the per capita money. Let's say this individual was adopted into the tribe and had an adopted child that was not biologically theirs. Because of adoption laws a non-Indian child takes on the blood of the parent. Therefore, it made this individual, this nonmember child, a tribal member. In contrast, the direct descendants of tribal members who were 1/16 GTB were not able to be enrolled. So this is the situation: we have 1/8 historic Grand Traverse Band members that can't be enrolled because they're not quarter Indian; we have adopted members into the tribe that are receiving benefits even though they aren't even historic Grand Traverse Band members; and we have descendants, lineal descendants, that don't receive any benefits. This created a huge conflict, a huge fight. We have seen where families are getting torn apart because of the membership issue. Some of the children are members and some of the children are not members because of this bar that the federal government placed on us for determining who's an Indian and who's not an Indian. The 1/4 blood quantum is putting a great strain on our community and it's building pressure. We never got into physical violence. That's not to say that it's not going to. That's the whole reason for changing our constitution and really getting particular about what a federally recognized Indian tribe means.

For the four years that we've been going through this we've been fighting a lot with the community in the committee hearings. Of the Grand Traverse Band's 3,500 members, only 1,500 live within the jurisdiction of the tribe in the six-county service area surrounding the tribal reservation. And half of this 1,500, about 700, are adult voting members—they are the only ones that are interested and that come to the meetings. It's not even 700, it's only 10 or 12 people at a time. But they're real dissident, they're real disturbed, and they're very upset about things, and they're coming to the committee and beating the crap out of us because of the constitution that was written twenty years ago. We're trying to communicate to them and let them know that what we're trying to do is guarantee their rights for the future.

Money doesn't fix everything. Money, I think, creates more problems than what we had before, because money and greed divide communities. They divide our nation. People feel that only the wealthy or the people with more money or the people with families of power are the ones that can speak, the only ones that have a voice. We don't want to have that. We want to create a community, a nation that is equal and fair to everybody. Everybody's going to have a vote. Everybody over the age of eighteen should have a vote, should have a say, and have a right to be heard.

But we're stuck on the personalities and the money. Because the people who elected us to office will suddenly start pointing fingers at you. The first time that they get rejected from a program or their education check doesn't come in on time, they'll start saying that you're a rich bastard who doesn't care about the people anymore—even when you have good intentions and say, "Hey, I'm on the same side of the table with you." I think the generations of abuse on Indian people has had its effect on us and that's why we react that way. We have to get beyond that.

It's a difficult process because there are people that want to keep the enrollment numbers low so there'll be more benefits for current members of the tribe. Then there are people who want to preserve our identity and our culture and with that comes an acknowledgment that things change. It's obvious there are more non–Native Americans than there are Native Americans, and it's evident that our children are going to someday marry a non–Native American and that diminishes the blood quantum. Underneath the IRA constitutions we have set a bar—you have to be a quarter blood in our tribe to be an Indian. We don't agree with that, I don't personally agree with that because I think it's in, it's in a person's heart and in a person's values. I'm at odds with tribal members that want to keep it low. It means less for their children, and I can see their point of view, but I also see in the future that if we don't end that type of mentality, we're going to diminish ourselves. We're going to lose ourselves because the quarter bloods are getting drawn out. That's the truth. So, it's a very difficult process, a tough and sensitive situation, and I want to learn from other Indian nations that are possibly going through the same thing.

On the committee we have a good balance because we have people that are in disagreement and we have people that are in agreement, and this helps the leadership think through everything and make good decisions. In selecting members of the committee we picked people from both sides of the aisle. People that want to stay small, people that see the need to change, and expand, and grow. There are people on the committee that don't agree with the per capita. They're not giving it back, but they didn't vote for the policy in the first place—it's an entitlement and they're going to take it. So we have a good mix on our committee and we have a draft of a new constitution. Instead of revising the whole constitution and then dropping it in the people's lap one day and saying "OK, now vote yes or no on this," we're going to take advisory votes on each section. Then, in the end, we're going to vote on the whole thing.

We've come up with our drafts from the community, from the grassroots people calling for preservation of the 1/4 blood quantum requirement for enrollment. I don't know if any other tribe is having that same issue, but we are and that's why we feel very strongly about the quarter-blood Indian. That's our justification and we don't mean to offend any other tribe that decides to go with the lineal descendants test. As a sovereign nation, that's going to be our position and it's our right, and it's your right to do it another way.

When the lawyers got involved things really went downhill fast because our constitution says Indian. One lawyer stood up and said well, does that mean Canadian Indian? Does that mean American Indian? What type of Indian does that mean? So we have to clearly define what *Indian* means in the constitution. After we told the lawyers what we wanted they brought us new drafts of the constitutional language in a big old, thick document. We said, "My God, you guys, can't we just come down to earth and find some simple language?" Obviously, their answer was no. But finally our committee just took a stand and said, "Look, we as members hired each and every one of you through our elected representatives. This is what we want you to say, this is how you are going to say it, but say it so it protects the interests of those historic Grand Traverse Band members so we don't have this flood of non–Grand Traverse Band Indian people. They're Indian people, but they're not Grand Traverse Band members."

And the definition that we came up with, after surveying and having a series of long discussions with the membership, is the following: Degree of Indian blood means total blood quantum derived from the tribe's bands or groups recognized by the federal government of the United

States of America. It does not include blood quantum derived from non–U.S. federally recognized tribes. So that, to us, defines what Indian blood means. It would mean United States of America Indian blood is all we're going to count. Therefore, we don't count the Indian blood of anybody from Canada that is a direct descendant of a GTB Ottawa. To me, that is a radical decision. This is just the draft that hasn't been voted on yet by the members, who must ultimately decide if this is what they want.

We're also putting in this new draft language about disenrollment. There's a procedure for a person to appeal a disenrollment decision to the tribal judiciary. But because a number of members requested it, we've also proposed a provision in the draft for people to challenge someone's enrollment status. If a member doesn't think that another person is a bona fide Grand Traverse Band member and is getting the benefit of their property interest, they want to be able to challenge that and get them off the rolls. The draft also allows for challenges from the opposite side. It allows for someone to be able to challenge the tribe to be able to get into the tribe, to prove that they are a GTB member. People feel that these challenges to membership are very important.

CONCLUSION

Our constitution is generally OK. The people are just worried about the enrollment and they're worried about the powers of the tribal council, what we're spending, where we're going, what we're doing. That's all they're concerned about. They're not really concerned about the land or the resources. It's not controversial. They're not worried about planting a tree for every tree that you take down. They're not worried about collecting back all of the old reservation lands or anything like that. What they're concerned about is the enrollment numbers as that translates into dollars. But I see the whole problem that Albert Hale and others are talking about with being a nation, and being a sovereign, taking out the secretarial approval clause and having our constitution reflect what our people want. That's sovereignty.

We're trying to create a living document that is fair and equal for all tribal members, and there's been talk about nationhood. But our constitution doesn't say nation, our constitution says tribal members. Until the constitution is changed all we're going to think about is tribal members. So we have this draft and we're excluding Canadian Indian blood from our rolls. In my mind I think that's wrong but we rule by consensus of the committee and I'm the committee chairman and the chairman doesn't vote. But we're excluding the Canadian Indian blood.

We're saying that Indians, to us, are a quarter GTB. That's what we're saying an Indian is. I think that's wrong because in the future my children will be enrolled members of the tribe, they have the blood quantum. But are their children going to be tribal members? Who knows. I would like for them to marry another tribal member. I'd like for them to stay within the tribe but it's unlikely, it's very unlikely. A lot of times today people won't marry another tribal member because they're related to them, or their clans cross, or somehow it's forbidden for them to get married. This needs to be addressed.

I'm trying to understand how other tribes are doing that. I don't know if there are other gaming tribes that are distributing per capita benefits, but for our tribe it's very disruptive, the benefits we are giving out, because the people are only thinking about today and they want the biggest per cap check they can get, so therefore they want the enrollment numbers to be as low as possible. They want us to be a three-hundred-member tribe so that way our per cap checks are $500,000 dollars. You know, that's just not going to happen and I don't think that's a good policy to have because what we are is a sovereign nation. We have to stand up, and we have to be strong, and we have to act like a nation. I can't think of any other nation in the world that gives their members ten or twenty thousand dollars a year just because they're a member of that nation. Ours does, however, and it has created a real problem for our tribe. For many people it's the only income that they have and all they look forward to. It's all they're living on and if it dries up and goes away, which eventually I think it will, where are they going to be? What will they be left with?

If our constitution is not corrected now, and if we don't plan for the future and anticipate this problem, our people are going to be destroyed and the U.S. government is going to accomplish its goal of exterminating Indians as we know them today. It's not like other countries where they are going through ethnic cleansing and are killing people to take over their property. It's not like that anymore today. It was. It's more methodical now in [that] they're setting the standards of what an Indian is. Eventually, if we don't plan for it, there are going to be no more Indians left and they'll have won.

I can see this process moving on for another five years, maybe longer. But we feel we don't need to rush because this is something that we're creating for our children, our grandchildren, and their children and the next seven generations. So the small piece of time that we're taking now, which could be ten, twelve years, is fairly insignificant to the next two hundred, three hundred years and beyond that we need to think about. I'm very proud of what I'm doing and I'm very proud to be taking the thoughts of our children, of our women, of our elders, of our citizens and putting that into the constitution, because I believe that they're our guiding light for the future.

LE ROY SHINGOITEWA, CHAIR, HOPI TRIBE
CONSTITUTIONAL REFORM COMMITTEE

One of the things we need to remember is that not all tribes are the same in dealing with royalties, in dealing with per capitas. For instance, with the Hopi people, debates over enrollment and membership have nothing to do with per capita. Our concern is continuing our bloodlines, keeping Hopis, having Hopis so that there continue to be Hopis. When we deal with our enrollment as an amendment to the constitution, it's about ensuring that there are Hopis still there in the future. Traditionally, you could belong to the Hopi if your mother was Hopi. Well, because of modern times and the intermarriages that have taken place—not only with other tribal members but also with outside nationalities—bloodlines have changed within our tribe. What we're asking is, "How do we maintain the tribe?" We ask this not because we want to give out money to our members but because we want to ensure the longevity of our continued existence and maintain our traditional lines.

So when we deal with enrollment we find ourselves in the opposite position of the Grand Traverse Band. We're trying to make sure the Hopis keep growing and are maintained because, traditionally, our Hopi women are the valued people. Because of them our clan lines continue to grow and grow. If we don't have that then, of course, we lose the identity of being Hopis. So when you go about reforming your constitution you need to think about how is it going to benefit, in the long run, those people that are there.

How are we doing it? Well, we only made one amendment to the constitution that we did pass. Like I said, traditionally, if your mother is Hopi, then you automatically become Hopi. But because of intermarriage, the blood in our tribe got thinner and thinner. So we said that anyone who can come in and give us at least a quarter blood will be included as a tribal member. And even that is now beginning to disappear. Because through intermarriages those who are half Hopi have children and their blood drops a fourth. And those that are a quarter Hopi get married and have children with 1/8 blood. And so forth [and] so on. So we're really starting to look not just at tomorrow but down the line. How does the Hopi survive? A related issue that will also become more pressing down the road is our continued ability to engage in our culture. In order to perform religious ceremonies you need to know the Hopi language. This is another factor that is finding its way into our discussions as we revise the constitution.

ALBERT HALE, FORMER PRESIDENT,
NAVAJO NATION

I think the question of enrollment and the process of determining citizenship goes back to an issue that all of us need to face as Indian nations. Once we start to move away from being a tribe to a nation, which a lot of us are doing, we have to start looking at that. What does that mean? What are the consequences? We can't continue to treat ourselves as tribes on the one hand and then try to define ourselves as sovereign nations, and act as sovereign nations. We have to start looking at expanding that, and looking at citizenship. How do we determine citizenship? I think that's going to be a major issue. I think there was an article recently in *Indian Country Today* that addressed this issue. It had to do with a conflict just outside of Las Vegas with a little Paiute tribe. The council got together and practically cut their membership. They had about eighty-five members, and they came down to forty members. This is a tribe that was now generating a lot of revenues from casinos and resorts so that came into play.

So the question really is how do you exercise your sovereignty, not only with regard to your relations with the people on the outside but also in relation to your own people. And that's what the government structure does. That's what a constitution does. That's what the Title 2 amendments of the Navajo Nation Code do with Navajo. It's looking at how we exercise our sovereign authority with regard to governing our own people and also non-Navajos who happen to be within our jurisdiction. So I would dare say that it's going to be an issue that we're going to have to deal with in the near future. Enrollment versus citizenship is going to be an issue that we're going to have to deal with pretty quickly. And, as an aside, in the process of doing government reform, if you start out at different points, you'll reach different results. If you start out defining yourself as a tribe, and treating yourself as a tribe, you'll develop a constitution, or governmental document that will only be applicable to your members. That's where you will end up. If you proceed with your government reform as a sovereign entity, as a nation, then where you end up is going to be entirely different because you're developing a governmental structure that will govern your entire nation, and all the people, regardless of race, who may be residents of that area.

LARRY FOSTER, FORMER CHAIR, NAVAJO NATION
COMMISSION ON GOVERNMENT DEVELOPMENT

We go by enrollment, by blood quantum. If you're one quarter Navajo, then you're Navajo. The blood quantum requirement is another requirement that was imposed by the federal government, arising out of the treaty situation, because they had to find a way to disseminate treaty provisions like farm implements and food. They didn't want to give it to anyone who couldn't prove that they were Navajo. And that's where we got a lot of our names—when our forefathers got in line to receive those treaty items that were promised. Our forefathers said, "My name is Cunkyia," or something like that, and they couldn't write it down, so they said, "Well, you're going to be Albert Hale." A lot of Indian people got their names through that process because they couldn't spell Indian names. Again, that comes from the federal government again. To me, it's another way of perpetuating this dependency, another way of exercising paternalism.

So, as a sovereign entity we have to take a look at that and determine whether it's conducive to our nation building, to our concept of nationhood, to continue to limit ourselves to only enrolled members or to expand that and talk about citizenship. And if we go in that direction, what are the elements that will require that citizenship be established?

As President Hale was saying, "How do we limit who's going to be part of the nation?" We have thousands of in-laws, thousands of in-laws. If we're going to be a nation, then how do they fit in? Will they fit in? If we're going to be a tribe then we're definitely just looking at Navajos. But if we're going to be a nation, then we have in-laws, we have Hopi in-laws, we have in-laws from a lot of other tribes. Where do they fit in? We went out there and had hearings. People said, "Well, my daughter is married to an Apache. Is there going to be some room in this government for him? Or what about my grandkids, they're going to be half Apache and half Navajo. Where do they fit in?" So, I think those are things that we're pondering. We need to take a good look at that.

It's just like me going to another Indian nation. If I were to marry into another Indian nation, how will I be accepted? I hope I will be accepted by that nation. But I know that, at least to my knowledge, I would be subject to their laws. A good example is when Russell Means comes down to Navajo land. He's one of our in-laws. He'll always be an in-law because he's got Navajo kids down there, and he's a good brother of mine. We've had a falling out because he told me, "You guys don't have any jurisdiction over me." I told him, "When I go to your reservation, which I do, I respect your ways and if I do something wrong up there I expect to face the consequences up there." But that's something where we're going to have to find common ground at some point in time.

The other question is on-reservation versus off-reservation. We have approximately 150,000 people living on-reservation. We have close to half of that living off-reservation. What about them? Right now we have Navajos in the Phoenix area, Albuquerque, and Flagstaff. They're off-reservation and want to form their own chapters. They want their own representation on the tribal council. So these are issues that we're still going to have to address.

Another question is the Navajo preference. If a non-Navajo marries a Navajo, they're entitled to pretty much all of the privileges except that they can't vote and we haven't addressed that yet. I know that one of our bigger communities, Chinle, with about seven or eight thousand people in the chapter, has already drafted some provisions. I know that a couple of years ago they wanted to include voting rights for non-Navajos. That's going to be a tough debate that's going to come up.

ROSS SWIMMER, FORMER PRINCIPAL CHIEF,
CHEROKEE NATION OF OKLAHOMA

We do not have an enrollment. When the Cherokee Nation reformed its government in 1971, we didn't really have an enrollment procedure. When we called for the first election of a chief, anyone who wanted to enroll, and claimed they were Cherokee, could sign up. And I think we had about six or seven thousand people who enrolled and said they were Cherokee. In 1975 we established, through the constitution, that one had to be either on — or a lineal descendant of — someone who was on the 1906 Dawes Commission roll. And on the Dawes Commission roll there were approximately 41,000 Cherokees enrolled. So in order to be a member of the tribe one has to prove his ancestry back to a person on that roll. And that's the same, I believe, under the proposed constitution. That's somewhat arbitrary. It also has created some difficulty because we have what are known as Texas Cherokees. During the troubles of the Cherokee Nation in the 1850s, some of the Cherokees went to Texas and settled there, and they were not in Oklahoma or Indian territory in 1906, and they did not enroll. And some of our full blood Cherokees are not, technically, legal members of the Cherokee Nation. No less Cherokee, but they didn't enroll in 1906, and they're not on the roll today.

It was an arbitrary decision. The reason the 1906 roll was chosen was because it was the first census taken under oath. And it was taken under oath because it also resulted in an allotment of land to those people who were enrolled. One of the reasons why we oppose blood quantum for membership is that there really is no way of determining what blood quantum is from historic records. At the very least it would be very difficult because in 1906, and some of you I'm sure are affected by this, blood quantum was marked down as a way of determining whether an allotment could be restricted or unrestricted. It was a competency test. Generally, if you were a half degree of blood or more your land allotment would be restricted. You could not manage it and it would have to be managed by the Bureau of Indian Affairs. If you registered yourself as less than a half degree, then you could do what you wanted. You could sell the property the next day. So, a lot of ingenious Cherokees who were full blood, registered as a quarter, eighth or sixteenth blood so they could sell their property. And a lot of those who really were a quarter or an eighth or a sixteenth and who didn't want to pay taxes registered as full blood so that they could have their land restricted and nontaxable. So, it's a hodgepodge now, and we treated membership as citizenship in a nation, not blood quantum. I've never heard anyone claim they were a quarter Canadian, a quarter American or a quarter Mexican. But for some reason tribes got into this and part of it started when the Bureau was trying to administer services and said you needed to be a quarter blood.

JOHN PETERS, JR., EXECUTIVE DIRECTOR,
MASSACHUSETTS COMMISSION ON INDIAN AFFAIRS

At Mashpee Wampanoag, we've been dealing with the
English since the 1620s. And over the course of time, a lot of people
have left, their families have left the community, and now they want to
come back. Those who have always lived there have a different view on
life than those who left and want to come back—we're concerned about
what impact they would have on the way we perceive things. So we've
been fighting over this issue for a long time, about abandoning your
tribal rights by leaving and not coming back for a number of generations.
But it gets to be a very complex discussion about how do you really
limit someone's rights and be fair about it. We talked about a naturalization process like they have in the United States or other procedures that
could help maintain the outlook we have on our community. We're
still debating this and we don't know exactly how to pull all these pieces
together.

The other point is that we've been together so long in our community
that everybody is my cousin. I had to go to Narragansett in order to find
a wife. We're all that close, through intermarriage. So, you're going to
find yourself in a situation where you're not going to be able to keep that
quarter blood requirement, or criteria like that, in future generations.

CARRIE IMUS, VICE CHAIR, HUALAPAI NATION

There is a lot of discussion that we hear now in Indian
Country, especially with the changes that are coming about in the Indian
Child Welfare Act and children that are not enrolled in any tribe. Those
kids [not a 1/4 blood of any tribe] are in limbo and tribes need to
look at the big picture and say, Where will this kid go? What's going to
happen to them? Part of me feels we need to lower the blood quantum.
Ours is a quarter, and it's a hard decision that all the nations need to
make. We're a small tribe but we're growing, and with all the intermarriages that we're having within our community, it's something I know
has to be addressed whether we like it or not. It's either going to be
lowered or be maintained at a quarter. Hopefully, some of the kids will
be enrolled, but I know that there are going to be a handful that aren't
going to be eligible anywhere based on their blood quantum. So, that's
something that I know we're going to be talking about.

LINDA HAVATONE, FORMER COUNCIL MEMBER,
HUALAPAI NATION

The thing that has happened most frequently is that a lot
of our people want to relinquish their enrollment with the Hualapai
Nation because they see that other tribes have gaming casinos and have
something to offer to their tribal members. That's the reason why they
want to relinquish their enrollment with us and have left. It's been six to
ten a month that have relinquished their enrollment.

MARTHA BERRY, DELEGATE, 1999 CHEROKEE
NATION CONSTITUTION CONVENTION

Of all the issues with which our delegation dealt, the very
most difficult issues—blood quantum for citizenship and elected officials,
council representation for nonresidents, and allegiance to the United
States Constitution—were all related to two basic questions: What is a
Cherokee? And how do Cherokees fit into the world as a whole? These
are not questions that arose from the constitutional crisis of that particular
time in Cherokee history. These are questions of identity.

When all Cherokees had been lined up along pro- [former Principal
Chief Joe] Byrd and anti-Byrd lines for months and months, we suddenly
found ourselves divided along blood lines. On both sides of the issue, the
arguments were emotional, and they were hurtful. Not surprisingly, in a
nation with an average quantum of 16ths and 32nds, no blood requirements were added for either citizenship or eligibility for elected office.
When the arguing was done and the vote taken, however, delegates from
both sides of the blood quantum issue found themselves in little clusters,
shaking their heads, crying and comforting one another, in the auditorium, the foyer, and the rest rooms. We came to within a handful of delegates of being unable to conduct business for lack of a quorum. There
we sat, in the closing days of the twentieth century on the Christian
calendar, struggling with what can only be called an identity crisis. Of all
the cruel and subtle gifts bestowed upon the Cherokee by colonization,
this is perhaps the cruelest and most subtle of them all.

Joseph Kalt

Six   # Constitutional Rule and the Effective Governance of Native Nations

> *Constitutional reform is an exercise of sovereignty. With constitutional reform we're talking about Indian nations doing what they have to do, or can do, in forming a structure that will bring them together . . . to address common problems. The question should be, as a truly sovereign nation, is this constitution, this form of government, acceptable to us? To our people? That should be the question. And that should be the only question. And if it is acceptable to our people, then it is and that's the way it should be. That is sovereignty.*
> HON. ALBERT HALE, FORMER PRESIDENT, NAVAJO NATION[1]

INTRODUCTION: CONSTITUTIONS AND THE WEALTH AND HEALTH OF TRIBAL NATIONS

Native America is at a critical juncture in its drive for self-determination and political sovereignty. With their de jure sovereignty under persistent attack,[2] it has become critical for tribes to demonstrate their capacity for effective self-governance. Without this capacity, Indian nations are sitting ducks for those who would wish to limit tribal sovereignty by pointing to examples of political disarray, unenforced law, and irrationally enforced law. At the same time, the evidence is overwhelming that political self-rule is the only policy that has enabled at least some tribes to break out of a twentieth-century history of federal government–dominated decision-making that yielded social, cultural, and economic destruction.[3] By the 1990s, American Indians living on reservations were the poorest identifiable group in the United States.

Notwithstanding the importance of sovereignty to tribes' political, social, cultural, and economic futures, like other nations in the world, Indian nations that succeed in (re)establishing and/or protecting de jure[4] and de facto[5] powers of self-rule can, nevertheless, fail to meet their citizens' needs and desires. Success in securing *rights of self-government* must be backed up by the *ability to self-govern*. Like other nations in the world, an Indian nation may fight mightily for recognition of its sovereignty—and, upon winning such recognition, fall flat on its face unless it can effectively exercise that sovereignty both in its internal affairs and vis-à-vis other sovereigns.

As they have set about the challenge of building and rebuilding societies that are successful according to their communities' own self-determined standards of "success," many Indian nations are finding that they are severely hampered by governing structures that are not of their own making. More than 180 tribes adopted constitutions boilerplated by the federal government in the 1930s under the Indian Reorganization Act (IRA),[6] and many more have ended up with constitutions that were either modeled after the IRA systems or otherwise externally designed. Even where tribes historically were more in the driver's seat when it came to designing their governance systems, many are finding that systems adopted decades ago are not up to the on-the-ground challenges of tribal self-government today. Thus, much like the nations of post-colonial Africa (which generally inherited the colonials' structures) and the former Soviet Bloc countries (many of which grabbed a Western European–style constitution "off the shelf" after the demise of the USSR), many Indian Nations are now in the midst of the struggle to implement governing structures that will work for them to achieve their goals.

The process of constitutional reform in Indian Country is fraught with political turmoil and uncertainty. Not surprisingly, current systems create vested interests in and loyalties to the status quo. Thus, for example, deeply embedded traditions giving cultural legitimacy to local self-rule at the Navajo Nation, the Tohono O'odham Nation, the Oglala Sioux Tribe, Hopi, and many others prod those nations to look for decentralizing responsibility for structural governmental change. Yet extant centralized systems are the systems through which external federal dollars and resources have been channeled for decades, and tribal governments are often the largest employers on reservations. It should hardly be surprising that even culturally legitimate constitutional reform would face tough sledding when it seeks to change the fundamental centralized structures that the decades of federal domination have engendered.

Needed reform of tribal constitutions can also be impeded by uncertainty and lack of knowledge: Why should we change our governing structures? What will happen if we do? What changes would work for us? What process should we use to arrive at reforms that will be legitimate and more likely to work for us? Questions of these sorts drive home the point that constitutional reform is at once momentous and fraught with risk. It is not undertaken lightly, and it is not guaranteed to improve the lives of tribes' citizens. At the same time, it is a critical need for a good many Indian nations.

This chapter examines questions of content, rather than process, in constitutional reform. What does the evidence say about the role of tribes' constitutions? And what constitutional provisions recommend themselves for serious consideration? As discussed at length below, the first of these questions turns out to be amenable to conceptual answers of broad applicability across not only U.S. Indian nations, but nations generally. The second question—what kind of constitutional provisions work best?—is a different story. Here, the logic and the evidence compel the conclusion that one size will not fit all. To serve a nation's needs and desires, governing structures must be practically efficacious in the face of the real-world problems and opportunities the community faces. At the same time, they must be legitimate in the eyes of the people who live their lives within those structures; and to be legitimate, they must resonate in quite concrete dimensions with the community's cultural norms regarding the holding and wielding of power and authority. Because Native communities differ in the objective challenges they face and, most especially, in their relevant cultural norms, what works for one Native nation is hardly guaranteed to work for another.

Section II below asks when, and even *whether,* American Indian nations need constitutions. Are constitutions and constitutionally based tribal governments, in fact, symptomatic of assimilation into the dominant society's norms and modus operandi? Regardless of the answer to this question, are constitutions and constitutionally based tribal governments nevertheless necessary for tribes to serve the interests of their citizens in today's world with the challenges it presents for contemporary Indian nations? Or are there models of contemporary self-rule that eschew constitutionalism that can work for Indian nations? With perspective on these questions in hand and with an eye toward those Native nations for whom constitutionalism is desired and perhaps necessary, Section III then turns to examinations of the kinds of generic problems that constitutions inherently must address in establishing a rule of law that is legitimate in the eyes of citizens, and that is effective in the face of the practical economic, social, and political challenges of the day. Section IV discusses the range of choices that tribal constitutional reformers confront as they consider specific structural provisions, and assesses alternative choices in light of the twin criteria of practical effectiveness and cultural "match."

CONSTITUTIONALISM AND NATIVE SELF-RULE

This is our long-term strategic plan.
RICHARD REAL BIRD, FORMER CHAIR, CROW TRIBE OF MONTANA[7]

The term *constitutionalism* seems quintessentially Western, conjuring up mainstream America's high school civics textbooks, the dominant society's Grecian-rooted ideologies and foundation stories, and high-minded parchment protected in the National Archives. At the same time, for many Indian nations, the formation of constitution-based governments in the 1930s signaled the end of official federal policies of trying to terminate the notion of geographic areas of tribal control by allotting reservation lands to individuals. Tribes' constitutions, moreover, have provided a recognizable locus of decision-making that has had to be reckoned with when other governments and external parties have come calling for control over resources and jurisdiction. For better or for worse, constitutionally based tribal government has meant that an outside party wanting to sign a contract to mine the ore on tribal land, or the state government wanting to build a cross-reservation road, or federal officials seeking to enforce U.S. endangered species law, have had a "there" there to deal with. While the origins of wanting a "there" to be there may have been to make it easier for non-Indians to gain access to reservations' resources,[8] many tribal citizens see and remember the adoption of their nation's contemporary constitution as the moment at which a barrier to the otherwise irresistible erosion of tribal political sovereignty was affirmatively erected.

So, are tribal constitutions inherently "Western," or "dominant society," in their origins and function, albeit perhaps necessary as adaptations to contemporary circumstances? When we conceive of a "constitution" as a society's rules for making and enforcing its collective rules and decisions, including the legitimate allocation of power and authority over rule-making and decision-making, it seems incontrovertible that constitutions are ubiquitous across human societies and hardly a conceit of Western culture. The point is driven home by the many cases of nations—Native and otherwise—that have no written constitution, yet function as polities with respect to both internal affairs and external interactions with other polities. From Great Britain and Israel to the Navajo Nation and a number of the New Mexico Pueblos, constitutional rule—replete with institutional structure, tradition-laden rules of procedure, claims to de jure primacy, and de facto practical acceptance as the monopoly wielder of legitimate force—exists in fact despite the absence of a written "constitution."

Indeed, the cases of Pueblos such as Cochiti are particularly telling. In the face of the Spanish invasion, the Cochiti took their precontact systems of community organization and decision-making literally underground. At least from the time of the Spanish occupation to the present, and extending through all manner of foreign attempts to stamp out those systems over the centuries, Cochiti Pueblo has sustained continuity of collective organization for collective decision- and rule-making, although this organization was never written down as a "constitution." The Pueblo continues to function under a theocratic system of governance in which governors, lieutenant governors, and other officials are appointed from socioreligious medicine societies by theocratic authority exercised under procedures and standards that are every bit as compelling and recognized by the people as the dominant society's pieces of paper on display at the National Archives.[9] Although it doesn't look at all like the constitution one would expect to find in a mainstream high school civics textbook, *Cochiti's* constitution is what Cochiti governs itself under.[10]

Similar conclusions regarding the presence of constitutional self-rule—i.e., indigenously derived structures and modes of legitimate collective rule-making, decision-making, and rules enforcement through the legitimate allocation and use of authority and power—apply throughout precontact, and certainly preconquest, North America. From the strong, democratically selected chief executive systems of the Western Apache[11] to the Iroquois Confederacy's Great Law of Peace to the Lakotas' essentially parliamentary system of a council and multiple executive ministers ("shirtwearers") with an independent judiciary (in the *akicita* societies)[12] to the Cherokees' written constitution of 1827, preconquest tribes operated under constitutions—*their* constitutions.

It is not dispositive to argue that such examples of indigenous governance were "not really" examples of constitutionalism (or even "government") because they were not written, or because they were not adopted by democratic vote, or because they were embedded in an entirely indigenous worldview or cosmology, or because they were not conceived of as constitutions undergirding nations. While a tradition of scholarship once more commonly described indigenous preconquest government as "informal"[13] or nonexistent because, for example, "[t]he concept of government is rooted in European political philosophy and tradition, and it denotes a bureaucratic organizational system of legitimate public power,"[14] such a definition of *government* is unsupportable, and such characterizations are problematic in the extreme. A society that operates under a council presided over by four appointed chiefs who attained their positions by performing appropriately within a system that considered it proper that those considered "supreme elder clansmen" preside over council deliberations[15] is not an informal system—unless *formal* must mean written down in codified form and bureaucratized, as described in the high school civics textbooks. Nor does the fact that such council chiefs wielded only such authority as their prestige and persuasiveness could engender among the most prestigious men of the community who formed the council mean that those chiefs "had no actual power,"[16] much less that the community lacked a formal government. In fact, the logic and structure of "the most prestigious men of the community forming a council and selecting from among their members the most prestigious and persuasive as the heads of the council to serve so long as they have the support of the council" sounds very much like what one might find in a high school civics textbook in a number of European parliamentary democracies.

What is true in the critique of constitutionalism as being "Western" or "of the dominant society" is that "Western" or "dominant society" norms and standards of *proper, prestigious, legitimate,* and the like—which undergird the "Western" or "dominant society" understanding of why a constitution is or should be of a particular form and authority—do not provide particular understanding of how Cochiti's constitution is understood and is conceived of by the citizens of Cochiti Pueblo. The non-Cochiti observer may be able to recognize that contemporary Cochiti operates under a quintessentially Cochiti constitutional government. Yet the non-Cochiti observer—whether that observer is a contemporary Oglala or a "Western" academic—is unlikely to be able to understand Cochiti's constitutionalism *from the perspective of Cochiti understanding and perception.* With community-specific cultural norms regarding power and authority serving as the support for Cochiti's constitution, and with cultural norms acting to influence individuals' conduct through interpersonal networks of shared signaling of felt psychological penalties and approbations,[17] it is unlikely that the non-Cochiti can feel what it is like to live under Cochiti's constitution—just as it is unlikely that a typical citizen of, say, Beijing can understand what it felt like to Americans to live through the Bush-Gore crisis. There is meaning when the outsider is told, "Man, you don't understand Cochiti government."

In fact, at least for more-or-less sovereign democracies, constitutional rule is everywhere and always ultimately founded on the informal cultural norms that glue people into an "us" rather than a "them." A recent stark example—the Bush-Gore constitutional crisis—makes the point. Looking for statistical regularity across similar situations in world history, we might have expected that Vice President and presidential candidate Gore might have used his office, prestige, and persuasiveness to mount what is commonly seen in the world—an attempt at a military solution for himself. Why did he not? The answer cannot be that the U.S. Constitution and its derivative institutions prevented him from doing so; the night of the U.S. Supreme Court's final edict, the U.S. Constitution sat placidly in its box in the National Archives, unable to take action. Rather, the citizens (including Vice President Gore) of a culture in which the norm, or idea, of constitutional rule and derivative institutions is sacred according to the iconic, tradition- and ceremony-laden values of its founding fathers (should we say "elders" or "grandfathers"?) did not even seem to take the possibility of such otherwise common strategies seriously.

To be sure, the cultural, economic, sociological, psycho-sociological, and numerous other dimensions of the peaceful resolution of the Bush-Gore constitutional crisis are far beyond the scope of this study. The point to be made, however, is the point increasingly emphasized by scholars of self-determined polities. At least where governing systems are not coerced by dictatorial power, constitutions and constitutional self-rule are everywhere and always founded on the informal, organic, and indigenous shared cultural traits of the self-governing society.[18] In such settings, there is no outside "meta-enforcer"[19] by which to ultimately compel adherence to some actual or veil-of-ignorance original agreement as to the rules by which individuals "agree" to make their rules. Down that path is "infinite regress."[20]

Thus, the claim here is that constitutional rule is neither "Western" nor Native; it is human. Human societies that sustain the capacity for collective action and coexistence through other than the brute force of tyrannical dictatorship do so by establishing via their own culturally dependent paths and mechanisms the rules by which they make and enforce the rules of collective decision-making and permissible individual conduct. That is, they establish constitutions. Without them, would-be polities are not sustained as such. They are consigned to the Hobbesian pre-constitutional struggle.

THE TWIN CHALLENGES OF *EFFECTIVE* AND *LEGITIMATE* CONSTITUTIONAL RULE

I believe that friend, family, and foe should be treated equally.
SAM McCLELLAN, CONSTITUTIONAL REFORM
COMMITTEE, GRAND TRAVERSE BAND OF OTTAWA
AND CHIPPEWA INDIANS[21]

A constitution, written or not, is a polity's rules for how it will make and enforce its rules. Constitutions are necessary for the sustainability of a polity and arise as human inventions most fundamentally because humans are social animals for whom (1) collectively coordinated action is advantageous in certain situations, (2) "defection" and "free riding" are often individually rational and otherwise feasible even when interpersonal coordination is collectively rational, and (3) even when not defecting or free riding, individuals are not identical in their preferences and/or their perceived opportunities, such that there is not always unanimous and voluntary adherence to collective means and ends.

Within groups of human beings, constitutions are not the only means of overcoming such problems. At some level, social institutions such as families, churches, ceremonies, clans, and the like are conscious or unconscious inventions for capturing the advantages of collective coordination in the face of prospective disputes arising from heterogeneous ends and perceptions and opportunities for defection and free riding. But, while the conceptual dividing lines are not bright, groups of people spill over into being a "polity" and their collective institutions spill over into being "government" as at least some of their institutions are endowed with coercive power to enforce those institutions' decisions and rules.[22] The rules for making and enforcing the rules and decisions of a society's coercive institution(s) of collective action and dispute resolution are a *constitution*.[23]

The Necessity of Effective Constitutional Rule

A wave of constitutional reform has been sweeping across Indian Country since federal policies of tribal self-determination and government-to-government relations began to be implemented in the mid-1970s.[24] This is not surprising, with so many tribal constitutions not being of the Indian nations' own making, and with so many tribal constitutions designed at a time when reservation governments were hardly conceived as becoming *real* governments (with their own taxes, police, courts, jails, business codes, criminal procedures, land use and environmental policies, traffic laws, child welfare systems, and the rest of the panoply of powers that Indian nation governments now push for). Native nations are changing their constitutions because they are finding that foreign and/or outdated systems are not working for them.

It is striking how commonly one finds constitutional reform occurring within Indian nations now well-known for their political, social, cultural, and economic success. Examples include Mississippi Choctaw,[25] Citizen Potawatomi,[26] and the Confederated Salish and Kootenai Tribes of the Flathead Reservation.[27] At this stage in the history of America's Indian nations, effective constitutions are a make-or-break necessity to success in nation building and the exercise of tribal self-determination. "Success" here refers to self-defined success. As with most if not all nations in the world, political identity and political sovereignty are preeminent goals of American Indian nations. But, like nations elsewhere, Indian nations also are seeking cultural and social well-being and sovereignty (i.e., control over the cultural and social dynamics of their societies), as well as economic development of the level and type that is consonant with their particular communities' values and that can support individual and collective well-being at a level at which it can be said: "It used to be that everyone wanted to move away, but now they're all coming back."[28] One is reminded of the cruel experiment that the world ran in Germany over the half-century that followed World War II: The ruling powers took a group with a common culture, a common language, an approximately common resource base, a common starting point (wartime devastation and subjugation)—and then gave East Germany and West Germany different political systems. At the end of the "experiment," West Germany was the world's third largest economy[29] and a desired destination for émigrés and refugees; East Germany's economy collapsed and its government had to use barbed wire and machine guns to keep its citizens from leaving.

The "necessary but not sufficient" character of effective constitutional rule lies in the fact that a polity's written or unwritten constitution is the meta-rules of the game. These rules and their derivatives (e.g., by act of the legislature, proclamation of the executive, ruling of the court) structure the incentives and risks that determine whether and how much individuals, families, enterprises, and institutions are willing to invest (in terms of their efforts, energy, ideas, and capital) in the nation. From the perspective of contemporary Native nations, "investors" may mean outside capital owners (such as a corporation), but it more importantly means the nation's citizen who is contemplating opening a small restaurant on the reservation, or the recent college accounting major who is contemplating whether she should go to work for her tribe instead of staying in Phoenix, or the nonprofit foundation which is contemplating funding prenatal education programs if it can find the right tribal partners.

The challenge of successful nation building for contemporary Native nations is to put in place rules of the game that are both effective and legitimate in the eyes of the governed. Satisfying these criteria only proceeds so far as the nation's constitution permits. Let us examine certain salient dimensions of what is required for constitutional self-rule to be effective and legitimate.

The Rules of the Game

At a quite general level, effective constitutional rule requires that the "rules of the game"—from personnel policies to a tribal court's decisions to the enforceability of contracts—be able to establish a rule of law that is both legitimate in the eyes of citizens and effective (i.e., up to the practical tasks of dealing with contemporary economic, social, and political affairs).

A Rule of Law

The essence of an effective constitution is its written or unwritten *rule of law*. At the ideal extreme, this means that the rules of conduct and procedure emanating under a polity's constitution are applied, and applied with equal force, independent of the relationship between an actor and those who wield the authority of government. As the opening quote of this section expresses it so straightforwardly from a Grand Traverse perspective: "friend, family, and foe should be treated equally."[30]

The necessity of a rule of law for effective governance is seen in its converse. A universal challenge of effective governance arises from the difficulty of governing the governors: Having given the power (including coercive power) to a party to serve as the rule maker, rule enforcer, and dispute resolver, how does a polity prevent that party from turning these powers toward serving its own personal interests? The power to govern can be the power to transfer wealth, and much of world political history is a history of governing powers turned against the interests of the governed and in favor of the interests of the governors. From the stark cases of the amassing of personal wealth by Ferdinand Marcos in the Philippines or the excesses of the former Soviet Union's ruling clique to petty corruption in the tribal housing office, application of the powers of governance for the purpose of improving the wealth, power, or status of those who control the means of government subverts the role of government as the instrument of compelling collectively rational conduct and coordination. Such conduct and coordination suffer in the process; the power and authority of government are diverted from promoting collective ends, particularly those that improve the lives of individuals and families in the polity lacking the capacity or influence to control those who govern.[31]

The difficulties that arise when the rule of law breaks down are at least twofold. First, individuals and organizations have an incentive to devote their resources and energy, their best and their brightest, to trying to turn the outcome of the governmental process in their favor by investing in the factors—political influence, having the right allies, wielding raw power, corrupting the right judge—that result in increasing the size of their pieces of the economic and social "pie." Such "rent-seeking" is socially unproductive as it allocates a society's scarce resources to a competitive process of slicing the pie of material and intangible wealth, rather than to processes of augmenting such wealth. To some extent, forms of such conduct are part and parcel of democracy, including lobbying, demonstrating, and making campaign contributions. But when investing in control of the government's apparatus of coercive force is left unstructured by constitutional rule and becomes the dominant method for accumulating wealth, influence, and/or status, it is destructive of the overall wealth and well-being of the community.

Second, as government moves away from the rule of law and toward the rule of power and influence, it undermines the values that otherwise support individuals' voluntary commitment to eschewing defection and free-riding on collectively rational coordination. As if by an invisible hand, non-rent-seeking conduct tends to be weeded out insofar as it proves to be inferior as a strategy of social survival. The results are well-documented cases in which the dominant political culture of a polity becomes some version of a "culture of corruption," "class warfare," "dog eat dog," and the like.

Neither the fact nor the concept of a rule of law is uniquely Anglo-European or Western. Nor are Anglo-European or Western versions of a rule of law the only conceivable or workable rules of law.[32] When a Native person voices the view that factionalism needs to be shut down and "we should be guided by our traditions in deciding the course to take as a people," that person is invoking a rule of Native law in which conduct and/or choices are guided by "tradition," rather than, say, what promotes the personal, familial, or factional interests of a particular tribal council member. When a traditionally governed Pueblo could and can remove its most senior theocrat from governing status for "negligence or wrongdoing"[33] (e.g., because he has entered into "social entanglements"[34] by, perhaps, attempting to appoint an unqualified family member to run a sophisticated tribal enterprise when the Pueblo's indigenous constitution requires that he "not enter into any of the economic functions of the [P]ueblo"),[35] the rule of the Pueblo's law is obviously being enforced. A Native rule of law operates, as it has for centuries, when Haudenosaunee clan mothers can remove chiefs for self-serving conduct in office.[36]

Within at least Anglo-European or Western political systems, the rule of law is quite closely tied to the concept of the separation of powers. Classically, the separation of powers (or balance of powers) is seen as a means by which to provide durability to a rule of law, with the various branches of government able to check transgressions by one another. To be sure, many Native nations' constitutions, both contemporary and historic, have exhibited strong separations of powers. The Lakotas' *akicita* societies illustrate an institutional mechanism historically employed by a number of tribes that possessed law enforcement societies or branches with the constitutionally provided power to discipline even council members.[37] Obviously, the Haudenosaunee clan mothers' appointment and impeachment powers over chiefs (noted above) illustrates separation of powers under the Great Law of Peace. Puebloan theocracy is striking in its separation of powers, with the government officials appointed by the senior theocrat coming from separate medicine societies, and both serving and retired government officials forming a council of *principales* which could "punish[ ], depose[ ], or even execute[ ]" the senior theocratic leader for official misconduct.[38]

Today, establishment of separation of powers is a common theme of many tribes' constitutional reform efforts. Thus, for example, the 1992 amendments to the Constitution and Bylaws of the Turtle Mountain Band of Chippewa Indians (North Dakota) added Article XIV, "Separation of Powers (Judiciary)," in order "[t]o provide for a separate branch of government free from political interference and conflicts of interest for the development and enhancement of the fair administration of justice."[39] In the case of the Constitution and By-Laws of the Pawnee Indians of

Oklahoma, Article II (amended 1982) states: "The Pawnee Indian Tribe of Oklahoma is empowered to establish a Law and Order and Judicial System to protect peace, safety, health and welfare of the members of the tribe; provided the concept of separation of the Executive and Judicial powers is maintained."[40] Article III, Section 3, of the 1994 Constitution of the Ho-Chunk Nation provides: "*Separation of Functions.* No branch of the government shall exercise the powers and functions delegated to another branch."[41]

Notwithstanding the utility and legitimacy that many Native (and other) nations have found over time in constitutional separation of powers, the historical evidence does not quite give such separation "necessary" status.[42] For example, at least historically, polities of collective adherence and action have been sustained and have prospered culturally, politically, and economically under governance systems in which single chieftains wielded legitimate authority and power without check by other than the consent of the governed. In the aforementioned case of the historic Apache, for example, single chieftains had the legitimate authority to select their own councils of vice chiefs, to serve as chief justices of distinctly indigenous judicial systems, and to select leaders for the execution of military campaigns.[43] Yet, as suggested, this rule was democratic,[44] insofar as head chieftains were selected by "direct election" on the basis of demonstrated wisdom and communication skills as the *non-rent-seeking* one "who convinces us,"[45] "our smart one."[46] The fact that an Apache head chief was required to consult with others of influence "gave weight to the opinions of others,"[47] and that he could be removed from office upon being found by the governed to be incapacitated or feeble[48] suggests that the strength of social norms of the governed was sufficient to check chieftain rent-seeking. One noted scholar of the historic Apache reported that, as of 1942, "no Apache could recall an unsatisfactory chief nor one who had been removed because of incompetence."[49]

Hence, the Apache case suggests the exception to the rule that a rule of law in nondictatorial government needs to be protected by separations of the powers within such a government. While theories of collective choice would suggest that the relative success enjoyed by the historic Apache as a polity up to approximately the 1880s was bolstered by a (relatively) culturally homogeneous Apache populace and a relatively small Apache population,[50] the case is not without contemporary relevance to Native nations. As so many of them now seek to reform their constitutions in the struggle to assert and exercise their sovereignty before the era of self-determination closes, Native nations are often tempted to quickly adopt separations of power built on the American or Western European models. Such models, however, may fail to resonate with certain particular contemporary tribal cultures. As I discuss below, failing the test of legitimacy in the eyes of citizens is likely to render any model of self-government unstable and unsatisfactory.

LEGITIMACY AND CULTURAL "MATCH"

As discussed earlier, the immediate wake of the 2000 Bush-Gore presidential election demonstrates the impotence of the U.S. Constitution—a paper document housed in a protected case—as a per se bar to political unrest and rebellion. Instead, governance depending on the consent of the governed hinges critically upon shared conceptions of legitimacy in the use of power and authority. Legitimacy in the institutions of self-government is the motivator of participation and protection by citizens when would-be rent-seeking usurpers of the rule of law arise. The felt impetus to action from private sentiments such as moral righteousness and outrage is what pushes individuals, socially acculturated to norms of the proper and improper, to act in support of legitimate political conduct.[51] "Legitimacy" of a nation's constitutional rule brings the turnout to the council meeting that tries to block the nation's chair from firing appointees of his political opponents in a culture that regards employment as legitimately founded on qualifications, rather than political connection. "Illegitimacy" of constitutional rule either leaves the citizenry at home "because all those politicians are crooked anyway," or urges the ambitious to invest in getting control of the system for the benefit of themselves and their supporters.

As Cornell and Kalt have argued, constitutional legitimacy inheres in a nation's social norms regarding the structure, scope, location, and source of governing authority. By these, we mean:

> *Structure of Authority*: The division of powers and
> responsibilities across such tasks as dispute resolution (judi-
> cial affairs), enforcement (coercion and policing), law and
> rulemaking (legislative affairs), administration and implemen-
> tation of public initiatives and investments (executive and
> bureaucratic functions), and external . . . affairs (international
> relations).
>
> *Scope of Authority*: The range of powers and responsibili-
> ties wielded by the government over the foregoing areas of
> authority . . .

> *Location of Authority*: The level of social organization —
> family, local community, . . . the tribe—in which political
> power and responsibility are properly vested, according to a
> society's cultural norms.
> *Source of Authority*: The mechanisms by which
> individuals who assume governmental roles . . . acquire
> *legitimate* authority . . .[52]

When the superstructure of governance provided by the constitution is consonant with a community's norms regarding these dimensions of authority, that constitution is culturally matched to the community. Legitimacy to rule under the constitution is the result.

Cultural match in contemporary practice is relatively straightforward for, say, the Cochiti, where cultural solidarity and historic governance structures remain relatively intact. On the other hand, the vast majority of American Indian nations have had their cultures actively targeted for destruction by foreign powers, have been compelled to abandon traditional governing structures, and have been pressured or enticed to adopt nontraditional governing structures over several centuries. Even absent concerted attempts to eliminate or assimilate Native societies and people, the Indian nations would not have been immune to the cultural changes brought on by the revolutions in technology, transportation, and communication over the centuries.

Accordingly, the challenge of devising legitimate governing structures today is not a matter of "going back"; it is rather the challenge of finding governing structures that match the reality of the contemporary cultures of Native communities. Relevant political norms are notably durable,[53] and for compelling reasons.[54] Hence, historic forms of governance often carry some resonance today—as in the cases of the Apache and Mississippi Choctaw and their relative success under the IRA's strong chief executive constitutions. But most Indian nations today face daunting challenges wrought by rapid and diversifying cultural change. The results of such changes include notable heterogeneity within and across tribes of religion (from the traditional to evangelical Christianity), cultural practice, economic mores, gender relations, educational attainment and systems, acculturation to American government and its precepts, and on and on across the dimensions of civic life in the contemporary world.[55]

Whether historic or new, the tribe that finds itself with strong allegiances to its villages or districts (such as Hopi or Tohono O'odham) is more likely to find a cultural match with a federated system that empowers local communities than the tribe for whom legitimate power and authority are seen as *located* at its national level. The tribe whose citizens see *sources* of political wisdom in its elders (such as, perhaps, the Lakota or the Ojibwe) may find therein a judicial system that taps such wisdom. The reservation that is the home to an amalgam of historically separate sovereigns that did not share a political culture (such as the Flathead reservation) may find that contemporary norms support a parliamentary *structure* (in which chairs serve at the will of a council of mixed tribal affiliations) as being more legitimate than a system with a U.S.-style directly elected chief executive (in which the chief executive would, perforce, be from one of the reservation's tribes or another). A tribe with little of its religious and cultural traditions even known, such as the Wampanoag Tribe of Gay Head (Aquinnah) on Martha's Vineyard in Massachusetts, may see no legitimacy in extending the *scope* of government to contemporary religious affairs, while any number of, say, Pueblos see a mixing of "church and state" as eminently proper.

PRACTICAL EFFECTIVENESS

The concept of cultural match is not a blank check—as if a Native nation could just find the constitution that is legitimate in its cultural setting and thereby be guaranteed self-defined success in its exercise of self-governing powers. In addition to cultural congruity, such success requires constitutional rule that is practically effective at dealing with the problems the Nation confronts today.

Consider, for example, the tribe whose social norms regarding the structure of authority do not support a judiciary that is separate from the control of its duly chosen elected council (it is sometimes said in such situations that "it is the job of the council to settle disputes"). If this tribe is also a tribe in which social norms do not support the scope of authority extending to the ownership of business enterprises by the government (as in much of Sioux country), this tribe is in a bind economically: It is culturally "matched" for a constitution that eschews an independent judiciary for at least commercial affairs, but such a constitution is not up to the economic tasks the Nation faces. Business development needed for employment and citizens' sense of self-sufficiency will need to come from the fostering of a private sector of member-owned or non-member-owned enterprises; but in approximately seventeen years of working with hundreds of tribes across the United States and Canada, the Harvard Project on American Indian Economic Development has yet to uncover cases in which a thriving private sector on a reservation is not accompanied by a politically independent court for, at least, business disputes. In fact, the existence of an independent court yields substantial increases in economic development on average across a large statistical sample of tribes,[56] and the existence of an independent tribal court is a dominant predictor of whether a tribal bureaucracy is well run (e.g., as reflected in financial soundness and meeting citizens' needs).[57]

When cultural norms and practical effectiveness are in conflict, cultural norms are placed under strain. This does not mean that Native nations caught in such binds are compelled to choose between practical failure in self-governance or abandonment of their cultural values in favor of adoption of "mainstream" norms. It does mean adaptive evolution of norms and creative, *self-determined* design of constitutions and the institutions of contemporary self-governance. Let us turn to an examination of key choices confronted by many Native nations.

KEY CHOICES IN CONSTITUTIONAL DESIGN

A nation's laws are the deepest expression of its culture.
HON. JOSEPH FLIES–AWAY[58]

There is a tremendous variety of constitutional forms represented in Indian Country. Constitutional structures range from Cochiti's and other Pueblos' theocratic systems, to a "textbook" parliamentary system with an independent judiciary at Flathead, to a general council system at Yankton Sioux, to Onondaga's system in which clan mothers select chiefs under the Great Law of Peace,[59] to the distinctly three-branch government with a directly elected president and strong separation of powers at the Navajo Nation, to many IRA tribes' unicameral tribal council systems with weak separations of powers. The question naturally arises as to which systems are working best to meet citizens' needs and protect tribes' sovereignty. Let us examine options and outcomes.

The Architecture of Powers and Functions

Perhaps the most basic of all choices in the design of a government is *who* does *what*. As the maker of coercively enforceable rules and decisions, government has tasks broken down into the basic three of legislation (policy, law, and collective organization decisions),[60] execution (implementing and administering the government's policies, laws, and collective organization decisions), and enforcement (including resolving disputes among parties and emanating from the nation's policies and laws). This natural three-part breakdown and the strong case for separations of powers discussed above, however, do not necessarily compel a three-branch government of the type adopted by the United States or the Navajo Nation or the Northern Cheyenne. Each nation faces the challenge of establishing the legislative, executive, and judicial systems that work, and that work within the distinctive culture and circumstances of that nation.

Executive Powers

The original IRA constitutions that scores of Native nations in the U.S. operate under are typically remarkable for their lack of separations of powers and for the power typically created for the tribal chairperson. Judicial appointments, funding, and functions are usually delegated to the council under provisions as vague in their entirety as:

> [The Tribal Council shall have the power to] promulgate and enforce ordinances, which shall be subject to review by the Secretary of the Interior, governing the conduct of members of the tribe, and providing for the maintenance of law and order and the administration of justice by establishing a reservation court and defining its duties and powers.[61]

The chairperson-centric character of government under such systems commonly emanates from the fact that the tribal chairperson simultaneously (1) is the chief executive administrator of the tribal government's various departments, programs, and enterprises, (2) chairs the tribal council, and (3) has secured a majority of the tribal council votes by explicitly or implicitly bringing into office his or her own factional slate of council members. The chairperson's power is further enhanced when she or he is directly elected by the tribal citizens (as opposed to being appointed parliamentary-style by, and hence more beholden to, the tribal council).

Notwithstanding the lack of separations of powers and the concentrations of power in the chairperson under IRA and IRA-derived constitutions, such governing structures are not without their successes. Both Mississippi Choctaw and Mescalero Apache, for example, operate under strong chief executive systems, and both have been notable for their aggressive assertions of sovereignty, investments in indigenous identity, and economic development. It is instructive that, in both cases, long-standing cultural norms have sanctioned chief executives and chiefs with powers to control national community affairs, appoint sub-executives, and otherwise wield substantial legitimate authority.[62] The very long length of service of Chief Philip Martin at Mississippi Choctaw and the late Chairman Wendell Chino at Mescalero is consistent with cultural support for strong chief executives in their respective societies.

But just as there are cases of effective chairperson-centric government under IRA-style constitutions, there are also numerous cases in which the combination of the lack of separation of powers and a powerful chief executive has led Indian nations down the path of hardship. Perhaps no case is as illustrative of this as that of the Oglala Sioux Tribe (OST) of the Pine Ridge Reservation under the Richard Wilson administration of the first half of the 1970s. Culminating in the civil strife and violence of Wounded Knee II, Wilson's control over the IRA government's council and OST law enforcement and the rebellion against that control have left lasting wounds and mistrust of the OST government to this day.[63] The generic shortcomings of IRA-style chairperson-centric government are most evident in the absence of cultural match between such government and indigenous norms eschewing the centralization of power in a strong national government with a powerful chief executive. The decentralizing and parliamentary cultural norms of the Lakota, for example, clearly have been out of synch with OST's IRA constitution. In the cases of nations such as Hopi and Tohono O'odham, long-standing cultural norms may expect and respect empowerment of single individuals, but see legitimate political authority as properly vested at the sub-national district or village level.[64] After decades of IRA-originating centralization of power, money, and employment options, it is understandably hard to budge the status quo through constitutional reform that might more closely accord with Hopi, Tohono O'odham, and many other tribes' cultural norms.[65]

In addition to mismatches between cultural norms that do not support concentration of power and authority in single offices or individuals at the national level, governmental failures under such concentration can also be laid at the feet of poor leadership and poor organization. When cultural norms support concentration of power and authority in the hands of the chief executive, what happens when the officeholder turns out to be unable to perform required functions because of lack of knowledge, poor leadership capacities, and/or systems and affairs that are too much for one individual to handle? Here, the case of the Mississippi Choctaw is instructive. With thousands of employees, hundreds of millions of dollars of business enterprises, and assumption of the entirety of governmental programs and services, Chief Martin has directed a focused process of building up the nation's bureaucratic and managerial capacity; the nation's operations have simply become too large and complicated to be run entirely out of the chief executive's office.[66]

The contrary outcome appears to have become the fate of the White Mountain Apache Tribe of Arizona. Touted in the late 1980s and early 1990s as one of the success stories of policies of self-determination and boasting a strong economy and improving social conditions, the nation had followed a path of aggressively asserting its sovereignty under the leadership of a long-serving, forceful, and charismatic chairman. This chairman and his successors, however, have operated in a setting in which chief executive authority is culturally sanctioned to the point of permitting it to overrun the nation's institutional framework. The inability to build and solidify organizational structures—from personnel systems to budgeting processes—that are durable in the face of citizens' expectation that the chief executive should and will control the details of tribal affairs has left the tribe in managerial and political disarray.[67] This has reversed the trend toward economic well-being and sociocultural sovereignty. Driving home the point that effective constitutional rule requires both cultural match and operational effectiveness, the White Mountain Apache are under considerable pressure for cultural change. Norms of strong, centralized leadership are in conflict with the need to build institutional capacity that can handle large and sophisticated enterprises, programs, and policies that are beyond the capacity of any one individual.

Council Powers

The extreme of the lack of separation of powers in Indian governments occurs under General Council constitutions. The "General Council" is typically the entire adult population of the nation, and constitutes its law-making body. A number of Indian nations' constitutions leave such matters as referendum, removal of elected officials from office, approval of constitutional changes, and approval of land transfers to the General Council, but also provide for a representative legislature (e.g., an elected tribal council, executive committee, or business committee) with true law-making and related legislative powers.[68] When this is not done and essentially all substantive decisions are left to the general populace acting as the General Council, results are typically disastrous for the nation.

The Crow Tribe of Montana is perhaps the preeminent example of the consequences of governance under a General Council system. Crow operated until 2001 under a 1948 constitution that was first drafted by a non-Crow, non-Indian attorney from a town bordering the reservation. The 1948 constitution provided for a quarterly General Council meeting of all voting-age adults. A quorum was achievable with only one hundred attendees (in a tribe numbering more than six thousand as of 2000), and an executive committee had governing powers that were effectively limited to setting the agenda for General Council meetings.[69] Under such a regime, which bore no resemblance to the Crows' traditional system of a Council of Clans and a Council of Warriors with parliamentary selection of executives, the implied power vacuum was filled by well-organized factions led by persuasive and charismatic individuals. Unchecked by constitutional delineations and separations of powers, the Crow government in which power was nominally shared in common by all became a primary vehicle for commandeering resources and employment, creating a political tragedy of the commons in which instability and disorganization were extreme. Despite abundant natural resources and a deep cultural respect for education, by the end of the reign of the 1948 Constitution, only about 10 percent of adults at Crow had employment, simmering political violence constantly threatened national well-being, non-Crow economic and political interests generally were able to steamroll over disorganized and unstable tribal institutions, and the last three tribal chairs were convicted of federal felonies.

With the vested interests and political culture developed under the 1948 constitution, it is hardly surprising that the effort in 2001 to create an otherwise commendable three-branch system that draws upon the legitimacy of local leaders as legislators and provides for strong separations of powers[70] was adopted amid turmoil and with little consensus, and has faced numerous grassroots and legal challenges. It remains to be seen whether the Crow will extract their nation from dysfunction. But it is clear that this dysfunction has not been the product of something inherently *Crow;* it has been the product of the cruel experiment that was run at Crow by placing it under a culturally foreign and practically inept constitution.

While IRA and IRA-derived constitutions have tended toward empowerment of the chief executive at the expense of the legislature, and the General Council systems, at the extreme, turn the legislature into an all-powerful mob, in the middle are systems that strike varying balances between executive and legislature. A number of Indian nations have begun indigenously to rebuild their constitutional structures so as to enhance the separation of powers between executive and council. At the Navajo Nation and under the new Crow constitution of 2001, for example, the tribal chief executive no longer chairs the tribal council (legislature). Rather, a speaker of the legislature serves as chair of the council, with the chief executive required to submit budgets, appointments, and legislative proposals at arm's length. In the case of the Confederated Salish and Kootenai Tribes of the Flathead Reservation, as noted, the tribal chairperson is a member of the council and is selected parliamentarily from the council by fellow council members. Separation of powers is achieved through the constitutional office of an executive secretary, a well-developed civil service system for personnel, and a strikingly efficient and independent tribal court.[71]

The Confederated Salish and Kootenai Tribes of the Flathead Reservation illustrate another aspect of effective Indian government—stability through constitutional structure. Under the Flathead constitution, council members serve staggered four-year terms and are elected at the district level through a system of primary elections and then a final election contest between the top two vote getters from the primary election. For those tribes choosing to elect their council members, staggered terms of office provide for continuity of policy and transference of procedural and issue knowledge from "seniors" to "juniors" (as one Flathead council member described it).

Policy continuity is largely destroyed if wholesale turnover of a council occurs, and is magnified in systems where turnover of elected officials is accompanied by removal of appointed tribal administrators allied with outgoing council members: Where do the negotiations with the senator on needed federal legislation stand? What have our practices been on finding a contractor for trash removal? What's the deadline for submitting the grant proposal for the anti-diabetes program? Have we met the terms of the financing agreement with Merrill Lynch? Answers to such questions not only determine whether a tribe can act appropriately to meet its needs; they also determine how nontribal actors perceive the Indian nation and its reliability and competence. Primary elections aid stability by reducing the cycling endemic to multi-option democratic voting, and they aid legitimacy by ensuring that successful candidates have the support of at least the majority of voting citizens.

An ongoing legacy of the eras of first federal Indian agents employing tribal councils to deliver those agents' edicts, employment, and goods, and then tribal councils serving as the conduits for all manner of federal programs, is that tribal councils on many reservations have long-running histories of being intimately involved in departments, programs, and enterprises. Indeed, numerous tribes operate under a system of administration in which individual council members serve, effectively, as executive department heads (often accompanied by commensurate additions to their compensation). Thus, one council member may chair the Natural Resources Committee, another the Enterprise Board, another the Housing Committee, and yet another the Education Committee . . . and so on.

The combination of at least two forces is increasingly putting pressure on the Council-as-Administrator approach to Native nations' executive functions. First, such intimate day-to-day involvement of a nation's lawmakers maximizes opportunity for council members to micromanage administrative affairs and employment—to their own and/or their supporters' advantage. The resulting damage to the nation's rule of law (e.g., as the contract for the headquarters' office cleaning service is let on criteria other than performance, as the ability to get and hold a job is weighted toward political influence or connection, as the tribal court decision is overturned by removing the tribal judge, and so forth) manifests itself as inefficiency in communities that can hardly afford wasting budget dollars and, even more critically, a loss in citizen respect for tribal government. The latter shows itself in the frequency with which the lack of separation of powers between council-as-legislature and executive administration is met with citizen complaints to the effect that "those council members are just like other politicians" (as opposed to legislative leaders who are setting policy for and charting the course of the nation). Conversely, more than one tribal council member and chairperson has remarked to the effect that putting in place an independent personnel grievance system, clear hiring standards, or a formal contract bidding system "gives me the insulation I need so that I can do my job and I'm not always having to respond to every little complaint or request."

The deleterious effects of a lack of delineation of a separation of powers between council and executive functions are increasingly compounded by a second factor: the demands placed on council members by the increasing role and sophistication of tribal government. As Indian nations take over (e.g., under P.L. 638 and related legislation) more and more of governmental functions, as they initiate more and more programs and policies to meet needs that state and federal governments simply do not address on reservations, and as economic development and business enterprises grow, tribal council members simply cannot be expected to handle the workload of executive administration. This "practical fact," however, can be a source of political and even cultural strain. The change and job insecurity that accompany the pressure on Indian governments to get increasingly formalized, computerized, and regimented can paint itself in tribal politics as the conflict between "the Native way" and "the way of the dominant society." Where this political reaction speaks to underlying cultural reality (as in tribes where long-standing traditions and norms expect tribal leaders to administer directly to the needs of individual community members), those cultural traditions and norms are under strain—because failing to separate politics from day-to-day administration repeatedly shows up across Indian Country as a primary cause of failed programs, policies, and enterprises.

Cultural stress of the foregoing type does not imply that assimilation to the dominant society's methods of governmental administration is necessary or desirable. First, "culture" is made of innumerable subtle actions and practices. When sovereignty is exercised and a community's own are in charge, the injection of a Native community's distinctly indigenous values and norms into a well-run health program,[72] a top-flight school,[73] a tribal foster care program that is so efficiently run that it usurps the neighboring county's role and moves placement of Indian children in Indian homes from zero to 100 percent,[74] or a crackerjack court system,[75] occurs consciously and unconsciously across myriad dimensions—from the hours of operation to the demeanor of the staff to the reasons certain days are no-work days. Second, increasing anecdotal evidence suggests that being in charge is what counts. Well-documented cases of extremely well-run tribal institutions, such as the enterprises and governmental programs of the Mississippi Choctaw, the for-profit and not-for-profit activities of HoChunk Inc., the recognized competency of governmental administration at Gila River, and the wholesale assertion of self-governance at Flathead,[76] appear to be accompanied by a resurgence in community pride (including, in some instances, increases in Native language use and observance of Native traditions). That is, without recognition under any of a number of stereotypes, effective tribal governance creates communities where "it used to be that everyone wanted to move away, but now they're all coming back."

Judicial Powers

Perhaps in no other dimension of self-government are Indian nations better teaching the world that universal tasks of government— i.e., law enforcement and dispute resolution—need not be prototypically Western than in the area of judicial affairs. They are doing so by answering the universal challenge of independent enforcement and dispute resolution with distinctly Native approaches.

Arguably, no dimension of self-government embodies political sovereignty more than a community's running of its own law enforcement and court system. For it is in such conduct, with its potential and (if need be) actual use of coercive force, that a community's institutions of self-determination most starkly cross over from civic organization to *government*. In so doing, they directly or indirectly compel the conduct of their own citizens, but they also challenge the jurisdiction of other governments who might wish to assert governmental authority over those same citizens. From *Oliphant v. Suquamish Indian Tribe* and extending through to *Nevada v. Hicks* and *U.S. v. Lara,* it is no wonder that so many key U.S. legal challenges to Indian nation sovereignty in the present era of aggressive self-assertion by tribal governments center on the powers of Indian nation courts and police.[77]

In this environment, the premium on politically independent and functionally competent tribal judicial systems is particularly high. The U.S. courts consistently reveal a certain mistrust of tribal judiciaries, particularly as they relate to civil rights and U.S. constitutional protections for non-Indians. The reining in of Indian nation sovereignty is commonly threatened and implemented on such grounds.[78] Toward the end of defending tribes' jurisdiction and sovereignty, many tribes' constitutions contain a bill of rights. The Chickasaw Nation Constitution's bill of rights, for example, provides:

> Nothing in this Constitution shall be interpreted in a way
> which would change the individual rights and privileges the
> tribal members have as citizens of the Chickasaw Nation, the
> State of Oklahoma, and the United States of America. . . . All
> political power is inherent in the people, and all free governments are founded on their authority, and instituted for their
> benefit; and they have at all times the inalienable right to
> alter, reform or abolish their form of government in such a
> manner as they may think expedient; provided, such action is
> taken pursuant to this Constitution. . . . No religious test shall
> ever be required as a qualification for any office of public
> trust in this Nation. . . . Every citizen shall be at liberty to
> speak, write, or publish his opinions on any subject, being
> responsible for the abuse of that privilege, and no law shall
> ever be passed curtailing the liberty of speech, or of the press.
> . . . The citizens shall have the right, in a peaceable manner,
> to assemble together for their common good, and to apply to

those invested with powers of government for redress of grievances or other purposes, by address, or remonstrance.

As noted above, for so many Indian nations, the problem of an independent judiciary arises from the fact that their original constitutions were adopted at a time in which it was not foreseen that these nations would be seeking to exert such broad powers of sovereign jurisdiction as they do today. Accordingly, constitutional reform for many tribes has entailed adoption of explicit protections for the independence of the judiciary. The constitution of the Cheyenne River Sioux Tribe, for example, now provides that:

> . . . the Tribal Council shall establish courts for the adjudication of claims or disputes arising among or affecting the Cheyenne River Sioux Tribe or any Indian present on the Cheyenne River Indian Reservation, and for the trial and punishment of Indians charged with the commission of offenses prescribed [*sic*] by ordinances of the Tribal Council. Decisions of tribal courts may be appealed to the tribal appellate courts, but shall not be subject to review by the Tribal Council.[79]

The constitution of the Citizen Potawatomi Nation provides for both judicial independence and Potawatomi Supreme Court review of legislative constitutionality:

> The judicial power of the Citizen Potawatomi Nation is hereby vested in one Supreme Court consisting of seven (7) Justices and such inferior courts as may be established by Tribal law . . . The Courts of the Citizen Potawatomi Nation shall be courts of general jurisdiction and shall further have jurisdiction in all cases arising under the Constitution, Laws and Treaties of the Citizen Potawatomi Nation. The Supreme Court shall have original jurisdiction in such cases as may be provided by law, and shall have appellate jurisdiction in all cases . . . The Tribal Courts, in any action brought before them, shall have the power of judicial review, in appropriate cases, in order to declare that legislative enactments of the Business Committee or the Council, are unconstitutional under the Constitution or prohibited by federal statutes and void.[80]

In the case of Navajo, the Navajo Code protects judicial independence. Even more importantly, the Navajo Supreme Court, having had its independence and authority tested in the showdown over the Peter MacDonald affair,[81] is protected by the palpable, unwritten, cultural commitment of the nation's leadership to the three-branch separation of powers. As I noted above in making the point that judicial independence does not have to look at all "Western," Cochiti's traditional theocracy provides that its senior theocrat, the *cacique,* can be disciplined or removed from office for negligence of duty or wrongdoing. In their own versions of judicial authority and independence, tribes such as Yakama and Rosebud Sioux have experimented with tribal ethics boards, usually made up of elders, able to oversee the behavior of council members and other government officials.[82]

As noted above, the objective data indicate that an independent court system, not subject to usurpation of its authority and decisions by the legislature or the chief executive, adds substantially to the ability of Indian nations to sustain economic development and create employment on their respective reservations. In this regard, tribal governments are similar to states: The independence and adherence to a rule of law of U.S. state courts is positively related to a state's economic fortunes; and a politicized court is routinely associated with lower levels of citizen economic well-being.[83] States such as Mississippi, West Virginia, and Alabama are among the poorest in the nation. Not coincidentally, they are routinely ranked by the U.S. Chamber of Commerce as the worst state court systems in the United States on measures such as judges' impartiality, judges' competence, and fairness.[84]

In a similar vein, research on tribal governmental programs finds that a primary predictor of whether an Indian nation's housing programs are efficient and sustainable is the presence or absence of an independent tribal court. The presence of an independent court substantially improves the performance of governmental programs such as housing. The reasons for the clarity of these linkages lie, in part, in the fact that most tribes are relatively small polities; everyone seems to be related to everyone else. If, for example, the new tribal chair removes the past tribal chair's nephew from his position as a perfectly competent accountant for the housing department, in contravention of both the tribe's personnel policies and restrictions of tribal council meddling in hiring and firing, the independent tribal court can successfully overturn the new chair's actions and have its decision stick. If, on the other hand, faced with such a court ruling, the tribal chair can effectively overturn the court by firing the judges or getting the council to cut off the court's funding, two lessons are transmitted through the community: Political connectedness, rather than competence, is the path to job security, and the decisions of the tribal court can be disrespected to political or personal advantage. The politicization of the issue might even precipitate a political crisis, as the past tribal chair undertakes to recall the sitting tribal chair from office.

As the United States itself learned through *Marbury v. Madison* in 1803 and repeatedly through FDR's attempt at court-packing,[85] establishing and protecting the independence of a nation's judiciary is an unending challenge. Quite understandably, when the judiciary is endowed with "the last word" in litigation, removal of officials for office, and review of the constitutionality of legislative and executive actions, there are always those who are not satisfied and want to have the last word—by appealing to the council, by removing the deciding judge, by choking funding for the court. Yet there has to be a last word. Without it, the rules of the game are hostage to politics, individuals and institutions are perpetually incented to invest in influencing the outcomes of governmental processes, and the rule of tribal law is at risk. Investments of effort, ideas, energy, and money in such a community are discouraged. In no other area of self-governance is legitimacy so important. If citizen and leader support for the sanctity of the nation's judicial institutions wanes, opposition to raids on those institutions will not burn with indignation, and usurpation will be more likely.

The legitimacy of Indian nation judicial systems is enhanced by policies of self-determination and the exercise of de facto sovereignty by those nations' governments. When tribes can design and control their own courts, the prospects are improved for producing law enforcement and courts whose procedures and actions are consonant with the culture and values of the community. Indian nations that take over the policing on their reservations, for example, not only improve law enforcement service; they also help their citizens to be more satisfied with the policing, and to see the police and related institutions as being both their own and more legitimate.[86] The matching of cultural norms to governmental function is particularly obvious in the operation of indigenously designed courts and alternative dispute resolution systems. Innovations such as the Peacemaker courts of Navajo, Seneca, Grand Traverse, and a number of other Indian nations directly apply non-Western procedures and values in the adjudication of civil disputes. The description of Peacemaker courts at Navajo by the nation's chief justice at once illustrates the infusion of *Navajo* values into the Navajo Nation's judicial system and expresses the principle of the rule of law under which all are equal before the bar of justice:

> The Navajo Peacemaker Court takes advantage of the talents of a *naat'aanii*. That is a traditional Navajo civil leader who is chosen by the community to be the "peacemaker" for his or her demonstrated abilities—wisdom, integrity, good character, and respect by the community. The civil authority of a *naat'aanii* is not coercive or commanding; it is a leadership role in the truest sense of the word. A peacemaker is a person who thinks well, speaks well, shows a strong reverence for the basic teachings of life, and has respect for himself or herself and others in personal conduct. A *naat'aanii* functions as a guide, and views everyone—rich or poor, high or low, educated or not—as an equal. The peacemaker attempts to bring participants to a final decision that everyone agrees to for the benefit of all. A *naat'aanii* is chosen for knowledge, and knowledge is the power which creates the ability to persuade others.[87]

Interestingly, Peacemaker concepts are entering Western institutions: The initiation of family courts in the U.S. mainstream, which emphasize noncoercive and nonadversarial dispute resolution, represent Western institutions moving toward the Indian way. At the same time, the movement toward inculcation of *tribal* common law as the guiding principle of the substance and processes of Indian nations' judicial systems at nations such as Navajo, Pasqua Yaqui, Flathead, various Pueblos, and many others represents Native communities' use of a concept (common law) iconically associated with Anglo jurisprudence, but rendered distinctively indigenous in the hands of self-governing Native nations.[88] Same problems, different culturally matched solutions.

NOTES

The author of this chapter, Joseph P. Kalt, is the Ford Foundation Professor of International Political Economy, John F. Kennedy School of Government, Harvard University, and co-director of the Harvard Project on American Indian Economic Development (www.ksg.harvard.edu/hpaied).

1. Hon. Albert Hale, former president, Navajo Nation, Initiative on American Indian Constitutional Reform, Cambridge, Massachusetts, April 2, 2001.

2. Joseph Kalt and Joseph Singer, *"Myths and Realities of Tribal Sovereignty: The Law and Economics of Indian Self-Rule,"* Native Issues Research Symposium, Harvard University Native American Program, December 2003.

3. See the body of research of the Harvard Project on American Indian Economic Development, Harvard University, at http://www.ksg.harvard.edu/hpaied.

4. I.e., referring to sovereignty according to jurisprudence, or "under the law"; in this case, according to U.S. federal and/or international law. See Kalt and Singer, *Myths and Realities*.

5. I.e., referring to sovereignty "in fact," or in practice, being the actual making and successful implementing of governmental decisions (sometimes in the absence of or in contradiction to de jure sovereignty).

6. Robert Porter, "Strengthening Tribal Sovereignty through Government Reform: What Are the Issues," *Kansas Journal of Law and Public Policy* 7 (Winter 1997): 72.

7. Richard Real Bird, chairman, Crow Tribe of Montana, on the occasion of introducing a proposed new constitution for the Crow Tribe, April 1989.

8. See, for example, Vine Deloria, Jr., and Clifford Lytle, *The Nations Within: The Past and Future of American Indian Sovereignty* (Pantheon Press, 1984), 212.

9. Charles H. Lange, *Cochiti: A New Mexico Pueblo Past and Present* (University of New Mexico Press, 1990).

10. Stephen Cornell and Joseph P. Kalt, "Successful Economic Development and Heterogeneity of Governmental Form on American Indian Reservations," in *Getting Good Government: Capacity Building in the Public Sector of Developing Countries,* ed. Merilee S. Grindle (Harvard University Press, 1997).

11. Stephen Cornell and Joseph P. Kalt, "Where Does Economic Development Really Come From? Constitutional Rule among the Contemporary Sioux and Apache," *Economic Inquiry* 33 (July 1995): 402–426.

12. Ibid.

13. See, for example, Raymond J. DeMallie, "Pine Ridge Economy: Cultural and Historical Perspectives," in *American Indian Economic Development,* ed. Sam Stanley (The Hague: Mouton Press, 1978), 247.

14. Tracy Becker, Introduction, "Traditional American Indian Leadership: A Comparison with U.S. Governance," American Indian Policy Center, Washington, D.C., 1997.

15. DeMallie, "Pine Ridge Economy," 248.

16. Ibid.

17. Stephen Cornell and Joseph P. Kalt, "Cultural Evolution and Constitutional Public Choice: Institutional Diversity and Economic Performance on American Indian Reservations," in *Uncertainty and Economic Evolution: Essays in Honor of Armen A. Alchian,* ed. John Lott (Routledge Press, 1997).

18. To be sure, these shared cultural traits are not universal across societies; societies differ dramatically in the social norms that undergird their institutions,

including their institutions of government. Thus, for example, it can be true (albeit overgeneralized from a reading of Ojibwe tradition) that "[t]raditional American Indian leadership displayed several distinct characteristics that developed out of a longstanding history of cultural traditions and values. American Indians lived holistically. They understood themselves to be interconnected with all physical and spiritual forms of life, and they did not compartmentalize their physical, emotional, intellectual and spiritual lives. Spirituality was a fundamental cornerstone of American Indian culture, and leadership was one of the ways the culture was sustained and nurtured"; and that, as leaders, "Ojibwe elders, for example, had a special kinship with manitous, or spirits, that validated their status as elders and leaders" (from Tracy Becker, *Traditional American Indian Leadership,* citing B. Johnston, *Ojibway Ceremonies* [University of Nebraska Press, 1982], in the latter instance). At the same time, the social norms and cultural underpinnings of American and other Western European leadership and governance clearly link back to the special relationship of those cultures and its founding elders to the Greek classical philosophers. The subjugation of Ojibwe traditional governance by the Western European diaspora makes the desire to "deconstruct" governance to mean "rooted in European political philosophy and tradition, and [denoting] a bureaucratic organizational system of legitimate public power" (Becker, *Traditional American Indian Leadership,* Introduction) understandable, but misses the points that sustained Native and non-Native polities of collective adherence and action have universally required "organizational systems of legitimate public power," while the particular cultural foundations and practical designs of such systems have differed dramatically across such polities.

19. Jack Hirshleifer, "Comment," in *Journal of Law and Economics* (August 1976): 241–244.

20. James Buchanan and Gordon Tullock, *The Calculus of Consent* (University of Michigan Press, 1971), 5–6. The same concept is found in the work of scholars ranging from Robert Putnam, *Making Democracy Work: Civic Traditions in Modern Italy* (Princeton University Press, 1992), to Douglass C. North, *Institutions, Institutional Change, and Economic Performance* (Cambridge University Press, 1990).

21. Sam McClellan, Constitutional Reform Committee, Grand Traverse Band of Ottawa and Chippewa Indians, *Initiative on American Indian Constitutional Reform,* Harvard Project on American Indian Economic Development, at Executive Session, October 13, 2001.

22. The implicit linking of "coercion" and "Native" here contradicts contemporary popular "natural-man" stereotyping in which at least precontact indigenous peoples are represented as free of conflict and even the need for legitimate coercion. Such stereotyping is not only bizarrely counterfactual, but it is also dehumanizing of indigenous peoples: As human beings, indigenous people have always confronted the conflicting human tendencies of coordination and competition. As it influences contemporary Native self-perception, such stereotyping also diverts the challenges of Native nation building toward wishful recovery of some fanciful

golden age of unanimity and perfect voluntarism in collective action, and away from the real-world task of Native institution (re)building following the decades of non-Indian subjugation and destruction of Native institutions of self-rule.

23. Note that in this conception, externally coerced or dictatorially imposed constitutions are admitted. That is, a dictatorship can have a constitution by which it makes decisions and rules, and under which it structures its enforcement of decisions and rules of conduct. Our focus, here, however, is on polities in which there is, in substantial measure, "consent of the governed." Certainly, this describes U.S. American Indian tribes—if for no other reason than the fact that their citizens are accorded freedom of movement and can withdraw consent de facto by exiting the tribal polity and jurisdiction.

24. See the *Initiative on American Indian Constitutional Reform,* Harvard Project on American Indian Economic Development, at http://www.ksg.harvard.edu/reform.

25. See Peter J. Ferrara, *The Choctaw Revolution: Lessons for Federal Indian Policy* (Washington, D.C.: Americans for Federal Tax Reform Foundation, 1998).

26. See Stephen Cornell, *Statement to the House of Commons Standing Committee on Aboriginal Affairs and Northern Development,* Ottawa, June 6, 2000.

27. Cornell and Kalt, "Successful Economic Development."

28. Chief Philip Martin, Mississippi Choctaw, *Address,* Harvard University, September 29, 1998, on the occasion of being asked what the much-touted economic development at Mississippi Choctaw was doing to Choctaw society and culture (with the questioner apparently unaware of the investments in health, language, and public safety of the Mississippi Choctaw Nation). On the latter, see *Honoring Contributions in the Governance of American Indian Nations,* Harvard Project on American Indian Economic Development, 1999 and 2003; see also Ferrara, *The Choctaw Revolution.*

29. http://www.learningenrichment.org/germany_stud.html.

30. Sam McClellan, Constitutional Reform Committee, Grand Traverse Band of Ottawa and Chippewa Indians, *Initiative on American Indian Constitutional Reform,* Harvard Project on American Indian Economic Development, at Executive Session, October 13, 2001.

31. For a generalized discussion outside of the American Indian context, see Robert D. Cooter, "The Rule of State Law and the Rule-of-Law State: Economic Analysis of the Legal Foundations of Development," in *Annual World Bank Conference on Development Economics 1996* (World Bank, 1996), 191.

32. See note 18.

33. Lange, *Cochiti Pueblo,* 373.

34. Fr. Noel Dumarest, "Notes on Cochiti, New Mexico," in *Memoirs of the American Anthropological Association,* no. 3 (1919): 197.

35. Esther Schiff Goldfrank, "The Social and Ceremonial Organization of Cochiti," in *Memoirs of the American Anthropological Association,* no. 33 (1927): 40.

36. Jack McIver Weatherford, *Indian Givers* (Random House, 1988).

37. Royal B. Hassrick, "Teton Dakota Kinship System," in *American Anthropologist* 46, no. 3 (July–September 1944): 338–347; Clark Wissler, "Societies and Ceremonial Associations in the Oglala Division of the Teton Dakota," in *Anthropological Papers of the American Museum of Natural History,* Vol. 1, part 1 (New York: The Trustees, 1912). Among other tribes, perhaps the most well-documented case of such judicial societies is that of the Dog Soldiers of the Cheyenne; see George Bird Grinnell, *Cheyenne Indians: Their History and Ways of Life* (University of Nebraska Press, 1923).

38. Lange, *Cochiti Pueblo,* 373.

39. Constitution and Bylaws of the Turtle Mountain Band of Chippewa Indians, Belcourt, ND, at www.tribalresourcecenter.org.

40. Constitution and By-Laws of the Pawnee Indians of Oklahoma at http://www.tribalresourcecenter.org.

41. Constitution of the Ho Chunk Nation at http://www.tribalresourcecenter.org.

42. As in "necessary, but not sufficient" for sustained governance.

43. Morris E. Opler, *An Apache Life-Way: The Economic, Social, and Religious Institutions of the Chiracahua Indians* (University of Chicago Press, 1941), 46, 468; Morris E. Opler, *Childhood and Youth in Jicarilla Apache Society,* Vol. 5 (Los Angeles: Hodge Publication Fund, 1946); Morris E. Opler, "An Outline of Chiracahua Apache Social Organization," in *Social Anthropology of North American Tribes,* ed. Fred Eggan (University of Chicago Press, 1937), 171–239, 235; Morris E. Opler, "Lipan Apache Culture," in *Southern Journal of Anthropology* 9 (1953): 92–95; Greenville Goodwin, *The Social Organization of the Western Apache* (University of Chicago Press, 1942), 165, 179, 676 (citing firsthand account of a chief's daughter); Ralph H. Ogle, *Federal Control of the Western Apaches* (University of New Mexico Press, 1970), 24–25 (based on firsthand accounts); Keith H. Basso, "Western Apache," in *Southwest Handbook of North American Indians,* Vol. 10, ed. Alfonso Ortiz (Smithsonian Institution, 1983).

44. Goodwin, *The Social Organization of the Western Apache;* Opler, *An Apache Life-Way;* Opler, "Lipan Apache Culture"; Pliny E. Goddard, *Indians of the Southwest,* Handbook Series No. 2 (American Museum of Natural History, 1921).

45. Translation by Edgar Perry, tribal cultural director, White Mountain Apache Tribe, personal interview, 1987.

46. Goodwin, *The Social Organization of the Western Apache,* 131, 164. More generally, see note 43 above.

47. James L. Haley, *Apaches: A History and Culture Portrait* (Doubleday and Company, 1981), 155.

48. Opler, *An Apache Life-Way;* Opler, "Lipan Apache Culture."

49. Goodwin, *The Social Organization of the Western Apache,* 181.

50. For the classic treatment, see Mancur Olson, *The Logic of Collective Action* (Schocken Books, 1971).

51. In Cornell and Kalt, "Cultural Evolution," we put forth a model in which action in support of maintenance of public goods such as constitutions and derivative governing institutions is individually rational in individuals who have preferences over social sentiments such as guilt, self-righteousness, belonging, and the like, and who have been acculturated by growing up and/or living in particular cultural contexts. Within those contexts, acculturation attaches the social sentiments to specific (albeit widely varying across cultures) ideological content as to the proper and the improper in the political realm, via processes of the personal internalization of social norms. As a result, the social entity that is a human being receives private consumption benefits and penalties (as if they were sugar and poison) when acting in accord with or contrary to acquired social norms with respect to the legitimate use of power and authority. For a somewhat similar treatment, although without the appeal to biology, see Robert Cooter, "Three Effects of Social Norms on Law: Expressiveness, Deterrence, and Internalization," in *Oregon Law Review* (September 2000): 1–22.

52. Cornell and Kalt, "Where Does Economic Development Really Come From?"

53. See Putnam, *Making Democracy Work.*

54. Cornell and Kalt, "Cultural Evolution."

55. See Harvard Project on American Indian Economic Development, *Native America at the New Millennium,* at www.ksg.harvard.edu/hpaied/pubs.

56. Cornell and Kalt, "Where's the Glue? Institutional and Cultural Foundations of American Indian Economic Development," in *Journal of Socio-Economics* 29 (2000).

57. Miriam Jorgensen, *Bringing the Background Forward: Evidence from Indian Country on the Social and Cultural Determinants of Economic Development,* Ph.D. diss., John F. Kennedy School of Government, Harvard University, June 2000.

58. Justice Joseph Flies-Away, *Initiative on American Indian Constitutional Reform,* Harvard Project on American Indian Economic Development, Executive Session, Mashantucket Pequot Tribal Nation, October 17, 2002.

59. John C. Mohawk, "Onondaga," in *Encyclopedia of North American Indians* at http://college/hmco.com/history/readerscomp/naind.

60. By "collective organization decisions" I mean such decisions as whether the nation should go into gaming, should the nation file that lawsuit, should the nation create a department of education, and so on.

61. Taken from the *Constitution and Bylaws of the Rosebud Sioux Tribe of South Dakota* (as adopted in 1935 and as of amendments of 1973), www.tribalresourcecenter.org.

62. A brief synopsis of Choctaw political systems is provided by http://www.runningdeerslonghouse.com. On Western Apache, see Cornell and Kalt, "Where Does Economic Development Really Come From?"

63. See www.library.ucla.edu/libraries/college/nwsevnts/exhibits/wdknee/ for a brief history and links to further readings.

64. On Tohono O'odham indigenous political structure, see Peter MacMillan Booth, "Tohono O'odham (Papago)," in Encyclopedia of North American Indians at http://college.hmco.com/history/readerscomp/naind/html/na_039300_tohonooodham.htm. On Hopi indigenous political structure, see the Hopi Tribe's description at http://www.hopi.nsn.us/history.asp; see also, for example, http://www.nativeamericans.com/Hopi.htm. Some report that the original vote on the Hopi IRA constitution was widely boycotted by the Hopi, and only adopted because of BIA corruption; see http://www.cinprograms.org/history/1845topresent.html.

65. A constitutional reform effort has been under way at Hopi for a number of years, but is reportedly stalled, in part because of village leaders' dissatisfaction with proposed continuation of a relatively strong national-level system. Tohono O'odham reformed its constitution in 1986, but left budgetary control in the central national Tohono O'odham government. Discussion as to how to tap into the legitimacy of district-level government continues.

66. See Ferrara, *The Choctaw Revolution*.

67. See the ongoing press coverage and reader commentary in the *White Mountain Independent*. Sample issues include Jo Baeza, "'Pandemonium' Unleashed on the Apache Tribe" (re: personnel firings) (May 7, 2004) and Jo Baeza, "Independent Investigator Finds Evidence of Malfeasance; Tribe May Have to Return $13 Million to Federal Government" (March 26, 2004).

68. For an example, see Constitution of the Citizen Potawatomi Nation at www.thorpe.edu.

69. Constitution and Bylaws of the Crow Tribal Council of Montana, June 1948, at www.lib.lbhc.cc.mt.us.

70. Crow Tribal Constitution at www.tribalresourcecenter.org.

71. Cornell and Kalt, "Successful Economic Development."

72. See the numerous cases of health programs in *Honoring Contributions in the Governance of American Indian Nations,* Harvard Project on American Indian Economic Development, 1999–2003.

73. See the case of Ya Ne Dah Ah School in *Honoring Contributions in the Governance of American Indian Nations,* Harvard Project on American Indian Economic Development, 2002.

74. See the case of Fond du Lac foster care in *Honoring Contributions in the Governance of American Indian Nations,* Harvard Project on American Indian Economic Development, 1999.

75. See the cases of the Northwest Intertribal Court System and the Navajo Nation Supreme Court in *Honoring Contributions in the Governance of American Indian Nations,* Harvard Project on American Indian Economic Development, 2003 and 1999, respectively.

76. See the case of Flathead Trust Resource Management in *Honoring Contributions in the Governance of American Indian Nations,* Harvard Project on American Indian Economic Development, 2003.

77. Certainly, taxation cases run a close second—for similar reasons.

78. Kalt and Singer, "Myths and Realities," 16–21.

79. Constitution and By-Laws of the Cheyenne River Sioux Tribe at http://www.tribalresourcecenter.org/ccfolder/cheyenne_sioux_const.htm.

80. Constitution of the Citizen Potawatomi Nation at www.thorpe.edu.

81. See, for example, *New York Times,* February 12, 1989, Section 4, at 7.

82. Cornell and Kalt, "Reloading the Dice: Improving Chances for Economic Development on American Indian Reservations," in *What Can Tribes Do? Strategies and Institutions in American Indian Economic Development,* ed. Cornell and Kalt (UCLA American Indian Studies Program, 1992), 1–59.

83. See Harris Interactive (Harris Poll), *2003 U.S. Chamber of Commerce State Liability Systems Ranking Study* at http://www.caltax.org/HarrisSurvey2003.pdf.

84. Harris Interactive (Harris Poll) (2003).

85. See, for example, "Court-Packing Plan" at http://college.hmco.com/history/readerscomp/rcah/html.

86. Stewart Wakeling, Miriam Jorgensen, Susan Michaelson, and Manley Begay, *Policing on American Indian Reservations* (U.S. Department of Justice, National Institute of Justice, 2001).

87. See, for example, Robert Yazzie (Chief Justice, Navajo Supreme Court), "Life Comes from It: Navajo Justice," *Ecology of Justice* (Spring 1994): 29.

88. For a detailed analysis, see Robert D. Cooter and Wolfgang Fikentscher, "Indian Common Law: The Role of Custom in American Indian Tribal Courts (Part I)," in *American Journal of Comparative Law* 46 (September 1998): 287–330.

Firsthand Accounts

Steven Chestnut, Lawyer, Northern Cheyenne Tribe
Carroll Onsae, Member, Hopi Tribe Constitutional
Reform Committee

STEVEN CHESTNUT, LAWYER, NORTHERN CHEYENNE TRIBE

I've represented the Northern Cheyenne for a long time.
I've just finished my twenty-eighth year, and it's the first tribe that I ever
did work for. I didn't know anything about Indians or Indian law when
I began. I've done work for the Cheyenne continuously since then and
for a number of other tribes. But I have to confess that there's nothing
like the Cheyenne. It's a great Indian tribe, tremendous history, brilliant
people, very poor, very, very principled.

The Northern Cheyenne reservation is very much intact and has
grown over the years. It began with something less than 300,000 acres
and is now about 450,000 acres. It is pristine and is 99 percent in Indian
hands in terms of ownership. The tribe owns 75 percent of the surface.
Individual Northern Cheyenne own, in trust, another 24 percent or so.
There's about 1 percent fee land on the reservation. The entire, extremely valuable subsurface of the reservation is owned by the tribe as a whole.
Land use on the reservation is virtually entirely Northern Cheyenne.

One of the amazing untold stories is that the Cheyenne have tremendous mineral wealth on their reservation—mineral wealth that, particularly given the economic, socioeconomic conditions on the reservation,
would have been developed by anybody, long ago, Indian or non-Indian.
And the tribe is being encircled increasingly by intense development
efforts, particularly with respect to coal bed methane, which started in

Wyoming and is now in Montana. But they've maintained control of the reservation. And in an act of unbelievable discipline, unparalleled I would say, perhaps in the world, they have denied themselves financial benefits that they could obtain if they were willing to make some measured sacrifice with respect to the sanctity of that land. But the tribe, notwithstanding the tremendous need, cannot bring themselves to harm their reservation. This has nothing to do with constitutional revision, but I'm just telling you a little bit about what I know about the tribe. They are a phenomenal tribe.

I worked with the tribe on constitutional revision and I will try to get into the specifics of what the tribe did. There are only three events in the constitutional history of the Northern Cheyenne: the original 1935 IRA BIA-prepared constitution, which was similar to all the others that were done; then in 1960, they did some limited amendments; then they waited another thirty-six years and in 1996 did another round of amendments. That round, the modern round of amendments, is a work in progress. I believe there will be additional amendments and I am going to discuss that as well.

In the early 1990s there was a constitution revision committee which worked for years. It was a fairly extensive public process. After a lot of interaction with the tribal government, written reports, newspaper reports, and a fair amount of publicity, a series of amendments were prepared in a wide variety of areas. As we came closer to getting them in place, the tribe decided to focus on certain specific, critical areas in the first round of constitutional amendments. There were other things that were done which are on the shelf, ready to be dusted off and considered, but we focused on governmental reform principally.

In the area of governmental reform the Northern Cheyenne had a twenty-four-person council at that time, which increased in size every two years. It was a council where members had two-year terms that all expired at the same time. So every two years there was a total turnover on the tribal council. I might add that the tribal council has traditionally been the most powerful unit of government on the reservation, as is true on many other reservations. This was truly a powerful tribal council, perhaps due to the history of the tribe and the Council of 44.

There were also episodes with very, very powerful executives. The tribe had a history of tribal presidents elected for four-year terms by the people, who served for long periods of time. When I began working for the tribe, the tribal president was a fellow named Alan Rowland, who many people know. He was a great and powerful Northern Cheyenne tribal president, and he served for sixteen years. Before him, an equally great and powerful tribal president, John Wooden Legs, served for many years. In more recent times there's been greater turnover in the executive branch.

In any event, in terms of governmental reform, the tribe decided to reduce the size of the council, and made it a permanent ten. There are five districts on the reservation that are traditional, separate communities. People have their own allegiance to their community. One of the communities is Bernie, which is extremely small and remote, and that's at one end of the spectrum in terms of size. Another community is Lame Deer, which is at the other end of the spectrum. One of the problems we had in constitutional reform, and in reducing the council to a permanent size of ten, plus a vice president, was to figure out how we could apportion the council among five communities, where one community had probably twenty times the population of another. If you figure out the math, you really can't allocate ten council members proportionately to the district populations.

So, the tribe came up with a mechanism, which I think may be unique to the Cheyenne, that allocated five of the ten council seats at one per district. So each district got one automatic seat. Then the remaining five seats were apportioned based on population. At this point, the district of Lame Deer has, I believe, four representatives, and the smallest district of Bernie has one, even though Lame Deer is twenty times bigger than Bernie.

Now this raised the question about one man, one vote. We had a concern about that. There were federal court decisions, based on the Indian Civil Rights Act, and the equal protection provision in particular, which tended to apply the one man, one vote standard to tribal elections. Northern Cheyenne devised a system to more or less accommodate that. What we did was adopt a primary system for the first time. We provided that the primary elections for these ten council seats would occur district by district, so that each district would have a voice, the only voice, in selecting the two final candidates to represent that district. And then we went to a general election which was reservation-wide for all seats. We felt that this process avoided a one man, one vote problem.

Another aspect of governmental reform that was adopted in 1996 was to establish a popularly elected vice president for the first time. The Northern Cheyenne tribal president had always been elected reservation-wide, at least under the IRA, for a four-year term. But in the prior system, the tribal council would choose a vice president from its own membership. Our change was to provide for the direct election, reservation-wide, of the tribal vice president, but give the tribal vice president a seat on the council.

We also extended the terms of the council. The terms of the council members had been two years; we made them four years. We staggered them so that every two years, five seats were open. None of that is revolutionary. I think it's been done in many different places.

Another thing the tribe wanted to do, which perhaps other tribes have done, was to increase the potency of the Northern Cheyenne vote in federal and state elections. So one of our changes was to make the tribal election date the same as the congressional, or presidential election date. This has worked well.

We adopted some other rules that were a product of the experience of the tribe. In the past, the twenty-four-person council met on a part-time basis. They met once a month except for special meetings. They had some committees which were more or less full time, but basically it was a part-time council. Going to a smaller council enabled the tribe to make the council a full-time body.

We also provided in the constitution that council members would receive a salary to the extent commensurate with the tribe's ability to pay, and that that would be all that they would get. Typically, the president, vice president, and council members have other responsibilities, like sitting on committees or on boards of tribal enterprises. Our change was to prohibit any additional compensation for service in these positions. As tribal leaders know, working for a tribe is more than a full-time job. And at Northern Cheyenne that's the case. Our concern was to avoid the appearance of council members supplementing their compensation by arranging for other assignments, other responsibilities, with additional compensation. At times, this has in fact created problems in Northern Cheyenne. So the tribe decided to ban this and said, if you're going to run for the council, or run for president or vice president, you're expected to serve the tribe full time, whatever that takes, and you'll get a specified salary which the tribe can afford. The tribe can't afford very much, by the way. It's a good deal for the tribe and it's accepted well on the reservation, and I think the people like that.

We got into a lot of other details. We did not follow the principle, which I think is probably a valid principle, of having a short, framework-oriented constitution. At least at Northern Cheyenne, we got into a lot of detail in the constitution. Mainly it was a product of the experience of the tribe. Over the years, elections and other issues created serious problems. The rules weren't clear. The council was, at times, fickle, at times arbitrary. I think it was felt by the Cheyenne that they wanted clear-cut, fairly detailed rules about how their government is going to work. So, when you look in the Northern Cheyenne constitutional revisions, you will notice that there's a fair amount of detail about the election process, about how the primaries work, about what happens if there's a tie in votes, provisions that lay out the rules as a matter of constitutional law for the tribe. The idea was to preempt the kind of creativity that the tribe has seen over the years in creating constitutional crises on the reservation in terms of the tribal government.

The Northern Cheyenne constitution, for the first time, now has a provision which adopts the principle of separation of powers for the Northern Cheyenne. They had not previously had that in their constitution. We pretty much used the standard language, and one of the kind of continuing matters of curiosity, and sometimes pretty intense, is what does that mean? What is separation of powers? It's certainly hard for me to explain, even though I was involved in putting that in. I've given some thought to it.

So the principle is there, but implementation is another question. What the tribe did, as a first step in implementing separation of powers, after the constitutional amendments were adopted, was to work on a new election ordinance, which is very detailed and tries to minimize post-election problems, post-election challenges. That effort took, I would say, about six or eight months to get everything in place after we passed the constitution. Then we used it in the first election under the new constitution. We have now used it in maybe seven or eight Northern Cheyenne reservation-wide elections since then, and it's worked pretty well. It was part of implementing the constitutional arrangement.

The second big step in implementing the constitutional arrangement was to draft a separation of powers ordinance to try to define, in some respects, what that means. We focused on the tribal court. The Northern Cheyenne tribal court is not a strong court. It's never been a strong court. The history had been that judges were appointed by the president with consent of the council. When unpopular decisions were made, the kind of normal things happened: judges were removed, decisions were reversed, decisions were disregarded. So the tribe created a new system for the tribal court in this very detailed separation of powers ordinance. It provided for the first time the election of tribal judges. And since 1997 the tribe has elected tribal judges on the reservation.

The separation of powers ordinance also attempts to address the issue of judicial review, which for nonlegal types means the question of whether or not the tribal court has authority to review and strike down actions of the tribal council. That had been an open question on the Northern Cheyenne reservation, and had never been clearly resolved. There is a point of view that the tribal court should not have power to strike down actions of the council. The Northern Cheyenne reservation has traditionally had, as I said earlier, a very strong tribal council, and there is a view that some people have that the tribal court should not have authority to strike down its actions. This is not the American view, but I think there are people in Indian Country who have that view, who believe that the tribal council should be supreme. There are also people, I believe, internationally, in other countries, who believe that the legislature is the ultimate authority, the most representative body. So it wasn't a given for the Northern Cheyenne that Northern Cheyenne courts would have authority to review the actions of this very powerful tribal council.

But in this separation of powers ordinance the Cheyenne took a first, measured step toward judicial review. They created, for the first time, a kind of blue ribbon court, which they called the Constitutional Court—a panel of three judges which has a very limited jurisdiction. It doesn't hear run-of-the-mill cases. It hears cases brought by litigants to strike down actions of the tribal council. The Northern Cheyenne Constitutional Court is given that limited jurisdiction and is given limited authority. The authority of the Northern Cheyenne Constitutional Court is, in a proper case, to review those actions, and to declare whether they are lawful or unlawful, and that's it. The ordinance says that the Court's declarations are binding on all branches of tribal government. So currently in the Northern Cheyenne system there is no authority to seek any relief, vis-à-vis an allegedly unlawful tribal council action other than a declaration, a binding declaration, on whether it's valid or invalid. There's no authority to seek damages, for example, against the tribe if the council action is declared invalid. This is an experiment for the tribe.

We also included in the separation of powers ordinance provisions which invite other courts—federal courts or state courts, which may be hearing a case with respect to the validity of tribal council action—to certify that question to the Northern Cheyenne Constitutional Court, and get a judgment of the Northern Cheyenne Constitutional Court with respect to the validity of the council action. We don't recognize jurisdiction in any other court to make that determination. About a week or so ago we got a certification from a state court in Forsyth, a local court, certifying a question to the Northern Cheyenne tribal court. These are experiments and we'll see how it all works out.

Another thing that the Constitutional Court does is have jurisdiction to hear complaints against tribal judges. I think it's similar to what the Cherokee have done with their [proposed] Court on the Judiciary, which, as I take it, is a court that polices the judicial branch in a sense. And the Northern Cheyenne, without any awareness that Cherokee did it, created similar jurisdiction in the Northern Cheyenne Constitutional Court. There had been a long history at Northern Cheyenne of people running to the council, dissatisfied with the decision of the court, asking the council to fire the judge or reverse the decision. It still happens, even after this ordinance. But under this new system the exclusive authority for hearing complaints for the removal of tribal court judges in this new system is the Constitutional Court. Again, this three-judge panel is likely to be the most nonpolitical decision-making body on the reservation. Having said all that, I recently got a call from the tribal president, who told me that the tribal council had just voted six to two to remove a judge. So you can write things down . . . Anyway, the separation of powers ordinance was very important for the tribe, and, I think, should be of some interest.

I didn't tell you all of the things that have been done in the first round of constitutional amendments. There were a lot of other detailed things that were done. But there are also a number of other subjects that the tribe intends to address, in a measured way, in the future. They want to address the qualifications of tribal officers. They want to upgrade the qualifications for president, vice president. One issue that has been a big headache at Northern Cheyenne, and I think has been a headache on many other reservations, is removal of the president and removal of council people. The tribe has never had recall on the reservation, which may be unique. Instead, there's an antiquated removal provision in the tribe's original constitution which has created tremendous mischief on the reservation. We simply have a removal provision that lacks due process procedures. This occurs when there's been a loss of confidence by the electorate in a particular member. You don't have to have any grounds. In response, the tribe has drafted a spiffy and well-thought-out removal provision which is going to be part of the next round. The tribe also wants to institute a recall procedure in the constitution.

We want to address enrollment standards and that's a difficult issue. I'm not sure how it's going to turn out. There's nothing drafted on this issue, but the principle, it's on the table. The tribe does want to address it.

We want to add a judicial article to the constitution. At this point the constitution, like others like it, simply says the tribal council has the authority to establish a tribal court and define its jurisdiction. That's still in the Northern Cheyenne constitution. I think we all view the separation of powers ordinance as a kind of a precursor to putting some of these protections directly into the tribal constitution. The last three years or so has been a dry run on seeing whether or not our changes are working. It's still an experiment.

One area that's important is the desire, in some way, to instill greater recognition for traditional matters in the tribal constitution, and to put in some sort of provision which tries to address some of the issues many members of the tribe are interested in. Talking about language, I can't speak the Cheyenne language. But, ironically, I've been going to Northern Cheyenne council meetings for twenty-eight years, and I think there's more Cheyenne spoken at Northern Cheyenne council meetings now, than ever before in my memory. There are more Cheyenne-speaking councilmen on the council than ever before. In the old days, when they didn't want me to understand, they would start talking Cheyenne. Now they do it routinely. Maybe they don't want me to understand anything, I don't know.

We have a few other ideas that we're thinking about. Sovereign immunity has been a problem, as we know, a problem in Congress, potentially. And since the tribal constitution only delegates powers to the council and to the officers, they only hold the powers that are delegated to them. We think that it may be good to limit the delegation with respect to sovereign immunity. So, irrespective of what Congress does, in terms of the powers that have been delegated by the people to their officers, there are restrictions that are inherent in that contract between tribal government and its people that Congress can't change. So we're thinking about putting in some sort of sovereign immunity type protection. We're giving it a shot, and seeing whether or not we can give the tribe another layer of protection that they don't currently have, instead of relying simply on general principles of sovereign immunity.

CARROLL ONSAE, MEMBER, HOPI TRIBE
CONSTITUTIONAL REFORM COMMITTEE

One of the reasons why the Hopi Tribe has engaged in constitutional reform is that things are changing, not only in the surrounding environment but within Hopi as well. Tradition, values, and culture are in a change process at this time within the Hopi people, and that process is pulling people apart in many ways. The tribal council thought that a revised constitution reflecting the basic core of Hopi values and tradition would help to pull back together the people as a group. The main thrust was to look at the constitution and its reform as a way to help keep intact the Hopi way of life and the traditional form of government, but yet develop a relationship with the outside world. Based on that, the tribe formed a constitution committee.

The Hopi Tribe is made up of twelve individual villages which are autonomous villages with their own governance, their own leaders, their own council and so on. However, the big difference is that the leadership in these villages cannot be equated to, for instance, the President of the United States, because the leadership is based on religion. The leader whom we call the *kikmongwi* is a religious leader.

We are an IRA tribe and we adopted a constitution back in 1936. One of the reasons why the Hopi Tribe developed its constitution is because the federal government wanted some organization to deal with. By dealing with this organization the federal government could send in dollars; and because of these dollars coming in the tribe needed some way to make decisions on how to use these dollars. The tribal government itself, because of the way the Hopi villages are set up, had to go out to these villages for some kind of concurrence or approval on expenditures. The people they would go to would be these traditional leaders, these religious leaders. But because it isn't their traditional role to say, "OK, this is how you spend this money," it created conflict and ambiguity in terms of the traditional form of governance. In some cases, unfortunately, these traditional leaders, the *kikmongwis,* used this to gain a form of power. They would say, "OK, we'll use it in this way and that way," in order to pull people in who supported these decisions. This began to split the people apart. Because these incidents have continued to occur, the tribal council recognized it and felt it had to do something about it. This constitutional reform effort is one of the means through which they are trying to do something to correct that.

The constitution reform committee began the process in 1998. They looked at the current constitution and identified some main problems, and they basically came up with four areas:

1. Lack of sovereignty and limited jurisdiction;
2. No separation of powers between the branches of government;

3. Unclear village powers, including limits on the form of village government; and
4. Weak civil rights for people.

So these were the four areas that they identified as key.

1. *Lack of Sovereignty and Limited Jurisdiction*

The first problem, as I indicated, is that the constitution makes no mention of the Hopi Tribe's sovereignty and allows for only limited jurisdiction. It does not indicate that the tribe has inherent sovereignty. So the committee wants to specifically say this in the current constitution. The other is that the constitution limits the tribe's territory and jurisdiction. It only talks about people living on the reservation, meaning the Hopi living on the reservation. But what if someone other than a Hopi comes onto the reservation. Should they be held to the same rules? Another concern is that the constitution allows the Navajo to object to Hopi exercising jurisdiction outside the villages. This could have come from the fact that the Hopi Tribe, if you've ever seen our reservation, is located right in the middle of the larger Navajo Nation reservation. So, perhaps to account for things like rights of ways, the constitution requires that Hopi go to the Navajo for permission to do so. But the Hopi Tribe in exercising its sovereignty wants to shore up its jurisdiction so it can operate as it so desires.

A final concern regarding sovereignty and jurisdiction is the fact that the constitution allows the BIA to have final say over certain tribal council decisions. The Hopi Tribe wants to get away from that and to do the things that they want to do based on their way of doing business. The Secretary of the Interior has to approve a lot of things and, again, the Hopi Tribe feels that it should not have to go to the BIA for a lot of things that it does for approval. One of them is membership. That's been one of the hotter debated issues on the reservation. There's a lot of debate because the Hopi people are matrilineal and if the offspring come from the mother they are automatically considered Hopi in the Hopi traditional way. But in order to define a Hopi in terms of the white society, as expressed in our current constitution, you have to define it in terms of blood quantum. If any changes will be made to the current constitution it will be in the membership area.

2. No Separation of Powers between the Branches of Government

In our current constitution there is no separation of powers between the branches of government. The constitution is based on a corporate type of structure where you have a board of directors. In our case the tribal council is the board of directors. So everything moves up to that level and there is no separation of powers. Even the chairman in our case is responsible or answers to the tribal government or tribal council.

One of the things that, as I mentioned, is unique about Hopi, are the villages. So when we're looking at restructuring the tribal government or the separation of powers concept, rather than have the three branches—the legislative, judicial, and executive—we want to include in there the villages as well. So in our case we would end up with four branches of government.

We have an organization chart which shows how the Hopi is organized at this point. At the very top of the 1936 IRA constitution is the BIA. Then you have the tribal council, and then you have the villages, and then of course the chairman and the various departments.

Everything that's happening within the tribal government ultimately ends up at the tribal council, and yet it has to be approved or decided upon by the BIA. The constitution committee sees this as a major problem for the Hopi Tribe. In response to that, we're proposing an alternative structure. You can pretty much say that it's based on the U.S. Constitution with the Hopi people on top, and then the four branches of government with the villages part of that.

We are proposing a system of separation of powers and checks and balances where power is shared among different people and different branches. One of the proposed checks on the authority of the council is a requirement that the council vote in public. This is a major issue within our Tribe because right now the council can go into executive session and decide things without going through the public process. And that really created a big mess just recently because the council wanted to go into a big project using the natural resources of the Tribe without getting consent or agreement from the people. It really threw a monkey wrench into that project and so now it's gone. This is one of the major things that the committee wants to include into the new constitution—that the council has to go through a public process.

The legislative process is another proposed area of reform. The 1936 constitution states that the council has the power to adopt resolutions providing the way in which it shall conduct its business. A minimum eight-day notice of a special executive session meeting of the council is required. Now the committee is proposing that a public legislative process is required—no more executive sessions. Legislative proposals are introduced as written bills and so forth. But the main thing is that the council must deliberate and make decisions in public, through this legislative process.

The new constitution clearly explains what the roles of each branch would be. For example, the tribal council would have all of the legislative powers, make all the laws, and pass an annual budget. The Executive, meaning the chairman, would have all executive powers and carry out and administer the laws. The judiciary would hear cases through a trial court and court of appeals. And finally the people really would have expanded village powers, with freedom to choose their form of village government and disputes between the villages handled by a mediator and the tribal court.

Right now, even though the constitution says that a village can choose its own form of government, it goes on to say that if they don't, then they either have to have a traditional form of government or go through an election process to come up with a formal government. So the constitution right now forces the villages either to have a constitution form of government or have a traditional form. But the committee is arguing that there are various different forms of government in the villages and that they should be able to choose and establish their own form without being forced to adopt any one form.

3. Unclear Village Powers

There has been a major discussion as well on village disputes. The 1936 constitution says that for powers reserved to the villages, uncertainty about who resolves any disputes involving these powers may be resolved by the tribal court or may be passed back and forth between the village and the court. The tribal council may also get involved in these disputes.

One of the problems currently is that when a village brings a matter to the tribal council the council automatically says "take it back, resolve it at your village because it's a village matter." And the village takes it back, talks about it, comes up with a possible resolution, and then goes back to the tribal council. And the tribal council may for some reason not want to accept it or not want to decide on it and they'll throw it back to the village. It goes back and forth like this and it creates a lot of problems, the largest one being a lack of trust for the tribal council because they're being perceived as indecisive, not addressing the problem, and maybe even furthering the problem by not taking appropriate action. The new constitution wants to correct that. It says that all disputes involving these powers are resolved by the village unless the village decides to send the matter to tribal court, which issues a final decision. The tribal council would not be involved with any of these matters.

Village government is another related issue. As I mentioned earlier, the current constitution says that each village shall decide for itself how it shall be organized. This is in the current constitution. However, in a separate section it says until a village shall decide to organize in another manner it shall be considered as being under the traditional Hopi organization and the *kikmongwi* in such village shall be recognized as its leader. A lot of our Hopi villages don't have a *kikmongwi*. They don't have a traditional form of government as it was seen and practiced in the past. A lot of them are new villages who have adopted a board of directors or some similar form of governance where the *kikmongwi* is not a player in that village government. So the current constitution's language would be inapplicable.

But again, the *kikmongwi* is not a leader in the political sense. He would be considered a religious leader where he would be heading a religious ceremony and provide direction to different societies in the village to perform their part of the ceremonies. So he would be a leader in that sense but not as a decision-maker in terms of how we should expend our funds. Again, the constitutional delegation of this power to the *kikmongwi* has really weakened the Hopi traditional form of government because it creates factions. It creates groups of people following the *kikmongwi* because he makes decisions for their benefit while leaving others out. Because it is based on money, basically, there is a lot of dissension and a lot of mistrust among the people. People say, "How come that person is driving in a truck and he doesn't even work?" That type of thing.

4. Weak Civil Rights

Someone mentioned that the civil rights section in many tribal constitutions may not or even should not follow what's given in the U.S. Constitution. One of the challenges of the committee is trying to align these words with Hopi values and the way Hopi sees things. We have committee members who are elders and committee members who are real young. It is interesting to see how they communicate with each other, trying to help the other person understand where they are coming from. In a lot of ways they're both right. It is interesting to see an elder say, "You're right." Because they would kind of step back in the explanation of what they were saying and somehow the two would fall at the same level, at the same place. Their ways of thinking about the concepts are the same but their explanations of it may be slightly different.

Freedom of speech, expression, and the press, for example, operate differently in the Hopi culture. You can't go in and interrupt an activity or even a ceremony with your opinions or with what you want to say because everything is set, and the speech part is given. You say certain things to help complete the ceremony. So if a person comes in and starts to talk about other things that's not related to it, that's not something that you should do. But because there is freedom of speech in the constitution, the elders said, "OK, we value what you're saying but this is not the place, we'll talk about it when the ceremony is over if what you're saying promotes the welfare of the tribe and the purpose of what that ceremony is all about." In a lot of cases that turns into a teaching, a form of discipline. If a person didn't know of these protocols and interrupted the ceremony they would be out of place. But through this process they learn and it helps to bring organization and control in the ceremonies.

PART III

Eric Lemont

Seven   REALIZING CONSTITUTIONAL
CHANGE THROUGH CITIZEN
PARTICIPATION

Practically speaking, how can American Indian nations realize the goals discussed throughout this book? Who within tribal nations will be charged with balancing traditional methods of political decision-making with the demands of globalization? Or wrestling with often competing cultural, legal, and economic pressures over membership criteria? Or determining how political power can be separated among branches of government?

For many Indian nations, resolving these deeply ambitious and politicized challenges requires citizen input and approval. Yet the seemingly simple notion of citizen participation is a real concern for constitutional reformers as well as tribal citizens. Within Indian Country, constitutional reformers are often committed citizens—bankers,[1] planners,[2] or educators[3]—who are charged with planning their nation's reform process. They can be, but often are not, elected government officials. As much as reformers desire to realize constitutional change in ways that reflect their community's values, they often lament what they see as a disengaged and apathetic citizenry. At the same time, tribal citizens *themselves* express a range of negative reactions, from muted mistrust to outright anger, over their feelings of exclusion from constitutional reform initiatives.

Of course, citizen participation—the opportunity both to provide input into and vote to approve or disapprove new and revised constitutions—is not the goal of all tribal governments or all individuals working within tribal government. This chapter addresses the narrow topic of how interested tribal constitutional reformers can address citizen concerns over lack of participation. It addresses two related questions: Why are complaints of nonparticipation so common in Indian Country? And how have some constitutional reformers succeeded in mobilizing citizen participation in their nation's constitutional reform initiatives?

The following sections dissect some of the different reasons citizens may not participate in constitutional reform initiatives and share innovative solutions developed by different Indian nations. The cited examples are drawn from two primary sources: a year-long investigation into the constitutional reform processes of four Indian nations and a series of national working group meetings attended by constitutional reformers from twelve Indian nations. The year-long research project took place in 2000 and consisted of in-depth interviews with reform leaders and citizens of the Cherokee Nation of Oklahoma, Hualapai Nation, Navajo Nation, and Northern Cheyenne Tribe.[4] All four engaged in fundamental constitutional and governmental reform between 1989 and 2002. The working group meetings took place at Harvard University's John F. Kennedy School of Government in 2001 and 2002 and brought together presentations and discussions from more than two dozen constitutional reformers from fifteen different Indian nations.[5]

SOURCES OF AND SOLUTIONS TO NONPARTICIPATION

In the mid-1990s, the Northern Cheyenne Tribe's constitutional reform committee organized a series of public meetings and designed and distributed to the tribal membership a survey regarding proposed constitutional changes. During the Hualapai Nation's constitutional revision in 1990, constitutional reform committee members hosted a series of community meetings. In 1998, the Cherokee Nation Constitutional Commission offered public hearings on and off the reservation, developed an internet chatroom on the Nation's website for discussions about the constitutional change process, and posted status reports on the Nation's website and in its newspaper in the months leading up to its 1999 Constitution Convention.

Despite these efforts, tribal members today at all three nations express frustration, even anger, at their feelings of exclusion from being full participants in the reform process. Almost uniformly, tribal members relate that they either were unaware that their nation was undertaking governmental or constitutional reform or did not feel there was an appropriate forum within which to learn and comment on the process. Within one nation, many citizens, especially elders, complain that the constitutional reform committee was a selective group that did not adequately seek out their input. In another, community leaders criticize the constitutional reform committee for failing to adequately explain the purpose of proposed changes, leaving tribal citizens without a sufficient understanding of their amended constitution.

Importantly, reformers have their own complaints about the difficulty of obtaining citizen participation. For more than ten years, Beverly Wright, the Chair of the Wampanoag Tribe of Gay Head, has sought to engage tribal members in a conversation over strengthening the nation's constitution. So far, Wright says, her best efforts have not proved fruitful. A report she commissioned on options for constitutional reform has "sat on a shelf" for more than five years.[6] Attendance has been sparse at meetings she has planned to discuss the need for a more updated constitution. In a recent paper, Wright argues that a lack of citizen education in tribal governance, competing demands on citizens' time, and family prejudices have combined to create a culture of citizen "apathy" regarding governmental reform.[7]

While these vignettes convey a broad sense of the problems surrounding citizen involvement, disentangling specific sources of nonparticipation is not easy. The reasons why a citizen may not participate in a reform initiative vary. Some are simply too busy to participate. Some don't see the value in a written constitution. Some don't trust the process. Some live off-reservation or out of state and are unaware of the existence of public hearings. Nonparticipation can be a symptom of simple logistics or a sign that an existing constitution is not truly valued as a society's highest law. Exploring the range of potential reasons for nonparticipation provides a window into the very meaning and purpose of tribal constitutions.

Reason No. 1: The Constitution Is Not My Constitution

If a constitution and its institutions are truly to be accepted as "higher law," they must do more than offer a simple governmental architecture. In his book *The Origins of American Constitutionalism*, noted political scientist Donald Lutz speaks forcefully to the connection between a constitution and a society's fundamental values:

> Every constitution uses principles of design for achieving the kind of life envisioned by its authors, and the principles will vary according to that vision. This is nothing more, though a good deal less, than what Aristotle said when he characterized the Greek understanding of the relationships between the polis and politea. The polis was a way of life, and [the] politea, or constitution, was the plan for a way of life. The constitution describes what that life should be like and the

institutions by means of which will be achieved that way
of life. The first description enunciates the values that
support the good life, thereby providing a definition of
justice. The second includes an enumeration of political
offices, the duties of each office, how each is to be filled,
how the offices interact to reach collective decisions, and
who is eligible to hold office—in effect a design for the
distribution of power.[8]

Lutz identifies several overarching American political values, including
legislative supremacy, majority rule, and individual liberty. These values
are incorporated clearly into the Constitution's institutional arrangements
and Bill of Rights, respectively. Lutz argues that these values did not origi-
nate in the U.S. Constitution. Rather, the Constitution itself represents
the culmination of centuries-long political and cultural understandings.
Indeed, the document most cited in the political literature during the
Founding era was the Bible.[9]

In stark contrast, American Indian nations have been denied the
privilege of governments and constitutions matching their fundamental
values—values that often are unwritten and more religious and cultural in
nature than political. In 1827, the citizens of the Cherokee Nation adopted
a written constitution—complete with a three-branch government—to
reassure the U.S. government that they were a "civilized" people. At the
turn of the century and through the 1920s, many American Indian nations saw their traditional governments replaced or eroded with the introduction of business committees and tribal councils. Beginning in 1934
and throughout the 1930s, dozens of Indian nations adopted standardized
constitutions developed as part of the Indian Reorganization Act. Even in
2001, the Chair of the Mashpee Wampanoag described his nation's ongoing process of constitutional development as one motivated more to satisfy
outside, Western investors than the demands of Mashpee citizens.[10]

What are traditional Native political values? There is of course no single
answer, and a thorough identification of Native political values is beyond
the scope of this inquiry. At the very least, commonly cited values include
a premium on individual leadership, local autonomy, and consensus-based
decision-making.[11] In the past, when tribal constitutions have failed to incorporate these values in favor of representative democracy, majority rule,
and the concentration of political authority in small, centralized councils,
the consequences have been grim. Mistrust, a lack of governmental accountability,[12] the production of "artificial elites,"[13] violent contestations

of political authority,[14] and dueling written and unwritten constitutions[15] reveal IRA constitutions' failure to connect with deeper tribal norms and understandings.

Given the mismatch between traditional tribal values and Western-introduced constitutions, it is not surprising that tribal citizens and constitutional reformers now comprise the front lines of a growing chorus calling for a realignment of tribal government and specific societal values. In his paper "Community, Culture, and the Lummi Constitution: Using Technology in the Reform Trenches," Lenny Dixon, the Lummi Nation's Constitution Outreach Coordinator, attributes the lack of interest in government reform among Lummi citizens to a widespread lack of association with the constitution:

> . . . there is one common thread that tends to surface from time to time among most tribal members: a feeling that the Lummi Constitution is just White Man's law and therefore is not important to their daily lives. These feelings stem from the fact that our constitution is modeled after the tribal constitution template of the Indian Reorganization Act of 1934 and is not connected to Lummi culture.

Dixon's views are not unique. Martha King, an attorney with the Office of Navajo Government Development who spends most of her days developing grassroots methods for strengthening the Navajo government, reaches similar conclusions. In 2001, King authored a report outlining a citizen-based approach to reform that detailed the current limitations of the Navajo government:

> The Navajo Nation Council was organized in 1923 to execute oil leases. The Bureau of Indian Affairs imposed the Rules for Governance for the Navajo Nation Council and recognized it as the governing body. These Rules have served as the foundation for the current government. And because the Navajo people have never formally established the Navajo Nation government, nor prescribed the nature and extent of its authority, it may not feel legitimate to the Navajo People. . . . Further, the government may not be tailored to reflect the Navajo People's needs, incorporate aspects of Dine culture and tradition, nor adequately empower chapters to handle local matters. This has resulted in

a general distrust of government, disharmony, confusion and controversy.[16]

The pressing question for Dixon, King, and other constitutional reformers isn't *whether* cultural values should be incorporated into governing institutions. The question is *how?* Reformers face a dilemma: the lack of ownership that tribal citizens feel toward their government creates a disincentive to participate in changing it. At the same time, the transition to a legitimate, culturally appropriate government usually requires citizens' individual participation.

More than twenty-five years ago, Robert LaFountain summarized the power and importance of citizen participation both to identify current traditional values and to forge consensus on how those values can be expressed in a constitution:

> If people participate, they have the voice in what the final decisions are for their government. Without the participation of the residents of the reservation, it's a minority group that governs even though it may be elected officials or hereditary officials. It's that minority group which is making the laws and the regulations and the policy decisions for the majority of the people who are silent. So this kind of participation — letting their own officials know what they think is the tradition of their tribe, what they think should be maintained, what kind of powers the tribe should have and what kind of authority it should exercise, what kinds of provisions and articles should be in the constitution because of what people say *now* and the kind of participation that's included *now*—is going to have an effect for decades in these constitutions.[17]

Citizen participation provides a powerful tool with which to identify common values, determine their current level of acceptance, and come to legitimate agreement (or disagreement) on how they can form the foundation of government. It is the bridge that allows nations to decide today what to take from the past to protect their future.

Of course, structuring citizen participation to help realign tribal values in new or revised constitutions is neither simple nor straightforward. The cumulative force of entrenched Western-style constitutional governments, demands of outside investors for mainstream political courts and procedures, and, in some instances, the need for formal approval of constitutional changes from the U.S. government temper the ability of Indian nations to incorporate fully traditional values into their constitutions. In addition, citizens' opinions will differ, sometimes greatly, over determinations of traditional values and the feasibility of melding these with written constitutions.

Despite these barriers, several Indian nations have crafted creative approaches for structuring these conversations. In 2000, the Navajo Nation Commission on Government Development hosted a series of traditional governance summits that allowed all interested Navajo citizens the opportunity to share their vision for the Nation's government. More than four hundred Navajo citizens provided testimony at the five summits regarding their suggestions for promoting more culturally appropriate and responsive government. The commission used this input as the foundation for its organization of a full-scale, national Government Reform Convention in May 2002. Each of the Nation's 110 chapters appointed two delegates to the convention, which succeeded in proposing twenty-six amendments to the Nation's governing code over the course of two days. Similarly, in 1999, the Cherokee Nation held a nine-day constitutional convention comprised primarily of citizen-delegates that also produced a proposed new constitution.

Importantly, reformers at Cherokee and Navajo structured citizen participation in ways that matched their nation's traditional process for reaching political decisions. The Cherokee Convention in 1999 was the Nation's third in its history. Navajo's use of local summits mirrored its historically local method of decision-making. These traditional processes of political action led to sweeping and historic discussions. Cherokee Convention delegates discussed the pros and cons of reverting back to a bicameral legislature and voted to reassert treaty rights unexercised for more than one hundred years. Navajo summiteers and delegates discussed the creation of a fourth branch of government charged with ensuring that Navajo laws reflect Navajo values, tradition, and philosophy.

Ultimately, some Indian nations, such as the San Manuel Band of Mission Indians, may reach the conclusion that their values and tradition don't require a written constitution at all. In the end, however, the specific outcomes of these summits, conventions, and conversations may be less important than the fact that they take place at all. With the provision of formal arenas where citizens' views are folded directly into the process of reform, ultimate substantive decisions are vested with a strengthened credibility and acceptance.

Reason No. 2: The Constitution Isn't a Concern to Me

Except in rare instances, a constitutional government is a foreign concept to Indian nations. Many individuals don't see how a constitution can affect their daily lives. Without this appreciation of a constitution's importance, tribal members aren't likely to attend public hearings, respond to surveys, or otherwise participate in reform processes. Reform leaders point to the lack of awareness of many tribal members of the basic structure and workings of their tribal government as a significant obstacle to effective public participation. While citizens' general lack of knowledge concerning their government is not unique to Indian Country, American Indians face the additional burden of overcoming years of systematic attempts by the U.S. government and religious missionaries to erase such knowledge. The forced removal of generations of Indians in the early to mid–twentieth century to distant federal government or religious boarding schools has been well documented. So too have the schools' policies against teaching tribal history and prohibiting students from talking in their Native languages.

Without a basic knowledge of tribal government and tribal history, many concerned members are neither comfortable participating in nor prepared to fully contribute to the process of reform. Reform leaders bemoan the difficulty of achieving broad-based citizen participation in a governmental or constitutional change process when many, if not most, tribal members don't have a detailed understanding of their nation's current government or constitutional structure. In many instances, tribal members feel that they don't understand proposed reforms fully enough to make an informed choice when voting on their approval. These feelings result in a lack of ownership over implemented changes. Just as important, those who can't trace the development of constitutional provisions—who don't know what the constitution says or why—can't use its provisions to promote and defend their individual and collective interests.

The Lummi Nation provides an example of how to make tangible to citizens the importance of a constitution. A representative from the constitutional reform committee regularly attends weekly meetings of a community group concerned about public safety on the reservation. At the end of the meeting, he delivers a presentation in which he demonstrates how these community concerns may be alleviated by restructuring the Nation's institutional structure to provide for more local decision-making. The connection between the constitution and everyday concerns is made clear.

Reform leaders from Hualapai, Northern Cheyenne, and Navajo nations argue strongly that in certain instances it is necessary to explain proposed governmental changes—and the rationale behind such changes—in the Native tribal language. For example, one of Northern Cheyenne's constitutional reform committee members, a respected traditionalist within the tribe, reminds us that official positions such as secretary and treasurer do not exist in most Native languages and that any English-only explanation of constitutional changes can never be fully effective. Recognizing this language gap, he effectively conveyed the meaning and purpose of proposed constitutional changes to tribal members uncomfortable with speaking English during the Tribe's constitutional reform initiative.

Early programs in civic education also are critical. The UCLA American Indian Studies Center's Project Peacemaker works with four tribal colleges to develop curricula examining the sources and origins of various constitutional provisions. These classes provide the next generation of tribal leaders with an important historical grounding in tribal constitutions, tribal law, and federal Indian law. They also serve as valuable, neutral space where constitutional reformers and interested citizens can discuss how their constitution is or is not facilitating community goals.[18] Northern Cheyenne's Lame Deer High School is one of several tribal high schools that offer classes in tribal government and tribal history. This past August, the tribal council passed a resolution formally recognizing these classes and resolving to meet periodically with a student advisory committee of the school.

Youth councils offer yet another way to introduce the next generation of leaders to issues of tribal government. At Fort Peck, members of the youth council attend meetings of the tribal council and interact regularly with tribal government officials. By obtaining an increased appreciation and understanding of government institutions, including constitutions, youth are more likely to participate in future reform initiatives.[19]

These early programs of civic education need not be limited to youth. Since 2001, the Cherokee Nation has enrolled more than seven hundred of its government employees in a mandatory week-long Cherokee Nation history course. By all accounts, the course has vested Cherokee citizens both with a stronger sense of national identity and the confidence and knowledge to exercise more fully their inherent powers of self-government.[20]

Reason No. 3: I Don't Trust the Process

A constitution that is "owned" by the people must flow from a reform process owned by the people. But people won't participate in a process they don't trust. Mistrust stems from citizens' belief that their input won't matter—or, worse, will be held against them. Some of the reasons citizens may not feel ownership in reform initiatives include: questions over the elected government's true position regarding participation, the dominance of lawyers in drafting tribal constitutions, and poisonous atmospheres at public meetings and hearings.

Often, reformers must battle citizens' perceptions that elected government officials don't truly desire widespread citizen participation. Beliefs range from a view that council members are indifferent or obstructionist to tangible fears of government retaliation for calls for reform. Of course, not all councils or council members can be depicted with a broad brush. True reformers exist in all governments and are often joined by other elected leaders who recognize that those whose voices are left out of the reform process will be first in line to question it.

But when councils, like any government, establish constitutional reform committees as "reporting" bodies, citizens' feelings of mistrust are well-placed. In Indian Country and around the world, the work and funding of constitutional reform committees often ends when reforms are introduced that are adverse to the interests of incumbent officials.[21] For reformers, the primary challenge is to develop a participatory process within the constraints of a political system usually dominated by a small council. Savvy citizens won't waste their time contributing their input to a reform committee that lacks sufficient political clout, funding, and political independence.

Nor will citizens trust and contribute to a reform process dominated by lawyers, an issue that produces some of the most heated emotions from reformers. Complaints abound of lawyers drafting constitutional provisions ahead of community input and guidance, often in confusing legalese. In some situations, reformers relate that lawyers themselves come to look at the constitution as *their* document, instead of that of the people.

Finally, mistrust surfaces when the forum created to offer input is tainted by fears of ridicule or retribution. Speaking for many other constitutional reformers, Chairperson Beverly Wright blames the verbal abuse members face at public meetings of the Wampanoag Tribe of Gay Head for contributing to citizens' decisions to stay home and remain uninvolved.

The common thread running through all of these sources of mistrust is a lack of citizen ownership in the process of reform. In response, constitutional reformers have devised a variety of innovative approaches to facilitate trust, citizen participation, and citizen ownership. For example, in 1999, the Cherokee Nation Constitution Commission organized a constitutional convention in which forty-eight of the seventy-nine delegates were lay citizens chosen by lottery or by their participation in public hearings. Since convention delegates had the power to submit a proposed new constitution directly to a national referendum, Cherokee citizens had a direct and unfiltered voice in the drafting of their national document. Similarly, in 2002, the Navajo Nation Commission on Government Development held a government reform convention to propose amendments to the Nation's governing code. Appointees of local government Navajo chapters were the overwhelming majority of convention delegates. Finally, by setting aside a minority of delegate positions for incumbent Council members, both Cherokee and Navajo were able to build an indispensable "buy-in" for reform from the elected leadership.

Other Indian nations have strengthened citizen ownership by clearly defining the role of lawyers in the reform process. At Northern Cheyenne, tribal leaders worked hand in hand with the Tribe's longtime lawyer to ensure that the final written product reflected the will of the community. In practice, this resulted in literally dozens of exchanges of drafts between the tribal lawyer and the constitutional reform committee. Ultimately, the lawyer and the committee succeeded in producing constitutional language that is as legally sound as it is accessible to current and future Cheyenne citizens.

To create an environment in which citizens feel comfortable contributing their input, numerous constitutional reform committees and commissions have institutionalized rules for taking public testimony. Both the Grand Traverse Band and Hopi Tribe constitutional reform committees open their deliberations to all interested participants and observers, including nontribal members. For Le Roy Shingoitewa, the Chair of the Hopi Tribe constitutional reform committee, this openness minimizes the influence of behind-the-scenes power brokers and quashes the spread of rumors that circulate easily in response to closed-door meetings. In addition to openness, a number of reform committees have adopted *Robert's Rules of Order* or other agreed-upon rules for taking testimony that reduce—and structure the resolution of—conflicts that arise over heated topics.

At the same time, written rules have their limits. As council member Shelly Carter points out, even after the Wampanoag Tribe of Gay Head implemented *Robert's Rules,* "the majority of the [members] that either sit on council or in the membership won't adhere to *Robert's Rules.* So we set standards, we passed them, we have it in writing, but at the very next meeting we're off and running again. It's another piece of paper of another document that sits on our shelf collecting dust." Indeed, for reformers like

King, Dixon, and Shingoitewa, lasting change can take place only when reformers set the example. Sam McClellan, a member of the Grand Traverse Band Constitutional Reform Committee, perhaps best sums up this consensus view:

> How do you get people out to even serve on a [constitutional reform] committee or even be involved in something like this? The one thing is that they have to see it in you. Do you believe what you're saying? Do you believe that the changes that you're going to make are best for your community and your tribe? Are you really becoming a sovereign nation? Do you believe in being sovereign? You have to bring that to your people. If you're going to be leaders and if you're going to be changing anything, you need to hear from the people and hear what they have to say.[22]

Reason No. 4: I'm Too Busy to Participate

Another broad explanation of nonparticipation can be attributed to simple problems of awareness and logistics. Many citizens live in rural areas, off-reservation or out of state. Others are busy with daily priorities and don't have time to attend public meetings and hearings. In these situations, typical outreach methods of surveys and advertisements for public meetings on community bulletin boards or in tribal newspapers are ineffective. In addition to the fact that such notices often fail to reach the entire membership, many members simply have too many other pressing concerns. Even when members give serious consideration to attending public meetings, many feel uncomfortable attending, not knowing what to expect at public meetings—and what, if anything, is expected of them.

These issues of awareness and logistics can be exacerbated by the resource limitations of ad hoc constitutional reform committees. At Hualapai and Northern Cheyenne, the tribal government created a constitutional reform committee comprised of volunteers. Both committees faced difficult problems of attrition. At Hualapai, the original twenty-five-member committee dwindled to seven. At Northern Cheyenne, the committee disbanded altogether at one point before reforming. Even when the committees were at their greatest number, members' outreach efforts had to compete with other, more immediate, personal and professional concerns.

Recognizing that people won't make a special trip to attend a public hearing or take a half hour to respond to a survey, reform leaders are going directly to the people. The Cherokee Nation Constitution Commission held hearings across the United States so off-reservation residents could contribute their input. The commission's efforts resulted in eight hundred pages of testimony from Cherokee citizens.[23] The commission's efforts are part of a wider "saturation" approach among constitutional reformers that involves reaching people where they live and work. Members of the Lummi Nation constitutional reform committee deliver presentations during regularly scheduled meetings of other community groups. Instead of attracting the handful of people who might otherwise show up to discuss constitutional issues, the committee capitalizes on a built-in audience of dozens of interested citizens. Theresa Two Bulls, the Vice President of Oglala Sioux, goes on the radio every week to update citizens on the progress of the government and visits schools to understand the concerns of Oglala Sioux youth. Albert Hale, the former President of the Navajo Nation, traveled the reservation on horseback in the mid-1990s to explain the purpose of the Local Governance Act to rural residents person-to-person. Often, these exchanges took place in the Navajo language, allowing Hale and Navajo residents to reach a level of understanding that otherwise would not have occurred.

CONCLUSION

Clearly, American Indian nations are not alone in their struggles over citizen political involvement. One need only pick up a newspaper or book to read of Americans' declining voting rates and participation in civic life. But for American Indian nations, with their relatively small size and limited human resources, the loss of every citizen who withdraws because she doesn't trust the process, doesn't view the constitution as her own, or doesn't feel the process warrants her concern, is more immediate and tangible. Given the experiences of the reformers described in this chapter, citizen participation clearly is critical to realign tribal constitutions with American Indian nations' most deeply held values, identify key issues for revision, develop consensus, instill understanding, and promote ownership. These idyllic-sounding goals translate into the reality of citizens better able and more willing to use their constitutions to defend their individual and collective interests. Given all of the pressing challenges facing tribal governments today, this is quite a high payoff indeed.

NOTES

1. Jay Hannah, Chair of the Cherokee Nation Constitution Convention.

2. Lenny Dixon, Lummi Nation Constitution Outreach Coordinator.

3. Le Roy Shingoitewa, Chair, Hopi Tribe Constitutional Reform Committee.

4. For an overview of these four nations' reform processes, see Eric Lemont, "Developing Effective Processes of Constitutional and Governmental Reform: Lessons from the Cherokee Nation, Hualapai Nation, Navajo Nation, and Northern Cheyenne Tribe," *American Indian Law Review* 26 (2001–2002): 147.

5. The first symposium, "Tribes Moving Forward: Engaging in the Process of Constitutional and Governmental Reform," took place on April 1–3, 2001. After the symposium, a working group called the Executive Session on American Indian Constitutional Reform was established. The first three meetings took place on October 11–13, 2001 ("Setting the Agenda"), May 9–11, 2002 ("Launching Effective Reform Processes and Maximizing Citizen Participation and Education"), and October 17–19, 2002 ("Traditional Values, Current Threats: The Meaning and Purpose of Tribal Constitutions"). Papers from these proceedings can be found at *www.ksg.harvard.edu/reform*.

6. Transcript from October 11–13, 2001, meeting of the Executive Session, note 5 herein.

7. See firsthand account of Beverly Wright in this book.

8. Donald Lutz, *The Origins of American Constitutionalism* (Louisiana State University Press, 1988), 13.

9. Ibid., 140. Lutz analyzed the references of 3,154 citations published between 1760 and 1805. Of these, 34 percent cited the Bible. In second place, Enlightenment thinkers such as Montesquieu, Blackstone, Locke, and Hume were cited in 22 percent of these publications. A full-length article detailing Lutz's study can be found in Donald S. Lutz, "The Relative Influence of European Writers on Late Eighteenth-Century American Political Thought," *American Political Science Review* 77 (1984): 189–197.

10. Transcript from April 1–3, 2001, symposium ("We've been running our government for quite some time and have been doing it in a different way that is consistent with [the] U.S. system and so forth. But I think of the years[,] of the excuses they used why they wouldn't invest into Native communities, and it was basically because they didn't have a system in place where companies could feel confident about investing in there without the fear of losing their investment. They were unable to collateralize. I look at constitutional development as a process we're going through in order to set up a government so that these investors will feel comfortable about investing in us, and have some assurance that they would get their money back out of it. So . . . the constitution really isn't about us, it's really about them, and about them having confidence and investing in us").

11. See generally Duane Champagne's chapter in this volume. See also Tom Holm, "The Crisis in Tribal Government," in *American Indian Policy in*

the Twentieth Century, ed. Vine Deloria, Jr. (University of Oklahoma Press, 1985).

12. As described by Abbott Sekaquaptewa, a former Chair of the Hopi Tribe, "It has only been since the adoption of a constitution and by-laws that there has been a tribal council, an entirely foreign concept in our case. It provided the opportunity for a democratic forum that did not exist before, but it also created a difficult problem. It created confusion in the people because now they had to deal with problems such as to whom is the council accountable?" quoted in *Tribal Constitutions: Their Past—Their Future: Proceedings of a Conference Held in Billings, Montana, August 12–13, 1977,* ed. James J. Lopach, Margery Hunter Brown, and Kathleen Jackson (Missoula: Bureau of Government Research, University of Montana, 1978), 31.

13. See Holm, "The Crisis in Tribal Government."

14. Ibid.

15. James J. Lopach, Margery Hunter Brown, and Richmond L. Clow, *Tribal Government Today: Politics on Montana Indian Reservations* (University Press of Colorado, 1998).

16. *Engaging the People of the Navajo Nation in the Process of Nation Building,* Report of the Office of Navajo Government Development Staff (July 26, 2001), 1.

17. Quoted in Lopach et al., *Tribal Constitutions: Their Past—Their Future,* 67 (emphasis added).

18. For an overview of Project Peacemaker, see Carole Goldberg, "Drafting Tribal Colleges into Constitution Reform," paper presented at May 9–11, 2002, Executive Session, available at *www.ksg.harvard.edu/reform.*

19. The Gila River Youth Council received a recent award by Honoring Contributions in the Governance of American Indian Nations, a Harvard Project on American Indian Economic Development national awards program designed to recognized innovative tribal government programs.

20. More information on the Cherokee Nation history course can be found on the Honoring Nations page of the Harvard Project on American Indian Economic Development website, www.ksg.harvard.edu/hpaied.

21. See Lemont, *Developing Effective Processes of Constitutional and Governmental Reform,* 161, concerning the experience of the Northern Cheyenne Tribe's constitutional reform committee. See also Ian Record, "Broken Government: Constitutional Inadequacy Spawns Conflict at San Carlos," *Native Americas* (Spring 1999), concerning the experience of the constitutional reform committee of the San Carlos Apache.

22. Transcript of October 11–13, 2001, meeting of the Executive Session, note 5 herein.

23. Jay Hannah, "The 1999 Constitution Convention of the Cherokee Nation: Process of a Sovereign People." A copy of the paper can be found at *www.ksg.harvard.edu/reform.*

Steven Haberfeld

Eight   THE PROCESS OF
CONSTITUTIONAL REFORM

T hese are exciting times. American Indian nations across the country are taking steps to revise their constitutions and reform their governments. They are "reinventing" their political systems to better fit their own cultures, traditions, and relationships, and to better cope with changing political and economic realities. The significance of these current reform efforts cannot be overestimated. To the extent there is widespread involvement by the community in this "reformation" process, American Indians will have a greater sense of ownership of their political institutions and a greater willingness to view such institutions as legitimate—something that has been seriously lacking under their current systems of government.

Moreover, in the drive to reform existing institutions and to create new ones, citizens of these communities are rejecting many aspects of the constitutions and institutions that were effectively imposed on them by the U.S. government as a precondition for the receipt of official "recognition" and federal funding. In effect, these communities are changing their relationship with the U.S. government. They are choosing to move from a former relationship of subjugation and dependency to a liberating and transforming exercise of their own inherent sovereignty. They are taking a significant step in establishing their own identity and taking responsibility for their own destiny. This shift alone can be the breakthrough that will enable American Indian nations to truly realize their fullest potential.

In other chapters of this book, a number of general observations have been made about differences between the IRA government model and the values and governing institutions typically found in traditional Indian societies. There also has been considerable discussion about a range of issues that currently concern contemporary Indian communities as citizens question how to enhance the effectiveness of their current political systems.

This chapter is not concerned with the "what" of constitutional reform but rather with the "how." How do communities go about surfacing, addressing, and resolving constitutional issues in a systematic and constructive way? Other than the requirements in many tribal constitutions for a specified percentage of eligible voters to ratify a new or amended constitution and subsequent review and approval by the Secretary of the Interior (for IRA constitutions), most tribal constitutions are silent on how to initiate and obtain citizen approval of constitutional reform. Since there is no blueprint to follow, reformers are presented with the challenge of designing and implementing a process that will get the job done in their communities.

But what should that process look like? In answering this question, we can begin with a basic premise that is reflected in this entire book. No matter what traditional societies had to say about participation in tribal government, members of Indian communities today expect their governments to function according to democratic principles. They expect tribal government to be "of, by, and for" the people. No matter the shortcomings of the IRA constitutional template, the typical IRA constitution embodies basic democratic principles of "one man, one vote," representative government, majority rule, due process, popular election of tribal leaders, and leadership accountability to the people, with whom sovereignty ultimately rests. Over the years, tribal citizens have been conditioned to expect adherence to these democratic principles. In fact, typical criticisms of IRA governments are that they have not lived up to these expectations.

In this context, tribal citizens will also expect the reform process to be democratic. They will expect the process to be open and fair, to provide community leaders and members sufficient opportunity to participate in the deliberations, to have an impact on the content of the proposed changes, and ultimately to be in a position of approving the changes before they go into effect. Constitutional reformers will have to begin by designing a participatory process—before any substantive constitutional issue is addressed—that meets these democratic expectations of tribal citizens.

While each community will design a process that reflects its unique needs and values, I will endeavor to identify some basic characteristics that successful reform processes seem to contain. I will identify these by reviewing the experiences of successful reform efforts and of some failed attempts at reform as well. My impression is that there are more instances in which tribes have tried to revise their constitutions or, similarly, initiate new or revised government codes, ordinances, or other organic documents, and were unable to get these approved by the membership. The details of where and why these failed attempts went wrong also will reveal what pitfalls to avoid and how.

In the ensuing discussion, I will borrow from negotiation and mediation models as well as from community organizing models for insights into how to design good processes for reform. Negotiation and mediation models spell out how multiple parties with divergent interests can reconcile their differences and jointly craft agreements that meet mutual interests. Community organizing models are particularly concerned with how to make local government decision-making inclusive of people who may tend to be excluded or are otherwise reluctant to participate.

The following discussion is organized around a series of issues and questions that should be addressed when designing a constitutional reform process in the community. Under each, I discuss a variety of options and offer some recommendations based on actual experiences and observations.

PART I: WHO SHOULD ORGANIZE, DESIGN, AND MANAGE THE REFORM PROCESS?

Reform initiatives are sometimes initiated by elected leaders and sometimes by people in the community who are not currently in power. In any case, as a general rule, whenever the reform effort is *solely* identified with one group or faction or another, there will be significant segments of the community that will reject the initiative out of hand simply because of suspicions that the reformers have "partisan" motives not to their liking. If only the elected leaders are identified with the reform effort, they may be suspected of trying to perpetuate or increase their power and longevity. If, on the other hand, the reform effort is seen as being initiated by those currently not in power, elected officials and their followers may suspect that the effort is designed to supplant them. There are numerous examples in Indian Country of initiatives that have failed because they were seen as driven by people with partisan objectives. In one southern California tribe, the effort to initiate constitutional reform has become identified with those unhappy with the current leadership. Meetings to discuss the proposed reforms have bogged down in recriminations and accusations. Some meetings have even adjourned prematurely because of physical violence.

This happens in the reverse as well. Reform efforts are discredited when they appear to be dominated by those in power. A longtime attorney with California Indian Legal Services observed recently that he had been involved over the years in a number of Indian communities in which he was asked by the tribal council to prepare and revise constitutions and other enabling legislation. However, as "good" as the newly prepared documents were, he found he met resistance to and ultimate rejection of his proposals from significant factions simply because they were opposed to the elected leadership for which he worked. In one case he described, this changed only when the Administration for Native Americans Director took over responsibility for the initiative and formed a sponsoring group composed of representatives from all the major factions in the community.

This same phenomenon appears in another context—tribal elections. Where there is suspicion that the process for electing a tribal council is controlled by one faction, opposition groups typically will deem the election process illegitimate and challenge the validity of the results. There are numerous examples of tribes in California, Nevada, and elsewhere throughout the country where two tribal councils have emerged, each conducting its own elections and each claiming to be the legitimately elected tribal council. Invariably, each council and its followers have boycotted the other's election and repudiated its results as "unrepresentative." This behavior can go on for years until both factions can agree to sit down together to design and conduct one election that has built-in guarantees of objectivity and inclusiveness.

In my own experience, I have found that tribal communities split down the middle like this have difficulty reconciling their differences without an independent mediator or facilitator accepted by both parties to administer and certify the election. My organization has sometimes filled the role of a tribe's impartial election committee. Prior to the election, we bring representatives of the major factions together to jointly craft an elections procedures agreement. It spells out every detail of the upcoming election process, including who is eligible to vote; what announcements will be sent out and when; how candidates' eligibility will be determined and by whom; how the ballot will be structured; and criteria for disqualifying ballots. The contending parties sign this agreement and our organization monitors, administers, and certifies the election according to the agreed-upon process. The election process is rarely challenged after the election because the process itself had the endorsement of the major stakeholders.

The case study in this book on the Cherokee constitutional reform effort describes a very self-conscious attempt by the reformers to assemble a group of people that—from the outset—was to be regarded as nonpartisan and "above politics." The politically diverse group that initiated and orchestrated the constitutional reform process saw its role as that of an impartial facilitator that would not be identified with any one interest group and would not take any position on any substantive reform issue. Once assembled, members of this organizing group signed a pledge that they were independent and not beholden to any group. This group's apparent impartiality and noninvolvement in the substance of the reform proposals made it acceptable for driving the reform movement. The fact that this occurred at the height of political turmoil makes it even more remarkable.

Other communities are strongly advised to follow the Cherokee example and make sure that the "organizing group" is representative of a cross-section of interests in the community. It should limit its role to serving as the impartial facilitator of the process. Just as an impartial election committee that is not beholden to any one group should be formed to run a tribal election, an impartial group should be formed to spearhead the constitutional reform process.

How Formal and Detailed Should a "Process Design" Be?

Constitutional reform is not an event. It is a process—one that needs financial resources, organization, and management to succeed in its mission. The next step after forming an impartial organizing group is to define the specific steps in this process for crafting and passing constitutional reforms. It is important that this plan explicitly lay out the stages of the process as well as how and when various groups will be involved in decision-making. It should have a starting and ending date and should be accompanied by realistic timelines and a sufficient budget. Once these issues are addressed, the plan should be presented to the governing authorities as well as to the people.

It behooves reformers to establish credibility within the community from the outset, both in themselves as objective and fair facilitators and in the objectivity and fairness of the process. One way to ensure credibility is to make sure that tribal citizens understand the purpose of the reform process, how it will be implemented, and when important milestones will occur. They will then know what to expect and will see when and how they can get involved. At some stage early in the process, it will be very helpful to have a series of community meetings devoted to describing the constitutional reform process that is about to unfold. Graphic illustrations and timelines on huge spreadsheets provide people with pictures of what is to come. By using these informational meetings to encourage community members to review, comment on, and recommend modifications in the process design, the facilitators of the process may be made aware of problems and opportunities they did not anticipate. At the same time, groups and individuals in the community will acquire a greater sense of ownership of the process.

Overall, the predictability, visibility, and transparency of the process will lend it credence and build trust among community members. When citizens have the sense that a process is open and fair and they have had full opportunity to participate, they will have what is known in the field of dispute resolution as "process satisfaction." This will contribute significantly to people's willingness to accept the substantive reforms that are eventually proposed. Approaching the constitutional reform effort in this way is not unique. The approach has much in common with other efforts that involve multiple parties in solving complex problems. We will say more about this later. But first let me share some options to consider when designing the process.

PART II: DEVELOPING AND DRAFTING CONSTITUTIONAL REVISIONS—WHO DECIDES?

Ultimately, changes will be made in the tribe's constitution, and more often than not these changes will be put in writing to serve as the ongoing guide for conducting the community's political affairs far into the future. But who should draft the proposed changes, and at what stage of the reform process? This is one of the first questions the organizing group will want to address and resolve.

I have observed that there are at least two different approaches communities follow when developing new or revised constitutions and other organic documents. They reflect two different orientations with very different implications.

The "Technical" Approach

First, and certainly most common, is for a tribal government to request its attorney or program and planning staff to develop a proposed draft of a new document. Once this is complete and internally reviewed, the tribe usually holds a series of open meetings in which the proposal is shared, information is provided, and community input is taken. Community members ultimately are given a chance to approve or reject the proposed constitution in a community-wide referendum.

The Hoopa Valley Tribe in northern California has institutionalized a strategy for involving the community. By tribal law it is required to hold formal community hearings before it enacts new laws and regulations. Testimony is recorded and then considered by tribal government when the elected leaders and staff finalize the proposed changes. The last step is to take the proposal to the people for ratification.

Other communities may conduct meetings, either in addition to or instead of a structured hearing, in less formal settings, where citizens are given an opportunity to listen to the changes being contemplated, ask questions, and express their opinions. Many communities schedule open meetings to which everyone is invited. Other tribes announce a series of informational community meetings targeted at specific and significant segments of the population, such as elders, veterans, farmers, health workers, or students, and convened in various communities or neighborhoods. Tribes use various incentives to bring the people out. Serving meals and having entertainment seems to work in some places. The Turtle Mountain Tribe has offered high school and college credits in civics to students who attend and participate in deliberations about constitutional reform. The Lummi Tribe in western Washington has used another strategy for gathering community input. It has extended the community education and response period over several years to ensure ample time for the community to participate in constitutional reform discussions. It often reserves time in organizational and community meetings that were convened for an entirely different purpose to deal with given aspects of the contemplated constitutional changes.

However, one fundamental problem with the approach of having technical experts prepare the proposed document is its basic premise: a belief that what is technically and legally sound is the best solution for the community. Typically, experts will start with what is commonly referred to as a boilerplate document and modify it by drawing on examples from other written constitutions used in Indian or non-Indian communities. They will modify this prototype to fit the local situation and incorporate what they perceive is needed to make things work better.

The technical documents themselves may be problematic. It is likely that the document is written without the benefit of input from the community and therefore will not reflect tribal citizens' values, opinions, concerns, and priorities. Technical experts quite likely will also write in technical language, rather than in the lexicon of the average layman. The document may not resonate with the people, and they may not even know how or where to begin to evaluate or critique it. From this perspective, the document may simply feel like a foreign object that the system has to reject, as a transplanted organ may be rejected by the immune system.

There is another problem with constitutional documents drafted solely by technical experts. When they are shared with the community before being put up for a popular vote, there tends to be resistance on the part of the drafters to changes made to accommodate members of the community for reasons of "political expediency." Even when it becomes clear that an important element of the community will oppose the existing draft unless it is changed, the technical experts will be inclined to resist making the change on the grounds that the draft document's inherent integrity and technical purity will be sacrificed. This tension between technical experts and politically oriented pragmatists committed to passing the proposed legislation is legendary in almost every field. Ask anyone involved in the legislative arena.

There are additional problems that are a function of the way the document is shared with the community. Large open meetings often do not generate a large turnout in most Indian communities, despite all the special devices used to bring people out. People at Hoopa, for example, report that their legislative hearings do not generate a lot of interest or active participation. As a rule, many people are not inclined to attend community meetings unless there is some raging controversy. Yet if the meeting is expected to be volatile, there may be just as many or more people who will stay far away, having decided that such meetings are not only dangerous but unproductive and a waste of time. In either case, many community members who will be later asked to vote for the proposed reform document will not have been exposed beforehand to the issues. Nor will they have had an opportunity to hear the underlying rationale for the draft as it was presented or to express their own concerns and provide input.

The other problem is that large open meetings are hard to manage as two-way dialogues in which people can satisfactorily resolve differences of opinion. They are not conducive to the trust building and intimacy that one needs to work things out by talking them through. This is particularly true when dealing with the complex issues that arise in constitutional reform discussions. Open public meetings are best for sharing information and providing answers to specific questions. However, in the constitutional reform context, people who give input in these settings usually will not have the satisfaction that their views will be heard and taken into account. They do not see that they will have any impact on the process. When they go to vote, whatever concerns about the document they may have had most likely will remain unresolved. At this point, the only method remaining to register their concern may be to reject the entire document.

This experience of dissatisfaction is very much like meeting with a government agency that engages in consultation with tribes. The agency may ask for a tribe's input without any commitment to reaching an agreement that will satisfy mutual interests. Tribal spokespersons will suspect that they helped the agency officials meet their legal consultation requirements and that the officials will simply go back to their offices and do what they intended to do in the first place. There is just enough cynicism among tribal members about their own political processes and the hidden agendas of their leaders that we can expect people to have very low process satisfaction when their own governments "consult" with them. This will be the general case unless there are overt and sincere attempts to take the concerns expressed by people in the audience and make revisions on the spot.

Some tribes have learned how to overcome some of the inherent problems with the technical-expert model we are describing here. Over the years most tribal reformers have concluded, as a result of trial and error, that when proposing a major change in how the tribe will operate, the change is more likely to be supported if it is accompanied by a deliberate and systematic strategy to educate and inform the membership. For example, many years ago the membership of the Bishop Paiute Tribe in central California failed to approve a comprehensive joint venture agreement with outside developers to build and operate a shopping center. One problem was that the tribal council that negotiated the agreement had little contact with the membership during two years of negotiations. Once the agreement was ready for ratification and the council began to share information, the lack of previous consultations—combined with misinformation in the community—doomed the agreement to oblivion. Years later, when the same tribe sought member approval of a casino proposal, this too was defeated. According to the leadership, a handful of people with incomplete or faulty information were able to disrupt the few community meetings that the council scheduled.

Some months later the outcome was very different. The tribal council implemented a step-by-step process to inform and involve the membership. It conducted a series of well-planned and well-orchestrated meetings in the community. A great deal of time was set aside for the community education and approval phase. Moreover, the council invested time and money in preparing well-organized and easy to understand graphics and quantitative and qualitative data on the scope and projected impact of the project.

The Klamath Tribes in southern Oregon learned some important lessons in process design as well. They tried several times to get their revised constitution passed by the membership and each time failed to get a majority. Ultimately, the tribal council decided that it was a mistake to try to get all of the many changes in the proposed revision approved at the same time. The sheer number of changes was probably hard for the tribal membership to fully understand and feel comfortable with at one time. But simple arithmetic was working against ratification as well. Enough different groups were finding something they did not like with the document and so were opposing the entire proposal at the polls. By contrast, when the tribal council went to the citizens with one major change at a time, there was a smaller total amount of opposition each time and enough popular support to win approval.

The "Political" Approach

There is an alternative to having technical experts draft the language of the constitutional revisions and members of the community provide feedback on the internally prepared document. The proposed reforms can arise out of discussions among citizens themselves, in the interplay and resolution of different and competing interests articulated by an array of different constituencies. In this case, constitutional reform, or the creation of any new law or regulation, for that matter, is regarded as essentially a political process. It is assumed that since any new legislation spells out what behaviors will be acceptable and unacceptable under the new law, people who anticipate being affected will want to participate in shaping the new legislation before it goes into effect.

Rather than starting with changes recommended by technical experts and getting community feedback, reformers will create forums in which competing interests will have the opportunity to participate in a negotiation process. The draft of the reform document will consist essentially of a series of negotiated agreements about what the various constituencies participating in the process have decided they can live with and support. This gives the reformers the assurance that when a revised constitution comes up for a vote it will likely be widely supported and politically feasible.

The contrast between reform proposals drafted by technical experts and those drafted in the interplay of different and competing interests can be seen in terms of the stage at which agreement is sought. In the first case, the reformers are seeking input on an agreement *after* the document has been drafted. In the second, the reformers are inviting input and agreement among various interests *during* the drafting process itself. In the first case, citizens are brought into a consultation process. Their views are taken into consideration by the drafters, who reserve the right to decide unilaterally what modifications, if any, should be made to their initial draft proposals. In the second case, the citizen's role is essentially very different. Tribal citizens are given the opportunity, beyond being consulted, to be an integral part of the decision-making process itself. There is an understanding that they as constituents or stakeholders will be involved in a forum in which they and other stakeholders have full opportunity to review materials, hear pros and cons, and make proposals and counterproposals. They are given the added assurance that they, together with other interested parties, will have the opportunity to try to reconcile differences and reach agreements that satisfy mutual interests. Those agreements will form the basis of the draft document that is shared with the community and submitted to popular referendum.

Constitutional reformers in Indian Country have used both approaches, one we can characterize as the "technical expert approach" and the other as a political approach. Each has its strengths and weaknesses. It is my general observation that starting with a document prepared by a lawyer or planner and adding some limited consultations with the membership is by far the more common approach followed. Since many of these attempts fail to be ratified when put to the vote, it behooves us to explore the political approach in more detail.

PART III: MAKING THE POLITICAL APPROACH WORK—LESSONS FROM NEGOTIATED RULE-MAKING

Above, I discussed some of the possible reasons why constitutional reform efforts in Indian communities might not have been successful. I also suggested another approach—a political approach—that might be more successful in incorporating in the reform proposal features that will more accurately reflect the values, traditions, and needs of the community. By having citizens participate actively in the development of a new or revised constitution, this approach also ensures that there are sufficient numbers of people who understand the proposed reforms and support ratification—a critical ingredient to a reform initiative's ultimate success.

But how does one design and implement such a political approach that will not backfire and create even more disruption and distrust than currently exists? Not knowing how to answer this question has persuaded countless tribes to avoid the challenge of creating a new or revised constitution (or the challenge of devising or revising a wide range of different codes and ordinances that are needed in their communities). They have chosen to leave well enough alone rather than risk opening Pandora's box.

Before addressing this question directly, it is helpful to discuss a similar dilemma in a context outside the Indian community. The case in point is what is known as negotiated rule-making or "neg-reg." Federal agencies historically have implemented new congressional legislation after writing new regulations and publishing them in the *Federal Register* for public comment. The agencies' legal staffs and other Washington, D.C., technical experts routinely drafted these regulatory proposals. However, many agencies experienced enormous opposition to their proposed rules when they used this approach. They were accused of pandering to special interests, and their proposed regulations were said to be unrealistic, impractical, and out of touch with what was actually needed. Various constituencies were often able to tie the agency up in litigation and prevent or delay the introduction of the regulations for many years. When these controversies were settled by compromising with the constituency raising the objection, the agency then had to face other constituencies that raised strenuous objections to the agency's compromise in the subsequent round.

In 1992, Congress passed the Administrative Negotiated Rule Making Act, which allowed federal agencies to implement another approach. Negotiated rule-making should be familiar to Indian tribes because the Department of Housing and Urban Development, the BIA, and the Indian Health Service are among the agencies that have opted for this approach. What characterizes negotiated rule-making is the decision to bring together representatives from a cross-section of an agency's constituencies and let them negotiate the content of agency regulations. The various constituencies are invited to go beyond the consultation process. They are involved, along with agency officials, in wrestling with the issues, analyzing the implications of various options, understanding the perspectives and constraints of other parties, and reaching agreements that reconcile and accommodate the differences. The agreements become the basis of the new regulations that subsequently get published in the *Federal Register*. And there are substantially fewer contentious battles fought in the courts as a result.

Negotiated rule-making offers a model that can be used by constitutional reformers at the community level. By giving major stakeholders in the community the opportunity to meet to articulate their concerns, reconcile their differences, and jointly craft agreements that can be incorporated in a draft document, reformers can overcome the shortcomings of strategies that rely only on consultation meetings to introduce and generate support for their proposals.

Who Should Be at the Table?

This is actually a common question asked whenever parties to a conflict prepare for negotiations. Deciding who the stakeholders are and who should be invited to participate is an integral part of any process design. Agencies engaged in negotiated rule-making spend literally months identifying and inviting stakeholders to send representatives to the table. This is true for other complex negotiations as well. It also will be important when designing a constitutional reform process within the community.

In negotiations in general, it is highly important that no one significant is left behind. When people feel they are left out of the loop, they are often predisposed to oppose any decision or recommendation that parties involved in the negotiations finally make. If these recommendations still have to be ratified by the parties' constituencies and hierarchies before they take effect, stakeholders that were left out of the negotiations can have a devastating impact on the effort. Often the decision to exclude a particular stakeholder from a negotiation is not an oversight but rather a conscious decision at the outset stemming from the parties' fear that the inclusion of a particularly troublesome person or group would undermine their efforts. Most experienced negotiators will urge parties to include rather than exclude a prominent stakeholder and spend the extra time and effort bringing them around within the confines of the negotiation rather than risk being blindsided in public when it is harder to respond.

How Many Seats Should Be at the Table?

In making the decisions concerning who and how many should participate in a negotiation, there are two principles that need to be observed. The first is that there should be enough delegates to represent the full spectrum of different constituencies that have an interest in the issues being negotiated. For example, in the case of federal negotiated rule-making in Indian Country, at the very minimum there should be representatives from large and small tribes in every region of the country where there is a concentration of tribes. The second principle is that the size of the group should not be so great that it undermines the participants' ability to get to know each other and develop the trusting relationships that help support mutual understanding and mutual accommodation. It is hard to build this type of relationship and get traction in large impersonal groups that may also experience substantial internal turnover. This is especially true where the conflict is highly contentious and there is an atmosphere of distrust and antagonism.

Over the years, mediators in my organization have been involved in numerous highly charged conflicts within Indian communities where two major factions had been battling for many years. In each of these cases, we encouraged each party to identify no more than five or six people to represent their interests. When there are more than two parties you can usually expect to have to deal with even more at the table at one time. In a highly contentious "government to government" negotiation between the Timbisha Shoshone Tribe in Death Valley and four federal agencies in 1998 and 1999, the Tribe sent six people to the table and the agencies assembled.

To create the preconditions for relationship-building, we urged the parties of each of these negotiations to agree to having no alternates and no observers. They also agreed to schedule subsequent negotiation sessions only on dates and at times when everyone could attend. People learned that they could count on each other and they began to trust the process as well as one another.

It is safe to say that the group ultimately formed will be a compromise of the two principles. While ten to fifteen people may be the ideal number for developing a good consistent working relationship, this may not be enough to be representative of the diverse interests having a stake in the outcome. The federal agencies involved in the negotiated rule-making process usually seem to invite from forty to sixty representatives. Several years ago, the governor of Alaska invited the Alaska Native tribes to come and negotiate with him and his cabinet a mutually agreed-upon protocol for government-to-government relationships. After months of internal discussions, the 227 Native Alaskan groups, each regarding itself as sovereign and unique, grudgingly agreed to send forty-eight representatives to negotiate with the governor. In the Cherokee case study, it was reported that seventy-nine delegates were invited to participate in the Constitutional Convention. There, for nine consecutive days, the delegates negotiated the content of a draft of the revised tribal constitution.

Avoiding Chaos and Breakdowns in the Process

Substantial amounts of time need to be devoted by the parties to negotiate the framework or procedural ground rules to be followed during the negotiation. And this should be done before any substantive issues are discussed. Defining "how we are going to talk about what we are going to talk about," or defining the rules of engagement before the engagement, will provide the sense of safety, security, order, and predictability that parties need before they can settle down, listen, agree to share their perspectives, and take into consideration conflicting points of view.

In the examples discussed above, mediators in my organization who intervene in internal tribal conflicts often spend the better part of the first day facilitating negotiations over procedural issues. It is not unusual to have twenty-five to thirty different procedural agreements. Even before the first face-to-face session, the parties will usually negotiate the basic questions of how many representatives will be at the table, who they will be, and where, when, and for how long the first session will be convened.

In the negotiations referred to above, between the Timbisha Shoshone Tribe and four federal agencies, there were six months of procedural negotiations over the phone and in writing between the tribes and the federal agency officials before there were any face-to-face negotiations. These clarifications were necessary because of tremendous distrust after an ill-fated attempt several years before and no contact for almost two years in between. During the first face-to-face session, the parties spent the first day and a half writing the provisions of a "framework for bilateral negotiations" that incorporated procedural understandings already reached, as well as additional ones needed to define the scope and steps that would be followed.

Parties involved in the federal negotiated rule-making process also spend substantial time at the outset getting agreement on process among the participants. In negotiations over the implementation of the Native American Housing and Self Determination Act between HUD and federally recognized tribes, at least the first four days of the yearlong process were devoted to negotiating internal procedural issues. One of the agreements was to have the procedural as well as subsequent substantive negotiations facilitated by impartial professionals who were experienced in process design and in facilitating collaborative multiparty negotiations. This is common practice in any federal negotiated rule-making process. With hardly an exception, these processes are managed by impartial outside facilitator/mediators who are hired by the agency with the other parties' consent, and paid for by the agency or by the Federal Mediation and Conciliation Commission.

Anyone who has been a party to these processes knows that the participants will have initial concerns. Delegates will want to know how sincere the agency is about reaching mutual agreement and whether the agency will make the final decisions when push comes to shove. They invariably want to know whether all the delegates have an equal amount of authority or whether some will wield greater influence and have privileged access to the agency officials. These concerns are not unlike ones that will be raised by parties involved in negotiations about constitutional reforms. The understandings and safeguards the parties think are necessary will be proposed and resolved during the procedural negotiations.

Once again the Cherokee example is illustrative of how large groups of stakeholders can ensure that their time will be well spent. The Cherokee Nation's Constitutional Convention invited seventy-nine delegates from a cross-section of Cherokee communities both in Oklahoma and outside, from all sectors of their society. They had diverse backgrounds, experience, expertise, interests, and expectations. At the outset, before they began to deliberate the substantive issues, they reached agreement on a process they all felt would be fair and conducive to open and creative problem-solving.

The procedural issues that generally get resolved in these complex multi-party negotiations include: (1) where, when, and for how long they will meet; (2) how many people will be at the table and who they will be; (3) the presence of observers and the use of alternates; (4) how people will be permitted to talk to one another—for example, what constitutes acceptable language, and the ruling out of personal attacks; (5) the scope and limits of confidentiality; (6) the use, role, and authority of special working committees; (7) the use, role, and authority of technical experts; (8) the rules around the formal use by the parties of the "caucus" (special confidential session) to discuss issues away from the table, including time limits; (9) how decisions will be made—for example, by majority vote, consensus, or some limited form of consensus; (10) systems for representatives to consult regularly with their constituencies back home; (11) the authority of those at the table and the need for subsequent ratification by constituents and/or people higher up in the hierarchy; and (12) the intended form of the ultimate product of the negotiations—for example, a written report, a Memorandum of Understanding (MOU), or a written set of agreed-upon regulations signed by all the parties.

Before finishing this discussion about the general importance of negotiating procedural ground rules before tackling questions of substance, I must emphasize the importance of doing this when Indian communities are concerned. Many communities today do not have agreed-upon rules to guide their discussions during public meetings. The likelihood that certain people may come to disrupt the discussions and try to intimidate those with whom they disagree is the primary reason many tribal governments do not dare go public with constitutional reform proposals and hesitate as well to propose new or revised ordinances.

I am suggesting here that any public dialogue be considered a negotiation, one in which people try to "work things out by talking things through." Agreement on process, on procedural ground rules for meetings, can change this dynamic and create the environment for informed and orderly decision-making. Several years ago, the Enterprise Rancheria in northern California created an ordinance spelling out how tribal council members are expected to behave in council meetings and in the community. These same ground rules also define acceptable behavior by community members in other tribal meetings. This is not the only tribe that has done this.

Finally, procedural ground rules are an essential protection of tribal interests whenever tribes participate in external negotiations with outside local, state, and federal agencies and political jurisdictions. We know from the fields of negotiation and mediation that reaching agreement on a process at the outset is one of the basic prerequisites for a successful negotiation. But this appears to be especially true when parties come to the table apprehensive because they have a history of bad experiences in "negotiations." When the process itself is negotiable, the parties have the opportunity to ensure that they are being negotiated *with* rather than *upon*. Moreover, parties can be assured that the process will be responsive to their different cultural styles and preferences, including the language to be spoken, seating arrangements, time, location, ceremony, dress, titles, and how participants are to be addressed.

PART IV: COMMUNITY ORGANIZING AS A MODEL FOR STRENGTHENING CITIZEN PARTICIPATION

Reformers observe that they have difficulty getting people to come to meetings and to participate consistently over the long run. Before concluding this chapter let us explore what other people facing similar challenges have learned to do that is effective.

What is being asked here constitutes the primary challenge seasoned community organizers face each time they enter a new community and are expected to "persuade, convince and influence" heretofore disenfranchised people to get actively involved in taking greater control over their own destinies. The communities that organizers enter are not unlike Indian communities where historically there have been low levels of civic engagement. Many members are low-income and have relatively low levels of formal education. They may have some trepidation about communicating verbally in public. They are further dissuaded from participating in public forums because they are not made safe from personal attacks and ridicule. There are no established ground rules. In addition to these personal barriers are institutional ones. People in power, whether the Bureau of Indian Affairs or a tribal council with concentrated power and little accountability, may not have created the forums or incentives that would encourage the average tribal member to have input into government. In fact, just the opposite may have occurred. There may have been deliberate attempts to limit public participation and public scrutiny.

Community organizers who work in non-Indian communities are confronted by the same personal and institutional barriers. Over the years they have devised a methodology to overcome them. They have learned that it is not enough to invite people to come out to a meeting by sending them a flier or announcing the event in the newspaper. They have to spend a lot of time on a one-to-one basis to convert the people to active participation. They have to meet the people as equals on their turf and listen to and value the reasons they give for their hesitation. They have to listen also to their underlying hopes for different conditions in their community, and to persuade them that they are needed to help make the difference. The community members must experience that they have potential value and that they can make a valued contribution both in the initial discussions the organizer has with them and any time they participate. In other words, rather than the organizer trying to get the community members to do something the organizer wants them to do, the organizer tries to establish opportunities for community members to do what promises to satisfy their interests.

The organizer follows a step-by-step strategy for meeting and establishing relationships with community members. He or she will make appointments to sit down in a congenial location to have private, confidential, in-depth, one-to-one conversations. The next step is to persuade each member to invite some close friends and family home to meet with the organizer. They too have discussions about the community and what they would like to have changed. These meetings are safe and familiar and people feel free to speak candidly. In the course of these meetings, they start to see that there are others who share their perspectives and their hopes, and who are also considering doing something about it. Before the organizer leaves the house meeting, he or she asks those attending whether they are willing to organize similar meetings in their own homes and invite people from among their own friends and family. The organizer makes a similar request at each subsequent house meeting.

After several months of house meetings, the organizer will have been able to reach several hundred people in the community and learn a great deal about peoples' concerns and ideas. Moreover, the organizer will have been able to enroll and get commitments from people who are now willing to be part of the process. Natural leaders who enjoy credibility in the community will also have begun to emerge.

The next stage is to move out of these more intimate and familiar surroundings and hold larger community meetings, where committees can be formed and the next steps can be negotiated. Here too, though, it is important that there be structure and negotiated ground rules to ensure that community members will have a sense of safety and predictability and that the preconditions they need for informed and orderly decision-making are present.

The community organizing strategy that is outlined above is almost identical to the approach people use to sell Tupperware. They too start with one-on-one conversations in people's homes and encourage them to invite family members and friends to subsequent in-home meetings. But these commercial ventures aside, the approach is very commonly applied in other contexts in which people experience resistance to greater involvement. For example, mediators enlisting participation often find they have to persuade the parties that the mediation process can satisfy their interests. Private, confidential, and safe conversations with each of the parties in order to discover each party's interests, needs, and expectations, and to answer questions about the mediation process, are an integral part of the pre-mediation phase. These are often a prerequisite to getting parties to the table and encouraging them to participate in the negotiations. This incremental approach is often described as needed to develop trust first in the mediator, then in the process, and then, it is hoped, in the other party, with whom they eventually need to craft an "exchange of promises" or agreements.

The sequence of steps followed by the Cherokee organizing committee appears to follow the classical organizing model. Perhaps that is why it worked. It was designed to generate participation by a cross-section of the Cherokee Nation. It began small with an impartial and nonaligned group that took on the responsibility to design and facilitate the process. This group took the process to the people where they lived, held small meetings in which there could be informed and thoughtful discussions, and used these smaller meetings to identify the community's issues, form an agenda, and identify leaders who were willing to participate in later negotiations at the convention. Just as in the community organizing model, it prepared the way for later negotiations by first having consultations, during which it was able to create among key players an investment in and commitment to the constitutional reform process. It did this before going to a large public forum where there was a greater risk of confusion, multiple agendas, and the danger of having certain more articulate and aggressive people determined to take the process hostage.

Firsthand Accounts

Beverly Wright, Chairperson, Wampanoag Tribe of Gay
   Head/Aquinnah
Sheri YellowHawk, Council Member, Hualapai Nation
Larry Foster, Former Chair, Navajo Nation Commission
   on Government Development
Steve Brady, Sr., Member of Northern Cheyenne Tribe
   Constitutional Reform Committee and Instructor in
   Tribal History and Government
Theresa Two Bulls, Vice President, Oglala Sioux
   Tribe
Leonard D. Dixon, Former Outreach Coordinator,
   Lummi Nation Constitutional Reform Committee

BEVERLY WRIGHT, CHAIRPERSON, WAMPANOAG TRIBE OF GAY HEAD/AQUINNAH

My name is Beverly Wright and I'm chairperson of the
Wampanoag Tribe of Gay Head, Aquinnah. We are the people of the
first light. We are the tribe that met the Pilgrims. So, if it weren't for
us, all of you non-Natives wouldn't have been here. I always start off by
telling a little joke. When I first became chair, which was ten years ago, I
was in an elevator and a woman got on the elevator who saw my nametag. And she couldn't pronounce Wampanoag. She's squinting and she's
looking at it, so I said to her, "It's Wampanoag and we are the tribe that
met the Pilgrims." And just as straight-faced she said to me, "Oh, you
shouldn't have done that."

The membership of the Wampanoag Tribe of Gay Head/Aquinnah

consists of approximately 1,000 members. Of these members, 350 live and work on the island of Martha's Vineyard, the base and foundation of our government. Because our trust lands are located on an island, seven miles from the mainland, travel back to our ancestral lands is difficult and expensive at best. This has impacted members' participation and involvement in government. We also don't have the money to allow tribal council members to get paid sufficiently to really put their full effort into running the tribe. It's a sideline because they have to work and put food on the table for their family. The council meets twice a month on the first Saturday and the third Wednesday, and our agendas are so full that if we start at noon, sometimes we're still there until 6:00 or 7:00 at night.

General Membership meetings are held quarterly with a quorum of 50 members required to conduct business. An average of 65 members regularly attend General Membership meetings. Fifty percent of the General Membership meetings do not reach a quorum. Approximately one dozen members attend tribal council meetings, which are held twice each month. The meeting that generates the largest turnout—on average 250 members—is the General Membership meeting in November, which includes the annual election of tribal council members.

The Wampanoag Tribe has made a big stride in that we went self-governance. We're the only tribe in the east coast that has gone self-governance. But it seems like we always do something because we are caught, or this grant is coming down, or we jump to get involved with the latest opportunity. And we end up thinking about the bigger issues later.

We were federally recognized in 1987. Since that time, the Tribe has made progress in many areas. We provide affordable rental housing for eighteen families. There are eight tribally owned homes on tribal lands. We have a Natural Resource Department that has oversight and mainte-nance of our ancestral homelands. A Shellfish Hatchery has come online within the last month. The Aquinnah Wampanoag Health Department operates its own clinic, provides contract health services for tribal mem-bers living in the Dukes Country service area, and has a Human Resource Department that provides referral services to all members of the Tribe.

But we are a new and thriving government that needs to meet the growing needs of our increasing enrollment. We have had a constitution since 1990. I don't know where our constitution came from. I think it was worked on but it was a boilerplate document and where that boilerplate came from I don't know. The constitution, like the U.S.

Constitution, requires constant change. Since 1990 we have had six amendments, including two this year. So we are a government constantly in flux. And the reason we are in flux is because it only takes fifty tribal members to call a meeting, and those fifty tribal members can change our constitution according to how they feel or believe that it should run. Calls for constitutional change depend on who or what faction (traditional versus organizational) is in control of the tribal council. So we are very political. We do not think, or the tribal council or the general membership does not think, about what is the best for all of our tribal members. It's what's the best today and maybe six months down the road.

The decline in tribal participation seems to have occurred about five or six years into the process of building the government we presently recognize. When council member Shelly Carter and I were looking at the constitution, the first thing that we saw was our tribal members were not interested in our constitution. And I bet that I can say over 75 percent of our members probably have the constitution someplace in their house. The reason I know it is because we sent it out to everybody, and they've never read it, they don't know how it affects them. They are only interested when it affects them personally, if they can't get health services or if something happens and they don't get their scholarship for school, or some similar type of personal event.

About six or seven years ago, Joe Kalt and some other Harvard researchers came down and put together a report on strengthening our constitution. We went through the whole process and they tore our constitution apart, and they made recommendations and we have a nice report. And I have the report sitting on my shelf and it is covered with dust. The tribal members were not interested. I don't know why the tribal members do not want to come out to learn about our constitution, listen to our concerns, why they do not want to participate. I say I don't know why but I think I do know why. It's because they are very intent on putting food on their table for their children. They need to go to work. They need to take their kids to baseball. They need to worry about whether when they go to the dentist or go to the doctor or call into our clinic that there is funding for them to pay the bills. Forty-three percent of the people that live on Martha's Vineyard island, including our tribal members, do not have any kind of insurance. So our tribal members have to worry about these things. I think that's one of the reasons they don't participate.

The other issue is that there is no separation of government for our tribe. We're the judicial, we're the legislative, and we're the executive.

When we hire people and then we decide to terminate them, that person has no place to go. There's no process there. The constitution says you have an appeal process. But if we hired you and if we fired you, where's your appeal process? You're coming back to the same board that hired and fired you.

But the biggest drawback that we saw was apathy. How do we get the tribal members to participate? And I think we have banged our heads against the wall for ages on this question. My personal feeling is that we're a family. A tribe, no matter if you're 23,000 people or 1,000, like our tribe, is a family, and when we come together at council meetings we treat one another as family. We are a large and extended family. Old beliefs and festering wounds are still prevalent and hinder our growth and progress. The lack of education in the process of "tribal governance" along with the continued differences among tribal members create a negative atmosphere at general membership and tribal council meetings. Prejudice exists within the members of the tribe: "down-island versus up-island," "off-island versus on-island."

The lack of "standing rules" and respect for one another result in an inability to keep order during meetings and create a hostile environment. When we are out in the public sector with the dominant society, we get our point across without yelling or degrading one another.

When tribal members come to tribal council meetings or to general membership meetings, usually that's how they're treated. And the majority of the tribal members walk away and say, "I'm not interested, I can't handle this, I can't do this. I'll come and vote and I'll vote my choice," and then they're gone. This has led to the apathy and nonparticipation we face today.

I don't know how to get the members to participate. I think one of the issues is that as a tribal membership, we are still in a place where it's my way or no way; there's always a faction. We need to learn how to negotiate where we all give up something, we all gain something and the whole tribal membership gains. We need to get the tribal members to that place but it's still not happening.

The other issue that's happening with us is that we might have gaming in Massachusetts. So it's imperative for us to look at our constitution, to look at how our government structure and how the tribal council operates. Because if gaming happens, we're going to be constantly putting out fires and we need our infrastructure in place. We have two businesses that are floundering and it is draining the tribal resources and we can't stop the hemorrhaging. We can't stop the hemorrhaging because we haven't gotten beyond that process yet of where we're looking at what is best for the whole tribe and not what is best for me personally or what is best for my cousin, or friends, or aunt or uncle.

We have taken some measures to address members' lack of participation. Approximately eight years ago, the tribe instituted a newsletter, the *Toad Rock Times,* to keep members informed of programs, services, and alternative resources. It is mailed, free of cost, to the membership and the many agencies that provide service. It has served us well in some areas, but needs to be expanded upon and fine-tuned to bring more of the culture and heritage to the membership.

Through the efforts of the Wampanoag Education Department, tribal youth are dedicating themselves to the resurgence of the culture, history, and language of the Aquinnah / Wampanoag people. Young adult members have begun developing a curriculum to present to the institutions of learning on Martha's Vineyard and beyond.

The government is currently developing a judicial component to strengthen our sovereignty and enhance the principles that have been promulgated in our constitution. This judicial component will allow us to govern our land and our people with honor.

Despite our conflicts and issues we still progress in our mission to provide the best infrastructure for our tribal members to grow and prosper. Some type of mediation, be it peacekeeping, consensus building, or intervention by the outside society, may be warranted.

SHERI YELLOWHAWK, COUNCIL MEMBER,
HUALAPAI NATION

Well, I came in at the tail end of our constitution reform process. I lived in Peach Springs about five years of my childhood, and grew up on other reservations, but I returned to my reservation in April of 1990, when the tribe was completing its first major constitutional reform. At the age of twenty I really wasn't interested in too much, just coming out of my teenage years. But at that time tribal attorneys and BIA and community members were discussing the constitution and seeking public input, and that sparked my interest in tribal politics and government. I started looking at the draft amended constitution and I questioned what it was about and what was really happening on the reservation.

In February of 1991, the amended constitution went to the vote of the people and I voted no on the adoption of that draft, for a number of reasons. The first reason was that the old constitution required that 30 percent of the eligible voters must show up to vote. The tribe adopted another process that was not outlined in our old constitution, and it chose to register voters, and then count 30 percent of those registered. If you weren't registered, you couldn't vote. So I questioned the decision to exclude some voters on voting day.

There were supposed to have been meetings with the elderly and meetings with the youth but I didn't see any of those meetings. I think that people need to be more involved in the beginning of the reform process instead of just waiting, having meetings, and seeing what their opinions are at that time. But at any rate, the amended constitution passed with a vote of 141 for and 33 against, and I was one of those 33.

The constitution has been the governing document for the last ten years. It is a functional document. It's not the greatest, but who's to say what is the greatest document that could govern the tribe, or any tribe. And it provides for a separation of powers among our government branches, which is very important.

In June of 1998 I ran for tribal council. I ran for tribal council before when I was twenty-five. The first time I ran I lost by three votes. The second time I ran I lost by about two votes, and then, finally in 1998 I was elected for a four-year term. During the last ten years I also earned my bachelor's degree in business management, and master's degree in organizational management. So I've been setting myself up to be a good contributor to the tribe and to the council. Since that time I've been engaged in the daily barriers and opportunities of the tribe, and really get to see what's going on in terms of issues in Indian Country. Unfortunately, a lot of our community members don't get to see or hear that. They don't understand why the council takes the actions it does, and I think we need to spend a little bit more time educating our community as to what's really going on so they understand why we do the things that we do. Because when we don't educate them they end up saying that we're doing things that are against the community. It's not because they're trying to be mean or hateful, it's just because they don't understand what's really going on.

Like I said before, the constitution that we adopted has served its purpose. But within the past year the council, a lot of the council members, including myself, have made comments as to "Gee, we need to change this, or maybe we need to elaborate more on this," and that conversation has been arising more and more. So, I think that we are in the process of moving into another constitution reform. Our constitution actually says that we're supposed to readdress it on an annual basis, and we haven't done that, so I think we need to start adhering to our constitution.

When I'm thinking about our next reform, I think that we should go into it by not excluding any of our nation's members. Before anything is even drafted, anything is even talked about in terms of change, we need to start motivating our own community members, and educating them in terms of what our current constitution is, and does, and what has happened in the last ten years in terms of development and progress, and then start talking about the issues. Let them tell us what the process should look like, what kind of groups should be formed, who should be involved, and how we should go about it. Because change seems to occur more easily when people are more involved, and people are allowed to provide more input.

Then when the brainstorming is done we need to really include our young people, even if it means going into the schools, going into the high school, even going down to about third grade, and asking them what they think should happen in the future. Because really this document affects our young people. I've worked with our teenagers for the last 11 years in the summer youth programs, and they can tell you exactly what's wrong with the community, in a few words, and very clearly. And we often don't listen to them as to what their needs are. But if they're given that opportunity to express themselves, and they're not going to be punished for it, they will say what they think that they need.

Also, group meetings, community meetings, need to have structure and purpose. Often, we say OK, we're going to have a community meeting, we're going to meet at this time, and maybe we'll have some food. Then we go into the meeting and we have no purpose. We don't clearly define our goals for the meeting and we end up having a screaming match. Somebody gets mad, somebody cries, and there is nothing that you come away with. We thought we were going to come out with some ideas, and some sense of direction, but it doesn't occur. So, when we have our meetings I think we need to come to a consensus at the beginning about what our purpose is and whether we're going to continue meeting until we have accomplished our goals.

In addition, conflict resolution mechanisms need to be talked about before these meetings are conducted. How is conflict going to be resolved? What are we going to do when somebody starts getting irate? What are we going to do when somebody starts yelling, or putting down somebody else? This needs to be decided before you get into the meeting so that these incidents can be kept to a minimum.

I also believe that we need to look at the constitution as a way to plan for the future. For instance, we put a [1/4] blood quantum test for tribal enrollment in our constitution and now we have a child that's 1/8 Hualapai by blood, has no place to go, has no parents, and is going to end up being placed with a non-Indian family. We have no way of enrolling that child. So we need to start looking at the long-term effects of the changes that we make, and start running through some of the possible scenarios that they are going to create. We need to plan for these things instead of saying, "Oops, now we have a problem," and then waiting another ten years to try to resolve it. It's always good to try to look at what's going to happen out of the decisions that we have put in place.

I heard one tribe, and I'm not sure if they actually did this or not, but they wanted to make their native language a requirement for tribal council. Initially, I thought that might be a good idea. But then I realized that this provides for the exclusion of a group of people—those children whose parents went to boarding school [where they] were punished for speaking their language. I said to my Dad, "Why didn't you teach me to speak Indian?" He said, "Well, I went to boarding school for twelve years, because there were no schools where I grew up, and they slapped me, they yelled at me, they put me down for speaking my language and I thought you would just be better off if you knew English." Now I'm ridiculed for not knowing how to speak any language besides English.

So, I think when you start looking at reforming your constitution that your requirements for elected office don't exclude any members of your community or your tribe. One alternative is to require candidates to learn the language and the culture while they're on council. This provides for learning and development of the tribal culture and language, without excluding anyone. Because a lot of our young people bring the knowledge of education and outside experience, and can contribute to the economic development and growth of the community. Although they may not contribute a lot in terms of culture and language, they still can help the nation grow. So, when you take on reform just make sure you're not excluding anybody—even though it might be a small group of people—that you're not pushing certain groups away.

In closing, I want to stress the importance of maintaining an atmosphere where everybody's voice counts, no matter how irate somebody is. Because I know we all have people in our communities that, when they walk in the room it's like, "Oh no, they're going to complain again." But we need to start transforming that thinking into "What are they going to contribute to me today?" Because they're going to give you something. They're going to give you something if not a couple of thoughts or words to make some kind of change. We need to create that feeling that everybody counts, especially in our smaller communities, because change is not going to be taken unless they have input. That's the bottom line. It's not going to work unless somebody's had a voice in it. And if somebody hasn't contributed to changing a constitution in some way, shape or form, they're not going to accept it, and they are going to be the barrier that is going to always get in the way. Otherwise, the conflict and the individual agendas will prevail. So, involve your people.

LARRY FOSTER, FORMER CHAIR, NAVAJO NATION
COMMISSION ON GOVERNMENT DEVELOPMENT

We have a Commission on Government Development that is in charge of putting together a long-term government reform project for the Navajo Nation. It's a very diverse group of twelve members. One representative is selected by each of the five agencies [districts] of the Navajo Nation. Then the three branches of government—the President, the Chief Justice of the Navajo Nation Supreme Court, and the Speaker of the Council—each appoint a member. Because we wanted to involve the youth, we have one student representative that's selected by our tribal college. The graduate students also select a representative from their own membership.

Then we have a representative appointed by the Navajo women's commission. If you go to a lot of our chapter meetings back home, women are the dominant force in the politics. We needed to have a woman that sits on the commission to represent women. The last and very important person that sits on this commission is a traditional practitioner from the Navajo.

STEVE BRADY, SR., MEMBER OF NORTHERN
CHEYENNE TRIBE CONSTITUTIONAL REFORM
COMMITTEE AND INSTRUCTOR IN TRIBAL
HISTORY AND GOVERNMENT

The state of repression of our tribe existed for a very, very long time, and it still exists today. There's a tremendous amount of healing that needs to take place with our people. Just because I'm a traditional leader, doesn't necessarily mean I'm separate and apart from the existing Indian Reorganization Act system. I devote a tremendous amount of my time, personal time, to reforming our tribal government. I didn't like the way it ran. I didn't like what was going on, so I did something about it. I studied it. I also found out that we had a written constitution. For a long time I didn't know we had a written constitution. I thought it was an informally based system. I came to find out there was a written system.

Then I found out there was a way you could change the system. Article 10 [of the Northern Cheyenne constitution] says you can bring the people together and they can change the constitution. It's also subject to the review of the Secretary of the Interior's approval. So even though the people may change it, our changes are still subject to being revoked or denied by the U.S. government. This hasn't changed. I also found out that there was another constitution behind this written constitution—the Code of Federal Regulations, 25 (CFR), part 81—the other constitution. A very comprehensive system set of rules and procedures to change our constitution.

Our people ratified our IRA constitution in 1935, amended it once in 1960, and then made a series of major amendments in 1996. Today, I'm involved in the teaching of our young people, and I really, really appreciate the comments of other tribal leaders in terms of educating and keeping our young people involved. When I was in grade school and high school, I didn't know we had a tribal government. I didn't know we had a constitution. I had no idea, absolutely no idea. There's nowhere to learn this type of system other than what you learn out in the street. So I've been involved in an effort to help with this educational process. I currently teach tribal government and tribal history at Lame Deer High School on our reservation. In terms of actually making amendments, the amendment process, it is very, very helpful to have a supportive tribal administration and tribal council. But you cannot amend a constitution without public education, the education of your tribal membership. And the tribal council cannot do that on its own.

THERESA TWO BULLS, VICE PRESIDENT,
OGLALA SIOUX TRIBE

We've had two constitutional amendments in 1985 and 1997, and the people weren't involved in either process. It was just the president saying, "I want these changes, get them out there." There was no effort to solicit public input and that was part of the reason people felt they didn't have a say. So, last administration, a group of people calling themselves the grass roots took over our tribal building, stating that this is what they wanted. They have seven amendments that they want to see passed. They even had themselves appointed as a constitutional revision committee of this administration.

Being part of the tribal government I felt that we needed to be represented as well—the government along with the people. But there's so much distrust for our IRA government they don't want to compromise. They don't want to come together. They don't want to sit down. And it's sad to say that even this group is separated. They've separated into three factions. There's the original grass roots, who ironically were subsequently elected into the IRA elected positions. Then we have another group promoting traditional government. And we have a third group stressing international treaties. Now how can we get into international treaties when our people don't fully understand the treaties we have now? I think there needs to be a lot of education. We need to have a working relationship among each other. We all have to come together.

What keeps me going through all this is my traditional culture. I really depend on spirituality. That's what keeps me going. I ask for strength, patience, understanding, and most of all guidance. When I ran for this position, I told the people, "I will be your voice. I will listen to you. Your concerns will be my concerns which I'm going to take to the government." And I hold that dear to my heart. I go out and I listen and I talk. I go on the radio once a month and I let the people know what my office is doing for them. I encourage them to come to see me, or call me. I'm even trying to get involved with the schools and the youth because I feel they've had enough confidence in me to put me in this position where I could be a tool to make life better for the people.

Because for too long we have been made promises and they've never been kept. Even among our people. Even among the tribal government. And we all said this was a new millennium. This is a time for a change, and that's what we all want to work towards. But that change can only come if we work together. My vision is for all the Indian nations to work together so we can strengthen each other. And we can work together. Because if you remember in the beginning we were the only ones here. We need to remember that.

LEONARD D. DIXON, FORMER OUTREACH COORDI-
NATOR, LUMMI NATION CONSTITUTIONAL REFORM
COMMITTEE

Social mobilization is often associated with reform movements in response to perceived and unjust distribution of wealth and
goods. For the most part, that is a correct assumption. When individuals
begin to realize that they are not the only ones affected by laws, policies,
or processes, they seek out others with similar circumstances and begin
to organize and build coalitions. It seems that change is most readily accepted when it conforms to a recognized process. But what if the process
is not really known or no longer effective?

There are a number of pathways to ineffective government reform
processes, a common one being insufficient knowledge of government
laws and policies. Another problem is ignorance that a government
reform process even exists. Although I cannot speak for other Indian
nations, and can only selectively speak on behalf of the Lummi Nation,
I believe that our constitution is ineffective for a number of reasons, not
the least of which is that folks really are not interested in its contents
until it affects their daily lives.

Many tribal members have not read the Lummi Constitution, and
a large number of those who haven't read the constitution don't even
know where to obtain a copy.[1] There does, however, exist one common
thread that tends to surface from time to time among most tribal members: a feeling that the Lummi Constitution is just white man's law and
therefore is not important to their daily lives. These feelings stem from
the fact that our constitution is modeled after the tribal constitution
template of the Indian Reorganization Act of 1934 (IRA) and is not
connected to Lummi culture.

Culture is the most relevant and difficult aspect to incorporate in a tribal
constitution. As Indian people, we are reluctant to put our culture on
paper for anyone to pick up, read, criticize, condemn, and steal. Culture
in itself has many popular interpretations. I like to use the definition of the
compound Latin words *cult* (to worship) and *ure* (the earth). So culture really speaks to our relationship with the earth, to worship the earth. Culture
is geographically fixed to one specific area of the earth. Whereas religion
can be taken on the road and applied to any area of the earth, with little
or no regard to the natural environment (an ethos), true culture is not
portable. In Lummi, culture is referred to as *schelangen,* and speaks to our
relationship to the mountain, animals, streams, rivers, and the daylight.

In order for us to incorporate culture within the Lummi Constitution, we need to tie the constitution to the Point Elliot Treaty of 1855. It is the Treaty that comes closest to our culture, as it reserves and protects our "Usual and Accustomed Areas" for our continued right to hunt, fish, and gather.

While it is usually not a good idea to make assumptions, especially in Indian Country, it appears that most tribal members elect the tribal council to protect their treaty rights from other governments and jurisdictions. Tribal members expect and demand that the tribal officials protect their cultural rights under the Treaty. Yet even though the IRA-style Lummi Constitution is not tied to our culture, we use it to elect tribal officials to protect our treaty rights. When it is perceived that the tribal government is not protecting tribal rights, it creates a new layer of distrust.

This poses a fundamental and important question. What is more important to tribal members, their tribal constitution or the culture preserved in their Treaty? At this point in time, the constitution is our governing document even though it is common knowledge that treaties are the supreme law of the land—and, in our case, [our treaty] preserves rights to land that is the basis of our culture. Regardless of their importance, treaties too often are forgotten, overlooked, or swept under the rug.

If we are going to gain the type of community participation needed to fuel constitutional reform, we need to make it relevant to the people; and this will occur when we incorporate culture through the Treaty into the Lummi Constitution. But first, we need to better understand our current constitution and identify the strengths and weaknesses of the document.

How is the Lummi Constitution Office doing this? First, we are reaching out to educate and inform Lummi's leaders. Getting back to white law, it was never intended to protect the rights of Indians. This brings us to a familiar crossroad. Historically, Indian Country in general has a unique way of dealing with tribal leadership. Today we find three common characteristics associated with tribal government. We have tribal administrators (general managers and CEOs), tribal leaders, and tribal politicians (elected officials). There are instances when tribal administrators are running the tribe, as well as tribal politicians. However, it is not uncommon to find that a majority of the tribal leaders are not politicians or administrators but simply concerned tribal members who have volunteered their own time and energy to address different concerns throughout the tribal community. In short, not all leaders are politicians and not all politicians are leaders.

It is the tribal leaders that we wish to seek out and inform. For they are the true conduit to the community and carry credibility earned over a span of several years. These leaders are often supported by the elders and have a solid foundation and knowledge of the culture.

An important element of this effort is to increase members' level of interest and knowledge in the constitution. To do this, we are combining our previous approach—going door-to-door in the community with grassroots volunteers and hosting community dinners—with a high-tech approach. We see technology as an extremely useful tool to help members better understand our Treaty, the current constitution, and how we got here.

We have found that community members enjoy and are even impressed with PowerPoint presentations. We have contracted to install a twenty-three-foot screen and multimedia overhead projection unit at the Lummi Community Building. Once installed, we intend to host a family night once a week to view DVDs and VHS movies, provide snacks, enjoy one another's company, and just work on being a community. Although we often talk about nation building and its importance in Indian Country, at Lummi we are more concerned with community building and learning to be a people again.

One of our constitution committee volunteers created a CD containing our Treaty, the original Lummi Constitution, and all of its amendments to date, and several constitutions from other Indian Nations that we are sharing with interested community members. Currently, we are launching training sessions and workshops utilizing the big screen, and the Lummi Information Services Department has placed the Lummi Constitution on Intranet1, the internal website for employees of the Lummi Indian Business Council. We also are scripting training sessions that will be aired on our tribal TV channel, utilizing PowerPoint and in-line digital editing. The most challenging component is actually developing a constitution information booth utilizing a desktop computer to run a timed series of hyperlinked PowerPoint presentations and address frequently asked questions, such as the purpose and structure of the Lummi Constitution—and where copies can be located.

So far, our discussions have revolved around getting information to the people, but the most important aspect of communication is listening. If people know that you are listening to their concerns and are attempting to address those concerns, then they begin to trust and realize that they are in a safe place free of criticism and ridicule. Then they won't be afraid to share new ideas or to ask questions. This can potentially lead to people trusting one another and in turn helping one another—which is often the definition of a community or a people.

NOTE

1. Lummi Constitution Survey (1999).

Nine   OVERCOMING THE POLITICS
OF REFORM

*The Story of the Cherokee Nation of Oklahoma
Constitution Convention*

O n a cold night in February 1999, seventy-nine citizens of the Cherokee Nation of Oklahoma (hereinafter the Nation) gathered in the auditorium of a local university for the first day of the Nation's constitution convention. The gathering was historic not only because it was the Nation's third constitution convention and first since 1839. More important, it was taking place during the tail end of a constitutional crisis that had ripped the Nation in two. For two years, the Nation had suffered through a series of events leading to the existence of dual governments, complete with two courts and two police forces.

A split tribal council had stopped conducting regular business for almost a year. Skirmishes between sides loyal and opposed to the principal chief had led to violence and arrests at the Nation's courthouse. For a period of time, the incumbent administration had fired the editor of the Nation's newspaper. The *New York Times* and the *Washington Post* had reported on the crisis, the FBI had begun an investigation of the principal chief, and three Oklahoma lawmakers had called for additional federal investigations.[1] In the middle of everything, the warring sides somehow had agreed to a process bringing together seventy-nine delegates to review the Nation's constitution. As the delegates sized each other up on the convention's first night, feelings "ranged from mutual respect and admiration to loathing and even outright fear."[2]

Exploring how the Nation moved from crisis to convention to a proposed new constitution provides an important window into many questions faced by the large number of American Indian nations engaged in constitutional reform. Stories of intratribal conflicts, dual governments, and constitutional crises have been well documented in Indian Country.[3] This government instability has often been attributed to outdated, Western-introduced tribal constitutions—documents that to varying extents lack both legitimacy within tribal communities and the institutional foundations necessary for the effective exercise of government action.[4] A host of tribal leaders and scholars have called for American Indian nations to revise their constitutions and government institutions as an essential first step in strengthening government stability, exercising greater political sovereignty, and enhancing prospects for increased political and economic development.[5]

Although many American Indian nations have decided to reexamine their constitutions, the process of reform has proven incredibly difficult. First, American Indian nations' historical relationships with the United States complicate the nature of the questions they are seeking to answer through constitutional reform. Unlike the Founding Fathers of the United States Constitution, American Indian nations do not have the luxury of coming to agreement on the political rules of the game within well-accepted political and cultural norms. Rather, they are engaged in a fundamental rethinking of how to balance entrenched Western institutions with often competing traditional, cultural, and political values. Moreover, centuries of physical separations, cultural fragmentation, and various degrees of assimilation have diversified cultural and political viewpoints *within* tribal communities. This, in turn, has made the process of finding constitutional consensus—always a difficult proposition—even more elusive.

In addition to these unique constraints, American Indian nations also confront universal challenges associated with the politics of reform. Throughout the world, a central concern of political reformers has been preventing incumbent institutions and officeholders from directing reforms to their own self-interests. From Africa to Eastern Europe to individual American states, stories abound of parliaments and congressional bodies seeking to maintain the status quo by refusing to heed calls for reform, assuming complete control over the reform process, or creating commissions and other reform bodies that serve at their pleasure.

A central question therefore is how can nations engage in governmental and constitutional reform when those currently holding political power control the levers of change? This inquiry applies especially forcefully to Indian Country, where political power is often concentrated in small tribal councils and where constitutional reform realistically cannot take place without council approval. While a political or economic crisis can certainly help catalyze reform, there still remains the question of how to engage in a process of reform that is not overly influenced by the incumbent government. For all of these reasons, American Indian nations interested in constitutional and governmental reform face the critical challenge of first developing reform processes that create the necessary political space within which leaders and citizens can develop stronger, more accountable, and more culturally matched governments.

To date, there has been relatively little written about how American Indian nations have navigated this difficult, layered process of constitutional reform.[6] Unlike countries engaged in postcolonial constitution-making in Eastern Europe and Africa, most American Indian nations have traveled along their own roads of reform in a context of informational isolation. While the reform priorities of American Indian nations vary by political circumstance, history, and culture, examining the reform processes of individual American Indian nations can identify common issues, provide interested nations with insights and ideas for their own reform processes, and lay the groundwork for more in-depth comparative analysis.

The Cherokee Nation of Oklahoma is a good case study for two reasons. First, it demonstrates the power of tribal institutions to catalyze legitimate processes of reform. Specifically notable is the Nation's creation of an independent Cherokee Nation Constitution Commission that was successful both in overcoming biases toward retaining the political status quo and engaging widespread citizen participation in the reform process. Perhaps most important is the commission's success in organizing the Cherokee Nation Constitution Convention—a sovereign arena where deep issues of governance could be legitimately raised, debated, and decided. Second, the Nation's substantive debates at the constitution convention, such as blood quantum requirements for candidates for principal chief, judicial restructuring, and representation for nonresident members, reflect many of the substantive reform challenges faced by American Indian nations as they have assumed ever greater governmental responsibilities over the past twenty-five years. Together, the work of the commission and the debates at the convention provide a unique window into one Nation's successful *process* for addressing fundamental questions of governance.

The first part of this chapter gives a brief sketch of the Nation's history, including a short discussion of the origins and structure of its current 1976 constitution. The second part pulls together newspaper accounts, transcripts, and personal interviews to describe in detail how the Nation engaged in a legitimate process of constitutional reform during the middle of a searing political crisis. It discusses how the Nation formed an independent Cherokee Nation Constitution Convention Commission representative of the Nation's warring political factions. It also examines the commission's intensive approach to obtaining widespread citizen participation in all stages of the reform process and its unique method for choosing convention delegates. The third part highlights some of the major debates that took place during the Nation's nine-day constitution convention, including arguments over bicameralism, citizenship, and blood quantum, political representation for nonresident members, and judicial restructuring. The fourth part documents the Nation's four-year struggle to ratify the constitution adopted at the convention. This part discusses internal debates within the Nation over the proper meaning of a constitution, the Nation's struggle to obtain approval of the proposed constitution from the Bureau of Indian Affairs, and the massive public education initiative conducted by the constitution commission in preparation for the Nation's July 2003 national referendum ratifying the constitution. The fifth part offers concluding thoughts.

I. BACKGROUND

The original members of the Nation resided in the foothills of the Appalachian Mountains in Georgia and Tennessee. Political decision-making was decentralized to largely autonomous local villages and towns, which encountered problems with white settlers almost immediately.[7] By the early nineteenth century, the Nation began altering its traditional government structures and adopting U.S.-style governing institutions as a defensive strategy to ward off accusations that it was barbarous and unfit to keep its land.[8] In 1827, the Nation elected delegates to a constitution convention and adopted its first constitution, complete with a three-branch government, a bicameral legislature, and a bill of rights. Notwithstanding the Nation's best efforts, relations with the U.S. government soon reached a historic low point. In 1839, Andrew Jackson ordered the infamous "Trail of Tears" removal of thousands of Cherokees to Oklahoma. Upon arrival in Oklahoma, a dominant Cherokee faction organized another constitution convention and drafted the Nation's second constitution, based to a large extent on the earlier 1827 Constitution written in Georgia.

Although suffering in the 1840s from a period of internal conflict, exacerbated in part by the exclusion from the 1839 constitution-making process of several Cherokee political factions, the Nation soon entered into what is commonly known as its Golden Age. The Nation established more than one hundred college-level and public schools, a tribal newspaper, and an economy that made poverty "practically unknown."[9] The Nation's Golden Age ended abruptly with the U.S. Civil War. Its 1866 Reconstruction Treaty with the victorious Union forced the Nation to surrender land and open its territory to railroads.[10] During the 1880s and

1890s, the United States placed increasing pressure on the Nation to sell land to burgeoning railroads and, later, to incorporate the Nation into a territory of the U.S. government.[11] In 1893, the U.S. government formed the Dawes Commission to create a roll of citizens of five Oklahoma tribes, including the Nation, for the purpose of dividing up the Nation's land into individual allotments. In 1898, the U.S. Congress passed legislation accelerating the process of allotment and formally mandating the abolition of the Cherokee government by 1906.[12]

From 1907 through 1970, the Cherokee Nation functioned without a government. During this time, the U.S. government appointed a principal chief, who did little more than approve leases and sign documents transferring out the last of the allotments. More than sixty years later, the Nation reconstituted itself and obtained recognition by the U.S. government to elect its own leaders in 1971. The intervening decades without a functioning government, however, had taken their toll. Through a combination of allotment forgeries, embezzlements, misuse of notary seals, and other crimes, the overwhelming majority of land allotted to Cherokee citizens had found its way into white hands.[13] The Nation's population had fallen to only 40,000 citizens, and federal government agencies had taken over responsibility for delivering services to individual Cherokee allottees.

A. Current 1976 Constitution

Before serving as principal chief of the Nation from 1975 to 1985 and heading the U.S. Department of the Interior's Bureau of Indian Affairs in the Reagan Administration, Ross Swimmer played a large role in helping to construct the Nation's modern government. With the beginning of the U.S. government's policy of self-determination in the mid-1970s, Swimmer and other Cherokee leaders began looking for ways to access the new flow of federal funds into tribal communities. Swimmer saw federal funds as "a big impetus" for the Nation to organize its government and adopt a new constitution.[14] By the time Swimmer was elected principal chief in 1975, a cluster of community representatives had already been working on a new constitution for over ten years.[15] According to Swimmer, the process of reform "was all over the place" with some people "wanting to re-create the 1839 constitution." Soon after being sworn in, Swimmer, frustrated at the slow pace of reform, decided to form a small group that would complete work on a new constitution.[16]

The Nation's current 1976 Constitution supersedes completely the 1839 Constitution. It divides the Cherokee government into three branches.

The legislature consists of a single-body tribal council, composed of fifteen members elected at large[17] from the Nation's fourteen districts.[18] Executive power is vested in a principal chief and a deputy principal chief, elected to four-year terms of office. The deputy principal chief also serves as president of the council, with the power to cast tie-breaking votes.[19] The Judiciary consists of a three-member "Judicial Appeals Tribunal" (the Nation's Supreme Court) and other courts that the council may choose to establish.[20] The constitution incorporates the protections of the 1968 Indian Civil Rights Act and contains provisions for referendum and initiative.

Swimmer says he viewed the Cherokee Nation "not necessarily as a government but as an organization," a cross "between a non-profit and a profit-making business" whose specific "purpose was to enhance the living conditions of the people."[21] He therefore based the constitution on "a corporate model" with council members serving in positions akin to members of a Board of Directors.[22] In Swimmer's view, a bicameral legislature, considered at length in discussions leading up to the new constitution, would have been too "unwieldy" and not useful for the quick receipt and disbursement of federal funds:

> [A bicameral legislature] would have meant about sixty or
> seventy-five people in the government of the tribe. And it was
> a personal privilege. I didn't like that. I thought we'd never
> get anything done. And so I said let's cut that out and let's just
> have a tribal council to act as a legislature and we pegged the
> number at fifteen. There wasn't a lot of thought that went into
> that, but we decided on fifteen as a good number.[23]

Swimmer grounds his preference for a unicameral, corporate form of government in the context of the time. For almost seventy years, the Nation had had no enrollment and no government. Services were delivered directly from the U.S. government to individual Cherokee allottees. Swimmer says that before the era of self-determination, he never could have imagined that the Nation would one day exercise taxing powers or have a court system that could incarcerate Cherokee citizens and handle adoption cases. Instead of creating a government, Swimmer simply wanted to organize a system for the improvement of the delivery of services to individual Cherokees:

> The court, for instance, its only purpose at the time was
> to handle disputes between the executive and legislative

bodies. It had no outside function. It was going to be an internal court. The legislative body was there to review programs and sign off for the most part on federal programs and appropriations to the tribe. And, of course, the executive body was to administer those programs that came in and do whatever it could to improve the living conditions of Cherokees in Eastern Oklahoma.[24]

Two specific provisions in Article XV of the 1976 constitution later proved to play key roles in the Nation's recent constitutional reform process. Article XV, Section 9, requires that the question of a proposed constitution convention be submitted to the members of the Cherokee Nation at least once every twenty years.[25] Article XV, Section 10, requires that any new constitution or amendment receive the approval of the President of the United States or his authorized representative. While Section 9 helped to launch the Nation's process of political reform, Section 10 proved responsible for producing a four-year delay in the ultimate ratification of the Nation's constitution.

B. 1997–1999 Constitutional Crisis

It would have been very difficult to predict in the early 1990s the emergence of the Nation's constitutional crisis several years later. With approximately 230,000 members, the Cherokee Nation of Oklahoma is the second largest American Indian nation in the United States. From the mid-1970s through the mid-1990s, the Nation prospered under its 1976 constitution and enjoyed a reputation as one of the most stable and autonomous nations in Indian Country. Swimmer served as principal chief for ten years before becoming the head of the Department of the Interior's Bureau of Indian Affairs in 1985. His successor, Wilma Mankiller, became the Nation's first woman principal chief, also served for ten years, and became a prominent national leader.

The Nation's stability began to unravel in the 1995 election for principal chief. Mankiller's choice as her successor was disqualified by the Nation's election board and, in a runoff election, Joe Byrd was elected as principal chief with less than five thousand votes. The real trouble, however, began in February of 1997, when the Nation's highest court authorized Cherokee marshals to search Byrd's offices for evidence of illegal activity. In retaliation, Byrd and half of the council impeached all three justices, replaced the Nation's marshal service with a private security force, and forcibly took over the Nation's courthouse.[26] The crisis became a national affair when a melee erupted as the fired marshals and justices tried to retake the courthouse in August 1997.[27] With the threat of congressional intervention hanging over them, the two sides reluctantly agreed to a meeting mediated by Interior Secretary Bruce Babbitt in the summer of 1997.[28] But the truce did not last long. In the early months of 1998, Byrd moved the district court—responsible for hearing obstruction of justice charges against him—out of the tribal courthouse and into the tribal administration building near his office.[29] Beginning in April 1998, six council members boycotted scheduled council meetings for more than a year in order to prevent a quorum and delay official council actions until the district court was moved back to the courthouse.[30]

II. LAUNCHING A PROCESS OF CONSTITUTIONAL REFORM

A. Creation of Independent Constitution Convention Commission

In early 1999, during the middle of the crisis that was tearing the Nation apart, a group of seventy-nine Cherokee citizens were spending nine days at a local university trying to lay a foundation for putting the Nation back together. How the Nation pulled together a true cross-section of Cherokee citizens to serve as delegates in a full-fledged constitution convention during the middle of a political crisis is a powerful story that begins several years before the crisis.

The year 1995 marked the twentieth anniversary of the Nation's present constitution. Pursuant to Article XV, Section 9, it also marked the constitutional twenty-year deadline for asking the Cherokee citizenry to vote on the question of a constitution convention. In the summer of 1995, Cherokee voters at a general election overwhelmingly approved the calling of a convention.[31] Importantly, although the constitution required a vote on calling a convention, it did not specify when the convention actually needed to take place. For three years, the tribal administration did not take any action to plan a convention and the issue faded off the political map.[32]

As the years slowly crept by, the Cherokee voters' mandate for a convention collided with the Nation's political crisis. At various points during the crisis, several individuals on both sides of the political fence began pushing the Nation's government to begin work on the convention.

Charles Gourd, a member of the Byrd administration, and Troy Wayne Poteete, the chair of the council's rules committee, along with others, ultimately were successful in getting the rules committee to begin laying the groundwork for the convention.[33]

Planning a convention in the middle of a constitutional crisis was no easy task. Poteete, the point person on the rules committee, was most concerned about the political challenges of beginning the reform process. The difficulty lay in obtaining council approval for launching a constitutional reform process without letting the process become subject to the same political forces associated with the crisis. Faced with the monumental nature of the task, Poteete and others reached out to a variety of outside experts before finally deciding to form a constitutional commission.

In March 1998 each of the three branches of government appointed two representatives to serve on a newly formed Cherokee Nation Constitution Convention Commission. The six commissioners then collectively chose a seventh member.[34] The selection process was modeled on that of the Nation's election commission.[35] Byrd appointed two representatives from the executive branch, whose interests were countered by the judiciary's two representatives. A council split between Byrd supporters and opponents named the remaining two representatives. By allowing for appointees from each branch of government, both the pro- and anti-Byrd camps thought that they could gain something from inclusion on the commission.[36] At the same time, the commission's structure allowed it to operate without being unduly influenced and controlled by either side.

In order to reinforce the perception of political neutrality, commission members were sworn in at Sequoyah High School, and not at the tribal administration building.[37] After creating the commission, the council left it up to the commissioners to develop their own empowering legislation.[38] Assuaging their own mutual mistrust and signaling their credibility as a body, the commissioners decided collectively to take an oath of political neutrality, refrain from holding political office, hold open meetings, and act only upon unanimity.[39]

Almost immediately the commissioners, compensated with a stipend of $250 per month, began asserting their independence. When representatives from the Bureau of Indian Affairs tried to persuade the commission to amend the constitution under the Oklahoma Indian Welfare Act, commission members refused.[40] The real test of the commission's strength, however, came in the summer of 1998, when it sought council ratification of its enabling legislation. The commissioners not only had to call the divided council together for a special meeting to approve the legislation (no easy task during the period of council meeting boycotts by six of its members), but also had to break free from the council's oversight. At first, the council wanted to limit the commission's authority to that of a recommending body.[41] Poteete admits he was "a little apprehensive" about an independent commission and initially asked that the commission "go out to the public, get their feelings, report back to council, tell us what is legislative (should be put in ordinance), what should be in the constitution and we'll decide what to put on the ballot." By this time, however, the commission had already established an identity of its own. After earlier agreeing to an oath of political neutrality, the seven commissioners responded to the council with an ultimatum: "We stay independent or we walk."[42]

After what one commission member described as a "dogfight" to preserve the commission's independence, the council eventually approved the commission's enabling legislation in 1998.[43] The legislation contained language confirming the commission as "an independent commission" whose authority "shall not be subject to direction or supervision by the executive, legislative or judicial branch of the Cherokee Nation government."[44] It granted the commission "sole responsibility and explicit authority for the conduct of the Constitution Convention" and allowed the commission to place a new constitution or set of amendments directly on the ballot for a referendum vote by the citizens of the Nation.[45] Importantly, the council allocated the commission an initial budget of $250,000 to begin its work. Cumulatively, the combination of a willful commission, a weak council, and a perception by both political sides of potential benefits from reform contributed to securing the commission's independence.

B. Engaging and Informing the Public

The enabling legislation placed an overarching priority on the commission's responsibility for educating Cherokee citizens about the initiation of the Nation's constitutional reform and achieving widespread citizen participation in the process. The commission's first step was to foster a culture of openness, which the commissioners felt was essential due to the crisis atmosphere at the time. The commission made this commitment concrete by publishing a schedule of all of its meetings and making them open to everyone, including nontribal media sources.[46]

The heart of the commission's outreach efforts, however, consisted of a well-planned series of public hearings, both within and outside the Nation's fourteen-county jurisdictional area in Oklahoma. From September 1998 through January 1999 the commission held approximately twenty public hearings, providing citizens with the opportunity to give both written and oral testimony expressing their views on constitutional changes. A critical decision, and one that would later have a significant impact on the convention itself, was the commission's commitment to hold several public hearings outside of the Nation's jurisdictional area, home to approximately 40 percent of the Nation's citizens.[47] The commission held public hearings in several cities, including Tulsa, Dallas, Houston, Los Angeles, and Sacramento.

Altogether, attendance at the public hearings ranged from two people to two hundred and generated more than eight hundred pages of testimony.[48] To ensure consistency, the commission developed and published rules for the taking of testimony, required the presence of at least three commissioners at each hearing, and determined hearing locations based on voter precinct locations established by the Election Commission.[49] The commission made use of both direct mail pieces and media releases to publicize awareness of the hearings, and kept a permanent record of all testimony.[50]

The commission supplemented its public hearings with innovative uses of the Nation's website—posting testimony from public hearings, providing status reports of the commission's work on a periodic basis, and establishing a chatroom for citizens to post additional suggestions and reactions about proposed constitutional revisions.[51] The commission later posted on the website the transcripts from the nine-day convention itself.

The commission made use of the testimony from the public hearings and other sources of community input to develop and disseminate an "issues list" for focusing additional debate and discussion. Ultimately, the commission concluded that the public comments were too wide-ranging, diverse, and in some instances contradictory to be translated into amendments to the Nation's current constitution. Instead, the commission used the issues list to draft a proposed new constitution that would serve as the basis of debate at the convention.

C. Choosing Convention Delegates

The most difficult task faced by the commission was determining a method for choosing delegates to the convention, a process Poteete described later as "an opportunity to undo ourselves."[52] A formidable challenge under any circumstance, the ongoing political crisis involving all three branches placed an even higher premium on developing a process that all sides would accept as legitimate.

The commission decided against the traditional practice of electing convention delegates for several reasons, including the logistical and financial difficulties of determining nominating processes, apportioning delegates by electoral districts, and holding an election. Instead, the commission developed an original and multifaceted method for choosing the seventy-nine convention delegates. The first twenty-four delegates consisted of eight appointees from each of the three branches of government. The commission then selected the second twenty-four delegates from a pool of citizens who had given testimony at public hearings. The commission chose the third set of twenty-four delegates by lottery from a pool of applicants. The drawing was held in an open meeting with considerable media attendance. The seven commission members themselves filled the remaining delegate seats.

The commission's method ensured representation in the convention of all political parties. Not surprisingly, executive branch delegates were pro-Byrd, judicial appointees were Byrd opponents, and legislative branch delegates—like the council itself—were split between pro- and anti-Byrd delegates. As Poteete said, "we had every faction represented."[53] The delegates to the constitution convention were a cross-section of Cherokee society, one whose members differed by age, degree of Cherokee blood quantum, and educational and occupational background.[54] While a few delegates were current or former elected tribal officials, most had no previous political experience.[55] Only nineteen of the seventy-nine delegates resided outside of the historic boundaries of the Nation.[56]

D. Overview and Ground Rules of Constitution Convention

On February 26, 1999, the seventy-nine delegates to the Cherokee Nation Constitution Convention assembled for the first day of a nine-day convention at Northeastern State University, just outside the Nation's capitol in Tahlequah, Oklahoma.[57] As one delegate later described, "the tension between the pro- and anti-Byrd administration delegates was so thick you could cut it with a knife," and "there were times . . . when it was just downright hard to breathe."[58] Consistent with its approach throughout the reform process, the commission opened the convention proceedings to nondelegates, including nontribal media sources.[59] In order to accommodate the views of seventy-nine delegates in a finite amount of time, the commission introduced *Robert's Rules of Order,* which the delegates voted to accept as the convention's procedural ground rules.[60]

Just as the commissioners had asserted their independence from the council, the delegates quickly asserted their independence from the commission. The very first motion replaced the commission's choice for convention chair—seen as too closely aligned with Byrd—with Jay Hannah, another commission member and an Oklahoma banker seen as more politically neutral.[61] The delegates then moved to amend the ground rules for raising and debating constitutional amendments during the convention. Feeling that limiting debate only to the commission's proposed constitution would undercut the convention's autonomy and range of options, the delegation voted to allow any delegate to introduce proposed new language.

Convention delegates agreed to vote on proposed amendments to the Nation's current constitution on a section-by-section basis. When voice votes were inconclusive, the convention utilized standing votes and roll call votes. Once delegates worked their way through the entire 1976 constitution in this fashion, a final vote was to approve the proposed new constitution in its entirety.[62]

Finally, although this issue was never explicitly addressed, the fourteen delegates who were also Cherokee lawyers were treated just like the other sixty-five delegates. In the vast majority of instances, the delegation suggested, discussed, and debated proposed new constitutional language as a group. For certain sections with legal "terms of art," particularly sections pertaining to the powers of the judiciary, lawyer-delegates took a leading role in suggesting, defining, and clarifying proposed language.[63] In other instances, lawyers joined nonlawyers in small breakout groups to draft language that they then reported back to the convention as a whole for further discussion and debate. On one occasion, lawyer-delegates even passed around copies of *Black's Law Dictionary* so that other delegates could review definitions of legal terms. At least one delegate reported that the convention's "lawyers helped with the proper format of amendments even if they didn't agree with its substance."[64]

III. MAJOR AREAS OF REFORM DEBATED AT CONSTITUTION CONVENTION

Topics dominating discussion at the commission's public hearings and the convention itself fell into two broad categories. The first set consisted of concrete proposals for strengthening the accountability and effectiveness of the Nation's government. Many of these concerns were raised in direct response to the Nation's crisis. During the commission's public hearings, citizens called for procedures allowing for the recall of elected officials, the holding of mandatory community meetings by council members in their respective districts, open financial records of the Nation's government, publication of the Nation's laws, the creation of an independent election commission, and better publicized notices of open council meetings.

A number of these concerns subsequently were addressed at the convention, with delegates voting to create a permanent record of the Nation's laws, remove language requiring their approval by the Bureau of Indian Affairs, stagger terms and implement term limits for council members, create an independent election commission, and remove the deputy principal chief from service as president of the council.

A second set of reform proposals stemmed from the growing disconnect between the constitution's corporate model of government and the Nation's phenomenal growth in population, diversity, and assumption of governmental responsibilities over the preceding three decades. Between 1970 and 1999, the Nation's population had grown from 40,000 to more than 200,000. The government had contracted or compacted with the U.S. government in a host of different areas, including housing, health, economic development, elderly programs, education, and environmental management. As a result, the Nation's budget had ballooned from $10,000 to $192 million.[65] This change in the size of the Nation's government matched an equally dramatic change in the Nation's demographics. The absence of a blood quantum requirement in the constitution and the passing of a generation had combined to lower the average blood quantum of the Nation's citizenry by the time of the convention. And the Nation's citizens, once concentrated in Oklahoma, were increasingly living in places as far-flung as Texas and California.

In the minds of many citizens, Swimmer's 1976 constitution simply could not keep up with the Nation's increased governmental responsibilities and the competing demands of a larger and more diverse citizenry—one whose interests diverged by residency, blood quantum, and culture. These pressures manifested themselves in debates over a return to a bicameral form of government, a stronger and more independent judiciary, political representation for nonresident Cherokee members, and minimum blood quantum requirements for candidates for principal chief. The following sections briefly summarize the convention debates on these four topics. To varying extents, they reflect similar discussions engaged in by other American Indian nations. They also serve as important bridges to larger questions of American Indian citizenship, governance, and nationhood. Collectively, they demonstrate how the difficult task of reforming entrenched governmental institutions can be achieved.

A. Bicameralism

One of the first major convention debates involved whether the Nation should return to the bicameral form of government of its 1827 and 1839 constitutions. Across Indian Country, the overwhelming majority of tribal governments concentrate legislative power in unicameral tribal councils. During the nineteenth century, the U.S. government, frustrated at tribes' slow, consensus-oriented method of political decision-making, began pressuring tribes to form small tribal bodies capable of quickly approving treaties and agreements. The trend became entrenched with the adoption by dozens of tribes of generic constitutions developed under the 1934 Indian Reorganization Act. IRA constitutions generally follow a similar format, including the vesting of legislative power in unicameral tribal councils that often consist of fewer than fifteen members.

Tribal councils were never intended to reflect and balance sociocultural groupings within tribes, such as family allegiances, clans, or bands. Nor were they intended to allow for the efficient operation of sovereign tribal governments. As in Swimmer's 1976 constitution, the motivation for unicameral councils was to facilitate the receipt and disbursement of federal funds through a corporate structure. Underscoring the point, many IRA constitutions include "bylaws" naming and describing the duties of individual members of the council as president, secretary, and treasurer. Relative to other branches of government, most tribal councils have vast unchecked powers. The limitations of tribal councils have been exacerbated as American Indian nations have grown and diversified. Noting the need for more responsive, capable, and culturally grounded institutions, Indian scholar Duane Champagne has underlined the ability of bicameral legislatures to both enhance government stability and give formal political recognition to sociopolitical groupings within tribes.[66]

On the second day of the convention, John Keen introduced a motion for the convention to consider a return to bicameralism. Keen argued that the Nation's current unicameral form of government had allowed nine persons—the principal chief and eight council members—to control the Nation's entire government and only six boycotting councilors to bring that government to a halt. Keen's motion called for a lower house (tribal council) apportioned by district population and an upper house (senate) apportioned by one delegate per district. The move to two houses of government would increase the total number of legislators from fifteen to thirty-three and reduce the ratio of legislators to citizens from 1:12,000 to 1:5,500.[67]

Quoting James Madison's *Federalist No. 51*, Keen argued that a bicameral legislature's dual legislative track structure and form of election as well as its increased size would prevent a small bloc of united council members from controlling the levers of the Nation's government. A supporter of the motion said the lower house could address local concerns while the upper house would provide "balance" and "stability" by ensuring that the legislature did not get bogged down in debates over local issues. Another argument raised in favor of Keen's bicameral proposal was its consistency with the Nation's bicameral system of government in the 1827 and 1839 constitutions.

In response, several delegates proffered a series of counterarguments against the adoption of a bicameral legislature. Some feared that two houses of government would double the potential for stonewalling and make it more difficult for the Nation to reach consensus. Another delegate argued that, unlike the Founding Fathers of the U.S. government, who wanted to develop a mechanism for distributing power among states of unequal population, the Nation did not have a problem with regard to unequal power among its districts. Several members of the convention commission reported that bicameralism had been raised during public hearings but felt that such a change would present too many practical difficulties.[68] Commission members said they were "stymied" in their attempt to figure out a way to implement a bicameral legislature without affecting other constitutional provisions.[69] The Nation's Chief Justice quickly and forcefully denounced the commission's concerns, describing it as "mindboggling" that the leaders at the convention couldn't figure out how to form a bicameral legislature.[70]

Surprisingly, the argument that appeared to seal victory for opponents of a bicameral legislature was the simple one of cost. Numerous delegates felt that the Nation's annual budget should be spent on delivering services to Cherokee citizens rather than creating a bigger government. Although several delegates said the issue was important enough to justify a fuller examination of structure, powers, and cost, the delegation ultimately voted down the proposal.

B. Judiciary

Much focus at the convention was spent on restructuring the Nation's judiciary. The provisions in the 1976 constitution concerning

the judiciary had not kept up with the spectrum of civil jurisdiction powers increasingly exercised by Indian nations. The corporate model of the
constitution vested the Nation's three-member Judicial Appeal Tribunal
with powers only "to hear and resolve any disagreements arising under any
provisions of this Constitution or any enactment of the Council." In addition to wanting to strengthen the judiciary's powers, the delegates were
concerned about its political independence. Great concern was placed on
preventing a reoccurrence of the impeachments, standoffs, lockouts, dual
court systems, and other problems between the judiciary and the other
two branches that had taken place during the crisis.

To strengthen the powers of the judiciary, the delegates agreed to a
two-tiered court system consisting of a Supreme Court (formerly the Judicial Appeals Tribunal) and lower district courts. The proposed constitution vests the Nation's district courts with original jurisdiction to hear
and resolve disputes arising under the laws or constitution of the Nation,
whether criminal or civil in nature.[71] It vests the Supreme Court with
powers of original jurisdiction over all cases involving the Nation or its
officials named as a defendant and with exclusive appellate jurisdiction
over all district court cases.[72] To improve the scope and depth of decision-
making of the Supreme Court, the proposed constitution raises the number of justices from three to five.[73]

The delegates also took a series of steps to strengthen the judiciary's independence while providing checks on the exercise of its powers. To protect the Judiciary's independence from various interest groups, delegates
voted to have judges and justices appointed by the principal chief rather
than elected. Under the proposed constitution, judges and justices also
serve longer terms (ten years for Supreme Court justices) and cannot have
their salaries diminished during their terms.[74] To prevent court stacking,
the proposed constitution staggers the terms of the judges and justices so
they do not overlap with the terms of the principal chief more than twice
in any five-year period.

At the same time, the proposed constitution contains several checks.
First, it keeps judges and justices subject to removal by the council for
specified causes. The most innovative check, however, is the proposed
constitution's Court on the Judiciary. After suffering through the recent
impeachment of the entire judiciary by the principal chief and council,
the delegates wanted to preserve the judiciary's integrity without allowing
it to police itself entirely. Similar to European-style constitutional courts
with their discipline-keeping role, the Court on the Judiciary is a seven-
member panel vested with powers of suspension, sanction, discipline, and

recommendation of removal of judges and justices.[75] With a form borrowed from that of a similar body in the Oklahoma Constitution, the Court is composed of two appointees from each of the Nation's three branches of government, who collectively appoint a seventh. One of the two appointees of each branch must be a member of the Cherokee Nation Bar Association and the other a nonlawyer.[76]

C. Representation on Tribal Council for Nonresident Members

Federal relocation programs, forced removals, a lack of well-paying jobs on many reservation lands, and routine migration have left many American Indian nations with high numbers of off-reservation citizens. The situation is especially pronounced for American Indian nations lacking a sufficient number of well-paying reservation-based jobs. With approximately 40 percent of its 200,000 citizens living outside of its jurisdictional area, the Cherokee Nation is at the forefront of this trend of dispersed Indian citizenry.

The Nation's current 1976 constitution does not provide for specific representation on the tribal council for nonmember residents. Instead, nonmember residents select a district or precinct within the Nation's jurisdictional area for purposes of registration and voting. Nonresident members claim this has led many candidates to solicit their votes before elections and ignore them afterwards.[77]

Gaining representation on the council proved to be the foremost priority of the fourteen convention delegates who did not reside within the Nation's jurisdictional area. Julia Coates Foster, a Cherokee citizen living in New Mexico, organized a meeting of all fourteen delegates on the night before the convention's first day to develop a strategy for gaining representation. An initial step in the strategy was to become better able to identify those delegates who were players on both sides of the crisis troubles.[78]

On the convention's second day, Foster introduced a motion requesting representation for nonresident members. Foster's motion called for 20 percent of council seats to be reserved for representation of the Nation's nonresident members. If nonresident Cherokees were included as delegates to the convention, she asked, why shouldn't they have a seat at the legislative table? Foster argued that representation would provide nonresidents with the information necessary to advocate for Cherokee issues against outside public and private interests. She also pointed to the need for stronger bonds among Cherokee's diverse citizenry: "Our land base is minimal . . .

but in some sense our Nation exists from coast to coast and border to border because our Nation exists in our people, our citizens and our citizens are everywhere."[79] Opposition by delegates residing within the Nation's jurisdictional area was swift to appear. Delegate David Cornsilk reminded delegates that nonresident members were adequately represented in the Nation.[80] Contrasting Foster's view of the Nation being made up of its citizens, wherever they were, Cornsilk countered that the "Cherokee Nation is a real place, that it is here.

"That it is within the exterior boundaries of the Cherokee Nation as described in our treaties, and that the focus of the people who live outside the Cherokee Nation should be to strengthen the Nation, the place here."[81] Other delegates argued that the Nation's current system of having nonresidents choose a district within which to register and vote was sufficient. Couldn't a group of nonresidents simply form an organization and agree to register in the same district as a bloc?[82]

The tide turned when a well-respected current council member, Barbara Starr-Scott, unexpectedly stood up in support of nonresident representation with the simple declaration that "[w]hen everybody represents you, nobody represents you."[83] The motion then became renamed the Starr-Scott proposal.[84] Eventually, the two sides reached a compromise calling for the council to be expanded from fifteen to seventeen members, with the additional two at-large seats reserved specifically for representation of nonresidents.

D. Blood Quantum Requirements for Candidates for Principal Chief

At the end of the nineteenth century, the U.S. government terminated its official recognition of the Nation's government. To transfer land out of the Nation's ownership, the U.S. government created the Dawes Commission to compile a list of individual Cherokees eligible to receive individual land allotments. Under the Nation's current constitution, citizenship is granted to any descendant by blood of a Cherokee originally listed on the Dawes Commission Rolls. By 1999, the descent test, along with time and intermarriage, had allowed the Nation to grow to over 200,000 citizens. These same forces had also worked to greatly lower the Indian blood quantum of the Nation. At the time of the convention, approximately 90 percent of the Nation was one-quarter Indian blood or less, with the most common degree of blood quantum being one-sixteenth or one-thirty-second.[85]

The tension between full-blooded and non–full-blooded Cherokees manifested itself on the convention's fifth and sixth days, when delegates introduced motions to establish a minimum blood quantum requirement for candidates for principal chief. The first motion was for candidates to be one-sixteenth or greater blood quantum and to be bilingual in Cherokee and English. The motion was immediately and strongly opposed by several delegates. One, referring to the low blood quanta of the Nation's citizenry, argued:

> If we put this kind of limitation on ourselves, we are simply saying that we don't trust ourselves to lead our own Nation. We're trying to say that the people, our own children, our own grandchildren, at some point are not capable of leading this Nation, simply because they have some federally imposed degree of Indian blood.[86]

A second delegate opposed the motion with a warning for the future:

> We're saying that we are going to put a time and date on the existence of the Cherokee Nation. If we put a grade of Indian blood on it . . . we're saying that in a hundred years or two hundred years, that we will cease to exist as a people, at least with a leader.[87]

The motion was quickly voted down.[88] The next day, however, the issue was raised again, this time through a motion presented on behalf of a bloc of nondelegates calling for a one-quarter blood quantum for candidates for principal chief.[89] The sponsor based the motion on the "pride of not one day seeing a blond-haired, blue-eyed Chief representing me."[90] Supporters of the motion associated low blood quantum Cherokees with dominating the convention by talking in fast legalese that they couldn't understand.[91] One expressed his desire for a blood quantum requirement as a way to maintain the "integrity of the Cherokee Nation."[92] Another felt that a blood quantum requirement for Chief would serve as an important symbol for Cherokee children: "I would like for our Cherokee children, our dark-skinned Cherokee children to be able to look at their Chief and see someone like them. I think that's essential for their self-esteem."[93]

In opposition, delegates argued along several lines: the blood quantum requirement could not stand up against the test of time and the Nation's ever-decreasing Native bloodlines;[94] citizens' opportunities to run for office should not be limited by their blood; those favoring higher blood quantum could express their desire for such a candidate at the ballot box;[95] blood quantum is a nontraditional value introduced by the federal government and not an appropriate criterion for determining the Nation's Chief;[96] the Dawes Commission made mistakes in its original blood quantum determination, therefore making it inherently inaccurate;[97] and blood quantum is not a perfect match for "Indianness."[98] A final argument was that such a change would never be approved by Cherokee voters at a referendum.[99]

In the end, the delegates voted to reject a minimum blood quantum requirement for candidates for principal chief.

IV. RATIFICATION

Notwithstanding the scope of the convention's work, there was no guarantee that the Cherokee people would vote to ratify the proposed new constitution. Indeed, the sweeping nature of the changes in the proposed constitution posed a significant obstacle to ratification.

In the aftermath of the convention, several high-ranking officials and lawyers in the Nation's current administration felt the proposed constitution contained "too much legislation."[100] Citing the document's mandate of attendance at council meetings and the "unwieldy" language concerning representation for nonresident members, they expressed concern that the proposed constitution's specificity would work to constrain effective government action.[101] These arguments were usually wrapped up in a larger preference for limited, framework-based constitutions that serve primarily to outline institutional arrangements.[102]

In response, other delegates defended the proposed constitution's "legislation" as necessary. Foster said there was "much legislation in the document because it was written during a crisis. The more words, the hotter the issue."[103] Indeed, transcripts from the convention reveal a frustration with the Nation's minimalist, framework-oriented constitution. Simply charging the council to implement legislation, some delegates argued, was not sufficient when the council had not acted in the past.[104]

In addition to debates over constitutional "legislation," a second concern revolved around the decision of the commission and convention delegates to replace the current constitution in a wholesale manner, rather than by a series of amendments. David Mullon, former general counsel for the Nation, worried that the commission's introduction of a replacement constitution would present a "big target" for opposition, where individual opposition to a single proposed provision might lead to a vote against the constitution as a whole.[105] Others, including a Supreme Court justice, feared that the wholesale replacement of the Nation's current constitution would lead to the loss of the precedential value of the Nation's entire body of case law.

The commission defended its decision as necessary, arguing that the sheer amount of recommended changes brought forth by Cherokee citizens during the public hearings and comment period precluded revising the current constitution by amendment. Citing the Nation's need for the significant amount of changes in the proposed constitution, Hannah expressed concern about individuals wanting to "throw the baby out with the bathwash."[106]

Notwithstanding these points of disagreement, reform leaders on both sides of the aisle affirmed the legitimacy of the Nation's constitutional revision process and the substance of the proposed constitution. Even Swimmer, the primary author of the current constitution, agreed at the time that "the constitution convention and the product they developed seems to be pretty well accepted by most people."[107]

In fact, the most significant obstacle to ratification did not result from internal debates within the Nation. Rather, a referendum vote to approve the convention's proposed constitution was delayed for more than four years because of the Nation's interactions with the Bureau of Indian Affairs. The delay stemmed from Article XV, Section 10, of the 1976 constitution, which included language requiring that any amendment or new constitution be approved by the "President of the United States or his authorized representative."[108] Because the Cherokee Nation did not organize its government pursuant to the Indian Reorganization Act, it was not required by U.S. law to obtain federal approval for new and amended constitutions. Swimmer said he included the language as a defensive measure to ensure the recognition of the Nation's 1976 constitution by the U.S. government.[109]

Following the constitution's self-imposed requirement, the commission sought BIA approval of the proposed constitution adopted by delegates to the convention. After not hearing from the Bureau for several months, the commission began to lobby the Bureau with calls and letters from September through December 1999.[110] After nine months of review by two separate field offices, the solicitor's office, and several internal levels in the Bureau's Washington central office, the Bureau finally decided on December 14, 1999, not to approve the convention's proposed constitution.[111] In a lengthy disapproval letter to the Nation, the Bureau delivered a series of mandated and recommended changes to specific articles of the proposed constitution.

Instead of proceeding with a referendum without the Bureau's blessing, the commission decided not to spend $350,000 on a special election on the proposed constitution only to be told subsequently by the U.S. government that it is null and void. At least one member of the commission feared that governing under a constitution not recognized by the U.S. government would lead the BIA to cease its recognition of council actions and jeopardize the Nation's operation of its federally funded government programs.[112] Instead, the Nation's tribal council responded to the Bureau's decision on February 26, 2000, by proposing a single amendment to the 1976 constitution striking the requirement to obtain U.S. government approval.[113]

Finally, in April 2002, after a change in administration at the Bureau and much behind-the-scenes discussions, the Department of the Interior approved the council's proposed amendment removing the need for approval of constitutional amendments by the U.S. government. With the legal path clear, Cherokee citizens voted on May 24, 2003, to strike the 1976 constitution's requirement of U.S. governmental approval of all constitutional amendments. A final referendum on the constitution adopted by convention delegates in 1999 was scheduled for July 26, 2003.

In preparation for the final vote, the commission conducted a public education initiative unprecedented in Indian Country. The commission inserted 100,000 copies of a fourteen-page "Constitution Education Tabloid" into the tribal newspaper and mailed an additional 26,000 copies to all Cherokee registered voters.[114] The commission also conducted forty-one Constitution Education forums throughout the Nation and the United States, including forums in Texas, California, and Kansas, where there were high concentrations of Cherokee citizens. The schedule for the education forums was advertised by means of five hundred posters printed and posted throughout the Cherokee Nation, direct mailings of 26,000 oversized postcards to registered voters, and press releases to more than forty newspapers. The commission also made ample use of the Nation's website to disseminate critical information regarding the referendum.[115]

Finally, on July 26, 2003, more than four years after the conclusion of the convention, the Cherokee citizens voted to approve a new constitution replacing the Nation's current 1976 constitution.[116] Ironically, notwithstanding the vote of the Cherokee people and the election's certification by the Cherokee Nation Election Commission, as of the date of this writing, implementation of the new constitution has been delayed indefinitely. The delay stems from the Bureau of Indian Affairs' recent decision to review the results of the May 24, 2003, Cherokee election removing the requirement of presidential approval of any amendment or new constitution.[117]

CONCLUDING THOUGHTS

It is difficult to draw conclusions from the experiences of one nation. However, some tentative lessons can be drawn from the Nation's story.

First, the Nation's story is important because it demonstrates the power of institutions to catalyze and legitimize reform processes. The provision in Article XV, Section 10, of the Nation's current constitution requiring periodic referenda for the calling of a constitution convention allowed for the crucial introduction of citizen voices demanding change.[118] To fulfill the will of the Cherokee voters, however, the Nation still had to develop a reform process viewed as legitimate and independent from the incumbent government. Somewhat counterintuitively, the Nation created an independent constitution commission by *including* appointees from all three branches of government. This allowed incumbent officeholders the comfort of having representation on the commission while at the same time preventing any single government body from controlling it. The Nation then lent teeth to the commission's independence by granting the commission exclusive authority over the reform process and investing it with the power to place its proposed reforms directly on a referendum without the requirement of initial approval by any branch of government.

Together, the constitutional language for the "automatic referendum" every twenty years and the independent nature of the commission allowed the Nation to begin a legitimate process of reform at a time of widespread mistrust and heightened instability. The commission's method of engaging public input and support for its work, as well as its inclusive method for choosing convention delegates, added the crucial final steps. Cumulatively, they led to the creation of a legitimate and accepted forum—the convention—within which to debate complex and often divisive issues of governance.

Second, the substance of the convention debates themselves is enlightening for revealing how the Nation pursued reform in two distinct areas. The Nation desired not only to create stronger and more accountable governmental institutions (e.g., debates over bicameralism, separation of powers, and judicial reform), but also to address primary questions of citizenship and national identity (e.g., representation for off-reservation residents and blood quantum requirements for citizens and candidates for principal chief). This dual-track nature of constitutional reform most likely will resemble the reform processes of other American Indian nations as they continue to assume governmental responsibilities from the U.S. government, see their populations geographically and demographically diversify, and face cultural, political, and economic pressures to confront issues of citizenship.

For these reasons, analyzing how the commission and the convention delegates resolved such issues is relevant to a larger number of American Indian nations. Procedurally, the commission included delegates of all political and demographic stripes. The adoption of *Robert's Rules of Order* then allowed for the input of all seventy-nine delegates. While this led to instances of intense debate, it also vested the delegates' decisions with legitimacy. For especially controversial or technically complex proposed amendments, the convention formed caucuses to hammer out agreements. Together, these procedural devices helped the Nation create a sovereign arena within which to plan the government of its future.

A broader observation from the convention concerns the method by which delegates addressed substantive constitutional concerns. Invariably, delegates moved from discussions of immediate and pressing concerns to more general and deeper issues of governance. The demands by nonresidents for political representation, for example, evolved into debates over whether Cherokees were "members of a tribe" or "citizens of a nation." Calls for blood quantum requirements for the principal chief led to deeper questions of citizenship and the definition of who is a Cherokee. Ultimately, the delegates didn't resolve these issues at the convention. Nonetheless, this pattern of discussion exemplifies how preliminary discussions of concrete problems of governance may be necessary lead-ins to reaching larger questions of governmental transformation and national identity.[119]

To the extent that the Cherokee Nation's story is representative, American Indian nations *are* engaged in a process of creating more effective and legitimate constitutions. However, instead of re-envisioning their governing institutions or refashioning their national identities out of whole cloth, they are tying their discussions of reform to tangible concerns associated with day-to-day government operations. In the end, the Nation's story demonstrates how a well-designed, inclusive, and politically independent constitutional reform process can help achieve the monumental task of transforming such concerns into the development of new constitutions and governing institutions.

NOTES

The author is a lawyer at Goodwin Procter, LLP, in Boston, Massachusetts; a research fellow at the Harvard Project on American Indian Economic Development; and Founding Director of the Initiative on American Indian Constitutional Reform, Harvard Project on American Indian Economic Development.

1. See Anne Farris, "Controversy over Tribal Funds Splits Cherokee Nation into Warring Camps; BIA Called in for Law Enforcement Duty after Marshals Fired," *Washington Post,* July 5, 1997, A6; Sam Howe Verhovek, "Cherokees Reopen Courthouse in Step to Resolve Tribal Crisis," *New York Times,* August 28, 1997, A24.

2. Martha Berry, Delegate to 1999 Cherokee Nation Constitution Convention, Address at John F. Kennedy School of Government Symposium on American Indian Constitutional and Governmental Reform (April 2, 2001) (transcript on file with author).

3. For examples, see Sean Paige, "Rewriting Tribal Law," *Insight Magazine,* May 29, 2000, 10; Jeff Hinkle, "Constitutional Crisis: Can Tribal Governments Take the Heat?" *American Indian Report,* May 2000, 12; Ian Wilson Record, "Broken Government: Constitutional Inadequacy Spawns Conflict at San Carlos," *Native Americas* (Spring 1999): 10–16; Robert B. Porter, "Strengthening Tribal Sovereignty through Government Reform: What Are the Issues?" *Kansas Journal of Law and Public Policy* 7 (1997): 72.

4. See Duane Champagne chapter in this book; Porter, "Strengthening Tribal Sovereignty through Government Reform."

5. For arguments tying strengthened governmental institutions to greater stability and the exercise of increased political sovereignty, see Porter, "Strengthening Tribal Sovereignty through Government Reform." For a connection between strengthened American Indian governmental institutions and enhanced economic development, see Stephen Cornell and Joseph P. Kalt, "Sovereignty and Nation-Building: The Development Challenge in Indian Country Today," *American Indian Culture and Resource Journal* 22 (1998): 3.

6. One exception is Record, "Broken Government," 10–16.

7. For an in-depth historical analysis of Cherokee politics and government, see Duane Champagne, *Social Order and Political Change: Constitutional Governments among the Cherokee, the Choctaw, the Chickasaw, and the Creek* (Stanford University Press, 1992).

8. See Duane Champagne, *American Indian Societies: Strategies and Conditions of Political and Cultural Survival* (Cambridge, MA: Cultural Survival, 1989), 42.

9. Rennard Strickland and William M. Strickland, "Beyond the Trail of Tears: One Hundred Fifty Years of Cherokee Survival," in *Cherokee Removal: Before and After,* ed. William L. Anderson (Athens: University of Georgia Press, 1991), 112, 114–115.

10. Ibid., 117.

11. See generally Morris L. Wardell, *A Political History of the Cherokee Nation, 1838–1907* (Norman: University of Oklahoma Press, 1938), chapter 8.

12. Curtis Act, ch. 517, 30 Stat. 495 (1898), repealed by Indian Reorganization Act of 1934, 25 U.S.C. §§ 461–479 (2000).

13. Records from 1985 from the Bureau of Indian Affairs show that "fewer than 65,000 acres of the 20 million allotted [to Cherokee citizens] remain in tribal hands." Strickland and Strickland, "Beyond the Trail of Tears," 126.

14. Swimmer said that, in Eastern Oklahoma,

> a lot of federal help was being given to tribes in the west, but none in Oklahoma, because again we didn't have organized tribes. This was also an impetus, a big impetus, for the adoption of a constitution. . . . I saw this opportunity with the federal money that was coming in that we could use that and turn it into a useful tool that we could do some things in Eastern Oklahoma.

Interview with Ross Swimmer, former principal chief, Cherokee Nation of Oklahoma, Tulsa, Oklahoma, September 4, 2000.

15. Swimmer elaborated on the representatives:

> In 1967 or '68, Bill Keeler had assembled a group of Cherokees in Eastern Oklahoma to look at the formation of a constitution, not necessarily, I think, with the idea in mind of a governing document but something that would, from a social point of view, give more people the opportunity to focus on the services, the Indian health services, the BIA services, and provide some input to the leadership, to the chief, for how those services could be better delivered to tribal members.

Ross Swimmer, former principal chief, Cherokee Nation of Oklahoma, Address at John F. Kennedy School of Government Symposium on American Indian Constitutional and Governmental Reform (April 2, 2001). (Transcript on file with author.)

16. Swimmer explained the dilemma as follows:

> At that time we had all these myriad of drafts, we've been holding public hearings, we've gone through the community reps and it had just . . . seemed that we just weren't going to get there. So I had

several people that I gathered together and we sat down and drafted a final version of the constitution and said "This is it." And we put it out for a vote and it got passed.

Interview with Ross Swimmer (September 4, 2000). Swimmer said later in a separate context:

And then there were a couple of other things that needed some revision, I felt, from what the constitutional committee had been putting together. I had some opposition and people said well, it's not ready yet, you can't do this, one thing after another. I went ahead and took it to the Bureau of Indian Affairs, we got them to sign off on it, and in 1976 we took it to a vote and it was overwhelmingly adopted. I don't think the people had a clue as to what they were voting on. They accepted that we needed something, but they still, you can imagine, I mean up until that time the only government the Cherokee people were aware of in Eastern Oklahoma was county, state, city and local government. They were totally under the law of the state. They were totally under county police jurisdiction, that kind of thing. And in fact, in 1975 if somebody had suggested to me that the Cherokee Nation had tax powers, or that I, as principal chief, had the opportunity to incarcerate my fellow Cherokees for crimes they might commit, I would have said they were crazy. I would have said there is no such thing. We don't have that kind of sovereignty. In fact, as I recall, we were operating a restaurant and a motel and we were still collecting sales taxes to send to the state. That went on for several years until I finally woke up and said well why are we doing this.

Address at John F. Kennedy School of Government Symposium on American Indian Constitutional and Governmental Reform (April 2, 2001) (transcript on file with author).

17. Cherokee Nation of Oklahoma Constitution, art. V, § 3.

18. Alison Vekshin, "BIA Declines to Take up Cherokee Chief Challenge," *Times Record* (Ft. Smith, Arkansas), August 8, 2003, available at http://www.swtimes.com.

19. Cherokee Nation of Oklahoma Constitution, art. VI, § 11.

20. In 1990, the Nation passed legislation creating a District Court with one or more judges. 20 Cherokee Nation Code § 11 (1993).

21. Swimmer said that, in Oklahoma,

[t]here's such an assimilation that we look to the local, state, county, federal governments for primary services and the Cherokee

Nation sort of then overlaps all of these services, yet they have to be careful where they go because their jurisdiction is only over certain areas. It's real complicated. And that's why I had not envisioned, and perhaps I was being shortsighted, I don't know, but when we adopted the constitution I said it was more of a corporate document, a development authority. I mean our job was to help improve lives. It wasn't to create a government. I never envisioned having 2,000 or 3,000 people working for the government. I envisioned them working . . . and I always thought at some point we would reach a peak and then we would start declining in employment because we would be able to say, "We have created the result that we want, people are working, we don't need to be there any longer. We can have fewer social workers than we had yesterday."

Interview with Ross Swimmer (September 14, 2000).
22. Swimmer commented on his thoughts:

I think actually I was probably thinking again of a corporate model. I was thinking more of a Board of Directors. . . . And the rest of it, the executive branch and the judicial branch is pretty straightforward. It was mainly in the legislative arena that I suggested we make those changes and make it a fifteen-member council.

Ibid.
23. Address at John F. Kennedy School of Government Symposium on American Indian Constitutional and Governmental Reform (April 2, 2001) (transcript on file with author).

Swimmer said in a different context that "the final document that was being considered as I recall would have two houses of the legislature and we would wind up electing around one hundred people. And that's the part that I took out. I just said, 'Look, we're not going to do that.'" Interview with Ross Swimmer (September 4, 2000).

24. Interview with Ross Swimmer (September 4, 2000). Swimmer said in a different context that he wanted to "give more people the opportunity to focus on the services [delivered by HIS and BIA] and provide some input to the leadership, to the chief, for how those services could be better delivered to tribal members." Address at John F. Kennedy School of Government Symposium on American Indian Constitutional and Governmental Reform (April 2, 2001) (transcript on file with author).

25. Swimmer said he had come across a similar provision in another state or tribal constitution. Interview with Ross Swimmer (September 4, 2000).

26. Rob Martindale, "Tribal Foes Talk after Big Ruckus," *Tulsa World,* August 15, 1997, A1.

27. Ibid.

28. The sides agreed to accept the opinion of an independent investigation into the constitutionality of the impeachment of the justices, the reopening of the Nation's courthouse, and a moratorium on all legal action related to the crisis. Jim Myers and Rob Martindale, "Cherokee Negotiations Break Down; Byrd Refuses to Recognize Justices, Official Says," *Tulsa World,* August 23, 1997, A1.

29. Rob Martindale, "BIA Chief Vows to Help Forge Resolution to Cherokee Crisis," *Tulsa World,* June 9, 1998, 7.

30. Associated Press, "Judge Orders Boycotting Cherokee Council Members to Attend Meetings" (June 14, 1999).

31. Jay Hannah, "The 1999 Constitution Convention of the Cherokee Nation: Process of a Sovereign People," available at *www.ksg.harvard.edu/hpaied/pubs.*

32. Troy Wayne Poteete, former chair, Cherokee Nation of Oklahoma Tribal Council Rules Committee, said, "I don't remember any political focus on the question. I don't remember so much as a press release or a footnote to a memorandum." Poteete believes that the three-year delay was due to other pressing priorities. The government was tackling election and campaign contribution law reforms and was also deeply involved in negotiations with the Delaware and Shawnee Indians over their desire to separate from the Nation and form their own independent nations. For all of these reasons, Poteete said, the "Constitution Convention . . . it could wait. It kept getting pushed back." Interview with Troy Wayne Poteete, Tahlequah, Oklahoma (September 2, 2000).

33. Interview with Charles Gourd, Member, Cherokee Nation Constitution Commission, Tahlequah, Oklahoma (June 25, 2000).

34. Hannah, "The 1999 Constitution Convention."

35. Interview with Troy Wayne Poteete (September 2, 2000). Commissioner Marion Hagerstrand said, in reference to the system of appointment, "That's the way Cherokees do things." Interview with Marion Hagerstrand, Member, Cherokee National Constitution Commission, Tahlequah, Oklahoma (June 25, 2000).

36. Swimmer said "the move was on both sides" to begin the process of reform. Interview with Ross Swimmer (September 4, 2000).

37. Interview with Jay Hannah, Member, Cherokee Nation Constitution Commission, Tahlequah, Oklahoma (June 24, 2000).

38. "While the Rules Committee of the Tribal Council had promulgated the creation of the commission and outlined its primary mission, empowering legislation was left to the newly appointed commissioners to write and submit to the Tribal Council for approval." Hannah, "The 1999 Constitution Convention."

39. Interview with Charles Gourd (September 2, 2000).

40. Interview with Jay Hannah, Member, Cherokee Nation Constitution Commission, Tahlequah, Oklahoma (June 25, 2000).

41. Interview with Charles Gourd (September 2, 2000).

42. Ibid.

43. As recalled by Commissioner Charles Gourd, it was a "dogfight to keep the commission completely independent from the three branches of government and make it a citizen's commission." Interview with Charles Gourd (September 2, 2000).

44. Act Creating a Constitution Convention Commission § 4A, Legislative Act No. 10-98 (Cherokee Nation, May 15, 1998), available at http://www.cherokee .org/TribalGovernment.

45. Id. §§ 4A, 4D.

46. Id.

47. The commission's enabling legislation required public hearings in all out-of-state major metropolitan centers having more than five hundred Cherokee citizens. Id. § 4(D)(6).

48. One commissioner attributed the low numbers at several meetings to a lack of access to mailing lists of tribal members and a lack of funds to perform targeted mailings. He believes that attendance could have been improved with improved cooperation with the Nation's newspaper and website.

49. Id. §§ 4(D)(4), 4(D)(5).

50. Id. § 4(D)(8).

51. Even with all of the commission's efforts to reach out to Cherokee citizens through public meetings, newsletters, and website materials, however, certain individuals have criticized it for not sufficiently reaching out to all Cherokees, including those residing in the Nation's more traditional communities.

52. Interview with Troy Wayne Poteete (September 2, 2000).

53. Ibid.

54. Hannah, "The 1999 Constitution Convention."

55. Ibid.

56. Ibid.

57. The commission originally planned the Convention to last for only three days.

58. Address by Martha Berry at John F. Kennedy School of Government Symposium on American Indian Constitutional and Governmental Reform (April 2, 2001) (transcript on file with author).

59. The commission's chair, Ralph Keen, Jr., said that the commission was aware that the U.S. Constitutional Convention was held in secret, but "disagreed with that philosophy." Interview with Ralph Keen, Jr., Member, Cherokee Nation Constitution Commission, Tahlequah, Oklahoma (June 25, 2000).

60. Hannah said *Robert's Rules* was "absolutely essential to the success of the convention. Everyone embraced that there had to be order and structure to what we were doing." Interview with Jay Hannah (June 24, 2000).

61. 1 Cherokee Nation Constitution Convention Transcript of Proceedings, 7–15 (1999) (transcript of February 26, 1999) (hereinafter Cherokee Constitution Convention Transcripts).

62. Another interesting and important ground rule was developed halfway through the Convention to address the problem of spectator lobbying of delegates. Delegates who smoked, for example, were lobbied consistently during breaks. One lobbyist passed out information on delegates' chairs during a break in the proceedings. Others whispered in delegates' ears during votes. Some nondelegates even tried to participate in voice votes. Some simply heckled. To counteract lobbying, Hannah required nondelegates to sit at least four rows back from delegates, hired a sergeant at arms, and moved furniture to physically separate delegates from nondelegates during breaks. Interview with Jay Hannah (June 24, 2000).

63. For examples, see 6 Cherokee Constitution Convention Transcripts, 44–46 (transcript of March 3, 1999) (describing legal definitions of mandamus, habeas corpus, and quo warranto, and discussion among delegates for need to use clearest possible language).

64. Interview with Julia Coates Foster, Delegate, Cherokee Nation Constitution Convention, Tahlequah, Oklahoma (June 24, 2001).

65. The $10,000 amount comes from an interview with Ross Swimmer. The $192 million comes from e-mail correspondence with Jay Hannah, the Nation's Treasurer.

66. See Duane Champagne chapter in this volume.

67. Keen's motion for a bicameral legislature is found in 2 Cherokee Constitution Convention Transcripts, 63–64 (transcript of February 27, 1999).

68. Hannah and other commissioners believed that a move to a bicameral legislature "would require an absolute dismemberment of the powers of the Cherokee Nation to redistribute among the two houses." Ibid., 68.

69. Ibid., 69.

70. Ibid., 70.

71. Proposed Cherokee Nation of Oklahoma Constitution, art. VIII, § 6.

72. Proposed Cherokee Nation of Oklahoma Constitution, art. VIII, § 4.

73. Proposed Cherokee Nation of Oklahoma Constitution, art. VIII, § 1. For discussion at the Convention of the need for additional justices, see 5 Cherokee Constitution Convention Transcripts, 80–81 (transcript of March 2, 1999).

74. Proposed Cherokee Nation of Oklahoma Constitution, art. VIII, §§ 2, 6. For discussion at Convention, see Cherokee Nation Constitution Convention Transcripts at 100.

75. Proposed Cherokee Nation of Oklahoma Constitution, art. VIII, § 5. For discussion at Convention, see 6 Cherokee Constitution Convention Transcripts, 54–61 (transcript of March 3, 1999).

76. Proposed Cherokee Nation of Oklahoma Constitution, art. VIII, § 5. For discussion at Convention, see 6 Cherokee Constitution Convention Transcripts, 62–64 (transcript of March 3, 1999).

77. Address by Martha Berry, John F. Kennedy School of Government Symposium on American Indian Constitutional and Governmental Reform (April 2, 2001) (transcript on file with author).

78. Interview with Julia Coates Foster (June 24, 2000).

79. See 2 Cherokee Constitution Convention Transcripts, 98–99 (transcript of February 27, 1999). Another delegate expressed a similar opinion: "I would like to think also that the Cherokee Nation is more than just its territory boundaries. I'd like to think that the Cherokee Nation is people, wherever we are." Ibid., 102 (testimony of Delegate MacLemore).

80. See ibid., 99–100 (testimony of Delegate Cornsilk).

81. Ibid., 100.

82. See ibid., 103–104 (testimony of Delegate Meredith).

83. See ibid., 101 (testimony of Deborah [*sic*] Scott).

84. Address by Martha Berry, John F. Kennedy School of Government Symposium on American Indian Constitutional and Governmental Reform (April 2, 2001) (transcript on file with author).

85. 5 Cherokee Constitution Convention Transcripts, 11 (transcript of March 2, 1999) (testimony of David Cornsilk).

86. Ibid.

87. Ibid. (testimony of Delegate Bill Baker).

88. Ibid., 12.

89. 6 Cherokee Constitution Convention Transcripts, 33 (transcript of March 3, 1999).

90. Ibid., 34.

91. See ibid., 85 (testimony of Delegate Silversmith).

92. Ibid., 34 (testimony of Delegate Silversmith).

93. Ibid., 36 (testimony of Delegate Hook).

94. See ibid., 34 (testimony of Delegate Hembree) ("[L]et's make this decision based on generations.").

95. Another delegate discussed the blood quantum requirement:

> Placing a blood quantum may be something we desire, and it
> may be something that we can show that desire by reflecting it at the
> ballot box by saying the candidate who is $\frac{1}{64}$ Cherokee, we may not
> want to split that person. But we should not put in our constitution
> that we are going to discriminate on the basis of blood quantum.

Ibid., 33 (testimony of Delegate Haskins, Jr.).

96. See ibid., 35 (testimony of Delegate Masters).

> [B]lood quantum by the way is not a traditional value. It was
> imposed on the people by the government. It's a government des-
> ignation, not a tribal designation that we have had. There are many
> people who have bought into this government designation that they
> can say what a Cherokee is by the surrender documents that they
> have held on us. But this is not a traditional value. . . . [I]f we want

> a blood quantum, we need to go back and reconsider, a Cherokee
> of the Cherokee Nation must be a one-quarter blood according
> to BIA and state standards. . . . So what we need to do if we want
> blood quantum, it needs to be in the membership category, and we
> need to limit the Cherokee Nation to one-quarter blood or more,
> according to government documents and government projects and
> government standards.

Ibid.

97. See ibid., 36–37 (testimony of Delegates Clarke and Scott).

98. See ibid., 37 (testimony of Delegate Hammons).

> [W]hile it makes me proud to see a leader of my Nation that
> looks like an Indian, I don't think that that ought to be the stan-
> dard for whether or not they represent me, ladies and gentlemen.
> Because, unfortunately, we've seen in the past few years that you can
> look like a Cherokee, and you can talk like a Cherokee and not care
> about the Cherokee people.

Ibid.

99. See ibid., 33 (testimony of Delegate Robinson).

100. Interview with David Mullon, Cherokee Associate General Counsel, and Chad Smith, principal chief, Tahlequah, Oklahoma (June 23, 2000).

101. Cherokee Nation Associate General Counsel David Mullon: "The more detailed a constitution is, the more of an imposition you are on the future." Interview with David Mullon (June 23, 2000). One delegate from the Byrd administration argues that the current administration opposes the constitution's detailed nature "because it constrains them." Interview with Charles Gourd (June 25, 2000).

102. See 3 Cherokee Constitution Convention Transcripts, 32, 89 (transcript of February 28, 1999); see also 4 Cherokee Constitution Convention Transcripts, 33 (transcript of March 1, 1999) (testimony of Delegate Chad Smith).

103. Interview with Julia Coates Foster (June 24, 2000).

104. The debate in some sense mirrors that between the "framework-oriented" U.S. Constitution and many more detailed state constitutions that contain legislation and policy. Some state constitutional scholars believe this divergence may be explained in part by the fact that the national constitution contemplated that additional details and policies would be filled in by its express delegation of powers to individual state constitutions. See G. Alan Tarr, *Understanding State Constitutions* (Princeton: Princeton University Press, 1998), 10. The drafters of state constitutions, on the other hand, could not rely on a separate document or government body to fill in ambiguous mandates. The push by delegates to hold the Nation's government accountable through detailed constitutional legislation may be

explained in part by similar reasoning. Tribal citizens, lacking the U.S. Government's abundance of federal regulations and long history of federal court decisions, have fewer avenues for "lawmaking" than states and therefore may look to a constitution as their sole guarantee of protection.

105. "An organic document presents a very big target. People with nothing in common except that they're against the document." Interview with David Mullon (June 25, 2000).

106. Interview with Jay Hannah, Member, Cherokee Nation Constitution Commission, Tahlequah, Oklahoma (September 2, 2000).

107. Interview with Ross Swimmer (September 2, 2000).

108. Cherokee Nation of Oklahoma Constitution, art. XV, § 7 (1976).

109. Swimmer commented regarding the 1976 Constitution:

> We were trying to adopt a constitution in place of the 1906 Act [terminating the Nation] and we felt that if we didn't have the federal imprimatur on this constitution that the BIA could come back and say, "Well, you're violating the '06 Act. Your constitution doesn't mean anything." By getting the signature of the Secretary of the Interior on our constitution, it meant to us that it would have to recognize this as the governing document of our tribe.

Interview with Ross Swimmer (September 2, 2000).

110. Hannah began attempting to contact the Bureau "on my speed dial every day." Interview with Jay Hannah (June 24, 2000).

111. Cherokee Nation Constitution Convention Commission Progress Report (February 2000).

112. A precedent for such action occurred in the Seminole Nation of Oklahoma, another nation with a constitution requiring approval by the U.S. government.

113. Open Letter from Convention Chairman Jay Hannah to Convention Delegates (February 15, 2000), available at http://www.cherokee.org.

114. The tabloid was also posted on the Nation's website in a printable format. Interview with Jay Hannah, Chairman, Cherokee Nation Constitution Convention, Tahlequah, Oklahoma (August 6, 2003).

115. The Cherokee Nation website contained a PDF version of the Education Tabloid, a webcast of one of the forums, a schedule of forums, press releases, and general contact information. A weekly reminder e-mail of Constitution Education Forums was sent to more than 100,000 e-newsletter subscribers. Ibid.

116. The final vote was 3,622 in favor and 3,059 against. Certification of Cherokee Nation Election Commission (August 7, 2003).

117. As discussed earlier, the BIA consented in an April 2002 letter to the removal of the U.S. government from the Nation's constitutional review process. However, the letter left open the possibility of Bureau review under a separate federal

act, the Principal Chiefs Act. In August 2003, several losing candidates in the May 24, 2003, general election wrote a letter to the Bureau of Indian Affairs claiming election irregularities and the disenfranchisement of Cherokee freedmen in both the May 24 general election and the July 26 runoff election. The BIA, claiming authority under the Principal Chiefs Act, announced that it would review the results of the May 24, 2003, election (the same election in which Cherokee voters approved an amendment to the 1976 Constitution removing the requirement for presidential approval of any amendment or new constitution). Although the BIA subsequently has upheld the reelection of Principal Chief Chad Smith, it has not yet stated its position concerning the portion of the May 24 general election in which citizens voted to amend the 1976 Constitution by removing the requirement of presidential approval.

118. Although such a periodic referendum is a strong initial catalyst, its power to trigger reform is not absolute. As one scholar of state constitutional revision has noted, periodic referenda may be scheduled at inopportune times, when other priorities crowd out concerns for constitutional reform. G. Alan Tarr, "State Constitutional Reform and Its Implications for Tribal Constitutionalism," paper presented at symposium "Tribes Moving Forward: Engaging in the Process of Constitutional and Governmental Reform" (April 3, 2001) (copy on file with author).

119. At the same time, full-fledged debates over novel ideas allowing for the expanding exercise of sovereignty or the restructuring of government were often cut short. Arguments for bicameralism, additional justices, sending a delegate to Congress, and representation for nonresidents, for example, were all initially or ultimately met by arguments of cost. In other instances, especially early in the convention, expansive ideas for restructuring government were also objected to on the basis that they would not receive Bureau approval, a fear later borne out in actuality.

Firsthand Account

OVERCOMING THE POLITICS OF REFORM

MARTHA BERRY, DELEGATE, CHEROKEE NATION
CONSTITUTION CONVENTION

Let me begin by saying some of the things I am going to say would be fighting words back in Cherokee Nation. So I want to make it very clear that these are my opinions, they're not that of the entire delegation. These are my words and mine alone.

My name is Martha Berry. I was raised in Northeastern Oklahoma, in Tulsa. Since moving with my family to South Texas in 1977 at the age of twenty-nine, I have never lived closer to Tahlequah than three hundred miles. I am a Cherokee tribal citizen, a homemaker, and an artist. I am here to tell you about the Cherokee Nation constitution reform process from a delegate's perspective.

Let me begin with a question. Why, in 1995, did Cherokee voters elect to put into motion a review of our constitution? The 1975 constitution had provided us with a great framework for our modern government. But as Native people always do, when given the opportunity to go our own way, at our own speed, we did not just fly, we soared. We had outgrown the constitution that had been so well crafted. Our citizen numbers and services had surpassed even the most ambitious dreams of the framers of that document. And many of us had come to feel very differently about what it was to be Cherokee in the last few years of the twentieth century. We wanted a document that reflected our understanding of tribal sovereignty, and our relationship to the world around us.

It is very, very important to understand that when we voted, in 1995, to review our constitution, none of the crisis events that I am about to describe had occurred. It was a smooth time for the Cherokees, perhaps a naive time. We were enjoying great, even legendary, leadership. No one had any idea what lay ahead.

The troubles all began about a year after the 1995 election. The new principal chief, a gentleman by the name of Joe Byrd, was asked to submit financial documents, pertaining to tribal spending, for review by some members of our council. When he refused, our judicial tribunal issued a warrant for our marshal service to seize these documents.

The marshals did, indeed, serve the papers and obtained the documents in question, during regular business hours, at the chief's office in the tribal complex. The chief was not in the building at the time. Enraged by this turn of events, the principal chief fired the entire marshal service, leaving us with no Cherokee law enforcement. Into this vacuum, he brought two elements that appalled many, many Cherokee citizens.

First, he requested that law enforcement officers be brought in from the Bureau of Indian Affairs to act as our police force, and then handed over our marshal service budget funds to the BIA to cover the cost. For many who had grown up with the presence of the BIA police, in Cherokee country and elsewhere, this was an unthinkable step backward and an insult, indeed a danger to our people. Next, Chief Byrd hired his own protection force.

The Justice Tribunal, reviewing the case of the fired Cherokee marshals, restored their positions. This so enraged Chief Byrd, that he called a tribal council meeting, without giving the required legal notice. As are all of our council meetings, this meeting was presided over by our deputy principal chief, obviously a member of the Byrd Administration. Without a quorum at this meeting, the council members in attendance voted to impeach the Justice Tribunal. The Justices on the Tribunal ignored their impeachment, arguing that the meeting was called illegally and there had not been a quorum present.

The months that followed were filled with one stunning development after another. Chief Byrd, angered by the coverage his actions had received in our tribal newspaper, fired the editor and the entire editorial staff. Then, in answer to criticism of this act, and claiming a "structural reorganization within the newspaper," rehired all of the staff, but not the editor. From that moment on, unbiased information was not a commodity available from within the Cherokee Nation. Our citizens were forced to obtain news from a variety of sources. There was already an opposition tribal newspaper, but their coverage was so slanted against Chief Byrd that most of us realized that the truth must lay somewhere between the two newspapers.

We began subscribing to mainstream newspapers from around the Tahlequah area and searched the Internet daily for articles from anywhere in the country about the Cherokee troubles. In my particular case, my eighty-seven-year-old father kept an open envelope on his kitchen table. He clipped every article about the troubles that appeared in the *Tulsa World,* the *Claremore Progress,* and the *Vinita Journal,* put them all into the envelope, and mailed them to me on a weekly basis. In turn, I kept my daughters, in Dallas and Austin, informed. And, needless to say, the passing of information via word of mouth was rampant.

The marshals, ousted from their offices within the tribal complex, took up office residence in the back of the Cherokee Nation courthouse, which also housed the Justices' offices. Cherokee citizens held community fundraisers and contributed money from their own pockets to finance the marshals, since the Byrd administration was no longer paying them.

Things came to a head in the summer of 1997. Chief Byrd wanted the Justices and the marshals thrown out of the Cherokee Nation courthouse, that venerable old building that is a part of the life of every Cherokee. When we go there, we know our ancestors have walked there, met there, conducted business there for scores of years. But suddenly, there seemed to be a disagreement as to whether or not the Cherokee Nation even owned this old Tahlequah landmark.

Very early one morning, police from several area law enforcement groups raided the building, removed the marshals, and sealed off the building with court records and the possessions of the Justices still inside. Of all the events that took place, this one has to be the most appalling. Our great festival was coming up at the end of that summer, bringing, as always, thousands of Cherokees from across the Cherokee Nation and the United States, into Tahlequah. Something had to give.

The BIA realized this and put pressure on Byrd to negotiate a reopening of the courthouse prior to the Cherokee national holiday. At the very last minute, Byrd agreed, and also agreed not to make the traditional appearance and State of the Nation address. It was on that day that the reality of all these events had the greatest impact on average Cherokee citizens. Those of us who do not live in Tahlequah, or in the small communities around it, or who do not work for the Nation or take advantage of its services, had only read or heard about the troubles. Even for Cherokee citizens residing elsewhere in northeastern Oklahoma, the unbelievable nature of the tale had made skeptics of the best of them.

But, on that day, celebrating the Cherokee national holiday on the courthouse lawn, we all understood. There were, as always, little children loitering about the snow cone machine, with various shades of red and blue tongues, fingers, and shirtfronts. There were elders, in lawn chairs, keeping the heat at bay with fans and sun hats. There were old friends greeting old friends, embracing. And above it all, on the rooftops surrounding Courthouse Square, were BIA and state police officers, decked out in their very best Kevlar, with binoculars, cameras, and automatic weapons. That day, there was no denying it and all of us then knew it was true. We had seen evidence of the crisis with our own eyes.

Perhaps the most debilitating development of the troubles was that the work of the tribal council ground to a halt. For months, knowing that the chief held the support of, and control of, a majority of council members, the minority council members boycotted the meetings. They knew if they attended, there would be a quorum and the Justices would be impeached with a full vote of the council. As it was, when the council did try to meet, anyone bringing up the troubles or criticizing Byrd or his administration was escorted out of the chamber by Byrd's police force.

So, in a matter of months, the Cherokee Nation had lost its freedom of information, the ability to police itself, its free press, its justice system had been stripped of power, not to mention its dignity, and the council was hamstrung. Most important of all, the Cherokee citizenry was polarized, divided along pro- and anti-Joe Byrd lines. In short, we were mad as hell and not going take it anymore.

It was into this volatile atmosphere that the constitution commission arrived. They began the hearing process and the citizens began giving testimony regarding a review of our 1975 constitution. The fairness and the integrity with which the commission and the citizens handled themselves and that process cannot be overstated. In my opinion, it is nothing short of a miracle that we accomplished what we did.

When we first began to hear about the opportunity to give testimony, to tell the commission what we believed needed to be changed in our constitution, there was a certain amount of disbelief on our part. Could this process be trusted when so much else was falling apart within our Cherokee Nation? Would our testimony be taken seriously? Or would we be asked to speak, and then our suggestions ignored?

As a citizen, never having been a part of any government except as a voter, I looked at this as the opportunity of a lifetime. It was a chance to take part in a very special event in Cherokee history. It was a chance to stand up and be counted. For me, it was a chance to make a statement for nonresident Cherokees and how we felt at the end of the twentieth century. But more than anything else, it was a chance for all of us to do something to repay our grandmothers and grandfathers, who had suffered so greatly in the past. A chance to do the right thing. For me, as for many of us, aside from raising children, just giving testimony was the most important thing I had ever done in my life. I was a nervous wreck.

When I stepped up to the registration table in Tahlequah, on the very first day of testimony, I could hardly speak. The magnitude of what I was about to do was overwhelming. Then, when the clerk began filling out my nametag, I noticed she put Witness No. 1, my jaw dropped. I asked her if that meant that I was about to become the very first person to give testimony in this historic event. When she said yes, I just began to shake. I shook so hard, in fact, I actually had to have help putting on the nametag. At that point, the concept of actually being asked to serve as a delegate to the convention never even entered my mind.

Giving testimony turned out to be a great experience. Although the situation was a little intimidating, the commissioners did, indeed, listen. They even took notes. For an ordinary person like me, and like most of us, that was an awesome experience. Later, as the hearings unfolded, the rules for giving testimony were relaxed a little, giving citizens more time and a slightly less intimidating atmosphere in which to speak.

Then, in February 1999, the experience of the convention began. It is difficult to know where to begin this part of the story. I will tell you that there were times, especially on that first evening, when it was just downright hard to breathe. The tension between the pro- and anti-Byrd administration delegates was so thick you could cut it with a knife. In addition, every ancestor and every descendent of every delegate, was in that auditorium with us. It was our chance to do them all proud, but it was pretty darn crowded.

Since that first day was our first meeting in the volatile atmosphere of the Cherokee Nation at the time, we did not know quite what to expect. Considering that there were council members and delegates from both sides of every issue that had come up in the previous months, believe me, it could have become a brawl. It was, from the beginning, very, very important to the delegates that the Cherokee Nation, the world, and the future, see our convention process as being credible. We did not, under any circumstances, want to be maneuvered, or be perceived as being maneuvered, by either the Byrd administration or by the Byrd administration opposition.

There is no better illustration of this desire for credibility than the very first thing we did. Many of us believe it to be the most important thing we did. Our first order of real business was to elect a chairman for the convention. The Byrd Administration had pretty much anointed the man who served as the commission chairman to also be the convention chairman. Word got out that first morning, over coffee and donuts in the foyer, that in addition to Byrd's choice, someone else was going to be nominated for that position. We knew it was important that we, the delegates, take control of the convention at the outset, and we saw this as our opportunity.

A precious little female Cherokee elder, loved and admired by all of us, from both sides of the troubles, had been given the honor of presenting the first proposal to this historic convention. She had been asked to nominate Byrd's anointed one for chairman. Many of us felt that this was a fairly sneaky maneuver and poor use of an elder. We are, after all, a matrilineal culture, one in which women are revered and occupy a very special role. Just nominating someone else could be seen as a bit of an insult to that precious, little elder woman's honor. We had a great many important items on our agenda, however, and so nominate and elect Jay Hannah as convention chairman we did. It was a crucial turn of events that marked the end of any hope of maneuvering, or even predicting the delegation.

One of the important items to be considered was a proposal to add nonresident representatives to the council. Now, I would love to be able to tell you that the Cherokee Nation boundaries are a dividing line between Cherokees and the rest of the world, but that is simply not the case. For over a century, our borders have been breached. We are overrun with, and often outnumbered by, non-Indians.

In addition, at the end of the twentieth century, as a result of allotment, economics and relocations, roughly 40 percent of Cherokee Nation citizens lived outside of the historic boundary in the fourteen-county area in northeastern Oklahoma. Also, about 40 percent of the qualified voters are nonresident Cherokees. Although as citizens, nonresidents have, of course, the right to vote, we do not have nonresident representation on the council.

If a Cherokee lives outside the Nation, he or she selects a district or precinct in which to register to vote. Since many Cherokees have never lived within the boundaries, some select the district of their ancestors, but many select the district containing Tahlequah, or a district near their own homes if they live in an area adjacent to the Nation. This situation creates two problems. First, the residents of the districts burdened with overwhelming numbers of nonresident voters, suffer an overwhelming influence on their elections from nonresident voters. Second, nonresidents, who find themselves buried in literature, phone calls, and videotapes from candidates just prior to an election, then find themselves ignored by these candidates after those candidates receive their votes.

To the credit of the commission, the hearing process carefully included nonresident Cherokees. The convention delegation also included a large number of nonresident Cherokees, roughly the same percentage as the Cherokee population. Many of us felt it was time to present the possibility of adding Cherokee council positions to represent these nonresident voters.

Julia Coates, a Cherokee from New Mexico, and a convention delegate, organized a meeting the evening prior to the first day of the convention. Nonresidents were invited there to meet one another, identify issues that would be important to us, and become better able to identify those delegates who were players on both sides of the crisis troubles. Many of us had read their names over and over again, but could not recognize their faces. It was important to understand who was who, and who was behind each of the issues as they were presented to the convention.

It was at this meeting that we hatched a plan for presentation of the nonresident representative issue. As luck would have it, of all the touchy issues facing the convention, this one occurred near the beginning in the order of the constitution, and so was the first touchy issue to be tackled by the delegation. When the proposal was first introduced onto the convention floor, it received the expected cold reception from most of the delegation. Although there were some resident Cherokees who supported us, and even some who spoke up for us, not even all of the nonresident delegates embraced nonresident council representation. For every impassioned argument for it, there was one equally impassioned against it.

It soon became apparent that the first thing we needed to do was come up with a total number of council positions, thereby giving the resident delegates confidence that they would not lose any positions, but that new, nonresident positions would simply be added. So, the proposal for nonresident representation was tabled and we spent most of the rest of the day arguing the number of council positions.

At last, we agreed to add two new seats to the council. The next move, most of us expected, would be for Julia Coates to table her proposal for nonresident representation. But just before that would have taken place, an amazing thing occurred. Barbara Starr Scott, a council member and a delegate to the convention, is a tall, striking Cherokee woman. She has much clout and influence. She happened to be sitting across the room from the microphone that the nonresidents had just sort of adopted. Many noticed her rise and walk around the room toward us. They watched as she and Julia Coates put their heads together and spoke in whispers. Then, it was Barbara Starr Scott who stepped up to the microphone. And it was she who proposed that the two new council positions that had just been created be given to nonresident Cherokees.

Our nonresident council representation proposal then became the Starr Scott proposal. Although we had lost control of it, this move put our issue right in the hands of an established Cherokee politician, with all of her clout and experience. It gave great credibility to the proposal and made it far easier for the resident delegates to swallow. Before it was all over, even the person who had argued the strongest against nonresident reps actually came back to the microphone and said that even he had changed his mind and would support the two new nonresident council positions.

Not only was this important to Cherokee citizens at the end of the twentieth century, but it was pivotal to the convention. The delegates voted overwhelmingly to adopt this proposal. Of all things, it was the issue of nonresident council representatives that brought about the very first overwhelming agreement of any sort within the Cherokee Nation for many, many months. When the gavel went down at the end of that evening's proceedings, a cheer went up. We knew then that we could do this thing.

It was during the course of ironing out a grandfather clause for the nonresident representation section in the constitution that one of the drawbacks to a convention of and by the people occurred. By far, the majority of delegates were much like me, just plain folks, passionate about the Cherokee Nation, to be sure, but just plain folks. We were not the ex-presidents of our high school student councils. Most of us had little or no experience with parliamentary procedure.

The commission anticipated this and brought in a respected expert in parliamentary procedure to give us a little lesson the first evening. Although she gave a good lesson, we were a delegation just about one or two events, or even rumors, shy of violence. Our feelings toward other delegates ranged from respect and admiration to loathing and even outright fear. The otherwise orderly parliamentary procedure lesson included a generous sprinkling of pointed questions to the commission regarding the fairness of various issues dealing with the preparations for the convention. Actually, it did not take us long to understand the wisdom of parliamentary procedure and *Robert's Rules,* and to become pros at obeying them, and even using them to our advantage. It was a wonderful learning process, the ultimate on-the-job training.

Those rules and that decorum helped us through some of the very, very tough issues, one of which was allegiance to the United States government. Many of us felt that, in the future, there might come a time when Cherokee officials, dealing with tribal sovereignty issues, might have to make a choice when dealing with the federal government. That to carry out the duties of the offices to which they had been elected, they might have to actually choose the Cherokee Nation. It was not that we were activists or rabble-rousers; we just simply felt that we should remove the phrase requiring allegiance to the U.S. Constitution from the oaths of office in the Cherokee Constitution. Others saw us as dissident firebrands, middle-aged hippies who had no respect for the United States flag and constitution for which they had fought. In our defense, I must say that many of us, and our loved ones, had fought for that same flag and constitution.

References to these oaths of office appear more than once in our constitution. When the first of these came up for review, the voice vote was close. One delegate even called for a roll call after the first vote had removed the U.S. allegiance phrase from this reference. He said, "I want to know just who it is in here that voted against the United States of America." That comment drew angry jeers and accusations of harassment. But even after being accused of being traitors to our United States, those of us who believed so strongly in tribal sovereignty, said our yeas when our names were called. It took courage, but we did it. I stress this because those of you who will study this process, and this new constitution in the future, will not see this change. Even though the majority of the delegates voted to remove the U.S. allegiance phrase from this first oath of office reference twice, it was later reinstated by an action of the convention's style committee.

And so it went. Nine twelve-hour days. Breakfasts, lunches, and dinners together. Getting to know each other, agreeing on some issues, vehemently disagreeing on others. Bonds and friendships forming that will last a lifetime. The entire experience was a wonderful example of what ordinary people can do, especially when there is much at stake.

One outcome of the convention that I want to share with you is the fresh leadership windfall, which has occurred in the Cherokee Nation as a result of the circumstances prior to the convention, and the crucible of the convention itself. There were many delegates who, like me, lived half their lives as interested but quiet observers. We were ordinary voters, not politicians, not political operatives, not bureaucrats, not even lawyers. Many of us had never even written our council representatives or donated money to campaigns. Through the convention experience, we became reluctant leaders. That process has changed our lives for the better and our confidence has grown. For the most part, we are well informed, ethical, intelligent people, very interested in the future of the Cherokee Nation, her structure, and her government. I believe the Cherokee Nation will ultimately be blessed by this windfall of fresh leadership. It is a positive result of the convention that no one could have predicted. We may still be without a newly ratified constitution, but we are already enjoying a healthy new crop of leaders at the community level.

I am happy to report that things are now looking up in Cherokee Country. In 1999, we elected a new administration. Our marshal service has since been reinstated. Our justices were reinstated. Our newspaper editor was hired back, and our council, although still divided along some of the same old lines, is functioning again. A Cherokee history course has been created and is being taught by Cherokee Nation certified teachers, is now being taught to all tribal employees and to any interested citizens, both Cherokee and non-Cherokee, within our communities.

In July 2000, I am proud to say, our council created the Cherokee Independent Press Act. This legislation gives us a newspaper that, although still funded by the tribe, now has an independent editorial board of qualified journalists from throughout the Cherokee Nation.

There are few things on this earth of which I am more proud than I am of the Cherokee Nation. I consider the constitution review process that we accomplished to be a great achievement, especially given the circumstances surrounding it. For those of you who do write the history books, please, tell our story well.

ABOUT THE CONTRIBUTORS

JAIME BARRIENTOZ

Jaime Barrientoz is a member of the Grand Traverse Band of Ottawa and Chippewa Indians located in the northwest part of Lower Michigan. He is the former vice chair of the Grand Traverse Band, chair of the Band's Constitutional Reform Committee, and chair of its Economic Development Corporation. Prior to his service on the Band's Tribal Council and Economic Development Corporation, he worked in the Band's casinos for approximately eleven years. He currently serves on the Board of Directors of the Native American Rights Fund. He lives in Peshawbestown, Michigan, with his wife, Tara, and three children.

MARTHA BERRY

After spending twenty-five years as wife, mother, and travel agent, Martha Berry began teaching herself American Indian beadwork in 1994. After seven years of study, experimentation, and discipline, she is becoming well known as a Cherokee and Southeastern Woodlands beadwork artist. Her work, inspired by the creations of Southeastern Woodlands Native American beaders prior to 1840, can be found in museums and private collections throughout the United States and England. She served as a delegate to the Cherokee Nation's 1999 Constitution Convention. A Cherokee Nation citizen living in Tyler, Texas, she is actively involved in Cherokee community organizations in Texas and New Mexico as well as the Cherokee National Historical Society, and is a charter member of the First Families of the Cherokee Nation.

STEVE BRADY, SR.

Steve Brady, Sr. is a member of the Northern Cheyenne Tribe. He is fluent in the Cheyenne language and is a headsman of the Northern Cheyenne Crazy Dog Society. He is a teacher of tribal government, tribal history, and Cheyenne language at Lame Deer High School, president of the Northern Cheyenne Sand Creek Massacre Descendants, and co-chair of the Northern Cheyenne Sand Creek Massacre Site Committee. He served as vice chair and subsequently chair of the Northern Cheyenne Tribe's Constitution Revision Committee from 1990 to 1994. He has testified on numerous occasions before the U.S. Congress on sacred sites and religious freedom for Native Americans and legislation pertaining to the Sand Creek Massacre and treaty rights. His Cheyenne name is Taa'evaho'nehe, or Night Wolf.

DUANE CHAMPAGNE

Duane Champagne is a member of the Turtle Mountain Band of Chippewa from North Dakota. He is a professor of sociology and American Indian studies and a member of the Faculty Advisory Committee for the UCLA Native Nations Law and Policy Center, and is acting director of the Tribal Learning Community and Educational Exchange. He was Director of the UCLA American Indian Studies Center from 1991 to 2002 and editor of the *American Indian Culture and Research Journal* from 1986 to 2003. He has authored or edited more than ninety publications, including *Native America: Portraits of the Peoples, The Native North American Almanac,* and *Social Order and Political Change: Constitutional Governments among the Cherokee, Choctaw, Chickasaw, and Creek.*

STEVEN CHESTNUT

Steven Chestnut has been a partner since 1974 in Ziontz, Chestnut, Varnell, Berley & Slonim, a law firm representing Indian tribes for more than forty years. He is currently the firm's most senior partner. His practice focuses on the areas of tribal governance, environmental matters, cultural matters, commercial development, mineral development, timber development, water rights, litigation including United States Supreme Court litigation, and securing federal legislation. Mr. Chestnut has represented the Northern Cheyenne Tribe since 1973.

LEONARD D. DIXON

Leonard D. Dixon is a Persian Gulf War (Desert Shield/Desert Storm) veteran of the United States Navy and an enrolled member of the Lummi Nation. He is the past Community Education and Outreach Coordinator within the Lummi Nation Constitution Office. He continues to work for the Lummi Nation as a member of the policy team within the chairman's office. He is also a principal of LD Consulting Services, which provides environmental planning and policy support to tribal governments, and a partner of Chachoosen Enterprises, LLC, a land acquisition and development company intended to strengthen the development of the Lummi Nation's reservation economy at Lummi.

MICHELLE DOTSON

Michelle Dotson is Legal Counsel in the Office of the Navajo Nations President/ Vice President. Previously, she served as the Executive Director of the Navajo Nation's Office of Government Development. She is a member of the Navajo Nation.

JOSEPH THOMAS FLIES-AWAY

Joseph Thomas Flies-Away (Hualapai) is a community and nation-building consultant who also serves as the chief judge of the Karuk Tribe of California Tribal Court, a visiting justice for the Gila River Indian Community Court of Appeals, and a judge pro tem for the Hualapai Tribal Court and other tribal court benches in Indigenous North America. He served as the chief judge for the Hualapai Tribal Court from 1996 to 1998 and as an associate judge until 2001. Prior to his judicial work, he served as a member of the Hualapai Tribal Council and directed the Hualapai Department of Planning and Community Vision, where he developed comprehensive planning strategies and documents for the Hualapai Nation in the areas of human capital development, organizational development, community infrastructure development and environmental support, and economic development.

LARRY FOSTER

Larry Foster is the former chair of the Commission on Navajo Government Development, chair of the Navajo Nation's Statutory Reform Convention, and CEO for former Navajo Nation president Kelsey A. Begaye. He is the current president of Indigitec. He was instrumental in the development of Title 2, the Navajo Nation's organic law. He also helped lead the development of the Navajo Nation's Local Governance Act and hosted numerous workshops on strengthening the jurisdiction and control of local governance authorities within the Navajo Nation. He continues to spend a great deal of time participating in Navajo Nation governance issues. In addition, he is a staunch supporter of Native American religious freedom and continues to dedicate a great deal of time to protecting such rights.

Carole Goldberg

Carole Goldberg is professor of law and director of the Joint Degree Program in Law and American Indian Studies at UCLA School of Law. She also serves as faculty chair of the law school's Native Nations Law and Policy Center. She is co-author and co-editor of the leading treatise in the field of Indian law, Felix S. Cohen's *Handbook of Federal Indian Law* (1982 ed.), and also serves as co-author and member of the Executive Committee for production of the 2005 edition of that influential work. She is also co-author of one of the two teaching casebooks in the field, *American Indian Law: Native Nations and the Federal System* (4th ed., 2005), with Robert N. Clinton and Rebecca Tsosie. Among her other publications are *Planting Tail Feathers: Tribal Survival and Public Law 280* (UCLA American Indian Studies Center 1997) and "American Indians and 'Preferential' Treatment," 49 *UCLA Law Review* 943 (2002). She is also the founding director of UCLA School of Law's Tribal Legal Development Clinic, which provides assistance to Native nations in developing their legal codes, constitutions, and justice systems.

Steven Haberfeld

Steven Haberfeld, Ph.D., serves as the executive director and the senior mediator/facilitator on the staff of Indian Dispute Resolution Services, Inc. He has more than thirty-five years of experience as a community organizer, mediator, facilitator, and trainer in multicultural and multiethnic settings. He has also been involved as an intermediary facilitating dialogues and increasing collaboration between tribes and local, state, and federal agencies, political jurisdictions, and public institutions (public school districts) and their constituents. Prior to his work at IDRS, he served as a mediator and associate trainer with Cascade Alternative Resolution Services (Portland, Oregon) and with Conflict Resolution Institute-CRI (Tacoma, Washington), and as an adjunct professor in dispute resolution at D-Q University (Davis, California) and Fond du Lac Tribal and Community College (Cloquet, Minnesota).

Albert Hale

Albert A. Hale is the former president of the Navajo Nation. He served as the president from 1995 to 1998. While president, he pushed for further Navajo government reform by moving power, money, and access to information to the local units of Navajo Nation government, a concept he calls "local empowerment." The initiative was enacted as the Navajo Local Governance Act. He was the primary author of the "Title Two Amendments of 1990," a reform of the Navajo

Nation government. He is the co-author of the Navajo Judicial Reform Act of 1985, an act solidifying an independent Navajo judiciary. Mr. Hale is now in private law practice with offices located in St. Michaels, Arizona, and Albuquerque, New Mexico.

LINDA HAVATONE

Linda Havatone is a member of the Hualapai Nation.

CARRIE IMUS

Carrie Imus is the former vice chair of the Hualapai Nation, where she was actively involved in the development of the Nation's current 1991 constitution and subsequent discussions regarding additional constitutional revision.

JOSEPH KALT

Joseph P. Kalt is the Ford Foundation Professor of International Political Economy at the John F. Kennedy School of Government at Harvard University. He is also faculty chair of the Harvard University Native American Program, and along with professors Stephen Cornell and Manley Begay of the University of Arizona, directs the Harvard Project on American Indian Economic Development. In addition, he is the co-editor, with Stephen Cornell, of *What Can Tribes Do? Strategies and Institutions in American Indian Economic Development.* Since 1987, the Harvard Project has worked for and with tribes and tribal organizations, providing research, advisory services, and education on issues of nation building in Indian Country. In addition to his work on issues of economic development and self-determination in Indian Country, he is a specialist in the economics of antitrust and regulation, with particular emphasis on the natural resource and transportation sectors.

ERIC LEMONT

Eric Lemont is a transactional real estate lawyer at Goodwin Procter, LLP, in Boston, Massachusetts. Prior to joining Goodwin Procter, he worked in the

Washington, D.C., office of the Indian law firm Hobbs, Straus, Dean and Walker, LLP, where he represented Indian tribes on a variety of business, gaming, self-governance, and constitutional reform issues. He is also a research fellow at the Harvard Project on American Indian Economic Development, where he founded and directed its Initiative on American Indian Constitutional Reform. His publications include "Developing Effective Processes of Constitutional and Governmental Reform: Lessons from the Cherokee Nation of Oklahoma, Hualapai Nation, Navajo Nation and Northern Cheyenne Tribe," *American Indian Law Review* 26:2 (2002), and "Overcoming the Politics of Reform: The Story of the Cherokee Nation Constitutional Convention," *American Indian Law Review* 28:1 (2003).

CARROLL ONSAE

Carroll Onsae is a Hopi from the village of Hotevilla and currently lives in Flagstaff, Arizona. He worked in public education for twenty-one years in the field of human resources and as a counselor to Native American students. He joined the staff of the Hopi Tribe chairman in 2001 as the operations officer for the Tribe. He is involved with many projects reporting directly to the chairman of the Tribe, including the Tribe's efforts to reform its current constitution. This project has been ongoing since the year 2000 and is now under review for further action by the Tribal Council, and to present to the Hopi people for a referendum vote.

JOHN PETERS, JR.

John Peters has been the executive director of the Massachusetts Commission on Indian Affairs since May of 1999. He is a member of the Mashpee Wampanoag Tribe from Cape Cod, Massachusetts. Prior to joining the commission, he held a number of positions with New England tribes, most recently with the Mashantucket Pequot Tribe of Connecticut. He served as director of the Mashpee Wampanoag Indian Tribal Council on Cape Cod for fourteen years, and held the position of tribal planner and tribal programs administrator for the Narragansett Tribe in Rhode Island. He also served as a principal planner for the Town of North Kingstown in Rhode Island. He has participated in many cultural, social, and historic Native American events that have taken place in southern New England over the past thirty years.

Elmer Rusco

The late Elmer Rusco was professor emeritus of political science at the University of Nevada, Reno, where he taught mainly Western and U.S. political theory. He served for ten years as the university's director of the Bureau of Governmental Research. His primary research interest concerned United States law and governmental policy and their relation to ethnicity and race. His published works include *A Fateful Time: The Background and Legislative History of the Indian Reorganization Act* (University of Nevada Press, 2000), as well as scholarly articles on civil liberties provisions in tribal constitutions in the United States and Native American governance in the Great Basin. In addition, he wrote on black history (*Good Time Coming? Black Nevadans in the Nineteenth Century* [Greenwood Press, 1976]) and Chinese Americans and the law in Nevada.

Le Roy Shingoitewa

Le Roy Shingoitewa is a member of the Hopi Tribe and the Chair of its Constitutional Reform Committee.

Ross Swimmer

Since 2003, Ross Swimmer has served as the special trustee for American Indians within the U.S. Department of the Interior. He has also served as the assistant secretary for Indian Affairs, Department of the Interior, and as principal chief of the Cherokee Nation, a position he held for ten years. While principal chief, he played a significant role in the development of the Cherokee Nation's 1976 Constitution. In addition to his elected and appointed positions, he has practiced law in Oklahoma City, served as an attorney for the Cherokee Nation Housing Authority, and served as outside general counsel of the Cherokee Nation.

Theresa Two Bulls

Theresa Two Bulls is a mother of six—three girls and three boys—and a grandmother of four grandsons. She is an Oglala Lakota living on the Pine Ridge Indian Reservation, Pine Ridge, South Dakota. In 2004, she was elected as a state senator for District 27 serving Bennett, Shannon, and Todd Counties. Prior to her election, she served as a prosecutor for the Oglala Sioux Tribal Attorney General's Office. From 2000 to 2002, she served as the Oglala Sioux Tribe's first woman vice president. She also served as the Tribe's secretary from 1990 to 1998 and worked as a legal secretary for fifteen years.

DAVID WILKINS

David Wilkins is professor of American Indian studies, political science, and law at the University of Minnesota. He teaches and writes in the areas of comparative politics, American political theory, federal Indian policy, tribal government, and history of colonialism and Native peoples. Professor Wilkins has been at the University of Minnesota since 1999. He has previously served as an assistant professor for the Department of Political Science and American Indian Studies at the University of Arizona and as an instructor at the Navajo Community College, Tsaile, Navajo Nation, Arizona. He is the author of numerous books and articles on American Indian law and studies, including *American Indian Politics and the American Political System* (Rowman and Littlefield, 2002) and *Tribes, Treaties, and Constitutional Tribulations* (University of Texas Press, 1999).

BEVERLY WRIGHT

Beverly Wright served as chairperson of the Wampanoag Tribe of Gay Head/ Aquinnah for fifteen years, from 1991 to 2005. As chief elected official and chairperson of an eleven-member Tribal Council, she maintained the integrity and goals of the Wampanoag Tribe of Gay Head/Aquinnah. Before being elected chairperson she served the Tribe for eight years as a council member and two years as treasurer of the Tribal Council. She was one of the founding members of the Aquinnah Wampanoag Housing Authority. She is a commissioner of the Massachusetts Commission on Indian Affairs and a board member of the Native Nations Institute at the University of Arizona. She is a past vice president and secretary of the United South and Eastern Tribes.

SHERI YELLOWHAWK

Sheri Kathleen YellowHawk lives and works in Peach Springs, Arizona, the capital of the Hualapai Indian Reservation. She is currently the chief executive officer of the Grand Canyon Resort Corporation, which specializes in tours of the Grand Canyon both above and below the rim. Previously, she was the director of education and training with the government branch of the Hualapai Tribe for more than eleven years. She has served on the Hualapai Tribal Council for the past six years. She is committed to contributing to the success, prosperity, and self-sufficiency of the Hualapai Nation.

INDEX

Acoma Pueblo, 15, 26–27

Bicameralism, 23, 24, 290, 292, 300–302, 310

Bureau of Indian Affairs, 5, 18, 36, 50, 51, 112, 181, 230, 276, 325, 326

Centralized government, 16, 21, 202, 240

Checks and balances, 20–22, 230, 303

Cherokee Nation of Oklahoma, 41, 45, 84, 86, 97, 100–101, 124, 129, 180, 181, 183, 238, 240, 243, 245, 247, 255, 265, 267, 270, 287–339

Christianity, 24, 30, 198

Citizen participation in reform process, 7, 169, 238–249, 258–259, 262, 268–270, 274–280, 285, 289, 296–299, 309, 326, 327

Citizen Potawatomi Nation, 192, 209

Citizenship/membership, 36, 89, 101, 145–146, 147, 150, 158–162, 166–183, 229, 311; adoption, 131; blood quantum requirement, 107, 117–118, 121–124, 127–128, 130–131, 147, 161–162, 171–176, 178, 181, 183, 229, 279, 289, 300, 305–307, 311; considerations in designing constitutional provisions, 122–128; descent, 110–112, 118, 122, 128, 130, 181, 305, 306; enrollment,

150–153, 157, 171–173, 175–178, 180, 226, 229, 292; federal law and policy, 112–122; non-member residents, 153, 155, 157, 159, 161; non-resident members, 304–305, 328–330; relation to jurisdiction, 119, 156

Cochiti Pueblo, 15, 26–27, 188–190, 198, 210

Cohen, Felix, 50, 53–57, 60, 61, 64, 66–69, 70–73

Collier, John, 50, 52, 53, 54, 56, 57, 58, 61, 67–72

Commission on Navajo Government Development, 44, 95, 96, 98, 241, 243, 247, 280

Confederated Salish and Kootenai Tribes, 192, 200, 205, 207

Conflicts/crises, 44, 45, 86, 96, 107, 172–173, 240, 241, 254, 282, 287, 293–294, 299, 303, 324, 325, 326

Consensus decision-making, 14, 29, 31, 240, 301

Constitutional conventions, 30, 45, 112, 243, 247, 265, 267, 287, 288, 289, 290, 294, 297–307, 310–311, 327–332

Constitutional reform committees, 30, 168–169, 174, 221, 230, 238, 246, 247–249, 270, 289, 294, 296, 299, 302, 307–311, 326–327, 330

Constitutional reformers, 39–40, 237, 246, 254, 256

CPSIA information can be obtained
at www.ICGtesting.com
Printed in the USA
FSHW022007100719
59908FS